George Brinton

Letter of the secretary of war,

Transmitting report of the organization of the Army of the Potomac, and of its campaigns in Virginia and Maryland, under the command of Maj. Gen. George B. McClellan, from July 26, 1861, to November 7, 1862 - Vol. 1

George Brinton

Letter of the secretary of war,
Transmitting report of the organization of the Army of the Potomac, and of its campaigns in Virginia and Maryland, under the command of Maj. Gen. George B. McClellan, from July 26, 1861, to November 7, 1862 - Vol. 1

ISBN/EAN: 9783337810481

Printed in Europe, USA, Canada, Australia, Japan

Cover: Foto ©ninafisch / pixelio.de

More available books at **www.hansebooks.com**

LETTER

OF

THE SECRETARY OF WAR,

TRANSMITTING REPORT ON THE

ORGANIZATION OF THE ARMY OF THE POTOMAC,

AND OF

ITS CAMPAIGNS IN VIRGINIA AND MARYLAND,

UNDER THE COMMAND OF

MAJ. GEN. GEORGE B. McCLELLAN,

FROM

JULY 26, 1861, TO NOVEMBER 7, 1862.

IN THE SENATE OF THE UNITED STATES, *January* 20, 1864.

Resolved, That five thousand copies of the report of General George B. McClellan upo
the operations of the army of the Potomac, recently communicated by the Secretary of W
to the House of Representatives, be printed for the use of the Senate, without the accomp
nying documents and maps.

LETTER

FROM

THE SECRETARY OF WAR,

TRANSMITTING

The report of Major General George B. McClellan upon the organization of the Army of the Potomac, and its campaigns in Virginia and Maryland, from July 26, 1861, to November 7, 1862.

DECEMBER 23, 1863.—Laid on the table and ordered to be printed.

WAR DEPARTMENT,
Washington City, D. C., December 22, 1863.

SIR: In compliance with the resolution dated December 15, 1863, I have the honor to communicate herewith "the report made by Major General George B. McClellan, concerning the organization and operations of the army of the Potomac while under his command, and of all army operations while he was commander-in-chief."

I am, sir, very respectfully, your obedient servant,

EDWIN M. STANTON,
Secretary of War.

Hon. SCHUYLER COLFAX,
Speaker of the House of Representatives.

REPORT.

FIRST PERIOD.

CHAPTER I.

NEW YORK, *August* 4, 1863.

SIR: I have the honor to submit herein the official report of the operations of the army of the Potomac while under my charge. Accompanying it are the reports of the corps, division, and subordinate commanders, pertaining to the various engagements, battles, and occurrences of the campaigns, and important documents connected with its organization, supply, and movements. These, with lists of maps and memoranda submitted, will be found appended, duly arranged, and marked for convenient reference.

Charged, in the spring of 1861, with the operations in the department of the Ohio, which included the States of Illinois, Indiana, Ohio, and latterly Western Virginia, it had become my duty to counteract the hostile designs of the enemy in Western Virginia, which were immediately directed to the destruction of the Baltimore and Ohio railroad and the possession of the Kanawha valley, with the ultimate object of gaining Wheeling and the control of the Ohio river.

The successful affairs of Phillippi, Rich Mountain, Carrick's Ford, &c., had been fought, and I had acquired possession of all Western Virginia north of the Kanawha valley, as well as of the lower portion of that valley.

I had determined to proceed to the relief of the upper Kanawha valley, as soon as provision was made for the permanent defence of the mountain passes leading from the east into the region under control, when I received at Beverly, in Randolph county, on the 21st of July, 1861, intelligence of the unfortunate result of the battle of Manassas, fought on that day.

On the 22d I received an order by telegraph, directing me to turn over my command to Brigadier General Rosecrans, and repair at once to Washington.

I had already caused reconnoissances to be made for intrenchments at the Cheat Mountain pass; also on the Hunterville road, near Elkwater, and at Red House, near the main road from Romney to Grafton. During the afternoon and night of the 22d I gave the final instructions for the construction of these works, turned over the command to Brigadier General Rosecrans, and started, on the morning of the 23d, for Washington, arriving there on the afternoon of the 26th. On the 27th I assumed command of the division of the Potomac, comprising the troops in and around Washington, on both banks of the river.

With this brief statement of the events which immediately preceded my being called to the command of the troops at Washington, I proceed to an account, from such authentic data as are at hand, of my military operations while commander of the army of the Potomac.

The subjects to be considered naturally arrange themselves as follows:

The organization of the army of the Potomac. The military events connected with the defences of Washington, from July, 1861, to March, 1862. The campaign on the Peninsula, and that in Maryland.

The great resources and capacity for powerful resistance of the south at the breaking out of the rebellion, and the full proportions of the great conflict about to take place, were sought to be carefully measured; and I had also endeavored, by every means in my power, to impress upon the authorities the necessity for such immediate and full preparation as alone would enable the government to prosecute the war on a scale commensurate with the resistance to be offered.

On the fourth of August, 1861, I addressed to the President the following memorandum, prepared at his request:

MEMORANDUM.

The object of the present war differs from those in which nations are engaged, mainly in this: that the purpose of ordinary war is to conquer a peace, and make a treaty on advantageous terms; in this contest it has become necessary to crush a population sufficiently numerous, intelligent and warlike to constitute a nation. We have not only to defeat their armed and organized forces in the field, but to display such an overwhelming strength as will convince all our antagonists, especially those of the governing, aristocratic class, of the utter impossibility of resistance. Our late reverses make this course imperative. Had we been successful in the recent battle, (Manassas,) it is possible that we might have been spared the labor and expenses of a great effort.

Now we have no alternative. Their success will enable the political leaders of the rebels to convince the mass of their people that we are inferior to them in force and courage, and to command all their resources. The contest began with a class, now it is with a people—our military success can alone restore the former issue.

By thoroughly defeating their armies, taking their strong places, and pursuing a rigidly protective policy as to private property and unarmed persons, and a lenient course as to private soldiers, we may well hope for a permanent restoration of a peaceful Union. But in the first instance the authority of the government must be supported by overwhelming physical force.

Our foreign relations and financial credit also imperatively demand that the military action of the government should be prompt and irresistible.

The rebels have chosen Virginia as their battle-field, and it seems proper for us to make the first great struggle there. But while thus directing our main efforts, it is necessary to diminish the resistance there offered us, by movements on other points both by land and water.

Without entering at present into details, I would advise that a strong movement be made on the Mississippi, and that the rebels be driven out of Missouri.

As soon as it becomes perfectly clear that Kentucky is cordially united with us, I would advise a movement through that State into Eastern Tennessee, for the purpose of assisting the Union men of that region and of seizing the railroads leading from Memphis to the east.

The possession of those roads by us, in connexion with the movement on the Mississippi, would go far towards determining the evacuation of Virginia by the rebels. In the mean time all the passes into Western Virginia from the east should be securely guarded, but I would advise no movement from that quarter towards Richmond, unless the political condition of Kentucky renders it impossible or inexpedient for us to make the movement upon Eastern Tennessee through that State. Every effort should, however, be made to organize, equip and arm as many troops as possible in Western Virginia, in order to render the Ohio and Indiana regiments available for other operations.

At as early a day as practicable, it would be well to protect and re-open the Baltimore and Ohio railroad. Baltimore and Fort Monroe should be occupied by garrisons sufficient to retain them in our possession.

The importance of Harper's Ferry and the line of the Potomac in the direction of Leesburg will be very materially diminished so soon as our force in this vicinity becomes organized, strong and efficient, because no capable general will cross the river north of this city, when we have a strong army here ready to cut off his retreat.

To revert to the west. It is probable that no very large additions to the troops now in Missouri will be necessary to secure that State.

I presume that the force required for the movement down the Mississippi will be determined by its commander and the President. If Kentucky assumes the right position, not more than 20,000 will be needed, together with those that can be raised in that State and Eastern Tennessee, to secure the latter region and its railroads, as well as ultimately to occupy Nashville.

The Western Virginia troops, with not more than five to ten thousand from Ohio and Indiana, should, under proper management, suffice for its protection.

When we have re-organized our main army here, 10.000 men ought to be enough to protect the Baltimore and Ohio railroad and the Potomac, 5,000 will garrison Baltimore, 3,000 Fort Monroe, and not more than 20,000 will be necessary at the utmost for the defence of Washington.

For the main army of operations I urge the following composition:

250 regiments of infantry, say	225,000	men.
100 field batteries, 600 guns	15,000	"
28 regiments of cavalry	25,500	"
5 regiments engineer troops	7,500	"
Total	273,000	"

The force must be supplied with the necessary engineer and pontoon trains, and with transportation for everything save tents. Its general line of operations should be so directed that water transportation can be availed of from point to point, by means of the ocean and the rivers emptying into it. An essential feature of the plan of operations will be the employment of a strong naval force to protect the movement of a fleet of transports intended to convey a considerable body of troops from point to point of the enemy's sea-coast, thus either creating diversions and rendering it necessary for them to detach largely from their main body in order to protect such of their cities as may be threatened, or else landing and forming establishments on their coast at any favorable places that opportunity might offer. This naval force should also co-operate with the main army in its efforts to seize the important seaboard towns of the rebels.

It cannot be ignored that the construction of railroads has introduced a new and very important element into war, by the great facilities thus given for concentrating at particular positions large masses of troops from remote sections, and by creating new strategic points and lines of operations.

It is intended to overcome this difficulty by the partial operations suggested, and such others as the particular case may require. We must endeavor to seize places on the railways in the rear of the enemy's points of concentration, and we must threaten their seaboard cities, in order that each State may be forced, by the necessity of its own defence, to diminish its contingent to the confederate army.

The proposed movement down the Mississippi will produce important results in this connexion. That advance and the progress of the main army at the east will materially assist each other by diminishing the resistance to be encountered by each.

The tendency of the Mississippi movement upon all questions connected with cotton is too well understood by the President and cabinet to need any illustration from me.

There is another independent movement that has often been suggested and which has always recommended itself to my judgment. I refer to a movement from Kansas and Nebraska through the Indian territory upon Red river and western Texas for the purpose of protecting and developing the latent Union and free-State sentiment well known to predominate in western Texas, and which, like a similar sentiment in Western Virginia, will, if protected, ultimately organize that section into a free State. How far it will be possible to support this movement by an advance through New Mexico from California, is a matter which I have not sufficiently examined to be able to express a decided opinion. If at all practicable, it is eminently desirable, as bringing into play the resources and warlike qualities of the Pacific States, as well as identifying them with our cause and connecting the bond of Union between them and the general government.

If it is not departing too far from my province, I will venture to suggest the policy of an ultimate alliance and cordial understanding with Mexico; their sympathies and interests are with us—their antipathies exclusively against our enemies and their institutions. I think it would not be difficult to obtain from the Mexican government the right to use, at least during the present contest, the road from Guaymas to New Mexico; this concession would very materially reduce the obstacles of the column moving from the Pacific; a similar permission to use their territory for the passage of troops between the Panuco and the Rio Grande would enable us to throw a column of troops by a good road from Tampico, or some of the small harbors north of it, upon and across the Rio Grande, without risk and scarcely firing a shot.

To what extent, if any, it would be desirable to take into service and employ Mexican soldiers, is a question entirely political, on which I do not venture to offer an opinion.

The force I have recommended is large; the expense is great. It is possible that a smaller force might accomplish the object in view, but I understand it to be the purpose of this great nation to re-establish the power of its government, and restore peace to its citizens, in the shortest possible time.

The question to be decided is simply this: shall we crush the rebellion at one blow, terminate the war in one compaign, or shall we leave it as a legacy for our descendants?

When the extent of the possible line of operations is considered, the force asked for for the main army under my command cannot be regarded as unduly large; every mile we advance carries us further from our base of operations and renders detachments necessary to cover our communications, while the enemy will be constantly concentrating as he falls back. I propose, with the force which I have requested, not only to drive the enemy out of Virginia and occupy Richmond, but to occupy Charleston, Savannah, Montgomery, Pensacola, Mobile and New Orleans; in other words, to move into the heart of the enemy's country and crush the rebellion in its very heart.

By seizing and repairing the railroads as we advance, the difficulties of transportation will be materially diminished. It is perhaps unnecessary to state that, in addition to the forces named in this memorandum, strong reserves should be formed, ready to supply any losses that may occur.

In conclusion, I would submit that the exigencies of the treasury may be lessened by making only partial payments to our troops, when in the enemy's country, and by giving the obligations of the United States for such supplies as may there be obtained.

GEO. B. McCLELLAN,
Major General.

I do not think the events of the war have proved these views upon the method and plans of its conduct altogether incorrect. They certainly have not proved my estimate of the number of troops and scope of operations too large. It is probable that I did under estimate the time necessary for the completion of arms and equipments. It was not strange, however, that by many civilians intrusted with authority there should have been an exactly opposite opinion held on both these particulars.

The result of the first battle of Manassas had been almost to destroy the morale and organization of our army, and to alarm government and people. The national capital was in danger; it was necessary, besides holding the enemy in check, to build works for its defence, strong and capable of being held by a small force.

It was necessary also to create a new army for active operations and to expedite its organization, equipment, and the accumulation of the material of war, and to this not inconsiderable labor all my energies for the next three months were constantly devoted.

Time is a necessary element in the creation of armies, and I do not, therefore, think it necessary to more than mention the impatience with which many regarded the delay in the arrival of new levies, though recruited and pressed forward with unexampled rapidity, the manufacture and supply of arms and equipments, or the vehemence with which an immediate advance upon the enemy's works directly in our front was urged by a partiotic but sanguine people.

The President, too, was anxious for the speedy employment of our army, and, although possessed of my plans through frequent conferences, desired a paper from me upon the condition of the forces under my command and the immediate measures to be taken to increase their efficiency. Accordingly, in the latter part of October I addressed the following letter to the Secretary of War:

SIR: In conformity with a personal understanding with the President yesterday, I have the honor to submit the following statement of the condition of the army under my command, and the measures required for the preservation of the government and the suppression of the rebellion.

It will be remembered that in a memorial I had the honor to address to the President soon after my arrival in Washington, and in my communication addressed to Lieutenant General Scott, under date of 8th of August; in my letter to the President authorizing him, at his request, to withdraw the letter written by me to General Scott; and in my letter of the 8th of September, answering your note of inquiry of that date, my views on the same subject are frankly and fully expressed.

In these several communications I have stated the force I regarded as necessary to enable this army to advance with a reasonable certainty of success, at the same time leaving the capital and the line of the Potomac sufficiently guarded, not only to secure the retreat of the main army, in the event of disaster, but to render it out of the enemy's power to attempt a diversion in Maryland.

So much time has passed, and the winter is approaching so rapidly, that but two courses are left to the government, viz., either to go into winter quarters, or to assume the offensive with forces greatly inferior in numbers to the army I regarded as desirable and necessary. If political considerations render the first course unadvisable, the second alone remains. While I regret that it has not been deemed expedient, or perhaps possible, to concentrate the forces of the nation in this vicinity, (remaining on the defensive elsewhere,) keeping the attention and efforts of the government fixed upon this as the vital point, where the issue of the great contest is to be decided, it may still be that, by introducing unity of action and design among the various armies of the land, by determining the courses to be pursued by the various commanders under one general plan, transferring from the other armies the superfluous strength not required for the purpose in view, and thus re-enforcing this main army, whose destiny it is to decide the controversy, we may yet be able to move with a reasonable prospect of success before the winter is fairly upon us.

The nation feels, and I share that feeling, that the army of the Potomac holds the fate of the country in its hands.

The stake is so vast, the issue so momentous, and the effect of the next battle will be so important throughout the future, as well as the present, that I continue to urge, as I have ever done since I entered upon the command of this army, upon the government to devote its energies and its available resources towards increasing the numbers and efficiency of the army on which its salvation depends.

A statement, carefully prepared by the chiefs of engineers and artillery of this army, gives us the necessary garrison of this city and its fortifications, 33,795 men—say 35,000.

The present garrison of Baltimore and its dependencies is about 10,000. I have sent the chief of my staff to make a careful examination into the condition of these troops, and to obtain the information requisite to enable me to decide whether this number can be diminished, or the reverse.

At least 5,000 men will be required to watch the river hence to Harper's Ferry and its vicinity; probably 8,000 to guard the lower Potomac.

As you are aware, all the information we have from spies, prisoners, &c., agrees in showing that the enemy have a force on the Potomac not less than 150,000 strong, well drilled and equipped, ably commanded and strongly intrenched. It is plain, therefore, that to insure success, or to render it reasonably certain, the active army should not number less than 150,000 efficient troops, with 400 guns, unless some material change occurs in the force in front of us.

The requisite force for an advance movement by the army of the Potomac may be thus estimated:

Column of active operations	150,000	men,	400	guns.
Garrison of the city of Washington	35,000	"	40	"
To guard the Potomac to Harper's Ferry	5,000	"	12	"
To guard the lower Potomac	8,000	"	24	"
Garrison for Baltimore and Annapolis	10,000	"	12	"
Total effective force required	208,000	men,	488	guns,

or an aggregate, present and absent, of about 240,000 men, should the losses by sickness, &c., not rise to a higher percentage than at present.

Having stated what I regard as the requisite force to enable this army to advance, I now proceed to give the actual strength of the army of the Potomac.

The aggregate strength of the army of the Potomac, by the official report on the morning of the 27th instant, was 168,318 officers and men, of all grades and arms. This includes the troops at Baltimore and Annapolis, on the upper and lower Potomac, the sick, absent, &c.

The force present for duty was 147,695. Of this number, 4,268 cavalry were completely unarmed, 3,163 cavalry only partially armed, 5,979 infantry unequipped, making 13,410 unfit for the field, (irrespective of those not yet sufficiently drilled,) and reducing the effective force to 134,285, and the number disposable for an advance to 76,285. The infantry regiments are, to a considerable extent, armed with unserviceable weapons. Quite a large number of good arms, which had been intended for this army, were ordered elsewhere, leaving the army of the Potomac insufficiently, and, in some cases, badly armed.

On the 30th of September there were with this army 228 field guns ready for the field; so far as arms and equipments are concerned, some of the batteries are still quite raw, and unfit to go into action. I have intelligence that eight New York batteries are en route hither; two others are ready for the field. I will still (if the New York batteries have six guns each) be 112 guns short of the number required for the active column, saying nothing, for the present, of those necessary for the garrisons and corps on the Potomac, which would make a total deficiency of 200 guns.

I have thus briefly stated our present condition and wants; it remains to suggest the means of supplying the deficiencies.

First, that all the cavalry and infantry arms, as fast as procured, whether manufactured in this country or purchased abroad, be sent to this army until it is fully prepared for the field.

Second, that the two companies of the fourth artillery, now understood to be en route from Fort Randall to Fort Monroe, be ordered to this army, to be mounted at once; also, that the companies of the third artillery, en route from California, be sent here. Had not the order for Smead's battery to come here from Harrisburg, to replace the battery I gave General Sherman, been so often countermanded, I would again ask for it.

Third, that a more effective regulation may be made authorizing the transfer of men from the volunteers to the regular batteries, infantry and cavalry; that we may make the best possible use of the invaluable regular "skeletons."

Fourth, I have no official information as to the United States forces elsewhere, but, from the best information I can obtain from the War Department and other sources, I am led to believe that the United States troops are:

In Western Virginia, about	30,000
In Kentucky	40,000
In Missouri	80,000
In Fortress Monroe	11,000
Total	161,000

Besides these, I am informed that more than 100,000 are in progress of organization in other northern and western States.

I would therefore recommend that, not interfering with Kentucky, there should be retained in Western Virginia and Missouri a sufficient force for defensive purposes, and that the surplus troops be sent to the army of the Potomac, to enable it to assume the offensive; that the same course be pursued in respect to Fortress Monroe, and that no further outside expeditions be attempted until we have fought the great battle in front of us.

Fifth, that every nerve be strained to hasten the enrolment, organization and armament of new batteries and regiments of infantry.

Sixth, that all the battalions now raised for new regiments of regular infantry be at once ordered to this army, and that the old infantry and cavalry en route from California be ordered to this army immediately on their arrival in New York.

I have thus indicated, in a general manner, the objects to be accomplished, and the means by which we may gain our ends.

A vigorous employment of these means will, in my opinion, enable the army of the Potomac to assume successfully this season the offensive operations which, ever since entering upon the command, it has been my anxious desire and diligent effort to prepare for and prosecute. The advance should not be postponed beyond the 25th of November, if possible to avoid it.

Unity in councils, the utmost vigor and energy in action are indispensable. The entire military field should be grasped as a whole, and not in detached parts.

One plan should be agreed upon and pursued; a single will should direct and carry out these plans.

The great object to be accomplished, the crushing defeat of the rebel army (now) at Manassas, should never for one instant be lost sight of, but all the intellect and means and men of the government poured upon that point. The loyal States possess ample force to effect all this and more. The rebels have displayed energy, unanimity, and wisdom worthy of the most desperate days of the French revolution. Should we do less?

The unity of this nation, the preservation of our institutions, are so dear to me that I have willingly sacrificed my private happiness with the single object of doing my duty to my country. When the task is accomplished, I shall be glad to return to the obscurity from which events have drawn me.

Whatever the determination of the government may be, I will do the best I can with the army of the Potomac, and will share its fate, whatever may be the task imposed upon me.

Permit me to add that, on this occasion as heretofore, it has been my aim neither to exaggerate nor underrate the power of the enemy, nor fail to express clearly the means by which, in my judgment, that power may be broken. Urging the energy of preparation and action, which has ever been my choice, but with the fixed purpose by no act of mine to expose the government to hazard by premature movement, and requesting that this communication may be laid before the President,

I have the honor to be, very respectfully, your obedient servant,

G. B. McCLELLAN,
Major General.

Hon. SIMON CAMERON,
Secretary of War.

When I assumed command in Washington, on the 27th of July, 1861, the number of troops in and around the city was about 50,000 infantry, less than 1,000 cavalry, and 650 artillerymen, with nine imperfect field batteries of thirty pieces.

On the Virginia bank of the Potomac the brigade organization of General McDowell still existed, and the troops were stationed at and in rear of Fort Corcoran, Arlington, and Fort Albany, at Fort Runyan, Roach's Mills, Cole's Mills, and in the vicinity of Fort Ellsworth, with a detachment at the Theological Seminary.

There were no troops south of Hunting creek, and many of the regiments were encamped on the low grounds bordering the Potomac, seldom in the best positions for defence, and entirely inadequate in numbers and condition to defend the long line from Fort Corcoran to Alexandria.

On the Maryland side of the river, upon the heights overlooking the Chain bridge, two regiments were stationed, whose commanders were independent of each other.

There were no troops on the important Tenallytown road, or on the roads entering the city from the south.

The camps were located without regard to purposes of defence or instruction, the roads were not picketed, and there was no attempt at an organization into brigades.

In no quarter were the dispositions for defence such as to offer a vigorous resistance to a respectable body of the enemy, either in the position and numbers of the troops, or the number and character of the defensive works. Earthworks, in the nature of *têtes de pont*, looked upon the approaches to the Georgetown aqueduct and ferry, the Long bridge and Alexandria, by the Little river turnpike, and some simple defensive arrangements were made at the Chain bridge. With the latter exception not a single defensive work had been commenced on the Maryland side.

There was nothing to prevent the enemy shelling the city from heights within easy range, which could be occupied by a hostile column almost without resistance. Many soldiers had deserted, and the streets of Washington were crowded with straggling officers and men, absent from their stations without authority, whose behavior indicated the general want of discipline and organization.

I at once designated an efficient staff, afterwards adding to it as opportunity was afforded and necessity required, who zealously co-operated with me in the labor of bringing order out of confusion, re-assigning troops and commands, projecting and throwing up defensive works, receiving and organizing, equipping and providing for the new levies arriving in the city.

The valuable services of these officers in their various departments, during this and throughout the subsequent periods of the history of the army of the Potomac, can hardly be sufficiently appreciated. Their names and duties will be given in another part of this report, and they are commended to the favorable notice of the War Department.

The restoration of order in the city of Washington was effected through the appointment of a provost marshal, whose authority was supported by the few regular troops within my command. These troops were thus in position to act as a reserve, to be sent to any point of attack where their services might be most wanted. The energy and ability displayed by Colonel A. Porter, the provost marshal, and his assistants, and the strict discharge of their duty by the troops, produced the best results, and Washington soon became one of the most quiet cities in the Union.

The new levies of infantry, upon arriving in Washington, were formed into provisional brigades and placed in camp in the suburbs of the city for equipment, instruction, and discipline. As soon as regiments were in a fit condition for transfer to the forces across the Potomac, they were assigned to the brigades serving there. Brigadier General F. J. Porter was at first assigned to the charge of the provisional brigades. Brigadier General A. E. Burnside was the next officer assigned this duty, from which, however, he was soon relieved by Brigadier General S. Casey, who continued in charge of the newly arriving regiments until the army of the Potomac departed for the Peninsula, in March, 1862. The newly arriving artillery troops reported to Brigadier General William F. Barry, the chief of artillery, and the cavalry to Brigadier General George Stoneman, the chief of cavalry.

By the 15th of October, the number of troops in and about Washington, inclusive of the garrison of the city and Alexandria, the city guard and the forces on the Maryland shore of the Potomac below Washington, and as far as Cumberland above, the troops under the command of General Dix at Baltimore and its dependencies, were as follows:

Total present for duty	133, 201
" sick	9, 290
" in confinement	1, 156
Aggregate present	143, 647
" absent	8, 404
Grand aggregate	152, 051

The following table exhibits similar data for the periods stated, including the troops in Maryland and Delaware:

Date.	Present.			Absent.	Total present and absent.
	For duty.	Sick.	In confinement.		
December 1, 1861	169, 452	15, 102	2, 189	11, 470	198, 213
January 1, 1862	191, 480	11, 790	2, 260	11, 707	219, 707
February 1, 1862	190, 806	14, 363	2, 917	14, 110	222, 196
March 1, 1862	193, 142	13, 167	2, 108	13, 570	221, 987

For convenience of reference the strength of the army of the Potomac at subsequent periods is given.

Date.	Present.							Absent.		Grand aggregate present and absent.
	For duty.		Sick.		In arrest or confinement.		Aggregate.	By authority.	Without authority.	
	Officers.	Men.	Officers.	Men.	Officers.	Men.				
April 30	4,725	104,610	233	5,385	41	356	115,350	11,037	....	*126,387
June 20	4,665	101,160	496	10,511	44	320	117,226	27,700	887	†145,813
July 10	3,834	85,715	685	15,959	60	213	106,466	34,638	3,782	‡144,886

* Including Franklin. † Including McCall and Dix.
‡ Including two brigades of Shiel's division absent. 5,354 men.

In organizing the army of the Potomac, and preparing it for the field, the first step taken was to organize the infantry into brigades of four regiments each; retaining the newly arrived regiments on the Maryland side until their armament and equipment were issued and they had obtained some little elementary instruction, before assigning them permanently to brigades. When the organization of the brigades was well established, and the troops somewhat disciplined and instructed, divisions of three brigades each were gradually formed, as is elsewhere stated in this report, although I was always in favor of the organization into army corps as an abstract principle. I did not desire to form them until the army had been for some little time in the field, in order to enable the general offices first to acquire the requisite experience as division commanders on active service, and that I might be able to decide from actual trial who were best fitted to exercise these important commands.

For a similar reason I carefully abstained from making any recommendations for the promotion of officers to the grade of major general.

When new batteries of artillery arrived they also were retained in Washington until their armament and equipment were completed, and their instruction sufficiently advanced to justify their being assigned to divisions. The same course was pursued in regard to cavalry. I regret that circumstances have delayed the chief of cavalry, General George Stoneman, in furnishing his report upon the organization of that arm of service. It will, however, be forwarded as soon as completed, and will, doubtless, show that the difficult and important duties intrusted to him were efficiently performed. He encountered and overcame, as far as it was possible, continual and vexatious obstacles arising from the great deficiency of cavalry arms and equipments, and the entire inefficiency of many of the regimental officers first appointed; this last difficulty was, to a considerable extent, overcome in the cavalry, as well as in the infantry and artillery, by the continual and prompt action of courts-martial and boards of examination.

As rapidly as circumstances permitted, every cavalry soldier was armed with a sabre and revolver, and at least two squadrons in every regiment with carbines.

It was intended to assign at least one regiment of cavalry to each division of the active army, besides forming a cavalry reserve of the regular regiments and some picked regiments of volunter cavalry. Circumstances beyond my control rendered it impossible to carry out this intention fully, and the cavalry force serving with the army in the field was never as large as it ought to have been.

It was determined to collect the regular infantry to form the nucleus of a reserve. The advantage of such a body of troops at a critical moment, especially in an army constituted mainly of new levies, imperfectly disciplined, has been frequently illustrated in military history, and was brought to the attention of the country at the first battle of Manassas. I have not been disappointed in the estimate formed of the value of these troops. I have always found them to be relied on. Whenever they have been brought under fire they have shown the utmost gallantry and tenacity. The regular infantry, which had been collected from distant posts and which had been recruited as rapidly as the slow progress of recruiting for the regular service would allow, added to the small battalion with McDowell's army, which I found at Washington on my arrival, amounted, on the 30th of August, to 1,040 men; on the 28th of February, 1862, to 2,682, and on the 30th of April, to 4,603. On the 17th of May, 1862, they were assigned to General Porter's corps for organization as a division, with the fifth regiment New York volunteers, which joined May 4, and the tenth New York volunteers, which joined subsequently. They remained from the commencement under the command of Brigadier General George Sykes, major third infantry United States army.

ARTILLERY.

The creation of an adequate artillery establishment for an army of so large proportions was a formidable undertaking; and had it not been that the country possessed in the regular service a body of accomplished and energetic artillery officers, the task would have been almost hopeless.

The charge of organizing this most important arm was confided to Major (afterwards Brigadier General) William F. Barry, chief of artillery, whose industry and zeal achieved the best results. The report of General Barry is appended among the accompanying documents. By referring to it, it will be observed that the following principles were adopted as the basis of organization:

"1. That the proportion of artillery should be in the proportion of at least two and one-half pieces to 1,000 men, to be expanded, if possible, to three pieces to 1,000 men.

"2. That the proportion of rifled guns should be restricted to the system of the United States ordnance department; and of Parrott and the 'smooth bores' (with the exception of a few howitzers for special service) to be exclusively the twelve-pounder gun, of the model of 1857, variously called the 'gun-howitzer,' the 'light twelve-pounder,' or the 'Napoleon.'

"3. That each field battery should, if practicable, be composed of six guns, and none to be less than four guns, and in all cases the guns of each battery should be of uniform calibre.

"4. That the field batteries were to be assigned to divisions, and not to brigades, and in the proportion of four to each division, of which one was to be a battery of regulars, the remainder of volunteers, the captain of the regular battery to be the commandant of artillery of the division. In the event of several divisions constituting an army corps, at least one-half of the divisional artillery was to constitute the reserve artillery of the corps.

"5. That the artillery reserve of the whole army should consist of one hundred guns, and should comprise, besides a sufficient number of light 'mounted batteries,' all the guns of position, and until the cavalry were massed, all the horse artillery.

"6. That the amount of ammunition to accompany field batteries was not to be less than four hundred rounds per gun.

"7. A siege train of fifty pieces. This was subsequently expanded, for special service at the siege of Yorktown, to very nearly one hundred pieces, and comprised the unusual calibres and enormously heavy weight of metal of two 200-pounders, five 100-pounders, and ten 13-inch sea-coast mortars."

As has been before stated, the chief of artillery reports the whole of the field artillery of the army of the Potomac, July 28, 1861, was comprised of nine imperfectly equipped batteries, of thirty guns, 650 men, and 400 horses. In March, 1862, when the whole army took the field, it consisted of ninety two batteries, of 520 guns, 12,500 men, and 11,000 horses, fully equipped and in readiness for active field service; of the whole force thirty batteries were regulars, and sixty-two batteries volunteers. During the short period of seven months, all of this immense amount of material was issued by the ordnance department and placed in the hands of the artillery troops after their arrival in Washington. About one-fourth of all the volunteer batteries brought with them from their respective States a few guns and carriages, but they were nearly all of such peculiar calibre as to lack uniformity with the more modern and more serviceable ordnance with which the other batteries were armed, and they therefore had to be withdrawn and replaced by more suitable material. While about one-sixth came supplied with horses and harness, less than one-tenth were apparently fully equipped for service when they reported; and every one of these required the supply of many deficiencies of material, and very extensive instruction in the theory and practice of their special arm.

The operations on the Peninsula by the army of the Potomac commenced with a full field artillery force of fifty-two batteries of two hundred and ninety-nine guns. To this must be added the field artillery of Franklin's division of McDowell's corps, which joined a few days before the capture of Yorktown, but was not disembarked from its transports for service until after the battle of Williamsburg, and the field artillery of McCall's division of McDowell's corps, (four batteries, twenty-two guns,) which joined in June, a few days before the battle of Mechanicsville, (June 26, 1862,) making a grand total of field artillery, at any time with the army of the Peninsula, of sixty batteries of three hundred and forty-three guns. With this large force, saving in six corps d'armée of eleven divisions, and the artillery reserve, the only general and field officers were one brigadier general, four colonels, three lieutenant colonels, and three majors, a number obviously insufficient, and which impaired to a great degree, in consequence of the want of rank and official influence of the commanders of corps and division artillery, the efficiency of the arm. As this faulty organization can be suitably corrected only by legislative action, it is earnestly hoped that the attention of the proper authorities may be at an early day invited to it.

When there were so many newly organized volunteer field batteries, many of whom received their first and only instruction in the intrenched camps covering Washington during the three or four inclement months of the winter of 1861–'62, there was, of course, much to be improved. Many of the volunteer batteries, however, evinced such zeal and intelligence, and availed themselves so industriously of the instructions of the regular officers, their commanders, and the example of the regular batteries, their associates, that they made rapid progress, and attained a degree of proficiency highly creditable.

The designations of the different batteries of artillery, both regular and volunteer, follow within a few pages.

The following distribution of regiments and batteries was made, as a preliminary organization of the forces at hand, shortly after my arrival in Washington. The infantry, artillery, and cavalry, as fast as collected and brought into primary organization, were assigned to brigades and divisions, as indicated in the subjoined statements.

Organization of the division of the Potomac, August 4, 1861.

Brigadier General Hunter's brigade.—23d, 25th, 35th, and 37th regiments New York volunteers.

Brigadier General Heintzelman's brigade.—5th regiment Maine volunteers, 16th, 26th, and 27th regiments New York volunteers, and Tidball's battery, (A,) 2d United States artillery.

Brigadier General W. T. Sherman's brigade.—9th and 14th regiments Massachusetts volunteers, DeKalb regiment New York volunteers, 4th regiment Michigan volunteers, Hamilton's battery, (E,) 3d United States artillery, and company I, 2d United States cavalry.

Brigadier General Kearney's brigade.—1st, 2d, and 3d regiments New Jersey volunteers, Green's battery, (G,) 2d United States artillery, and company G, 2d United States cavalry.

Brigadier General Hooker's brigade.—1st and 11th regiments Massachusetts volunteers, 2d regiment New Hampshire volunteers, and 26th regiment Pennsylvania volunteers.

Colonel Keys's brigade.—22d, 24th, and 30th regiments New York volunteers, and 14th regiment New York State militia.

Brigadier General Franklin's brigade.—15th, 18th, 31st, and 32d regiments New York volunteers, Platt's battery, (M,) 2d United States artillery, and company C, New York (Lincoln) cavalry.

Colonel Blenker's brigade.—8th and 27th regiments New York volunteers, 27th regiment Pennsylvania volunteers, and Garibaldi guard, New York volunteers.

Colonel Richardson's brigade.—12th regiment New York volunteers, and 2d and 3d regiments Michigan volunteers.

Brigadier General Stone's brigade.—34th and Tammany regiments New York volunteers, 1st regiment Minnesota volunteers, and 2d regiment New York State militia.

Colonel William F. Smith's brigade.—2d and 3d regiments Vermont volunteers, 6th regiment Maine volunteers, 33d regiment New York volunteers, company H, 2d United States cavalry, and Captain Mott's New York battery.

Colonel Couch's brigade.—2d regiment Rhode Island volunteers, 7th and 10th regiments Massachusetts volunteers, and 36th regiment New York volunteers.

The 2d regiment Maine, the 2d regiment Wisconsin, and the 13th regiment New York volunteers, stationed at Fort Corcoran.

The 21st regiment New York volunteers, stationed at Fort Runyon.

The 17th regiment New York volunteers, stationed at Fort Ellsworth.

By October the new levies had arrived in sufficient numbers, and the process of organization so far carried on that the construction of divisions had been effected.

The following statement exhibits the composition of the army, October 15, 1861.

Organization of the army of the Potomac, October 15, 1861.

1. *Brigadier General George Stoneman's cavalry command.*—5th United States cavalry, 4th Pennsylvania cavalry, Oneida cavalry, (one company,) 11th Pennsylvania cavalry, (Harlan's,) and Barker's Illinois cavalry, (one company.)

2. *Colonel H. J. Hunt's artillery reserve.*—Batteries L, A, and B, 2d United States artillery, batteries K and F, 3d United States artillery, battery K, 4th United States artillery, battery H, 1st United States artillery, and battery A, 5th United States artillery.

3. CITY GUARD, BRIGADIER GENERAL ANDREW PORTER.

Cavalry.—Companies A and E, 4th United States cavalry.

Artillery.—Battery K, 5th United States artillery.

Infantry.—2d and 3d battalions United States infantry, 8th and 1st companies United States infantry, and Sturgis's rifles, (Illinois volunteers.)

4. BANKS'S DIVISION.

Cavalry.—Four companies 3d regiment New York cavalry, (Van Allen's.)

Artillery.—Best's battery E, 4th United States artillery, detachment 9th New York artillery, Matthews's battery E, 1st Pennsylvania artillery, Tompkins's battery A, 1st Rhode Island artillery.

Infantry.—Abercrombie's brigade: 12th Massachusetts, 12th and 16th Indiana, and 30th Pennsylvania volunteers. Stiles's brigade: 3d Wisconsin, 29th Pennsylvania, and 13th Massachusetts volunteers, and 9th New York State militia. Gordon's brigade: 2d Massachusetts, 28th and 19th New York, 5th Connecticut, 46th and 28th Pennsylvania, and 1st Maryland volunteers.

M'DOWELL'S DIVISION.

Cavalry.—2d New York cavalry, (Harris's Light,) Colonel Davis.

Artillery.—Battery M, 2d, and battery G, 1st United States artillery.

Infantry.—Keys's brigade: 14th New York State militia, and 22d, 24th, and 30th New York volunteers. Wadsworth's brigade: 12th, 21st, 23d, and 35th New York volunteers. King's brigade: 2d, 6th, and 7th Wisconsin, and 19th Indiana volunteers.

HEINTZELMAN'S DIVISION.

Cavalry.—1st New Jersey cavalry, Colonel Halsted.

Artillery.—Thompson's battery, C, United States artillery.

Infantry.—Richardson's brigade: 2d, 3d, and 5th Michigan, and 37th New York volunteers. Sedgwick's brigade: 3d and 4th Maine, and 38th and 40th New York volunteers. Jameson's brigade: 32d, 63d, 61st, and 45th Pennsylvania volunteers, and Wild Cat reserves, (Pennsylvania volunteers.)

F. J. PORTER'S DIVISION.

Cavalry.—3d Pennsylvania cavalry, Colonel Averill, and 8th Pennsylvania cavalry, Colonel Gregg.

Artillery.—Battery E, 2d, and battery *E, 3d United States artillery.

Infantry.—Morell's brigade: 33d Pennsylvania, 4th Michigan, 9th Massachusetts, and 4th New York volunteers. Martindale's brigade: 13th New York, 2d Maine, and 18th Massachusetts volunteers, and DeKalb regiment New York volunteers. Butterfield's brigade: 50th New York, 83d Pennsylvania, (Colonel McLean,) 17th and 25th New York volunteers, and Stockton's independent Michigan regiment.

FRANKLIN'S DIVISION.

Cavalry.—1st New York cavalry, Colonel McReynolds.

Artillery.—Batteries D and G, 2d United States artillery, and Hexamer's battery, (New Jersey volunteers.)

Infantry.—Kearney's brigade: 1st, 2d, 3d, and 4th New Jersey volunteers. Slocum's brigade: 16th, 26th, and 27th New York, and 6th Maine volunteers Newton's brigade: 15th, 18th, 31st, and 32d New York volunteers.

STONE'S DIVISION.

Cavalry.—Six companies 3d New York (Van Allen) cavalry.

Artillery.—Kirby's battery I, 1st United States, Vaughn's battery B, 1st Rhode Island artillery, and Bunting's 6th New York independent battery.

Infantry.—Gorman's brigade: 2d New York State militia, 1st Minnesota

* This battery was transferred to Sherman's expedition.

15th Massachusetts, and 34th New York volunteers, and Tammany regiment, (New York volunteers.) Lander's brigade: 19th and 20th Massachusetts, and 7th Michigan volunteers, and a company of Massachusetts sharpshooters. Baker's brigade: Pennsylvania volunteers, (1st, 2d, and 3d California.)

BUELL'S DIVISION.

Artillery.—Batteries D and H, 1st Pennsylvania artillery.

Infantry.—Couch's brigade: 2d Rhode Island, 7th and 10th Massachusetts, and 36th New York volunteers. Graham's brigade: 23d and 31st Pennsylvania, and 67th (1st Long Island) and 65th (1st United States chasseurs) New York volunteers. Peck's brigade: 13th and 21st Pennsylvania, and 62d (Anderson Zouaves) and 55th New York volunteers.

M'CALL'S DIVISION.

Cavalry.—1st Pennsylvania reserve cavalry, Colonel Bayard.

Artillery.—Easton's battery A, Cooper's battery B, and Kein's battery G, 1st Pennsylvania artillery.

Infantry.—Meade's brigade: 1st rifles Pennsylvania reserves, 4th, 3d, 7th, 11th, and 2d Pennsylvania reserve infantry. ——— brigade: 5th, 1st, and 8th Pennsylvania reserve infantry. ——— brigade: 10th, 6th, 9th, and 12th Pennsylvania reserve infantry.

HOOKER'S DIVISION.

Cavalry.—Eight companies 3d Indiana cavalry, Lieutenant Colonel Carter.

Artillery.—Elder's battery E, 1st United States artillery.

Infantry.——— brigade: 1st and 11th Massachusetts, 2d New Hampshire, 26th Pennsylvania, and 1st Michigan volunteers. Sickles's brigade: 1st, 2d, 3d, 4th, and 5th regiments Excelsior brigade, New York volunteers.

BLENKER'S BRIGADE.

Cavalry.—4th New York cavalry, (mounted rifles,) Colonel Dickel.

Artillery.—One battery.

Infantry.—8th and 29th New York, 27th and 35th Pennsylvania volunteers, Garibaldi guard and Cameron rifles, (New York volunteers.)

SMITH'S DIVISION.

Cavalry.—5th Pennsylvania cavalry, (Cameron dragoons,) Colonel Friedman.

Artillery.—Ayres's battery F, 5th United States artillery, Mott's 2d New York independent battery, and Barr's battery E, 1st Pennsylvania artillery.

Infantry.——— brigade: 2d, 3d, 4th, and 5th Vermont volunteers. Stevens's brigade: 35th and 49th New York and 6th Maine volunteers, and *79th New York State militia. Hancock's brigade: *47th and 49th Pennsylvania, 43d New York, and 5th Wisconsin volunteers. Companies B and E, Berden's sharpshooters.

Casey's provisional brigades.—5th, 6th, and 7th New Jersey volunteers, *Round-Head regiment, (Pennsylvania volunteers,) battalion District of Columbia volunteers, 40th Pennsylvania, 8th New Jersey, and 4th New Hampshire volunteers.

---

* The 79th New York State militia, the 47th Pennsylvania volunteers, and the Round-Head regiment, were transferred to General Sherman's expedition.

5. *Garrison of Alexandria.*—Brigadier General Montgomery, military governor. Cameron guard. (Pennsylvania volunteers.)

Garrison of Fort Albany.—14th Massachusetts volunteers.

Garrison of Fort Richardson.—4th Connecticut volunteers.

Garrison of Fort Washington.—Company D, 1st United States artillery, companies H and I, 37th New York volunteers, and United States recruits unassigned.

6. DIX'S DIVISION, BALTIMORE.

Cavalry.—Company of Pennsylvania cavalry.

Artillery.—Battery I, 2d United States artillery, 2d Massachusetts light battery, and a battery of New York artillery.

Infantry.—3d, 4th, and 5th New York, 17th and 25th Massachusetts, 21st Indiana, 6th Michigan, 4th Wisconsin, 7th Maine, 2d Maryland battalion, and Reading city guard, volunteers.

On the 8th of March, 1862, the President directed, by the following order, the organization of the active portion of the army of the Potomac into four army corps, and the formation of a fifth corps from the division of Banks and Shields.

The following is the text of the President's order:

"[President's General War Order No. 2.]

"EXECUTIVE MANSION,
"*Washington, March* 8, 1862.

"Ordered, 1st. That the major general commanding the army of the Potomac proceed forthwith to organize that part of the said army destined to enter upon active operations, (including the reserve, but excluding the troops to be left in the fortifications about Washington,) into four army corps, to be commanded according to seniority of rank, as follows:

"First corps to consist of four divisions, and to be commanded by Major General I. McDowell. Second corps to consist of three divisions, and to be commanded by Brigadier General E. V. Sumner. Third corps to consist of three divisions, and to be commanded by Brigadier General S. P. Heintzelman. Fourth corps to consist of three divisions, and to be commanded by Brigadier General E. D. Keyes.

"2. That the divisions now commanded by the officers above assigned to the commands of army corps shall be embraced in and form part of their respective corps.

"3. The forces left for the defence of Washington will be placed in command of Brigadier General James Wadsworth, who shall also be military governor of the District of Columbia.

"4. That this order be executed with such promptness and despatch as not to delay the commencement of the operations already directed to be undertaken by the army of the Potomac.

"5. A fifth army corps, to be commanded by Major General N. P. Banks, will be formed from his own and General Shields's (late General Lander's) division.

"ABRAHAM LINCOLN."

The following order, which was made as soon as circumstances permitted, exhibits the steps taken to carry out the requirements of the President's war order No. 2:

"ARMY CORPS.

"HEADQUARTERS ARMY OF THE POTOMAC,
"*Fairfax Court-house, Virginia, March* 13, 1862.

[GENERAL ORDERS No. 151.]

"In compliance with the President's war order No. 2, of March 8, 1862, the active portion of the army of the Potomac is formed into army corps, as follows:

"First corps, Major General Irwin McDowell, to consist for the present of the divisions of Franklin, McCall, and King. Second corps, Brigadier General E. V. Sumner; divisions, Richardson, Blenker, and Sedgwick. Third corps, Brigadier General S. P. Heintzelman; divisions, F. J. Porter, Hooker, and Hamilton. Fourth corps, Brigadier General E. D. Keyes; divisions, Couch, Smith, and Casey. Fifth corps, Major General N. P. Banks; divisions, Williams and Shields.

"The cavalry regiments attached to divisions will, for the present, remain so. Subsequent orders will provide for these regiments, as well as for the reserve artillery. Regular infantry and regular cavalry arrangements will be made to unite the divisions of each army corps as promptly as possible.

"The commanders of divisions will at once report in person, or where that is impossible, by letter, to the commander of their army corps.

"By command of Major General McClellan.

"A. V. COLBURN,
"*Assistant Adjutant General.*"

I add a statement of the organization and composition of the troops on April 1, commencing with the portion of the army of the Potomac which went to the Peninsula, giving afterwards the regiments and batteries left on the Potomac, and in Maryland and Virginia after April 1, 1862.

Troops of the army of the Potomac sent to the Peninsula in March and early in April, 1862.

1st. Cavalry reserve, Brigadier General P. St. G. Cooke.—Emery's brigade: 5th United States cavalry; 6th United States cavalry; 6th Pennsylvania cavalry. Blake's brigade: 1st United States cavalry; 8th Pennsylvania cavalry; Barker's squadron Illinois cavalry.

2d. Artillery reserve, Colonel Henry J. Hunt: Graham's battery K and G, 1st United States, 6 Napoleon guns; Randall's battery E, 1st United States, 6 Napoleon guns; Carlisle's battery E, 2d United States, 6 20-pounder Parrott guns; Robertson's battery, 2d United States, 6 3-inch ordnance guns; Benson's battery M, 2d United States, 6 3-inch ordnance guns; Tidball's battery A, 2d United States, 6 3-inch ordnance guns; Edwards's battery L and M, 3d United States, 6 10-pounder Parrott guns; Gibson's battery C and G, 3d United States, 6 3-inch ordnance guns; Livingston's battery F and K, 3d United States, 4 10-pounder Parrott guns; Howe's battery G, 4th United States, 6 Napoleon guns; De Russy's battery K, 4th United States, 6 Napoleon guns; Weed's battery I, 5th United States, 6 3-inch ordnance guns; Smead's battery K, 5th United States, 4 Napoleon guns; Ames's battery A, 5th United States, 6—4 10-pounder Parrott and 2 Napoleon—guns; Diedrick's battery A, New York artillery and battalion, 6 20-pounder Parrott guns; Vogelie's battery B, New York artillery and battalion, 4 20-pounder Parrott guns; Knierim's battery C, New York artillery and battalion, 4 20-pounder Parrott guns; Grimm's battery D, New York artillery and battalion, 6 32-pounder howitzer guns. Total, 100 guns.

3d. Volunteer engineer troops, General Woodbury: 15th New York volunteers; 50th New York volunteers.

Regular engineer troops, Captain Duane: Companies A, B, and C, United States engineers.

Artillery troops, with siege trains: 1st Connecticut heavy artillery, Colonel Tyler.

4th. Infantry reserve, (regular brigade,) General Sykes: 9 companies 2d United States infantry, 7 companies 3d United States infantry, 10 companies 4th United States infantry, 10 companies 6th United States infantry, 8 companies 10th and 17th United States infantry, 6 companies 11th United States infantry, 8 companies 12th United States infantry, 9 companies 14th United States infantry, and 5th New York volunteers, Colonel Warren.

SECOND CORPS, GENERAL SUMNER.

Cavalry.—8th Illinois cavalry, Colonel Farnsworth, and one squadron 6th New York cavalry.

RICHARDSON'S DIVISION.

Artillery.—Clark's battery A and G, 4th United States, 6 Napoleon guns; Frank's battery G, 1st New York, 6 10-pounder Parrott guns; Pettit's battery B, 1st New York, 6 10-pounder Parrott guns; Hogan's battery A, 2d New York, 6 10-pounder Parrott guns.

Infantry.—Howard's brigade: 5th New Hampshire, 81st Pennsylvania, and 61st and 64th New York volunteers. Meagher's brigade: 69th, 63d, and 88th New York volunteers. French's brigade: 52d, 57th, and 66th New York, and 53d Pennsylvania volunteers.

SEDGWICK'S DIVISION.

Artillery.—Kirby's battery I, 1st United States, 6 Napoleon guns; Tompkins's battery A, 1st Rhode Island, 6—4 10-pounder Parrott and 2 12-pounder howitzer—guns; Bartlett's battery B, 1st Rhode Island, 6—4 10-pounder Parrott and 2 12-pounder howitzer—guns; Owen's battery G, 6 3-inch ordnance guns.

Infantry.—Gorman's brigade: 2d New York State militia, and 15th Massachusetts, 34th New York, and 1st Maine volunteers. Burns's brigade: 69th, 71st, 72d, and 106th Pennsylvania volunteers. Dana's brigade: 19th and 20th Massachusetts, 7th Michigan, and 42d New York volunteers.

NOTE.—Blenker's division detached and assigned to the mountain department.

THIRD CORPS, GENERAL HEINTZELMAN.

Cavalry.—3d Pennsylvania cavalry, Colonel Averill.

PORTER'S DIVISION.

Artillery.—Griffin's battery K, 5th United States, 6 10-pounder Parrott guns: Weeden's battery C, Rhode Island; Martin's battery C, Massachusetts, 6 Napoleon guns; Allen's battery E, Massachusetts, 6 3-inch ordnance guns.

Infantry.—Martindale's brigade: 2d Maine, 18th and 22d Massachusetts, and 25th and 13th New York volunteers. Morell's brigade: 14th New York, 4th Michigan, 9th Massachusetts, and 62d Pennsylvania volunteers. Butterfield's brigade: 17th, 44th, and 12th New York, 83d Pennsylvania, and Stockton's Michigan volunteers.

First Berdan sharpshooters.

HOOKER'S DIVISION.

Artillery.—Hall's battery H, 1st United States, 6—4 10-pounder Parrott and 2 12-pounder howitzer—guns; Smith's battery, 4th New York, 6 10-pounder Parrott guns; Bramhall's battery, 6th New York, 6 3-inch ordnance guns; Osborn's battery D, 1st New York artillery, 4 3-inch ordnance guns.

Infantry.—Sickles's brigade: 1st, 2d, 3d, 4th, and 5th Excelsior, New York. Naglee's brigade: 1st and 11th Massachusetts, 26th Pennsylvania, and 2d New Hampshire volunteers. Colonel Starr's brigade: 5th, 6th, 7th, and 8th New Jersey volunteers.

HAMILTON'S DIVISION.

Artillery.—Thompson's battery G, 2d United States, 6 Napoleon guns; Beam's battery B, New Jersey, 6—4 10-pounder Parrott and 2 Napoleon—guns; Randolph's battery E, Rhode Island, 6—4 10-pounder Parrott and 2 Napoleon—guns.

Infantry.—Jameson's brigade: 105th, 63d, and 57th Pennsylvania, and 87th New York volunteers. Birney's brigade: 38th and 40th New York, and 3d and 4th Maine volunteers. ——— brigade: 2d, 3d, and 5th Michigan, and 37th New York volunteers.

FOURTH CORPS, GENERAL KEYES.

COUCH'S DIVISION.

Artillery.—McCarthy's battery C, 1st Pennsylvania, 4 10-pounder Parrott guns; Flood's battery D, 1st Pennsylvania, 4 10-pounder Parrott guns; Miller's battery E, 1st Pennsylvania, 4 Napoleon guns; Brady's battery F, 1st Pennsylvania, 4 10-pounder Parrott guns.

Infantry.—Graham's brigade: 67th (1st Long Island) and 65th (1st United States chasseurs) New York, 23d, 31st, and 61st Pennsylvania volunteers. Peck's brigade: 98th, 102d, and 93d Pennsylvania, and 62d and 55th New York volunteers. ——— brigade: 2d Rhode Island, 7th and 10th Massachusetts, and 36th New York volunteers.

SMITH'S DIVISION.

Artillery.—Ayre's battery F, 5th United States, 6—4 10-pounder Parrott and 2 Napoleon—guns; Mott's battery, 3d New York, 6—4 10-pounder Parrott and 2 Napoleon—guns; Wheeler's battery E, 1st New York, 4 3-inch ordnance guns; Kennedy's battery, 1st New York, 6 3-inch ordnance guns.

Infantry.—Hancock's brigade: 4th Wisconsin, 49th Pennsylvania, 43d New York, and 6th Maine volunteers. Brooks's brigade: 2d, 3d, 4th, 5th, and 6th Vermont volunteers. Davidson's brigade: 33d, 77th, and 49th New York, and 7th Maine volunteers.

CASEY'S DIVISION.

Artillery.—Regan's battery, 7th New York, 6 3-inch ordnance guns; Fitch's 8th New York, 6 3-inch ordnance guns; Bates's battery A, 1st New York, 6 Napoleon guns; Spratt's battery H, 1st New York, 4 3-inch ordnance guns.

Infantry.—Keim's brigade: 85th, 101st, and 103d Pennsylvania, and 96th New York volunteers. Palmer's brigade: 85th, 98th, 92d, 81st, and 93d New York volunteers. ——— brigade: 104th and 52d Pennsylvania, 56th and 100th New York, and 11th Maine volunteers.

5th. Provost guard: 2d United States cavalry; battalions 8th and 17th United States infantry.

At general headquarters: 2 companies 4th United States cavalry; 1 company Oneida cavalry, (New York volunteers;) and 1 company Sturges's rifles, (Illinois volunteers.)

The following troops of the army of the Potomac were left behind, or detached on and in front of the Potomac for the defence of that line, April 1, 1862. Franklin's and McCall's divisions, at subsequent and different dates, joined the active portion of the army on the Peninsula. Two brigades of Shields's division joined at Harrison's landing:

FIRST CORPS, GENERAL McDOWELL.

Cavalry.—1st, 2d, and 4th New York, and 1st Pennsylvania.
Sharpshooters.—2d regiment Berdan's sharpshooters.

FRANKLIN'S DIVISION.

Artillery.—Platt's battery D, 2d United States, 6 Napoleon guns; Porter's battery A, Massachusetts, 6—4 10-pounder Parrott and 2 12-pounder howitzer—guns; Hexamer's battery A, New Jersey, 6—4 10-pounder Parrott and 2 12-pounder howitzer—guns; Wilson's battery F, 1st New York artillery, 4 3-inch ordnance guns.

Infantry.—Kearney's brigade: 1st, 2d, 3d, and 4th New Jersey volunteers. Slocum's brigade: 16th and 27th New York, 5th Maine, and 96th Pennsylvania volunteers. Newton's brigade: 18th, 31st, and 32d New York, and 95th Pennsylvania volunteers.

M'CALL'S DIVISION.

Artillery.—Seymour's battery C, 5th United States, 6 Napoleon guns; Easton's battery A, 1st Pennsylvania, 4 Napoleon guns; Cooper's battery B, 1st Pennsylvania, 6 10-pounder Parrott guns; Kein's battery C, 1st Pennsylvania, 6—2 10-pounder and 4 12-pounder Parrott—guns.

Infantry.—Reynolds's brigade: 1st, 2d, 5th, and 8th Pennsylvania reserve regiments. Meade's brigade: 3d, 4th, 7th, and 11th Pennsylvania reserve regiments. Ord's brigade: 6th, 9th, 10th, and 12th Pennsylvania reserve regiments.

1st Pennsylvania reserve rifles.

KING'S DIVISION.

Artillery.—Gibbon's battery B, 4th United States, 6 Napoleon guns; Monroe's battery D, 1st Rhode Island, 6 10-pounder Parrott guns; Gerrish's battery A, New Hampshire, 6 Napoleon guns; Durrell's battery, Pennsylvania, 6 10-pounder Parrott guns.

Infantry.———— brigade: 2d, 6th, and 7th Wisconsin, and 19th Indiana volunteers. Patrick's brigade: 20th, 21st, 23d, and 25th New York State militia. Augur's brigade: 14th New York State militia, and 22d, 24th, and 30th New York volunteers.

FIFTH CORPS, GENERAL BANKS.

Cavalry.—1st Maine, 1st Vermont, 1st Michigan, 1st Rhode Island, 5th and 8th New York, Keyes battalion of Pennsylvania, 18 companies of Maryland, 1 squadron of Virginia.

Unattached.—28th Pennsylvania volunteers, and 4th regiment Potomac home brigade, (Maryland volunteers.)

WILLIAMS'S DIVISION.

Artillery.—Best's battery F, 4th United States, 6 Napoleon guns; Hampton's battery, Maryland, 4 10-pounder Parrott guns; Thompson's battery, Maryland, 4 10-pounder Parrott guns; Mathews's battery F, Pennsylvania, 6 3-inch ordnance guns; ——— battery M, 1st New York, 6 10-pounder Parrott guns; Knapp's battery, Pennsylvania, 6 10-pounder Parrott guns; McMahon's battery, New York, 6 3-inch ordnance guns.

Infantry.—Abercrombie's brigade: 12th and 2d Massachusetts, and 16th Indiana, 1st Potomac home brigade, (Maryland,) 1 company Zouaves D'Afrique, (Pennsylvania) volunteers. ——— brigade: 9th New York State militia, and 29th Pennsylvania, 29th Indiana, and 3d Wisconsin volunteers. ——— brigade: 28th New York, 5th Connecticut, 46th Pennsylvania, 1st Maryland, 12th Indiana, and 13th Massachusetts volunteers.

SHIELDS'S DIVISION.

Artillery.—Clark's battery E, 4th United States, 6 10-pounder Parrott guns; Jenks's battery A, 1st Virginia, 4 10-pounder Parrott and 2 6-pounder guns; Davy's battery B, 1st Virginia, 2 10-pounder Parrott guns; Huntington's battery A, 1st Ohio, 6 13-pounder James's guns; Robinson's battery L, 1st Ohio, 2 12-pounder howitzers and 4 6-pounder guns; and ——— battery, 4th Ohio artillery.

Infantry.— ——— brigade: 14th Indiana, 4th, 8th, and 67th Ohio, 7th Virginia, and 84th Pennsylvania volunteers. ——— brigade: 5th, 62d, and 66th Ohio, 13th Indiana, and 39th Illinois volunteers. ——— brigade: 7th and 29th Ohio, 7th Indiana, 1st Virginia, and 11th Pennsylvania volunteers. Andrew sharpshooters.

GENERAL WADSWORTH'S COMMAND.

Cavalry.—1st New Jersey cavalry, at Alexandria, and 4th Pennsylvania cavalry, east of the Capitol.

Artillery and infantry.—10th New Jersey volunteers, Bladensburg road; 104th New York volunteers, Kalorama heights; 1st Wisconsin heavy artillery, Fort Cass, Virginia; 3 batteries of New York artillery, Forts Ethan Allen and Marcy; depot of New York light artillery, Camp Barry; 2d District of Columbia volunteers, Washington city; 26th Pennsylvania volunteers, G street wharf; 26th New York volunteers, Fort Lyon; 95th New York volunteers, Camp Thomas; 94th New York and detachment of 88th Pennsylvania volunteers, Alexandria; 91st Pennsylvania volunteers, Franklin Square barracks; 4th New York artillery, Forts Carroll and Greble; 112th Pennsylvania volunteers, Fort Saratoga; 76th New York volunteers, Fort Massachusetts; 59th New York volunteers, Fort Pennsylvania; detachment of 88th Pennsylvania volunteers, Fort Good Hope; 99th Pennsylvania volunteers, Fort Mahon; 2d New York light artillery, Forts Ward, Worth, and Blenker; 107th and 54th Pennsylvania volunteers, Kendall Green; Dickerson's light artillery, 86th New York, and detachment of 88th Pennsylvania volunteers, east of the Capitol; 14th Massachusetts (volunteers) heavy artillery and 56th Pennsylvania volunteers, Forts Albany, Tillinghast, Richardson, Runyon, Jackson, Barnard, Craig, and Scott; detachments of 4th United States artillery and 37th New York volunteers, Fort Washington; 97th, 101st, and 91st New York, and 12th Virginia volunteers, Fort Corcoran.

In camp near Washington.—6th and 10th New York, Swain's New York, and 2d Pennsylvania cavalry, all dismounted.

These troops (3,359 men) were ordered to report to Colonel Miles, commanding railroad guard, to relieve 3,306 older troops ordered to be sent to Manassas to report to General Abercrombie.

GENERAL DIX'S COMMAND, BALTIMORE.

Cavalry.—1st Maryland cavalry and detachment of Purnell Legion cavalry.

Artillery.—Battery I, 2d United States; battery —, Maryland; battery L, 1st New York, and two independent batteries of Pennsylvania artillery.

Infantry.—3d and 4th New York. 11th, 87th, and 111th Pennsylvania, detachment 21st Massachusetts, 2d Delaware, 2d Maryland, 1st and 2d Eastern Shore (Maryland) home guards, and Purnell Legion (two battalions) Maryland volunteers.

In a staff charged with labors so various and important as that of the army of the Potomac, a chief was indispensable to supervise the various departments and to relieve the commanding general of details. The officer of chief of staff, well known in European armies, had not been considered necessary in our small peace establishment. The functions of the office were not defined, and, so far as exercised, had been included in the Adjutant General's department. The small number of officers in this department, and the necessity for their employment in other duties, have obliged commanding generals, during this war, to resort to other branches of the service to furnish suitable chiefs of staff.

On the 4th of September, 1861, I appointed Colonel R. B. Marcy, of the inspector general's department, chief of staff, and he entered upon service immediately, discharging the various and important duties with great fidelity, industry, and ability, from this period until I was removed from command at Rectortown. Many improvements have been made during the war in our system of staff administration, but much remains to be done.

Our own experience, and that of other armies, agree in determining the necessity for an efficient and able staff. To obtain this, our staff establishment should be based on correct principles, and extended to be adequate to the necessities of the service, and should include a system of staff and line education.

The affairs of the Adjutant General's department, while I commanded the army of the Potomac, were conducted by Brigadier General S. Williams, assisted by Lieutenant Colonel James A. Hardie, aide-de-camp. Their management of the department during the organization of the army in the fall and winter of 1861, and during its subsequent operations in the field, was excellent.

They were, during the entire period, assisted by Captain Richard B. Irwin, aide-de-camp, and during the organization of the army by the following-named officers: Captains Joseph Kirkland, Arthur McClellan, M. T. McMahon, William P. Mason, and William F. Biddle, aides-de-camp.

My personal staff, when we embarked for the Peninsula, consisted of Colonel Thomas M. Key, additional aide-de-camp; Colonel E. H. Wright, additional aide-de-camp and major, 6th United States cavalry; Colonel T. T. Gantt, additional aide-de-camp; Colonel J. J. Astor, jr., volunteer aide-de-camp; Lieutenant Colonel A. V. Colburn, additional aide-de-camp and captain, Adjutant General's department; Lieutenant Colonel N. B. Sweitzer, additional aide-de-camp and captain, 1st United States cavalry; Lieutenant Colonel Edward McK. Hudson, additional aide-de-camp and captain, 14th United States infantry; Lieutenant Colonel Paul Von Radowitz, additional aide-de-camp; Major H. Von Hammerstein, additional aide-de-camp; Major W. W. Russell, United States marine corps; Major F. LeCompte, of the Swiss army, volunteer aide-de-camp; Captains Joseph Kirkland, Arthur McClellan, L. P. D'Orleans, R. D'Orleans, M. T. McMahon, William P. Mason, jr., William F. Biddle, and E. A. Raymond, additional aides-de-camp.

To this number I am tempted to add the Prince de Joinville, who constantly accompanied me through the trying campaign of the Peninsula, and frequently rendered important services. Of these officers Captain McMahon was assigned to the personal staff of Brigadier General Franklin, and Captains Kirkland and Mason to that of Brigadier General F. J. Porter during the siege of Yorktown. They remained subsequently with those general officers. Major LeCompte left the army during the siege of Yorktown; Colonels Gantt and Astor, Major Russell, Captains L. P. D'Orleans, R. D'Orleans, and Raymond at the close of the Peninsula campaign. Before its termination Captains W. S. Abert and Charles R. Lowell, of the 6th United States cavalry, joined my staff as aides-de-camp, and remained with me until I was relieved from the command of the army of the Potomac. All of these officers served me with great gallantry and devotion; they were ever ready to execute any service, no matter how dangerous, difficult, or fatiguing.

ENGINEERS.

When I assumed command of the army of the Potomac I found Major J. G. Barnard, United States engineers, subsequently brigadier general of volunteers, occupying the position of chief engineer of that army. I continued him in the same office, and at once gave the necessary instructions for the completion of the defences of the capital, and for the entire reorganization of the department.

Under his direction the entire system of defences was carried into execution. This was completed before the army departed for Fort Monroe, and is a sufficient evidence of the skill of the engineers and the diligent labor of the troops.

For some months after the organization of the army of the Potomac was commenced there were no engineer troops with it. At length, however, three companies were assigned. Under the skilful management of Captain J. C. Duane, United States engineers, these new companies rapidly became efficient, and, as will be seen, rendered most valuable service during the ensuing campaigns.

The number of engineer troops being entirely inadequate to the necessities of the army, an effort was made to partially remedy this defect by detailing the 15th and 50th New York volunteers, which contained many sailors and mechanics, as engineer troops. They were first placed under the immediate superintendence of Lieutenant Colonel B. S. Alexander, United States engineers, by whom they were instructed in the duties of pontoniers, and became somewhat familiar with those of sappers and miners. Previous to the movement of the army for the Peninsula this brigade was placed under the command of Brigadier General D. P. Woodbury, major United States engineers.

The labor of preparing the engineer and bridge trains devolved chiefly upon Captain Duane, who was instructed to procure the new model French bridge train, as I was satisfied that the India-rubber pontoon was entirely useless for the general purposes of a campaign.

The engineer department presented the following complete organization when the army moved for the Peninsula:

Brigadier General J. G. Barnard, chief engineer; First Lieutenant H. C. Abbott, topographical engineers, aide-de-camp. Brigade volunteer engineers, Brigadier General Woodbury commanding: 15th New York volunteers, Colonel McLeod Murphy; 50th New York volunteers, Colonel C. B. Stewart. Battalion, three companies United States engineers, Captain J. C. Duane commanding; companies respectively commanded by First Lieutenants C. B. Reese, C. E. Cross, and O. E. Babcock, United States engineers. The chief engineer was ably assisted in his duties by Lieutenant Colonel B. S. Alexander, and First Lieutenants C. R. Comstock, M. D. McAlester, and Merrill, United States engineers. Captain C. S. Stuart and Second Lieutenant F. U. Farquhar, United States engineers, joined after the army arrived at Fort Monroe.

The necessary bridge equipage for the operations of a large army had been collected, consisting of bateaux with the anchors and flooring material, (French model,) trestles, and engineers' tools, with the necessary wagons for their transportation.

The small number of officers of this corps available rendered it impracticable to detail engineers permanently at the headquarters of corps and divisions. The companies of regular engineers never had their proper number of officers, and it was necessary, as a rule, to follow the principle of detailing engineer officers temporarily whenever their services were required.

TOPOGRAPHICAL ENGINEERS.

To the corps of topographical engineers was intrusted the collection of topographical information and the preparation of campaign maps. Until a short time previous to the departure of the army for Fort Monroe, Lieutenant Colonel John W. Macomb was in charge of this department, and prepared a large amount of valuable material. He was succeeded by Brigadier General A. A. Humphreys, who retained the position throughout the Peninsula campaign. These officers were assisted by Lieutenants H. L. Abbott, O. G. Wagner, N. Bowen, John M. Wilson, and James H. Wilson, topographical engineers. This number, being the greatest available, was so small that much of the duty of the department devolved upon parties furnished by Professor Bache, Superintendent of the Coast Survey, and other gentlemen from civil life.

Owing to the entire absence of reliable topographical maps, the labors of this corps were difficult and arduous in the extreme. Notwithstanding the energy and ability displayed by General Humphreys, Lieutenant Colonel Macomb, and their subordinates, who frequently obtained the necessary information under fire, the movements of the army were sometimes unavoidably delayed by the difficulty of obtaining knowledge of the country in advance. The result of their labors has been the preparation of an excellent series of maps, which will be invaluable to any army traversing the same ground

During the campaign it was impossible to draw a distinct line of demarcation between the duties of the two corps of engineers so that the labors of reconnoissances of roads, of lines of intrenchments, of fields for battle, and of the position of the enemy, as well as the construction of siege and defensive works, were habitually performed by details from either corps, as the convenience of the service demanded.

I desire to express my high appreciation of the skill, gallantry, and devotion displayed by the officers of both corps of engineers, under the most trying circumstances.

During the Maryland campaign I united the two corps under Captain J. C. Duane, United States engineers, and found great advantages from the arrangement.

MEDICAL DEPARTMENT.

For the operations of the medical department I refer to the reports, transmitted herewith, of Surgeon Charles S. Tripler and Surgeon Jonathan Letterman, who, in turn, performed the duties of medical director of the army of the Potomac, the former from August 12, 1861, until July 1, 1862, and the latter after that date. The difficulties to be overcome in organizing and making effective the medical department were very great, arising principally from the inexperience of the regimental medical officers, many of whom were physicians taken suddenly from civil life, who, according to Surgeon Tripler, "had to be instructed in their duties from the very alphabet," and from the ignorance of the line officers as to their relations with the medical officers, which gave rise to confusion and conflict of authority. Boards of examination were instituted, by which many ignorant officers were removed; and by the successive exertions of Surgeons Tripler and Letterman, the medical corps was brought to a very high degree of efficiency. With regard to the sanitary condition of the army while on the Potomac, Dr. Tripler says that the records show a constantly increasing immunity from disease. "In October and November, 1861, with an army averaging 130,000 men, we had 7,932 cases of fever of all sorts; of these, about 1,000 were reported as cases of typhoid fever. I know that errors of diagnosis were frequently committed, and therefore this must be considered as the limit of typhoid cases. If any army in the world can show such a record as this, I do not know when or where it was assembled." From September, 1861, to February, 1862, while the army was increasing, the number of sick decreased from 7 per cent. to 6.18 per cent. Of these, the men sick in the regimental and general hospitals were less than one-half; the remainder were slight cases, under treatment in quarters. "During this time, so far as rumor was concerned, the army was being decimated by disease every month." Of the sanitary condition of the army during the Peninsula campaign, up to its arrival at Harrison's landing, Dr. Tripler says: "During this campaign the army was favored with excellent health. No epidemic disease appeared. Those scourges of modern armies—dysentery, tupus, cholera—were almost unknown. We had some typhoid fever and more malarial fevers, but even these never prevailed to such an extent as to create any alarm. The sick reports were sometimes larger than we cared to have them; but the great majority of the cases reported were such as did not threaten life or permanent disability. I regret that I have not before me the retained copies of the monthly reports, so that I might give accurate statistics. I have endeavored to recover them, but have been unsuccessful. My recollection is, that the whole sick report never exceeded 8 per cent. of the force, and this including all sorts of cases, the trivial as well as the severe. The army of the Potomac must be conceded to have been the most healthy army in the service of the United States."

His remarks at the conclusion of his report upon our system of medical administration, and his suggestions for its improvement, are especially worthy of attention.

The service, labors, and privations of the troops during the seven days' battles had, of course, a great effect on the health of the army, after it reached Harrison's landing, increasing the number of sick to about 20 per cent. of the whole force.

The nature of the military operations had also unavoidably placed the medical department in a very unsatisfactory condition. Supplies had been almost entirely exhausted or necessarily abandoned; hospital tents abandoned or destroyed, and the medical officers deficient in numbers and broken down by fatigue.

All the remarkable energy and ability of Surgeon Letterman were required to restore the efficiency of his department; but before we left Harrison's landing he had succeeded in fitting it out thoroughly with the supplies it required, and the health of the army was vastly improved by the sanitary measures which were enforced at his suggestion.

The great haste with which the army was removed from the Peninsula made it necessary to leave at Fort Monroe, to be forwarded afterwards, nearly all the baggage and transportation, including medical stores and ambulances, all the vessels being required to transport the troops themselves and their ammunition; and when the army of the Potomac returned to Washington after General Pope's campaign, and the medical department came once more under Surgeon Letterman's control, he found it in a deplorable condition. The officers were worn out by the labors they had performed, and the few supplies that had been brought from the Peninsula had been exhausted or abandoned, so that the work of reorganization and resupplying had to be again performed, and this while the army was moving rapidly, and almost in the face of the enemy. That it was successfully accomplished is shown by the care and attention which the wounded received after the battles of South Mountain and Antietam.

Among the improvements introduced into his department by Surgeon Letterman, the principal are the organization of an ambulance corps, the system of field hospitals, and the method of supplying by brigades, all of which were instituted during the Maryland campaign, and have since proved very efficient.

QUARTERMASTER'S DEPARTMENT.

On assuming command of the troops in and around Washington, I appointed Captain S. Van Vliet, assistant quartermaster, (afterwards brigadier general,) chief quartermaster to my command, and gave him the necessary instructions for organizing his department, and collecting the supplies requisite for the large army then called for.

The disaster at Manassas had but recently occurred, and the army was quite destitute of quartermaster's stores. General Van Vliet, with great energy and zeal, set himself about the task of furnishing the supplies immediately necessary, and preparing to obtain the still larger amounts which would be required by the new troops, which were moving in large numbers towards the capital. The principal depot for supplies in the city of Washington was under charge of Colonel D. H. Rucker, assistant quartermaster, who ably performed his duties. Lieutenant Colonel R. Ingalls, assistant quartermaster, was placed in charge of the department on the south side of the Potomac. I directed a large depot for transportation to be established at Perryville, on the left bank of the Susquehanna, a point equally accessible by rail and water. Captain C. G. Sawtelle, assistant quartermaster, was detailed to organize the camp, and performed his duties to my entire satisfaction. Captain J. J. Dana, assistant quartermaster, had immediate charge of the transportation in and about Washington, as well as of the large number of horses purchased for the use of the artillery and cavalry. The principal difficulties which General Van Vliet had to encounter arose from the inexperience of the majority of the officers of his department in the new regiments and brigades.

The necessity of attending personally to minor details rendered his duties arduous and harassing in the extreme. All obstacles, however, were surmounted by the untiring industry of the chief quartermaster and his immediate subordinates, and when the army was prepared to move the organization of the department was found to be admirable.

When it was determined to move the army to the Peninsula, the duties of providing water transportation were devolved by the Secretary of War upon his assistant, the Hon. John Tucker. The vessels were ordered to Alexandria, and Lieutenant Colonel Ingalls was placed in immediate charge of the embarkation of the troops, transportation, and materiel of every description. Operations of this nature, on so extensive a scale, had no parallel in the history of our country.

The arrangements of Lieutenant Colonel Ingalls were perfected with remarkable skill and energy, and the army and its materiel were embarked and transported to Fortress Monroe in a very short space of time, and entirely without loss.

During the operations on the Peninsula, until the arrival of troops at Harrison's landing, General Van Vliet retained the position of chief quartermaster, and maintained the thorough organization and efficiency of his department. The principal depots of supplies were under the immediate charge of Lieutenant Colonels Ingalls and Sawtelle.

On the 10th of July, 1862, General Van Vliet having requested to be relieved from duty with the army of the Potomac, I appointed Lieutenant Colonel Ingalls chief quartermaster, and he continued to discharge the duties of that office during the remainder of the Peninsula and the Maryland campaigns in a manner which fully sustained the high reputation he had previously acquired.

The immediate amount of labor accomplished, often under the most difficult circumstances, the admirable system under which the duties of the department were performed, and the entire success which attended the efforts to supply so large an army, reflect the highest credit upon the officers upon whom these onerous duties devolved. The reports of General Van Vliet and Lieutenant Colonel Ingalls, with the accompanying documents, give in detail the history of the department from its organization until I was relieved from the command of the army of the Potomac.

SUBSISTENCE DEPARTMENT.

On the 1st of August, 1861, Colonel H. F. Clark, commissary of subsistence, joined my staff, and at once entered upon his duties as chief commissary of the army of the Potomac. In order to realize the responsibilities pertaining to this office, as well as to form a proper estimate of the vast amount of labor which must necessarily devolve upon its occupant, it is only necessary to consider the unprepared state of the country to engage in a war of such magnitude as the present, and the lack of practical knowledge, on the part of the officers, with reference to supplying and subsisting a large, and at that time, unorganized army. Yet, notwithstanding the existence of these great obstacles, the manner in which the duties of the commissary department were discharged was such as to merit and call forth the commendation of the entire army.

During the stay of the army of the Potomac in the vicinity of Washington, prior to the Peninsula campaign, its subsistence was drawn chiefly from the depots which had been established by the commissary department at Washington, Alexandria, Forts Corcoran and Runyon. In the important task of designating and establishing depots of supplies, Colonel Clarke was ably seconded by his assistants, Colonel Amos Beckwith, commissary of subsistence, U. S. A.; Lieutenant Colonel George Bell, commissary of subsistence, U. S. A.; Lieutenant Colonel A. P. Porter, commissary of subsistence, U. S. A.; Captain Thomas Wilson, commissary of subsistence, U. S. A.; Captain Brownell Granger, commissary of subsistence, U. S. volunteers; Captain W. H. Bell, commissary of subsistence, U. S. A.; Captain J. H. Woodward, commissary of subsistence, U. S. volunteers; and Captain W. R. Murphy, commissary of subsistence, U. S. volunteers.

For a full knowledge of the highly creditable manner in whic heach and all of the above-mentioned officers discharged their duties, I invite attention to the detailed report of Colonel Clarke. The remarks and suggestions contained in his report are worthy of attention, as affording valuable rules for the future guidance of the subsistence department in supplying armies in the field. The success of the subsistence department of the army of the Potomac was in a great measure attributable to the fact that the subsistence department at Washington made ample provision for sending supplies to the Peninsula, and that it always exercised the most intelligent foresight. It moreover gave its advice and countenance to the officers charged with its duties and reputation in the field, and those officers, I am happy to say, worked with it, and together, in perfect harmony for the public good. During the entire period that I was in command of the army of the Potomac there was no instance within my knowledge where the troops were without their rations from any fault of the officers of this department.

ORDNANCE DEPARTMENT.

This very important branch of the service was placed under the charge of Captain C. P. Kingsbury, ordnance corps, colonel and aide-de-camp. Great difficulty existed in the proper organization of the department for the want of a sufficient number of suitable officers to perform the duties at the various headquarters and depots of supply. But far greater obstacles had to be surmounted, from the fact that the supply of small arms was totally inadequate to the demands of a large army, and a vast proportion of those furnished were of such inferior quality as to be unsatisfactory to the troops, and condemned by their officers. The supply of artillery was more abundant, but of great variety. Rifled ordnance was just coming into use, for the first time in this country, and the description of gun and kind of projectile which would prove most effective, and should, therefore, be adopted, was a mere matter of theory. To obviate these difficulties, large quantities of small arms of foreign manufacture were contracted for; private enterprise in the construction of arms and ammunition was encouraged; and by the time the army was ordered to move to the Peninsula the amount of ordnance and ordnance stores was ample. Much also had been done to bring the quality, both of arms and ammunition, up to the proper standard. Boards of officers were in session continually during the autumn and winter of 1861, to test the relative merits of new arms and projectiles.

The reports of these boards, confirmed by subsequent experience in the field, have done much to establish the respective claims of different inventors and manufacturers. During the campaigns of the Peninsula and Maryland the officers connected with the department were zealous and energetic, and kept the troops well supplied, notwithstanding the perplexing and arduous nature of their duties. One great source of perplexity was the fact that it had been necessary to issue arms of all varieties and calibres, giving an equal diversity in the kinds of ammunition required. Untiring watchfulness was therefore incumbent upon the officers in charge to prevent confusion and improper distribution of cartridges. Colonel Kingsbury discharged the duties of his office with great efficiency until the —— day of July, 1862, when his health required that he should be relieved. First Lieutenant Thomas G. Baylor, ordnance corps, succeeded him, and performed his duty during the remainder of the Peninsula and Maryland campaigns with marked ability and success.

The want of reports from Colonel Kingsbury and Lieutenant Baylor renders it impossible for me to enter at all into the details of the organization of the department.

PROVOST MARSHAL'S DEPARTMENT.

Immediately after I was placed in command of the "Division of the Potomac," I appointed Colonel Andrew Porter, 16th regiment infantry, provost marshal of Washington. All the available regular infantry, a battery and a squadron of cavalry were placed under his command, and by his energetic action he soon corrected the serious evils which existed, and restored order in the city.

When the army was about to take the field, General Porter was appointed Provost Marshal General of the army of the Potomac and held that most important position until the end of the Peninsula campaign, when sickness, contracted in the untiring discharge of his duties, compelled him to ask to be relieved from the position he had so ably and energetically filled.

The Provost Marshal General's department had the charge of a class of duties which had not before, in our service, been defined and grouped under the management of a special department. The following subjects indicate the sphere of this department: suppression of marauding and depredations, and of all brawls and disturbances, preservation of good order, and suppression of disturbances beyond the limits of the camps.

Prevention of straggling on the march.

Suppression of gambling houses, drinking houses, or bar-rooms, and brothels.

Regulation of hotels, taverns, markets, and places of public amusement.

Searches, seizures and arrests. Execution of sentences of general courts-martial, involving imprisonment or capital punishment. Enforcement of orders prohibiting the sale of intoxicating liquors, whether by tradesmen or sutlers, and of orders respecting passes.

Deserters from the enemy.

Prisoners of war taken from the enemy.

Countersigning safeguards.

Passes to citizens within the lines, and for purposes of trade.

Complaints of citizens as to the conduct of the soldiers.

General Porter was assisted by the following named officers:

Major W. H. Wood, 17th United States infantry; Captain James McMillom, acting assistant adjutant general, 17th United States infantry; Captain W. T. Gentry, 17th United States infantry; Captain J. W. Forsurth, 18th United States infantry; Lieutenant J. W. Jones, 12th United States infantry; Lieutenant C. F. Trowbridge, 16th United States infantry; and Lieutenant C. D. Mehaffey, 1st United States infantry.

The provost guard was composed of the 2d United States cavalry, Major Pleasanton, and a battalion of the 8th and 17th United States infantry, Major Willard. After General Porter was relieved, Major Wood was in charge of this department until after the battle of Antietam, when Brigadier General Patrick was appointed Provost Marshal General.

COMMANDANT OF GENERAL HEADQUARTERS.

When the army took the field, for the purpose of securing order and regularity in the camp of headquarters, and facilitating its movements, the office of commandant of general headquarters was created, and assigned to Major G. O. Haller, 7th United States infantry. Six companies of infantry were placed under his orders for guard and police duty. Among the orders appended to this report is the one defining his duties, which were always satisfactorily performed.

JUDGE ADVOCATE.

From August, 1861, the position of judge advocate was held by Colonel Thomas T. Gantt, aide-de-camp, until compelled by ill health to retire, at Harrison's landing, in August, 1862. His reviews of the decisions of courts-martial during this period were of great utility in correcting the practice in military courts, diffusing true notions of discipline and subordination, and setting before the army a high standard of soldierly honor. Upon the retirement of Colonel Gantt the duties of judge advocate were ably performed by Colonel Thomas M. Key, aide-de-camp.

SIGNAL CORPS.

The method of conveying intelligence and orders, invented and introduced into the service by Major Albert J. Myer, signal officer United States army, was first practically tested in large operations during the organization of the army of the Potomac.

Under the direction of Major Myer a signal corps was formed by detailing officers and men from the different regiments of volunteers and instructing them in the use of the flags by day and torches by night.

The chief signal officer was indefatigable in his exertions to render his corps effective, and it soon became available for service in every division of the army. In addition to the flags and torches, Major Myer introduced a portable insulated telegraph wire, which could be readily laid from point to point, and which could be used under the same general system. In front of Washington, and on the Lower Potomac, at any point within our lines not reached by the military telegraph, the great usefulness of this system ofsignals was made manifest. But it was not until after the arrival of the army upon the Peninsula, and during the siege and battles of that and the Maryland campaigns that the great benefits to be derived from it on the field and under fire were fully appreciated.

There was scarcely any action or skirmish in which the signal corps did not render important services. Often under heavy fire of artillery, and not unfrequently while exposed to musketry, the officers and men of this corps gave information of the movements of the enemy, and transmitted directions for the evolutions of our own troops.

The report of the chief signal officer, with accompanying documents, will give the details of the services of this corps, and call attention to those members of it who were particularly distinguished.

TELEGRAPHIC.

The telegraphic operations of the army of the Potomac were superintended by Major Thomas J. Eckert, and under the immediate direction of Mr. ——— Caldwell, who was, with a corps of operators, attached to my headquarters during the entire campaigns upon the Peninsula and in Maryland.

The services of this corps were arduous and efficient. Under the admirable arrangements of Major Eckert they were constantly provided with all the material for constructing new lines, which were rapidly established whenever the army changed position; and it was not unfrequently the case that the operatives worked under fire from the enemy's guns; yet they invariably performed all the duties required of them with great alacrity and cheerfulness, and it was seldom that I was without the means of direct telegraphic communication with the War Department and with the corps commanders.

From the organization of the army of the Potomac up to November 1, 1862, including the Peninsula and Maryland campaigns, upwards of twelve hundred (1,200) miles of military telegraph line had been constructed in connexion with the operations of the army, and the number of operatives and builders employed was about two hundred, (200.)

To Professor Lowe, the intelligent and enterprising æronaut, who had the management of the balloons, I was greatly indebted for the valuable information obtained during his ascensions.

I have more than once taken occasion to recommend the members of my staff, both general and personal, for promotion and reward. I beg leave to repeat these recommendations, and to record their names in the history of the army of the Potomac, as gallant soldiers, to whom their country owes a debt of gratitude still unpaid, for the courage, ability, and untiring zeal they displayed during the eventful campaigns in which they bore so prominent a part.

CHAPTER II.

On the 15th of October the main body of the army of the Potomac was in the immediate vicinity of Washington, with detachments on the left bank of the Potomac as far down as Liverpool point, and as far up as Williamsport and its vicinity. The different divisions were posted as follows: Hooker at Budd's ferry, Lower Potomac; Heintzelman at Fort Lyon and vicinity; Franklin near the theological seminary; Blenker near Hunter's chapel; McDowell at Upton's hill and Arlington; F. J. Porter at Hall's and Miner's hills; Smith at Mackall's hill; McCall at Langley; Buell at Tenallytown, Meridian hill, Emory's chapel, &c., on the left bank of the river; Casey at Washington; Stoneman's cavalry at Washington; Hunt's artillery at Washington; Banks at Darnestown, with detachments at Point of Rocks, Sandy Hook, Williamsport, &c.; Stone at Poolesville; and Dix at Baltimore, with detachments on the Eastern Shore.

On the 19th of October, 1861, General McCall marched to Drainsville with his division, in order to cover reconnoissances to be made in all directions the next day, for the purpose of learning the position of the enemy, and of covering the operations of the topographical engineers in making maps of that region.

On the 29th, acting in concert with General McCall, General Smith pushed strong parties to Freedom hill, Vienna, Flint hill, Peacock hill, &c., to accomplish the same purpose in that part of the front. These reconnoissances were successful.

On the morning of the 20th I received the following telegram from General Banks's headquarters:

"DARNESTOWN, *October* 20, 1861.

"SIR: The signal station at Sugar Loaf telegraphs that the enemy have moved away from Leesburg. All quiet here.

"R. M. COPELAND,
"*Assistant Adjutant General.*

"General MARCY."

Whereupon I sent to General Stone, at Poolsville, the following telegram:

"CAMP GRIFFIN, *October* 20, 1861.

"General McClellan desires me to inform you that General McCall occupied Drainsville yesterday, and is still there. Will send out heavy reconnoissances to-day in all directions from that point. The general desires that you will keep a good look-out upon Leesburg, to see if this movement has the effect to drive them away. Perhaps a slight demonstration on your part would have the effect to move them.

"A. V. COLBURN,
"*Assistant Adjutant General.*

"Brigadier General C. P. STONE, *Poolsville.*"

Deeming it possible that General McCall's movement to Drainsville, together with the subsequent reconnoissances, might have the effect of inducing the enemy to abandon Leesburg, and the despatch from Sugar Loaf appearing to confirm this view, I wished General Stone, who had only a line of pickets on the river, the mass of his troops being out of sight of, and beyond range from, the Virginia bank, to make some display of an intention to cross, and also to watch the enemy more closely than usual. I did not direct him to cross, nor did I intend that he should cross the river in force for the purpose of fighting.

The above despatch was sent on the 20th, and reached General Stone as early as 11 a. m. of that day. I expected him to accomplish all that was intended on the same day; and this he did, as will be seen from the following despatch, received at my headquarters in Washington from Poolsville on the evening of October 20:

"Made a feint of crossing at this place this afternoon, and at the same time started a reconnoitring party towards Leesburg from Harrison's island. The enemy's pickets retired to intrenchments. Report of reconnoitring party not yet received. I have means of crossing one hundred and twenty-five men once in ten minutes at each of two points. River falling slowly.

"C. P. STONE,
"*Brigadier General.*

"Major General McCLELLAN."

As it was not foreseen or expected that General McCall would be needed to co-operate with General Stone in any attack, he was directed to fall back from

Drainsville to his original camp, near Prospect hill, as soon as the required reconnoissances were completed.

Accordingly he left Drainsville, on his return, at about 8½ a. m. of the 21st, reaching his old camp at about 1 p. m.

In the mean time I was surprised to hear from General Stone that a portion of his troops were engaged on the Virginia side of the river, and at once sent instructions to General McCall to remain at Drainsville, if he had not left before the order reached him.

The order did not reach him until his return to his camp at Langley. He was then ordered to rest his men, and hold his division in readiness to return to Drainsville at a moment's notice, should it become necessary. Similar instructions were given to other divisions during the afternoon.

The first intimation I received from Generel Stone of the real nature of his movements was in a telegram, as follows:

"EDWARDS'S FERRY, *October* 21—11.10 *a. m.*

"The enemy have been engaged opposite Harrison's island; our men are behaving admirably.

"C. P. STONE,
"*Brigadier General.*

"Major General MCCLELLAN."

At 2 p. m. General Banks's adjutant general sent the following:

"DARNESTOWN, *October* 21, 1861—2 *p. m.*

"General Stone safely crossed the river this morning. Some engagements have taken place on the other side of the river—how important is not known.

"R. M. COPELAND,
"*Acting Assistant Adjutant General.*

"General R. B. MARCY."

General Stone sent the following despatches on the same day at the hours indicated:

"EDWARDS'S FERRY, *October* 21, 1861—2 *p. m.*

"There has been sharp firing on the right of our line, and our troops appear to be advancing there under Baker. The left, under Gorman, has advanced its skirmishers nearly one mile, and, if the movement continues successful, will turn the enemy's right.

"C. P. STONE,
"*Brigadier General.*

"Major General MCCLELLAN."

"EDWARDS'S FERRY, *October* 21, 1861—4 *p. m.*

"Nearly all my force is across the river. Baker on the right; Gorman on the left. Right, sharply engaged.

"C. P. STONE,
"*Brigadier General.*

"General MCCLELLAN."

"EDWARDS'S FERRY, *October* 21, 1861—9.30 *p. m.*

"I am occupied in preventing further disaster, and try to get into a position to redeem. We have lost some of our best commanders—Baker dead, Cogswell a prisoner or secreted. The wounded are being carefully and rapidly removed; and Gorman's wing is being cautiously withdrawn. Any advance from Drainsville must be made cautiously.

"All was reported going well up to Baker's death, but, in the confusion following that, the right wing was outflanked. In a few hours I shall, unless a night attack is made, be in the same position as last night, save the loss of many good men.

"C. P. STONE,
"*Brigadier General.*

"Major General McCLELLAN."

Although no more fully informed of the state of affairs, I had, during the afternoon, as a precautionary measure, ordered General Banks to send one brigade to the support of the troops at Harrison's island, and to move with the other two to Seneca mills, ready to support General Stone if necessary. The 9.30 p. m. despatch of General Stone did not give me an entire understanding of the state of the case.

Aware of the difficulties and perhaps fatal consequences of recrossing such a river as the Potomac after a repulse, and from these telegrams supposing his whole force to be on the Virginia side, I directed General Stone to intrench himself, and hold the Virginia side at all hazards until re-enforcements could arrive, when he could safely withdraw to the Maryland side, or hold his position on the Virginia side, should that prove advisable.

General Banks was instructed to move the rest of his division to Edwards's ferry, and to send over as many men as possible before daylight to re-enforce Stone. He did not arrive in time to effect this, and was instructed to collect all the canal-boats he could find, and use them for crossing at Edwards's ferry in sufficient force to enable the troops already there to hold the opposite side.

On the 22d I went to the ground in person, and reaching Poolsville, learned for the first time the full details of the affair.

The following extract from the evidence of General Stone before the "Committee on the Conduct of the War" on the 5th of January, 1862, will throw further light on this occurrence.

General Stone says he received the order from my headquarters to make a slight demonstration at about 11 o'clock a. m. on the 20th, and that, in obedience to that order, he made the demonstration on the evening of the same day.

In regard to the reconnoissance on the 21st, which resulted in the battle of Ball's Bluff, he was asked the following questions:

Question. "Did this reconnoissance originate with yourself, or had you orders from the general-in-chief to make it?"

To which he replied, "It originated with myself—the reconnoissance."

Question. "The order did not proceed from General McClellan?"

Answer. "I was directed the day before to make a demonstration; that demonstration was made the day previous."

Question. "Did you receive an order from the general-in-chief to make the reconnoissance?"

Answer. "No, sir."

Making a personal examination on the 23d, I found that the position on the Virginia side at Edwards's ferry was not a tenable one, but did not think it wise to withdraw the troops by daylight. I therefore caused more artillery to be placed in position on the Maryland side to cover the approaches to the ground held by us, and crossed the few additional troops that the high wind permitted us to get over, so as to be as secure as possible against any attack during the day. Before nightfall all the precautions were taken to secure an orderly and quiet passage of the troops and guns.

The movement was commenced soon after dark, under the personal supervision of General Stone, who received the order for the withdrawal at 7.15 p. m.

By 4 a. m. of the 24th everything had reached the Maryland shore in safety.

A few days afterwards I received information which seemed to be authentic, to the effect that large bodies of the enemy had been ordered from Manassas to Leesburg, to cut off our troops on the Virginia side. Their timely withdrawal had probably prevented a still more serious disaster.

I refer to General Stone's report of this battle, furnished the War Department, and his published testimony before the "Committee on the Conduct of the War" for further details.

The records of the War Department show my anxiety and efforts to assume active offensive operations in the fall and early winter. It is only just to say, however, that the unprecedented condition of the roads and Virginia soil would have delayed an advance till February, had the discipline, organization, and equipment of the army been as complete at the close of the fall as was necessary, and as I desired and labored against every impediment to make them.

While still in command only of the army of the Potomac, namely, in early September, I proposed the formation of a corps of New Englanders for coast service in the bays and inlets of the Chesapeake and Potomac, to co-operate with my own command, from which most of its material was drawn.

On the first of November, however, I was called to relieve Lieutenant General Scott in the chief and general command of the armies of the Union. The direction and nature of this coast expedition, therefore, were somewhat changed, as will soon appear in the original plan submitted to the Secretary of War, and the letter of instructions later issued to General Burnside, its commander. The whole country indeed had now become the theatre of military operations from the Potomac to beyond the Mississippi, and to assist the navy in perfecting and sustaining the blockade, it became necessary to extend these operations to points on the sea-coast, Roanoke island, Savannah, and New Orleans. It remained also to equip and organize the armies of the west, whose condition was little better than that of the army of the Potomac had been. The direction of the campaigns in the west, and of the operations upon the seaboard, enabled me to enter upon larger combinations and to accomplish results, the necessity and advantage of which had not been unforeseen, but which had been beyond the ability of the single army formerly under my command to effect.

The following letters, and a subsequent paper addressed to the Secretary of War, sufficiently indicate the nature of those combinations to minds accustomed to reason upon military operations:

"HEADQUARTERS ARMY OF THE POTOMAC,
"*Washington, September* 6, 1861.

"SIR: I have the honor to suggest the following proposition, with the request that the necessary authority be at once given me to carry it out: to organize a force of two brigades of five regiments each, of New England men, for the general service, but particularly adapted to coast service—the officers and men to be sufficiently conversant with boat service, to manage steamers, sailing vessels, launches, barges, surf-boats, floating batteries, &c. To charter or buy for the command a sufficient number of propellers, or tug-boats, for transportation of men and supplies, the machinery of which should be amply protected by timber; the vessels to have permanent experienced officers from the merchant service, but to be manned by details from the command. A naval officer to be attached to the staff of the commanding officer. The flank companies of each regiment to be armed with Dahlgren boat guns, and carbines with water-proof cartridges; the other companies to have such arms as I may hereafter designate; to be uniformed and equipped as the Rhode Island regiments are. Launches and floating batteries with timber parapets of sufficient capacity to land or bring into action the entire force.

"The entire management and organization of the force to be under my control, and to form an integral part of the army of the Potomac.

"The immediate object of this force is for operations in the inlets of Chesapeake bay and the Potomac; by enabling me thus to land troops at points where they are needed, this force can also be used in conjunction with a naval force operating against points on the sea-coast. This coast division to be commanded by a general officer of my selection; the regiments to be organized as other land forces; the disbursements for vessels, &c., to be made by the proper department of the army upon the requisitions of the general commanding the division, with my approval.

"I think the entire force can be organized in thirty days, and by no means the least of the advantages of this proposition is the fact that it will call into the service a class of men who would not otherwise enter the army.

"You will immediately perceive that the object of this force is to follow along the coast, and up the inlets and rivers, the movements of the main army when it advances.

"I am, very respectfully, your obedient servant,

"G. B. McCLELLAN,
"*Major General Commanding.*

"Hon. SIMON CAMERON,
"*Secretary of War.*"

Owing chiefly to the difficulty in procuring the requisite vessels, and adapting them to the special purposes contemplated, this expedition was not ready for service until January, 1862. Then in the chief command, I deemed it best to send it to North Carolina, with the design indicated in the following letter

"HEADQUARTERS OF THE ARMY,
"*Washington, January* 7, 1862.

"GENERAL: In accordance with verbal instructions heretofore given you, yo will, after uniting with Flag-officer Goldsborough at Fort Monroe, proceed under his convoy to Hatteras inlet, where you will in connexion with him take the most prompt measures for crossing the fleet over the Bulkhead into the waters of the sound. Under the accompanying general order constituting the department of North Carolina, you will assume command of the garrison at Hatteras inlet, and make such dispositions in regard to that place as your ulterior operations may render necessary, always being careful to provide for the safety of that very important station in any contingency.

"Your first point of attack will be Roanoke island and its dependencies. It is presumed that the navy can reduce the batteries on the marshes, and cover the landing of your troops on the main island, by which, in connexion with a rapid movement of the gunboats to the northern extremity, as soon as the marsh battery is reduced, it may be hoped to capture the entire garrison of the place. Having occupied the island and its dependencies, you will at once proceed to the erection of the batteries and defences necessary to hold the position with a small force. Should the flag-officer require any assistance in seizing or holding the debouches of the canal from Norfolk, you will please afford it to him.

"The commodore and yourself having completed your arrangements in regard to Roanoke island, and the waters north of it, you will please at once make a descent on Newbern, having gained possession of which and the railroad passing through it, you will at once throw a sufficient force upon Beaufort, and take the steps necessary to reduce Fort Macon and open that port. When you seize Newbern, you will endeavor to seize the railroad as far west as Goldsborough, should circumstances favor such a movement. The temper of the people, the rebel force at hand, &c., will go far towards determining the question as to how far west the railroad can be safely occupied and held. Should circumstances render it advisable to seize and hold Raleigh, the main north and south line of railroad passing through Goldsborough should be so effectually destroyed for considerable distances north and south of that point, as to render it impossible for the rebels to use it to your disadvantage. A great point would be gained, in any event, by the effectual destruction of the Wilmington and Weldon railroad.

"I would advise great caution in moving so far into the interior as upon Raleigh. Having accomplished the objects mentioned, the next point of interest would probably be Wilmington, the reduction of which may require that additional means shall be afforded you. I would urge great caution in regard to proclamations. In no case would I go beyond a moderate joint proclamation with the naval commander, which should say as little as possible about politics or the negro; merely state that the true issue for which we are fighting is the preservation of the Union, and upholding the laws of the general government, and stating that all who conduct themselves properly will, as far as possible, be protected in their persons and property.

"You will please report your operations as often as an opportunity offers itself.

"With my best wishes for your success, I am, &c., &c.,

"GEO. B. McCLELLAN,

"*Major General Commanding in Chief.*

"Brigadier General A. E. BURNSIDE,

"*Commanding Expedition.*"

The following letters of instruction were sent to Generals Halleck, Buell, Sherman, and Butler; and I also communicated verbally to these officers my views in full regarding the field of operations assigned to each, and gave them their instructions as much in detail as was necessary at that time:

"HEADQUARTERS OF THE ARMY,

"*Washington, D C., November* 11, 1861.

"GENERAL: In assigning you to the command of the department of Missouri, it is probably unnecessary for me to state that I have intrusted to you a duty which requires the utmost tact and decision.

"You have not merely the ordinary duties of a military commander to perform; but the far more difficult task of reducing chaos to order, of changing probably the majority of the personnel of the staff of the department, and of reducing to a point of economy, consistent with the interests and necessities of the State, a system of reckless expenditure and fraud, perhaps unheard of before in the history of the world.

"You will find in your department many general and staff officers holding illegal commissions and appointments, not recognized or approved by the President, or Secretary of War. You will please at once inform these gentlemen of the nullity of their appointment, and see that no pay or allowances are issued to them until such time as commissions may be authorized by the President, or Secretary of War.

"If any of them give the slightest trouble, you will at once arrest them and send them, under guard, out of the limits of your department, informing them that if they return, they will be placed in close confinement. You will please examine into the legality of the organization of the troops serving in the department. When you find any illegal, unusual or improper organizations, you will give to the officers and men an opportunity to enter the legal military establishment under general laws and orders from the War Department; reporting in full to these headquarters any officer or organization that may decline.

"You will please cause competent and reliable staff officers to examine all existing contracts immediately, and suspend all payments upon them until you receive the report in each case. Where there is the slightest doubt as to the propriety of the contract, you will be good enough to refer the matter, with full explanation, to these headquarters, stating in each case what would be a fair compensation for the services, or materials rendered under the contract. Discontinue at once the reception of material or services under any doubtful contract. Arrest and bring to prompt trial all officers who have in any way violated their duty to the government. In regard to the political conduct of affairs, you will please labor to impress upon the inhabitants of Missouri and the adjacent States that we are fighting solely for the integrity of the Union, to uphold the power of our national government, and to restore to the nation the blessings of peace and good order.

"With respect to military operations it is probable, from the best information in my possession, that the interests of the government will be best served by fortifying and holding in considerable strength Rolla, Sedalia, and other interior points, keeping strong patrols constantly moving from the terminal stations, and concentrating the mass of the troops on or near the Mississippi, prepared for such ulterior operations as the public interests may demand.

"I would be glad to have you make as soon as possible a personal inspection of all the important points in your department, and report the result to me. I cannot too strongly impress upon you the absolute necessity of keeping me constantly advised of the strength, condition, and location of your troops, together with all facts that will enable me to maintain that general direction of the armies of the United States which it is my purpose to exercise. I trust to you to maintain thorough organization, discipline and economy throughout your department. Please inform me as soon as possible of everything relating to the gunboats now in process of construction, as well as those completed.

"The militia force authorized to be raised by the State of Missouri for its defence will be under your orders.

"I am, general, &c., &c.,

"GEORGE B. McCLELLAN,
"*Major General Commanding U. S. A.*

"Major General H. W. HALLECK, U. S. A.,
"*Commanding Department of Missouri.*"

"HEADQUARTERS OF THE ARMY,
"*Washington, November* 7, 1862.

"GENERAL: In giving you instructions for your guidance in command of the department of the Ohio, I do not design to fetter you. I merely wish to express plainly the general ideas which occur to me in relation to the conduct of operations there. That portion of Kentucky west of the Cumberland river is by its position so closely related to the States of Illinois and Missouri, that it has seemed best to attach it to the department of Missouri. Your operations there, in Kentucky, will be confined to that portion of the State east of the Cumberland river. I trust I need not repeat to you that I regard the importance of the territory committed to your care as second only to that occupied by the army under my immediate command. It is absolutely necessary that we shall hold all the State of Kentucky; not only that, but that the majority of its inhabitants shall be warmly in favor of our cause, it being that which best subserves their interests. It is possible that the conduct of our political affairs in Kentucky is more important than that of our military operations. I certainly cannot overestimate the importance of the former. You will please constantly to bear in mind the precise issue for which we are fighting; that issue is the preservation of the Union and the restoration of the full authority of the general government over all portions of our territory. We shall most readily suppress this rebellion and restore the authority of the government by religiously respecting the constitutional rights of all. I know that I express the feelings and opinion of the President when I say that we are fighting only to preserve the integrity of the Union and the constitutional authority of the general government.

"The inhabitants of Kentucky may rely upon it that their domestic institutions will in no manner be interfered with, and that they will receive at our hands every constitutional protection. I have only to repeat that you will in all respects carefully regard the local institutions of the region in which you command, allowing nothing but the dictates of military necessity to cause you to depart from the spirit of these instructions.

"So much in regard to political considerations. The military problem would be a simple one could it be entirely separated from political influences; such is not the case. Were the population among which you are to operate wholly or generally hostile, it is propable that Nashville should be your first and principal objective point. It so happens that a large majority of the inhabitants of eastern Tennessee are in favor of the Union; it thererore seems proper that you should remain on the defensive on the line from Louisville to Nashville, while you throw the mass of your forces, by rapid marches, by Cumberland Gap or Walker's Gap, on Knoxville, in order to occupy the railroad at that point, and thus enable the loyal citizens of eastern Tennessee to rise, while you at the same time cut off the railway communication between eastern Virginia and the Mississippi. It will be prudent to fortify the pass before leaving it in your rear.

"Brigadier General D. C. BUELL."

"HEADQUARTERS OF THE ARMY,
"*Washington, November* 12, 1863.

"GENERAL: Upon assuming command of the department, I will be glad to have you make as soon as possible a careful report of the condition and situation of your troops, and of the military and political condition of your command. The main point to which I desire to call your attention is the necessity of entering eastern Tennessee as soon as it can be done with reasonable chances of success, and I hope that you will, with the least possible delay, organize a column for that purpose, sufficiently guarding at the same time the main avenues by which the rebels may invade Kentucky. Our conversations on the subject of military operations have been so full, and my confidence in your judgment is so great, that I will not dwell further upon the subject, except to urge upon you the necessity of keeping me fully informed as to the state of affairs, both military and political, and your movements. In regard to political matters, bear in mind that we are fighting only to preserve the integrity of the Union and to uphold the power of the general government; as far as military necessity will permit, religiously respect the constitutional rights of all. Preserve the strictest discipline among the troops, and while employing the utmost energy in military movements, be careful so to treat the unarmed inhabitants as to contract, not widen, the breach existing between us and the rebels.

"I mean by this that it is the desire of the government to avoid unnecessary irritation by causeless arrests and persecution of individuals. Where there is good reason to believe that persons are actually giving aid, comfort, or information to the enemy, it is of course necessary to arrest them; but I have always found that it is the tendency of subordinates to make vexatious arrests on mere suspicion. You will find it well to direct that no arrest shall be made except by your order or that of your generals, unless in extraordinary cases, always holding the party making the arrest responsible for the propriety of his course. It should be our constant aim to make it apparent to all that their property, their comfort, and their personal safety will be best preserved by adhering to the cause of the Union.

"If the military suggestions I have made in this letter prove to have been founded on erroneous data, you are of course perfectly free to change the plans of operations.

"Brigadier General D. C. BUELL,

"*Commanding Department of the Ohio.*"

"HEADQUARTERS OF THE ARMY,
"*Washington, February* 14, 1862.

"GENERAL: Your despatches in regard to the occupation of Dafuskie island, &c., were received to-day. I saw also to-day, for the first time, your requisition for a siege train for Savannah.

"After giving the subject all the consideration in my power, I am forced to the conclusion that, under present circumstances, the siege and capture of Savannah do not promise results commensurate with the sacrifices necessary. When I learned that it was possible for the gunboats to reach the Savannah river, above Fort Pulaski, two operations suggested themselves to my mind as its immediate results.

"*First.* The capture of Savannah by a '*coup de main,*'—the result of an instantaneous advance and attack by the army and navy.

"The time for this has passed, and your letter indicates that you are not accountable for the failure to seize the propitious moment, but that, on the contrary, you perceived its advantages.

"*Second.* To isolate Fort Pulaski, cut off its supplies, and at least facilitate its reduction by a bombardment.

"Although we have a long delay to deplore, the second course still remains open to us; and I strongly advise the close blockade of Pulaski, and its bombardment as soon as the 13-inch mortars and heavy guns reach you. I am confident you can thus reduce it. With Pulaski, you gain all that is really essential; you obtain complete control of the harbor; you relieve the blockading fleet, and render the main body of your force disposable for other operations.

"I do not consider the possession of Savannah worth a siege after Pulaski is in our hands. But the possession of Pulaski is of the first importance. The expedition to Fernandina is well, and I shall be glad to learn that it is ours.

"But, after all, the greatest moral effect would be produced by the reduction of Charleston and its defences. There the rebellion had its birth; there the unnatural hatred of our government is most intense; there is the centre of the boasted power and courage of the rebels.

"To gain Fort Sumter and hold Charleston is a task well worthy of our greatest efforts, and considerable sacrifices. That is the problem I would be glad to have you study. Some time must elapse before we can be in all respects ready to accomplish that purpose. Fleets are en route and armies in motion which have certain preliminary objects to accomplish, before we are ready to take Charleston in hand. But the time will before long arrive when I shall be prepared to make that movement. In the mean time, it is my advice and wish that no attempt be made upon Savannah, unless it can be carried with certainty by a '*coup de main.*'

"Please concentrate your attention and forces upon Pulaski and Fernandina. St. Augustine might as well be taken by way of an interlude, while awaiting the preparations for Charleston. Success attends us everywhere at present.

"Very truly, yours,

"GEO. B. McCLELLAN,
"*Major General, Commanding United States Army.*

"Brig. Gen. T. W. SHERMAN,
"*Commanding at Port Royal, &c.*"

"Headquarters of the Army,
"*Washington, February* 23, 1862.

"General: You are assigned to the command of the land forces destined to co-operate with the navy in the attacks upon New Orleans. You will use every means to keep your destination a profound secret, even from your staff officers, with the exception of your chief of staff, and Lieutenant Weitzell, of the engineers. The force at your disposal will consist of the first thirteen regiments named in your memorandum handed to me in person, the 21st Indiana, 4th Wisconsin, and 6th Michigan, (old and good regiments from Baltimore.)

"The 21st Indiana, 4th Wisconsin, and 6th Michigan, will await your orders at Fort Monroe.

"Two companies of the 21st Indiana are well drilled as heavy artillery. The cavalry force already en route for Ship island will be sufficient for your purposes.

"After full consultation with officers well acquainted with the country in which it is proposed to operate, I have arrived at the conclusion that two (2) light batteries fully equipped, and one (1) without horses, will be all that are necessary.

"This will make your force about 14,400 infantry, 275 cavalry, 580 artillery; total, 15,255 men. The commanding general of the department of Key West is authorized to loan you, temporarily, two regiments; Fort Pickens can, probably, give you another, which will bring your force to nearly 18,000.

"The object of your expedition is one of vital importance—the capture of New Orleans. The route selected is up the Mississippi river, and the first obstacle to be encountered (perhaps the only one) is in the resistance offered by Forts St. Philip and Jackson. It is expected that the navy can reduce these works; in that case you will, after their capture, leave a sufficient garrison in them to render them perfectly secure; and it is recommended that, on the upward passage, a few heavy guns and some troops be left at the pilot station (at the forks of the river) to cover a retreat in the event of a disaster. These troops and guns will, of course, be removed as soon as the forts are captured.

"Should the navy fail to reduce the works, you will land your forces and siege train, and endeavor to breach the works, silence their fire, and carry them by assault.

"The next resistance will be near the English Bend, where there are some earthen batteries. Here it may be necessary for you to land your troops and co-operate with the naval attack, although it is more than probable that the navy, unassisted, can accomplish the result. If these works are taken, the city of New Orleans necessarily falls. In that event, it will probably be best to occupy Algiers with the mass of your troops, also the eastern bank of the river above the city. It may be necessary to place some troops *in* the city to preserve order; but if there appears to be sufficient Union sentiment to control the city, it may be best for purposes of discipline to keep your men out of the city.

"After obtaining possession of New Orleans, it will be necessary to reduce all the works guarding its approaches from the east, and particularly to gain the Manchac pass.

"Baton Rouge, Berwick bay, and Fort Livingston, will next claim your attention.

"A feint on Galveston may facilitate the objects we have in view. I need not call your attention to the necessity of gaining possession of all the rolling stock you can on the different railways, and of obtaining control of the roads themselves. The occupation of Baton Rouge by a combined naval and land force should be accomplished as soon as possible after you have gained New Orleans. Then endeavor to open your communication with the northern column by the Mississippi, always bearing in mind the necessity of occupying Jackson, Mississippi, as soon as you can safely do so, either after or before you have effected the junction. Allow nothing to divert you from obtaining full possession of *all* the approaches to New Orleans. When that object is accomplished to its fullest extent, it will be necessary to make a combined attack on Mobile, in order to gain possession of the harbor and works, as well as to control the railway terminus at the city. In regard to this, I will send more detailed instructions as the operations of the northern column develop themselves.

"I may briefly state that the general objects of the expedition are, *first*, the reduction of New Orleans and all its approaches; then Mobile and its defences; then Pensacola, Galveston, &c. It is probable that by the time New Orleans is reduced, it will be in the power of the government to re-enforce the land forces sufficiently to accomplish all these objects. In the mean time you will please give all the assistance in your power to the army and navy commanders in your vicinity, never losing sight of the fact that the great object to be achieved is the capture and firm retention of New Orleans.

"I am, &c.,

"GEO. B. McCLELLAN,
"*Major General, Commanding United States Army.*

"Major General B. F. BUTLER,
"*United States Volunteers.*"

The plan indicated in the above letters comprehended in its scope the operations of all the armies of the Union, the army of the Potomac as well. It was my intention, for reasons easy to be seen, that its various parts should be carried out simultaneously, or nearly so, and in co-operation along the whole line. If this plan was wise, and events have failed to prove that it was not, then it is unnecessary to defend any delay which would have enabled the army of the Potomac to perform its share in the execution of the whole work.

But about the middle of January, 1862, upon recovering from a severe illness, I found that excessive anxiety for an immediate movement of the army of the Potomac had taken possession of the minds of the administration.

A change had just been made in the War Department, and I was soon urged by the new secretary, Mr. Stanton, to take immediate steps to secure the re-opening of the Baltimore and Ohio railroad, and to free the banks of the lower Potomac from the rebel batteries which annoyed passing vessels.

Very soon after his entrance upon office I laid before him verbally my design as to the part of the plan of campaign to be executed by the army of the Potomac, which was to attack Richmond by the lower Chesapeake. He instructed me to develop it to the President, which I did. The result was, that the President disapproved it, and by an order of January 31, 1862, substituted one of his own. On the 27th of January, 1862, the following order was issued without consultation with me:

[President's General War Order No. 1.]

"EXECUTIVE MANSION,
"*Washington, January* 27, 1862.

"*Ordered*, That the 22d day of February, 1862, be the day for a general movement of the land and naval forces of the United States against the insurgent forces. That especially the army at and about Fortress Monroe, the army of the Potomac, the army of Western Virginia, the army near Munfordsville, Kentucky, the army and flotilla at Cairo, and a naval force in the Gulf of Mexico, be ready to move on that day.

"That all other forces, both land and naval, with their respective commanders, obey existing orders for the time, and be ready to obey additional orders when duly given.

"That the heads of departments and especially the Secretaries of War and of the Navy, with all their subordinates, and the general-in-chief, with all other commanders and subordinates of land and naval forces, will severally be held to their strict and full responsibilities for prompt execution of this order.

"ABRAHAM LINCOLN."

The order of January 31, 1862, was as follows:

[President's Special War Order No. 1.]

"EXECUTIVE MANSION,
"*Washington, January* 31, 1862.

"*Ordered*, That all the disposable force of the army of the Potomac, after providing safely for the defence of Washington, be formed into an expedition for the immediate object of seizing and occupying a point upon the railroad southwestward of what is known as Manassas Junction, all details to be in the discretion of the commander-in-chief, and the expedition to move before or on the 22d day of February next.

"ABRAHAM LINCOLN."

I asked his excellency whether this order was to be regarded as final, or whether I could be permitted to submit in writing my objections to his plan, and my reasons for preferring my own. Permission was accorded, and I therefore prepared the letter to the Secretary of War, which is given below.

Before this had been submitted to the President, he addressed me the following note:

"EXECUTIVE MANSION,
"*Washington, February* 3, 1862.

"MY DEAR SIR: You and I have distinct and different plans for a movement of the army of the Potomac: yours to be done by the Chesapeake, up the Rappahannock to Urbana, and across land to the terminus of the railroad on the York river; mine to move directly to a point on the railroad southwest of Manassas.

"If you will give satisfactory answers to the following questions, I shall gladly yield my plan to yours:

"1st. Does not your plan involve a greatly larger expenditure of *time* and *money* than mine?

"2d. Wherein is a victory *more certain* by your plan than mine?

"3d. Wherein is a victory *more valuable* by your plan than mine?

"4th. In fact, would it not be *less* valuable in this: that it would break no great line of the enemy's communications, while mine would?

5th. In case of disaster, would not a retreat be more difficult by your plan than mine?

"Yours, truly,

"ABRAHAM LINCOLN.

"Major General McCLELLAN."

These questions were substantially answered by the following letter of the same date to the Secretary of War:

"HEADQUARTERS OF THE ARMY,
"*Washington, February* 3, 1862.

"SIR: I ask your indulgence for the following papers rendered necessary by circumstances.

"I assumed command of the troops in the vicinity of Washington on Saturday, July 27, 1861, six days after the battle of Bull run.

"I found no army to command; a mere collection of regiments cowering on the banks of the Potomac, some perfectly raw, others dispirited by the recent defeat.

"Nothing of any consequence had been done to secure the southern approaches to the capital by means of defensive works; nothing whatever had been undertaken to defend the avenues to the city on the northern side of the Potomac.

"The troops were not only undisciplined, undrilled, and dispirited; they were not even placed in military positions. The city was almost in a condition to have been taken by a dash of a regiment of cavalry.

"Without one day's delay I undertook the difficult task assigned to me; that task the honorable Secretary knows was given to me without solicitation or foreknowledge. How far I have accomplished it will best be shown by the past and the present.

"The capital is secure against attack, the extensive fortifications erected by the labor of our troops enable a small garrison to hold it against a numerous army, the enemy have been held in check, the State of Maryland is securely in our possession, the detached counties of Virginia are again within the pale of our laws, and all apprehension of trouble in Delaware is at an end; the enemy are confined to the positions they occupied before the disaster of the 21st July. More than all this, I have now under my command a well-drilled and reliable army, to which the destinies of the country may be confidently committed. This army is young and untried in battle; but it is animated by the highest spirit, and is capable of great deeds.

"That so much has been accomplished and such an army created in so short a time, from nothing, will hereafter be regarded as one of the highest glories of the administration and the nation.

"Many weeks, I may say many months ago, this army of the Potomac was fully in condition to repel any attack; but there is a vast difference between that and the efficiency required to enable troops to attack successfully an army elated by victory and intrenched in a position long since selected, studied, and fortified.

"In the earliest papers I submitted to the President, I asked for an effective and movable force far exceeding the aggregate now on the banks of the Potomac. I have not the force I asked for.

"Even when in a subordinate position, I always looked beyond the operations of the army of the Potomac; I was never satisfied in my own mind with a barren victory, but looked to combined and decisive operations.

"When I was placed in command of the armies of the United States, I immediately turned my attention to the whole field of operations, regarding the army of the Potomac as only one, while the most important, of the masses under my command.

"I confess that I did not then appreciate the total absence of a general plan which had before existed, nor did I know that utter disorganization and want of preparation pervaded the western armies.

"I took it for granted that they were nearly, if not quite, in condition to move towards the fulfilment of my plans. I acknowledge that I made a great mistake.

"I sent at once—with the approval of the Executive—officers I considered competent to command in Kentucky and Missouri. Their instructions looked to prompt movements. I soon found that the labor of creation and organization had to be performed there; transportation—arms—clothing—artillery—discipline, all were wanting. These things required time to procure them.

"The generals in command have done their work most creditably, but we are still delayed. I had hoped that a general advance could be made during the good weather of December; I was mistaken.

"My wish was to gain possession of the eastern Tennessee railroad, as a pre liminary movement, then to follow it up immediately by an attack on Nashville and Richmond, as nearly at the same time as possible.

"I have ever regarded our true policy as being that of fully preparing ourselves, and then seeking for the most decisive results. I do not wish to waste life in useless battles, but prefer to strike at the heart.

"Two bases of operations seem to present themselves for the advance of the army of the Potomac:

"1st. That of Washington—its present position—involving a direct attack upon the intrenched positions of the enemy at Centreville, Manassas, &c., or else a movement to turn one or both flanks of those positions, or a combination of the two plans.

"The relative force of the two armies will not justify an attack on both flanks; an attack on his left flank alone involves a long line of wagon communication, and cannot prevent him from collecting for the decisive battle all the detachments now on his extreme right and left.

"Should we attack his right flank by the line of the Occoquan, and a crossing of the Potomac below that river, and near his batteries, we could perhaps prevent the junction of the enemy's right with his centre, (we might destroy the former;) we would remove the obstructions to the navigation of the Potomac, reduce the length of wagon transportation by establishing new depots at the nearest points of the Potomac, and strike more directly his main railway communication.

"The fords of the Occoquan below the mouth of the Bull run are watched by the rebels; batteries are said to be placed on the heights in the rear, (concealed by the woods,) and the arrangement of his troops is such that he can oppose some considerable resistance to a passage of that stream. Information has just been received, to the effect that the enemy are intrenching a line of heights extending from the vicinity of Sangster's (Union mills) towards Evansport. Early in January, Spriggs's ford was occupied by General Rhodes, with 3,600 men and eight (8) guns; there are strong reasons for believing that Davis's ford is occupied. These circumstances indicate or prove that the enemy anticipates the movement in question, and is prepared to resist it. Assuming for the present that this operation is determined upon, it may be well to examine briefly its probable progress. In the present state of affairs, our column (for the movement of so large a force must be made in several columns, at least five or six) can reach the Accatinck without danger; during the march thence to the Occoquan, our right flank becomes exposed to an attack from Fairfax station, Sangster's, and Union mills. This danger must be met by occupying in some force either the two first named places, or better, the point of junction of the roads leading thence to the village of Occoquan; this occupation must be continued so long as we continue to draw supplies by the roads from this city, or until a battle is won.

"The crossing of the Occoquan should be made at all the fords from Wolf's run to the mouth; the points of crossing not being necessarily confined to the fords themselves. Should the enemy occupy this line in force, we must, with what assistance the flotilla can afford, endeavor to force the passage near the mouth, thus forcing the enemy to abandon the whole line, or be taken in flank himself.

"Having gained the line of the Occoquan, it would be necessary to throw a column by the shortest route to Dumfries; partly to force the enemy to abandon his batteries on the Potomac; partly to cover our left flank against an attack from the direction of Aquia; and lastly, to establish our communications with the river by the best roads, and thus give us new depots. The enemy would by this time have occupied the line of the Occoquan above Bull run, holding Brentsville in force, and perhaps extending his lines somewhat further to the southwest.

"Our next step would then be to prevent the enemy from crossing the Occoquan between Bull run and Broad run, to fall upon our right flank while moving on Brentsville. This might be effected by occupying Bacon Race church and the cross-roads near the mouth of Bull run, or still more effectually by moving to the fords themselves, and preventing him from debouching on our side.

"These operations would possibly be resisted, and it would require some time to effect them, as, nearly at the same time as possible, we should gain the fords necessary to our purposes above Broad run. Having secured our right flank, it would become necessary to carry Brentsville at any cost, for we could not leave it between the right flank and the main body. The final movement on the railroad must be determined by circumstances existing at the time.

"This brief sketch brings out in bold relief the great advantage possessed by the enemy in the strong central position he occupies, with roads diverging in every direction, and a strong line of defence enabling him to remain on the defensive, with a small force on one flank, while he concentrates everything on the other for a decisive action.

"Should we place a portion of our force in front of Centreville, while the rest crosses the Occoquan, we commit the error of dividing our army by a very difficult obstacle, and by a distance too great to enable the two parts to support each other, should either be attacked by the masses of the enemy, while the other is held in check.

"I should perhaps have dwelt more decidedly on the fact that the force left near Sangster's must be allowed to remain somewhere on that side of the Occoquan until the decisive battle is over, so as to cover our retreat in the event of disaster, unless it should be decided to select and intrench a new base somewhere near Dumfries, a proceeding involving much time.

"After the passage of the Occoquan by the main army, this covering force could be drawn into a more central and less exposed position—say Brimstone hill or nearer the Occoquan. In this latitude the weather will for a considerable period be very uncertain, and a movement commenced in force on roads in tolerably firm condition will be liable, almost certain, to be much delayed by rains and snow. It will, therefore, be next to impossible to surprise the enemy, or take him at a disadvantage by rapid manœuvres. Our slow progress will enable him to divine our purposes, and take his measures accordingly. The probability is, from the best information we possess, that the enemy has improved the roads leading to his lines of defence, while we have to work as we advance.

"Bearing in mind what has been said, and the present unprecedented and impassable condition of the roads, it will be evident that no precise period can be fixed upon for the movement on this line. Nor can its duration be closely calculated; it seems certain that many weeks may elapse before it is possible to commence the march. Assuming the success of this operation, and the defeat of the enemy as certain, the question at once arises as to the importance of the results gained. I think these results would be confined to the possession of the field of battle, the evacuation of the line of the upper Potomac by the enemy, and the moral effect of the victory; important results, it is true, but not decisive of the war, nor securing the destruction of the enemy's main army, for he could fall back upon other positions, and fight us again and again, should the condition of his troops permit. If he is in no condition to fight us again out of the range of the intrenchments at Richmond, we would find it a very difficult and tedious matter to follow him up there, for he would destroy his railroad bridges and otherwise impede our progress through a region where the roads are as bad as they well can be, and we would probably find ourselves forced at last to change the whole theatre of war, or to seek a shorter land route to Richmond, with a smaller available force, and at an expenditure of much more time, than were we to adopt the short line at once. We would also have forced the enemy to concentrate his forces and perfect his defensive measures at the very points where it is desirable to strike him when least prepared.

"II. The second base of operations available for the army of the Potomac is that of the lower Chesapeake bay, which affords the shortest possible land route to Richmond, and strikes directly at the heart of the enemy's power in the east.

"The roads in that region are passable at all seasons of the year.

"The country now alluded to is much more favorable for offensive operations than that in front of Washington, (which is *very* unfavorable,) much more level, more cleared land, the woods less dense, the soil more sandy, and the spring some two or three weeks earlier. A movement in force on that line obliges the enemy to abandon his intrenched position at Manassas, in order to hasten to cover Richmond and Norfolk. He *must* do this; for should he permit us to occupy Richmond, his destruction can be averted only by entirely defeating us in a battle, in which he must be the assailant. This movement, if successful, gives us the capital, the communications, the supplies of the rebels; Norfolk would fall; all the waters of the Chesapeake would be ours; all Virginia would be in our power, and the enemy forced to abandon Tennessee and North Carolina. The alternative presented to the enemy would be, to beat us in a position selected by ourselves, disperse, or pass beneath the Caudine forks.

"Should we be beaten in a battle, we have a perfectly secure retreat down the Peninsula upon Fort Monroe, with our flanks perfectly covered by the fleet.

"During the whole movement our left flank is covered by the water. Our right is secure, for the reason that the enemy is too distant to reach us in time; he can only oppose us in front; we bring our fleet into full play.

"After a successful battle our position would be—Burnside forming our left—Norfolk held securely—our centre connecting Burnside with Buell, both by Raleigh and Lynchburg—Buell in eastern Tennessee and North Alabama—Halleck at Nashville and Memphis.

"The next movement would be to connect with Sherman on the left, by reducing Wilmington and Charleston; to advance our centre into South Carolina and Georgia; to push Buell either towards Montgomery, or to unite with the main army in Georgia; to throw Halleck southward to meet the naval expedition from New Orleans.

"We should then be in a condition to reduce at our leisure all the southern seaports; to occupy all the avenues of communication; to use the great outlet of the Mississippi; to re-establish our government and arms in Arkansas, Louisiana and Texas; to force the slaves to labor for our subsistence, instead of that of the rebels; to bid defiance to all foreign interference. Such is the object I have ever had in view—this is the general plan which I hope to accomplish.

"For many long months I have labored to prepare the army of the Potomac to play its part in the programme; from the day when I was placed in command of all our armies, I have exerted myself to place all the other armies in such a condition that they, too, could perform their allotted duties.

"Should it be determined to operate from the lower Chesapeake, the point of landing which promises the most brilliant result is Urbana, on the lower Rappahannock. This point is easily reached by vessels of heavy draught; it is neither occupied nor observed by the enemy—it is but one march from West Point, the key of that region, and thence but two marches to Richmond. A rapid movement from Urbana would probably cut off Magruder in the Peninsula, and enable us to occupy Richmond, before it could be strongly re-enforced. Should we fail in that, we could, with the co-operation of the navy, cross the James and throw ourselves in rear of Richmond, thus forcing the enemy to come out and attack us, for his position would be untenable, with us on the southern bank of the river.

"Should circumstances render it not advisable to land at Urbana, we can use Mobjack bay; or, the worst coming to the worst, we can take Fort Monroe as a base, and operate with complete security, although with less celerity and brilliancy of results—up the Peninsula.

"To reach whatever point may be selected as a base, a large amount of cheap water transportation must be collected, consisting mainly of canal-boats, barges, wood-boats, schooners, &c., towed by small steamers, all of a very different character from those required for all previous expeditions. This can certainly be accomplished within thirty days from the time the order is given. I propose, as the best possible plan that can, in my judgment, be adopted, to select Urbana as a landing place for the first detachments; to transport by water four divisions of infantry with their batteries, the regular infantry, a few wagons, one bridge train and a few squadrons of cavalry, making the vicinity of Hooker's position the place of embarkation for as many as possible; to move the regular cavalry and reserve artillery, the remaining bridge trains and wagons, to a point somewhere near Cape Lookout, then ferry them over the river by means of North River ferry-boats, march them over to the Rappahannock, (covering the movement by an infantry force near Heathsville,) and to cross the Rappahannock in a similar way. The expense and difficulty of the movement will then be very much diminished, (a saving of transportation of about 10,000 horses,) and the result none the less certain.

"The concentration of the cavalry, &c., on the lower counties of Maryland can be effected without exciting suspicion, and the movement made without delay from that cause.

"This movement, if adopted, will not at all expose the city of Washington to danger.

"The total force to be thrown upon the new line would be, according to circumstances, from 110,000 to 140,000. I hope to use the latter number by bringing fresh troops into Washington, and still leaving it quite safe. I fully realize that in all projects offered, time will probably be the most valuable consideration. It is my decided opinion that, in that point of view, the second plan should be adopted. It is possible, nay, highly probable, that the weather and state of the roads may be such as to delay the direct movement from Washington, with its unsatisfactory results and great risks, far beyond the time required to complete the second plan. In the first case we can fix no definite time for an advance. The roads have gone from bad to worse. Nothing like their present condition was ever known here before; they are impassable at present. We are entirely at the mercy of the weather. It is by no means certain that we can beat them at Manassas. On the other line I regard success as certain by all the chances of war. We demoralize the enemy by forcing him to abandon his prepared position for one which we have chosen, in which all is in our favor, and where success must produce immense results.

"My judgment, as a general, is clearly in favor of this project. Nothing is certain in war, but all the chances are in favor of this movement. So much am I in favor of the southern line of operations, that I would prefer the move from Fortress Monroe as a base—as a certain though less brilliant movement than that from Urbana, to an attack upon Manassas.

"I know that his excellency the President, you, and I, all agree in our wishes; and that these wishes are, to bring this war to a close as promptly as the means in our possession will permit. I believe that the mass of the people have entire confidence in us—I am sure of it. Let us, then, look only to the great result to be accomplished, and disregard everything else.

I am, very respectfully, your obedient servant,

"GEO. B. McCLELLAN,

"*Major General, Commanding.*

"Hon. E. M. STANTON,

"*Secretary of War.*"

This letter must have produced some effect upon the mind of the President, since the execution of his order was not required, although it was not revoked as formally as it had been issued. Many verbal conferences ensued, in which, among other things, it was determined to collect as many canal-boats as possible, with a view to employ them largely in the transportation of the army to the lower Chesapeake. The idea was at one time entertained by the President to use them in forming a bridge across the Potomac near Liverpool point, in order to throw the army over that point; but this was subsequently abandoned. It was also found by experience that it would require much time to prepare the canal boats for use in transportation, to the extent that had been anticipated.

Finally, on the 27th of February, 1862, the Secretary of War, by the authority of the President, instructed Mr. John Tucker, Assistant Secretary of War, to procure at once the necessary steamers and sailing craft to transport the army of the Potomac to its new field of operations.

The following extract from the report of Mr. Tucker, dated April 5, will show the nature and progress of this well-executed service:

* * * * * * * * * *

"I was called to Washington by telegraph, on 17th January last, by Assistant Secretary of War Thomas A. Scott. I was informed that Major General McClellan wished to see me. From him I learned that he desired to know if transportation on smooth water could be obtained to move at one time, for a short distance, about 50,000 troops, 10,000 horses, 1,000 wagons, 13 batteries, and the usual equipment of such an army. He frankly stated to me that he had always supposed such a movement entirely feasible, until two experienced quartermasters had recently reported it impracticable, in their judgment. A few days afterwards, I reported to General McClellan that I was entirely confident the transports could be commanded, and stated the mode by which his object could be accomplished. A week or two afterwards I had the honor of an interview with the President and General McClellan, when the subject was further discussed, and especially as to the time required.

"I expressed the opinion that, as the movement of the horses and wagons would have to be made chiefly by schooners and barges, that as each schooner would require to be properly fitted for the protection of the horses, and furnished with a supply of water and forage, and each transport for the troops provided with water, I did not deem it prudent to assume that such an expedition could start within thirty days from the time the order was given.

"The President and General McClellan both urgently stated the vast importance of an earlier movement. I replied that if favorable winds prevailed, and there was great despatch in loading, the time might be materially diminished.

"On the 14th February you (Secretary of War) advertised for transports of various descriptions, inviting bids on the 27th February. I was informed that the proposed movement by water was decided upon. That evening the Quartermaster General was informed of the decision. Directions were given to secure the transportation—any assistance was tendered. He promptly detailed to this duty two most efficient assistants in his department. Colonel Rufus Ingalls was stationed at Annapolis, where it was then proposed to embark the troops, and Captain Henry C. Hodges was directed to meet me in Philadelphia, to attend to chartering the vessels. With these arrangements I left Washington on the 28th February.

* * * * * * * *

"I beg to hand herewith a statement, prepared by Captain Hodges, of the vessels chartered, which exhibits the prices paid, and parties from whom they were taken:

113 steamers, at an average price per day	....	$215 10
188 schooners, " " "	....	24 45
88 barges, " " "	....	14 27

"In thirty-seven days from the time I received the order in Washington, (and most of it was accomplished in thirty days,) these vessels transported from Perryville, Alexandria, and Washington to Fort Monroe (the place of departure having been changed, which caused delay,) 121,500 men, 14,592 animals, 1,150 wagons, 44 batteries, 74 ambulances, besides pontoon bridges, telegraph materials, and the enormous quantity of equipage, &c., required for an army of such magnitude. The only loss of which I have heard is eight mules and nine barges, which latter went ashore in a gale within a few miles of Fort Monroe—the cargoes being saved. With this trifling exception, not the slightest accident has occurred, to my knowledge.

"I respectfully, but confidently, submit that, for economy and celerity of movement, this expedition is without a parallel on record.

* * * * * * * *

"JOHN TUCKER,
"*Assistant Secretary of War.*"

In the mean-time the destruction of the batteries on the lower Potomac, by crossing our troops opposite them, was considered, and preparations were even made for throwing Hooker's division across the river, to carry them by assault. Finally, however, after an adverse report from Brigadier General J. G. Barnard, Chief Engineer, given below, who made a reconnoissance of the positions, and in view of the fact that it was still out of the power of the Navy Department to furnish suitable vessels to co-operate with land troops, this plan was abandoned as impracticable. A close examination of the enemy's works and their approaches, made after they were evacuated, showed that the decision was a wise one. The only means, therefore, of accomplishing the capture of these works, so much desired by the President, was by a movement by land, from the left of our lines, on the right bank of the Potomac—a movement obviously unwise.

The attention of the Navy Department, as early as August 12, 1861, had been called to the necessity of maintaining a strong force of efficient war vessels on the Potomac.

"HEADQUARTERS DIVISION OF THE POTOMAC,
"*Washington, August* 12, 1861.

"SIR: I have to-day received additional information which convinces me that it is more than probable that the enemy will, within a very short time, attempt to throw a respectable force from the mouth of Aquia creek into Maryland. This attempt will probably be preceded by the erection of batteries at Matthias and White House points. Such a movement on the part of the enemy, in connexion with others probably designed, would place Washington in great jeopardy. I most earnestly urge that the strongest possible naval force be at once concentrated near the mouth of Aquia creek, and that the most vigilant watch be maintained day and night, so as to render such passage of the river absolutely impossible.

"I recommend that the Minnesota and any other vessels available from Hampton Roads be at once ordered up there, and that a great quantity of coal be sent to that vicinity, sufficient for several weeks' supply. At least one strong war vessel should be kept at Alexandria, and I again urge the concentration of a strong naval force on the Potomac without delay.

"If the Naval Department will render it absolutely impossible for the enemy to cross the river below Washington, the security of the capital will be greatly increased.

"I cannot too earnestly urge an immediate compliance with these requests.

"I am, sir, very respectfully, your obedient servant,

"GEORGE B. McCLELLAN,
"*Major General Commanding.*

"Hon. GIDEON WELLES,
"*Secretary of the United States Navy.*"

It was on the 27th of September, 1861, that General Barnard, Chief Engineer, in company with Captain Wyman of the Potomac flotilla, had been instructed to make a reconnoissance of the enemy's batteries as far as Matthias point. In his report of his observations he says:

"Batteries at High point and Cockpit point, and thence down to Chopawampsic, *cannot* be prevented. We may, indeed, prevent their construction on *certain* points, but along here somewhere the enemy can establish, in spite of us, as many batteries as he chooses. What is the remedy? Favorable circumstances, not to be anticipated nor made the basis of any calculations, might justify and render successful the attack of a particular battery. To suppose that we can capture *all*, and by mere attacks of this kind prevent the navigation being molested, is very much the same as to suppose that the hostile army in our own front can prevent us building and maintaining field-works to protect Arlington and Alexandria by capturing them, one and all, as fast as they are built."

In another communication upon the subject of crossing troops for the purpose of destroying the batteries on the Virginia side of the Potomac. General Barnard says:

"The operation involves the forcing of a very strong line of defence of the enemy, and all that we would have to do if we were really opening a campaign against them there.

"It is true we hope to force this line by turning it, by landing on Freestone point. With reason to believe that this may be successful, it cannot be denied that it involves a risk of failure. Should we, then, considering all the consequences which may be involved, enter into the operation, merely to capture the Potomac batteries? I think not. Will not the Ericsson, assisted by one other gunboat capable of keeping alongside these batteries, so far control their fire as to keep the navigation sufficiently free as long as we require it? Captain Wyman says yes."

It was the opinion of competent naval officers, and I concur with them, that had an adequate force of strong and well-armed vessels been acting on the Potomac from the beginning of August, it would have been next to impossible for the rebels to have constructed or maintained batteries upon the banks of the river. The enemy never occupied Matthias point, nor any other point on the river, which was out of supporting distance from the main army.

When the enemy commenced the construction of these batteries, the army of the Potomac was not in a condition to prevent it. Their destruction by our army would have afforded but a temporary relief unless we had been strong enough to hold the entire line of the Potomac. This could be done either by driving the enemy from Manassas and Aquia creek, by main force, or by manœuvring to compel them to vacate their positions. The latter course was finally pursued, and with success.

About the 20th of February, 1862, additional measures were taken to secure the reopening of the Baltimore and Ohio railroad. The preliminary operations of General Lander for this object are elsewhere described.

I had often observed to the President and to members of the cabinet that the reconstruction of this railway could not be undertaken until we were in a condition to fight a battle to secure it. I regarded the possession of Winchester and Strasburg as necessary to cover the railway in the rear, and it was not till the month of February that I felt prepared to accomplish this very desirable but not vital purpose.

The whole of Banks's division and two brigades of Sedgwick's division were thrown across the river at Harper's Ferry, leaving one brigade of Sedgwick's division to observe and guard the Potomac from Great Falls to the mouth of the Monocacy. A sufficient number of troops of all arms were held in readiness in the vicinity of Washington, either to march *via* Leesburg or to move by rail to Harper's Ferry, should this become necessary in carrying out the objects in view.

The subjoined notes from a communication subsequently addressed to the War Department will sufficiently explain the conduct of these operations.

NOTES.

"When I started for Harper's Ferry, I plainly stated to the President and Secretary of War that the chief object of the operation would be to open the Baltimore and Ohio railroad by crossing the river in force at Harper's Ferry; that I had collected the material for making a permanent bridge by means of canal-boats; that from the nature of the river, it was doubtful whether such a bridge could be constructed; that if it could not, I would at least occupy the ground in front of Harper's Ferry, in order to cover the rebuilding of the railroad bridge; and finally, when the communications were perfectly secure, move on Winchester.

"When I arrived at the place I found the batteau bridge nearly completed; the holding-ground proved better than had been anticipated; the weather was favorable, there being no wind. I at once crossed over the two brigades which had arrived, and took steps to hurry up the other two, belonging respectively to Banks's and Sedgwick's divisions. The difficulty of crossing supplies had not then become apparent. That night I telegraphed for a regiment of regular cavalry and four batteries of heavy artillery to come up the next day, (Thursday,) besides directing Keyes's division of infantry to be moved up on Friday.

"Next morning the attempt was made to pass the canal-boats through the lift-lock, in order to commence at once the construction of a permanent bridge. It was then found for the first time that the lock was too small to permit the passage of the boats, it having been built for a class of boats running on the Shenandoah canal, and too narrow by some four or six inches for the canal-boats. The lift-locks, above and below, are all large enough for the ordinary boats. I had seen them at Edwards's ferry thus used. It had always been represented to the engineers by the military railroad employés, and others, that the lock *was* large enough, and, the difference being too small to be detected by the eye, no one had thought of measuring it, or suspecting any difficulty. I thus suddenly found myself unable to build the permanent bridge. A violent gale had arisen, which threatened the safety of our only means of communication; the narrow approach to the bridge was so crowded and clogged with wagons that it was very clear that, under existing circumstances, nothing more could be done than to cross over the baggage and supplies of the two brigades. Of the others, instead of being able to cross both during the morning, the last arrived only in time to go over just before dark. It was evident that the troops under orders would only be in the way, should they arrive, and that it would not be possible to subsist them for a rapid march on Winchester. It was therefore deemed necessary to countermand the order, content ourselves with covering the reopening of the railroad for the present, and in the mean time use every exertion to establish, as promptly as possible, depots of forage and subsistence on the Virginia side, to supply the troops, and enable them to move on Winchester independently of the bridge. The next day (Friday) I sent a strong reconnoissance to Charlestown, and, under its protection, went there myself. I then determined to hold that place, and to move the troops composing Lander's and Williams's commands at once on Martinsburg and Bunker Hill, thus effectually covering the reconstruction of the railroad.

"Having done this, and taken all the steps in my power to insure the rapid transmission of supplies over the river, I returned to this city, well satisfied with what had been accomplished. While up the river I learned that the President was dissatisfied with the state of affairs; but, on my return here, understood from the Secretary of War that upon learning the whole state of the case the President was fully satisfied. I contented myself, therefore, with giving to the Secretary a brief statement, as I have written here."

The design aimed at was entirely compassed, and before the first of April, the date of my departure for the Peninsula, the railroad was in running order. As a demonstration upon the left flank of the enemy, this movement no doubt assisted in determining the evacuation of his lines on the 8th and 9th of March.

On my return from Harper's Ferry, on the 28th of February, the preparations necessary to carry out the wishes of the President and Secretary of War in regard to destroying the batteries on the lower Potomac were at once undertaken. Mature reflection convinced me that this operation would require the movement of the entire army, for I felt sure that the enemy would resist it with his whole strength. I undertook it with great reluctance, both on account of the extremely unfavorable condition of the roads and my firm conviction that the proposed movement to the lower Chesapeake would necessarily, as it subsequently did, force the enemy to abandon all his positions in front of Washington. Besides, it did not forward my plan of campaign to precipitate this evacuation by any direct attack, nor to subject the army to any needless loss of life and material by a battle near Washington, which could produce no decisive results. The preparations for a movement towards the Occoquan, to carry the batteries, were, however, advanced as rapidly as the season permitted, and I had invited the commanders of divisions to meet at headquarters on the 8th of March, for the purpose of giving them their instructions, and receiving their advice and opinion in regard to their commands, when an interview with the President indicated to me the possibility of a change in my orders.

His excellency sent for me at a very early hour on the morning of the 8th, and renewed his expressions of dissatisfaction with the affair of Harper's Ferry, and with my plans for the new movement down the Chesapeake. Another recital of the same facts which had before given satisfaction to his excellency again produced, as I supposed, the same result.

The views which I expressed to the President were re-enforced by the result of a meeting of my general officers at headquarters. At that meeting my plans were laid before the division commanders, and were approved by a majority of those present. Nevertheless, on the same day two important orders were issued by the President, without consultation with me. The first of these was the general war order No. 2, directing the formation of army corps, and assigning their commanders.

I had always been in favor of the principle of an organization into army corps, but preferred deferring its practical execution until some little experience in campaign and on the field of battle should show what general officers were most competent to exercise these high commands, for it must be remembered that we then had no officers whose experience in war on a large scale was sufficient to prove that they possessed the necessary qualifications. An incompetent commander of an army corps might cause irreparable damage, while it is not probable that an incompetent division commander could cause any very serious mischief. These views had frequently been expressed by me to the President and members of the cabinet; it was therefore with as much regret as surprise that I learned the existence of this order.

The first order has been given above; the second order was as follows:

[President's General War Order No. 3.]

"EXECUTIVE MANSION,
"*Washington, March* 8, 1862.

"*Ordered*, That no change of the base of operations of the army of the Potomac shall be made without leaving in and about Washington such a force as, in the opinion of the general-in-chief and the commanders of army corps, shall leave said city entirely secure.

"That no more than two army corps (about fifty thousand troops) of said army of the Potomac shall be moved en route for a new base of operations until the navigation of the Potomac, from Washington to the Chesapeake bay, shall be freed from enemy's batteries, and other obstructions, or until the President shall hereafter give express permission.

That any movement as aforesaid, en route for a new base of operations, which may be ordered by the general-in-chief, and which may be intended to move upon the Chesapeake bay, shall begin to move upon the bay as early as the 18th March instant, and the general-in-chief shall be responsible that it moves as early as that day.

"*Ordered*, That the army and navy co-operate in an immediate effort to capture the enemy's batteries upon the Potomac between Washington and the Chesapeake bay.

"ABRAHAM LINCOLN.

"L. THOMAS, *Adjutant General.*"

After what has been said already in regard to the effect of a movement to the lower Chesapeake it is unnecessary for me to comment upon this document, further than to say that the time of beginning the movement depended upon the state of readiness of the transports, the entire control of which had been placed by the Secretary of War in the hands of one of the Assistant Secretaries, and not under the Quartermaster General; so that even if the movement were not impeded by the condition imposed, in regard to the batteries on the Potomac, it could not have been in my power to begin it before the 18th of March, unless the Assistant Secretary of War had completed his arrangements by that time.

Meanwhile important events were occurring which materially modified the designs for the subsequent campaign. The appearance of the Merrimack off Old Point Comfort, and the encounter with the United States squadron on the 8th of March, threatened serious derangement of the plan for the Peninsula movement. But the engagement between the Monitor and Merrimack on the 9th of March, demonstrated so satisfactorily the power of the former, and the other naval preparations were so extensive and formidable, that the security of Fort Monroe, as a base of operations, was placed beyond a doubt; and although the James river was closed to us, the York river, with its tributaries, was still open as a line of water communication with the fortress. The general plan, therefore, remained undisturbed, although less promising in its details than when the James river was in our control.

On Sunday, the 9th of March, information from various sources made it apparent that the enemy was evacuating his positions at Centreville and Manassas as well as on the upper and lower Potomac. The President and Secretary of War were present when the most positive information reached me, and I expressed to them my intention to cross the river immediately, and there gain the most authentic information, prior to determining what course to pursue.

The retirement of the enemy towards Richmond had been expected as the natural consequence of the movement to the Peninsula, but the adoption of this course immediately on ascertaining that such a movement was intended, while it relieved me from the results of the undue anxiety of my superiors, and attested the character of the design, was unfortunate in that the then almost impassable roads between our positions and theirs deprived us of the opportunity for inflicting damage usually afforded by the withdrawal of a large army in the face of a powerful adversary.

The retirement of the enemy and the occupation of the abandoned positions which necessarily followed presented an opportunity for the troops to gain some experience on the march and bivouac preparatory to the campaign, and to get rid of the superfluous baggage and other "impediments" which accumulate so easily around an army encamped for a long time in one locality.

A march to Manassas and back would produce no delay in embarking for the lower Chesapeake, as the transports could not be ready for some time, and it afforded a good intermediate step between the quiet and comparative comfort of the camps around Washington, and the rigors of active operations, besides accomplishing the important object of determining the positions and perhaps the future designs of the enemy, with the possibility of being able to harass their rear.

I therefore issued orders during the night of the 9th of March for a general movement of the army the next morning towards Centreville and Manassas, sending in advance two regiments of cavalry under Colonel Averill with orders to reach Manassas if possible, ascertain the exact condition of affairs, and do whatever he could to retard and annoy the enemy if really in retreat; at the same time I telegraphed to the Secretary of War that it would be necessary to defer the organization of the army corps until the completion of the projected advance upon Manassas, as the divisions could not be brought together in time. The Secretary replied, requiring immediate compliance with the President's order, but on my again representing that this would compel the abandonment or postponement of the movement to Manassas, he finally consented to its postponement.

At noon on the 10th of March the cavalry advance reached the enemy's lines at Centreville, passing through his recently occupied camps and works, and finding still burning heaps of military stores and much valuable property.

Immediately after being assigned to the command of the troops around Washington, I organized a secret service force, under Mr. E. J. Allen, a very experienced and efficient person. This force, up to the time I was relieved from command, was continually occupied in procuring from all possible sources information regarding the strength, positions, and movements of the enemy.

All spies, "contrabands," deserters, refugees, and many prisoners of war, coming into our lines from the front, were carefully examined, first by the outpost and division commanders, and then by my chief of staff and the Provost Marshal General. Their statements, taken in writing, and in many cases under oath, from day to day, for a long period previous to the evacuation of Manassas, comprised a mass of evidence which, by careful digests and collations, enabled me to estimate with considerable accuracy the strength of the enemy before us. Summaries showing the character and results of the labors of the secret service force accompany this report and I refer to them for the facts they contain, and as a measure of the ignorance which led some journals at that time and persons in high office unwittingly to trifle with the reputation of an army, and to delude the country with quaker gun stories of the defences and gross understatements of the numbers of the enemy.

The following orders were issued for the examination of persons coming from the direction of the enemy:

["Circular.]

"HEADQUARTERS ARMY OF THE POTOMAC,
"*Washington, December* 16, 1861.

"The major general commanding directs that hereafter all deserters, prisoners, spies, 'contrabands,' and all other persons whatever coming or brought within our lines from Virginia, shall be taken immediately to the quarters of the commander of the division within whose lines they may come or be brought, without previous examination by any one, except so far as may be necessary for the officer commanding the advance guard to elicit information regarding his particular post; that the division commander examine all such persons himself, or delegate such duty to a proper officer of his staff, and allow no other persons to hold any communication with them; that he then immediately send them, with a sufficient guard, to the provost marshal in this city for further examination and safe-keeping, and that stringent orders be given to all guards having such persons in charge not to hold any communication with them whatever; and further, that the information elicited from such persons shall be immediately communicated to the major general commanding, or to the chief of staff, and to no other person whatever.

"The major general commanding further directs that a sufficient guard be placed around every telegraph station pertaining to this army, and that such guards be instructed not to allow any person, except the regular telegraph corps, general officers, and such staff officers as may be authorized by their chief, to enter or loiter around said stations within hearing of the sound of the telegraph instruments.

"By command of Major General McClellan.

"S. WILLIAMS,
"*Assistant Adjutant General.*"

"Headquarters Army of the Potomac,
"*Washington, February* 26, 1862.

"General Order
No. 27.

* * * * * * * * * *

"All deserters from the enemy, prisoners, and other persons coming within our lines, will be taken at once to the provost marshal of the nearest division, who will examine them in presence of the division commander or an officer of his staff designated for the purpose. This examination will only refer to such information as may affect the division and those near it, especially those remote from general headquarters.

"As soon as this examination is completed—and it must be made as rapidly as possible—the person will be sent, under proper guard, to the Provost Marshal General, with a statement of his replies to the questions asked. Upon receiving him, the Provost Marshal General will at once send him, with his statement, to the chief of staff of the army of the Potomac, who will cause the necessary examination to be made. The Provost Marshal General will have the custody of all such persons. Division commanders will at once communicate to other division commanders all information thus obtained which affects them.

* * * * * * * * * *

"By command of Major General McClellan.

"S. WILLIAMS,
"*Assistant Adjutant General.*"

In addition to the foregoing orders, the division commanders were instructed, whenever they desired to send out scouts towards the enemy, to make known the object at headquarters, in order that I might determine whether we had the information it was proposed to obtain, and that I might give the necessary orders to other commanders, so that the scouts should not be molested by the guards.

It will be seen from the report of the chief of the secret service corps, dated March 8, that the forces of the rebel army of the Potomac, at that date, were as follows:

At Manassas, Centreville, Bull run, Upper Occoquan, and vicinity. 80,000 men.
At Brooks's station, Dumfries, Lower Occoquan, and vicinity.... 18,000 men.

At Leesburg and vicinity.................................... 4,500 men.
In the Shenandoah valley.................................... 13,000 men.

115,500 men.

About three hundred field guns and from twenty-six to thirty siege guns were with the rebel army in front of Washington. The report made on the 17th of March, after the evacuation of Manassas and Centreville, corroborates the statements contained in the report of the 8th, and is fortified by the affidavits of several railroad engineers, constructors, baggage-masters, &c., whose opportunities for forming correct estimates were unusually good. These affidavits will be found in the accompanying reports of the chief of the secret service corps.

A reconnoissance of the works at Centreville made by Lieutenant McAlester, United States engineers, on March 14, 1862, and a survey of those at Manassas, made by a party of the United States coast survey, in April, 1862, confirmed also my conclusions as to the strength of the enemy's defences. Those at Centreville consisted of two lines, one facing east and the other north. The former consisted of seven works, viz: one bastion fort, two redoubts, two lunettes, and two batteries; all containing embrasures for forty guns, and connected by infantry parapets and double caponiéres. It extended along the crest of the ridge a mile and three quarters from its junction with the northern front to ground thickly wooded and impassable to an attacking column.

The northern front extended about one and one-fourth mile to Great Rocky run, and thence three-fourths of a mile further to thickly wooded, impassable ground in the valley of Cub run. It consisted of six lunettes and batteries with embrasures for thirty-one guns, connected by an infantry parapet in the form of a cremaillère line with redans. At the town of Centreville, on a high hill commanding the rear of all the works within range, was a large hexagonal redoubt with ten embrasures.

Manassas station was defended in all directions by a system of detached works, with platforms for heavy guns arranged for marine carriages, and often connected by infantry parapets. This system was rendered complete by a very large work, with sixteen embrasures, which commanded the highest of the other works by about fifty feet.

Sketches of the reconnoissances above referred to will be found among the maps appended to this report.

From this it will be seen that the positions selected by the enemy at Centreville and Manassas were naturally very strong, with impassable streams and broken ground, affording ample protection for their flanks, and that strong lines of intrenchments swept all the available approaches.

Although the history of every former war has conclusively shown the great advantages which are possessed by an army acting on the defensive and occupying strong positions, defended by heavy earthworks; yet, at the commencement of this war, but few civilians in our country, and, indeed, not all military men of rank, had a just appreciation of the fact.

New levies that have never been in battle cannot be expected to advance without cover under the murderous fire from such defences, and carry them by assault. This is work in which veteran troops frequently faulter and are repulsed with loss. That an assault of the enemy's positions in front of Washington, with the new troops composing the army of the Potomac, during the winter of 1861–'62, would have resulted in defeat and demoralization, was too probable.

The same army, though inured to war in many battles, hard fought and bravely won, has twice, under other generals, suffered such disasters as it was no excess of prudence then to avoid. My letter to the Secretary of War, dated

February 3, 1862, and given above, expressed the opinion that the movement to the Peninsula would compel the enemy to retire from his position at Manassas and free Washington from danger. When the enemy first learned of that plan, they did thus evacuate Manassas. During the Peninsula campaign, as at no former period, northern Virginia was completely in our possession, and the vicinity of Washington free from the presence of the enemy. The ground so gained was not lost, nor Washington again put in danger, until the enemy learned of the orders for the evacuation of the Peninsula, sent to me at Harrison's bar, and were again left free to advance northward and menace the national capital. Perhaps no one now doubts that the best defence of Washington is a Peninsula attack on Richmond.

My order for the organization of the army corps was issued on the 13th of March; it has been given above.

While at Fairfax Court-house, on March 12, I was informed through the telegraph, by a member of my staff, that the following document had appeared in the National Intelligencer of that morning:

[President's War Order, No. 3.]

"EXECUTIVE MANSION,
"*Washington, March* 11, 1862.

"Major General McClellan having personally taken the field at the head of the army of the Potomac, until otherwise ordered, he is relieved from the command of the other military departments, he retaining command of the department of the Potomac.

"*Ordered further,* That the departments now under the respective commands of Generals Halleck and Hunter, together with so much of that under General Buell as lies west of a north and south line indefinitely drawn through Knoxville, Tennessee, be consolidated and designated the department of the Mississippi; and that, until otherwise ordered, Major General Halleck have command of said department.

"*Ordered, also,* That the country west of the department of the Potomac and east of the department of the Mississippi be a military department, to be called the mountain department, and that the same be commanded by Major General Frémont.

"That all the commanders of departments, after the receipt of this order by them, respectively report severally and directly to the Secretary of War, and that prompt, full, and frequent reports will be expected of all and each of them.

"ABRAHAM LINCOLN."

Though unaware of the President's intention to remove me from the position of general-in-chief, I cheerfully acceded to the disposition he saw fit to make of my services, and so informed him in a note on the 12th of March, in which occur these words:

"I believe I said to you some weeks since, in connexion with some western matters, that no feeling of self-interest or ambition should ever prevent me from devoting myself to the service. I am glad to have the opportunity to prove it, and you will find that, under present circumstances, I shall work just as cheerfully as before, and that no consideration of self will in any manner interfere with the discharge of my public duties. Again thanking you for the official and personal kindness you have so often evinced towards me, I am," &c., &c.

On the 14th of March a reconnoissance of a large body of cavalry with some infantry, under command of General Stoneman, was sent along the Orange and Alexandria railroad to determine the position of the enemy, and, if possible, force his rear across the Rappahannock, but the roads were in such condition that, finding it impossible to subsist his men, General Stoneman was forced to return after reaching Cedar run.

The following despatch from him recites the result of this expedition:

"HEADQUARTERS, UNION MILLS,
"*March* 16, 1862.

"We arrived here last evening about dark. We got corn for horses; no provisions for men. Bull run too high to cross. Had we stayed an hour longer we should not have got here to-day, owing to the high water in the streams. Felt the enemy cautiously, and found him in force at Warrenton Junction. Saw two regiments of cavalry and three bodies of infantry on the other side of Cedar run. Had we crossed, should not have been able to get back for high water. Had three men of 5th cavalry hit driving in enemy's pickets; one slightly wounded in the head. Enemy acted confidently, and followed us some way back on the road, but did not molest us in any way. Enemy's force consisted of Stuart's and Ewell's cavalry, a battery of artillery, and some infantry. Railroad bridges all burned down up to Warrenton Junction; still entire beyond, but all in readiness to burn at a moment's warning, having dry wood piled upon them. Heard cars running during night before last; probably bringing up troops from Rappahannock. Heard of two regiments of infantry at Warrenton engaged in impressing the militia and securing forage. Heard of a large force of infantry this side of Rappahannock river, having come up to Warrenton Junction from Aquia creek day before yesterday. Bridges all destroyed this side of Broad run. The aides who take this will give you further particulars.

"Very respectfully, &c.,

"GEORGE STONEMAN,
"*Brigadier General, Commanding.*

"Col. COLBURN."

The main body of the army was, on the 15th of March, moved back to the vicinity of Alexandria to be embarked, leaving a part of General Sumner's corps at Manassas until other troops could be sent to relieve it. Before it was withdrawn a strong reconnoissance, under General Howard, was sent towards the Rappahannock, the result of which appears in the following despatch:

"WARRENTON JUNCTION,
"*March* 29, 1862.

"Express just received from General Howard. He drove the enemy across the Rappahannock bridge, and is now in camp on this bank of and near the Rappahannock river.

"The enemy blew up the bridge in his retreat. There was skirmishing during the march, and a few shots exchanged by the artillery, without any loss on our part. Their loss, if any, is not known. General Howard will return to this camp to-morrow morning.

"E. V. SUMNER, *Brigadier General.*

"General S. WILLIAMS."

The line of the Rappahannock and the Manassas Gap railroad was thus left reasonably secure from menace by any considerable body of the enemy.

On the 13th of March a council of war was assembled at Fairfax Court-house to discuss the military status. The President's order No. 3, of March 8th, was considered. The following is a memorandum of the proceedings of the council:

"HEADQUARTERS ARMY OF THE POTOMAC,
"*Fairfax Court-house, March* 13, 1862.

"A council of the generals commanding army corps, at the headquarters of the army of the Potomac, were of the opinion—

"I. That the enemy having retreated from Manassas to Gordonsville, behind the Rappahannock and Rapidan, it is the opinion of the generals commanding army corps that the operations to be carried on will be best undertaken from Old Point Comfort, between the York and James rivers: *Provided*,

"1st. That the enemy's vessel, Merrimac, can be neutralized.

"2d. That the means of transportation, sufficient for an immediate transfer of the force to its new base, can be ready at Washington and Alexandria to move down the Potomac; and,

"3d. That a naval auxiliary force can be had to silence, or aid in silencing, the enemy's batteries on the York river.

"4th. That the force to be left to cover Washington shall be such as to give an entire feeling of security for its safety from menace. (Unanimous.)

"II. If the foregoing cannot be, the army should then be moved against the enemy, behind the Rappahannock, at the earliest possible moment, and the means for reconstructing bridges, repairing railroads, and stocking them with materials sufficient for supplying the army, should at once be collected, for both the Orange and Alexandria and Aquia and Richmond railroads. (Unanimous.)

"N. B.—That with the forts on the right bank of the Potomac fully garrisoned, and those on the left bank occupied, a covering force in front of the Virginia line of 25,000 men would suffice. (Keys, Heintzelman, and McDowell.) A total of 40,000 men for the defence of the city would suffice. (Sumner.")

This was assented to by myself, and immediately communicated to the War Department. The following reply was received the same day:

"WAR DEPARTMENT, *March* 13, 1862.

"The President having considered the plan of operations agreed upon by yourself and the commanders of army corps, makes no objection to the same, but gives the following directions as to its execution:

"1. Leave such force at Manassas Junction as shall make it entirely certain that the enemy shall not repossess himself of that position and line of communication.

"2. Leave Washington entirely secure.

"3. Move the remainder of the force down the Potomac, choosing a new base at Fortress Monroe, or anywhere between here and there, or, at all events, move such remainder of the army at once in pursuit of the enemy by some route.

"EDWIN M. STANTON,
"*Secretary of War.*

"Major General GEORGE B. McCLELLAN."

My preparations were at once begun in accordance with these directions, and on the 16th of March the following instructions were sent to Generals Banks and Wadsworth:

"HEADQUARTERS ARMY OF THE POTOMAC,
"*March* 16, 1862.

"SIR: You will post your command in the vicinity of Manassas, intrench yourself strongly, and throw cavalry pickets well out to the front.

"Your first care will be the rebuilding of the railway from Washington to Manassas and to Strasburg, in order to open your communications with the valley of the Shenandoah. As soon as the Manassas Gap railway is in running order, intrench a brigade of infantry, say four regiments, with two batteries, at or near the point where the railway crosses the Shenandoah. Something like two regiments of cavalry should be left in that vicinity to occupy Winchester, and thoroughly scour the country south of the railway and up the Shenandoah valley, as well as through Chester gap, which might perhaps be advantageously ccupied by a detachment of infantry, well intrenched. Block-houses should be built at all the railway bridges. Occupy by grand guards Warrenton Junction and Warrenton itself, and also some little more advanced point on the Orange and Alexandria railroad, as soon as the railway bridge is repaired.

"Great activity should be observed by the cavalry. Besides the two regiments at Manassas, another regiment of cavalry will be at your disposal, to scout towards the Occoquan, and probably a fourth towards Leesburg.

"To recapitulate, the most important points which should engage your attention are as follows:

"1. A strong force, well intrenched, in the vicinity of Manassas, perhaps even Centreville, and another force, (a brigade,) also well intrenched, near Strasburg.

"2. Block-houses at the railway bridges.

"3. Constant employment of the cavalry well to the front.

"4. Grand guards at Warrenton Junction and in advance, as far as the Rappahannock, if possible.

"5. Great care to be exercised to obtain full and early information as to the enemy.

"6. The general object is to cover the line of the Potomac and Washington.

"The above is communicated by command of Major General McClellan.

"S. WILLIAMS,

"*Assistant Adjutant General.*

"Major General N. P. BANKS,

"*Commanding Fifth Corps, Army of the Potomac.*"

"HEADQUARTERS ARMY OF THE POTOMAC,

"*March* 16, 1862.

"SIR: The command to which you have been assigned, by instructions of the President, as military governor of the District of Columbia, embraces the geographical limits of the District, and will also include the city of Alexandria, the defensive works south of the Potomac, from the Occoquan to Difficult creek, and the post of Fort Washington.

"I enclose a list of the troops and of the defences embraced in these limits.

"General Banks will command at Manassas Junction, with the divisions of Williams and Shields, composing the fifth corps, but you should, nevertheless, exercise vigilance in your front, carefully guard the approaches in that quarter, and maintain the duties of advanced guards. You will use the same precautions on either flank.

"All troops not actually needed for the police of Washington and Georgetown, for the garrisons north of the Potomac, and for other indicated special duties, should be moved to the south side of the river.

"In the centre of your front you should post the main body of your troops, and proper proportions at suitable distances towards your right and left flanks. Careful patrols will be made, in order thoroughly to scour the country in front, from right to left.

"It is specially enjoined upon you to maintain the forts and their armaments in the best possible order, to look carefully to the instruction and discipline of their garrisons, as well as all other troops under your command, and, by frequent and rigid inspections, to insure the attainment of these ends.

"The care of the railways, canals, depots, bridges and ferries, within the above-named limits, will devolve upon you, and you are to insure their security and provide for their protection by every means in your power. You will also protect the depots of the public stores and the transit of stores to troops in active service.

"By means of patrols you will thoroughly scour the neighboring country, south of the Eastern Branch, and also on your right, and you will use every possible precaution to intercept mails, goods and persons passing unauthorized to the enemy's lines.

"The necessity of maintaining good order within your limits, and especially in the capital of the nation, cannot be too strongly enforced.

"You will forward and facilitate the movement of all troops destined for the active part of the army of the Potomac, and especially the transit of detachments to their proper regiments and corps.

"The charge of the new troops arriving in Washington, and of all troops temporarily there, will devolve upon you. You will form them into provisional brigades, promote their instruction and discipline, and facilitate their equipment. Report all arrivals of troops, their strength, composition and equipment, by every opportunity.

"Besides the regular reports and returns, which you will be required to render to the Adjutant General of the army, you will make to these headquarters a consolidated report of your command, every Sunday morning, and monthly returns on the first day of each month.

"The foregoing instructions are communicated by command of Major General McClellan.

"S. WILLIAMS,
"*Assistant Adjutant General.*

"Brigadier General J. S. WADSWORTH,
"*Military Governor of the District of Columbia.*"

The Secretary of War had expressed a desire that I should communicate to the War Department my designs with regard to the employment of the army of the Potomac in an official form. I submitted, on the 19th of March, the following:

"HEADQUARTERS ARMY OF THE POTOMAC,
"*Theological Seminary, Va., March* 19, 1862.

"SIR: I have the honor to submit the following notes on the proposed operations of the active portion of the army of the Potomac.

"The proposed plan of campaign is to assume Fort Monroe as the first base of operations, taking the line of Yorktown and West Point upon Richmond as the line of operations, Richmond being the objective point. It is assumed that the fall of Richmond involves that of Norfolk and the whole of Virginia; also, that we shall fight a decisive battle between West Point and Richmond, to give which battle the rebels will concentrate all their available forces, understanding, as they will, that it involves the fate of their cause. It therefore follows—

"1st. That we should collect all our available forces and operate upon adjacent lines, maintaining perfect communication between our columns.

"2d. That no time should be lost in reaching the field of battle.

"The advantages of the peninsula between York and James rivers are too obvious to need explanation; it is also clear that West Point should as soon as possible be reached, and used as our main depot, that we may have the shortest line of land transportation for our supplies, and the use of the York river.

"There are two methods of reaching this point—

"1st. By moving directly from Fort Monroe as a base, and trusting to the roads for our supplies, at the same time landing a strong corps as near Yorktown as possible, in order to turn the rebel lines of defence south of Yorktown; then to reduce Yorktown and Gloucester by a siege, in all probability involving a delay of weeks, perhaps.

"2d. To make a combined naval and land attack upon Yorktown, the first object of the campaign. This leads to the most rapid and decisive results. To accomplish this, the navy should at once concentrate upon the York river all their available and most powerful batteries: its reduction should not in that case require many hours. A strong corps would be pushed up the York, under cover of the navy, directly upon West Point, immediately upon the fall of Yorktown, and we could at once establish our new base of operations at a distance of some twenty-five miles from Richmond, with every facility for developing and bringing into play the whole of our available force on either or both banks of the James.

"It is impossible to urge too strongly the absolute necessity of the full co-operation of the navy as a part of this programme. Without it the operations may be prolonged for many weeks, and we may be forced to carry in front several strong positions which by their aid could be turned without serious loss of either time or men.

"It is also of first importance to bear in mind the fact already alluded to, that the capture of Richmond necessarily involves the prompt fall of Norfolk, while an operation against Norfolk, if successful, as the beginning of the campaign, facilitates the reduction of Richmond merely by the demoralization of the rebel troops involved, and that after the fall of Norfolk we should be obliged to undertake the capture of Richmond by the same means which would have accomplished it in the beginning, having meanwhile afforded the rebels ample time to perfect their defensive arrangements, for they would well know, from the moment the army of the Potomac changed its base to Fort Monroe, that Richmond must be its ultimate object.

"It may be summed up in a few words, that, for the prompt success of this campaign, it is absolutely necessary that the navy should at once throw its whole available force, its most powerful vessels, against Yorktown. There is the most important point—there the knot to be cut. An immediate decision upon the subject-matter of this communication is highly desirable, and seems called for by the exigencies of the occasion.

"I am, sir, very respectfully, your obedient servant,

"GEORGE B. McCLELLAN,
Major General.

"Hon. E. M. STANTON,
Secretary of War."

In the mean time the troops destined to form the active army were collected in camps convenient to the points of embarcation, and every preparation made to embark them as rapidly as possible when the transports were ready.

A few days before sailing for Fort Monroe, while still encamped near Alexandria, I met the President, by appointment, on a steamer. He there informed me that he had been strongly pressed to take General Blenker's division from my command and give it to General Frémont. His excellency was good enough to suggest several reasons for not taking Blenker's division from me. I assented to the force of his suggestions, and was extremely gratified by his decision to allow the division to remain with the army of the Potomac. It was therefore with surprise that I received, on the 31st, the following note:

"EXECUTIVE MANSION,
Washington, March 31, 1862.

"MY DEAR SIR: This morning I felt constrained to order Blenker's division to Frémont, and I write this to assure you that I did so with great pain, understanding that you would wish it otherwise. If you could know the full pressure of the case, I am confident that you would justify it, even beyond a mere acknowledgment that the commander-in-chief may order what he pleases.

"Yours, very truly,

"A. LINCOLN.

"Major General McCLELLAN."

To this I replied, in substance, that I regretted the order, and could ill afford to lose ten thousand troops which had been counted upon in forming my plan of campaign, but as there was no remedy, I would yield, and do the best I could without them. In a conversation with the President a few hours afterwards I repeated verbally the same thing, and expressed my regret that Blenker's division had been given to General Frémont from any pressure other than the requirements of the national exigency. I was partially relieved, however, by the President's positive and emphatic assurance that I might be confident that no more troops beyond these ten thousand should in any event be taken from me, or in any way detached from my command.

At the time of the evacuation of Manassas by the enemy, Jackson was at Winchester, our forces occupying Charlestown, and Shields's reaching Bunker Hill on the 11th. On the morning of the 12th, a brigade of General Banks's troops, under General Hamilton, entered Winchester, the enemy having left at 5 o'clock the evening before, his rear guard of cavalry leaving an hour before our advance entered the place. The enemy having made his preparations for evacuation some days before, it was not possible to intercept his retreat. On the 13th the mass of Banks's corps was concentrated in the immediate vicinity of Winchester, the enemy being in the rear of Strasburg.

On the 19th General Shields occupied Strasburg, driving the enemy twenty miles south to Mount Jackson.

On the 20th the first division of Banks's corps commenced its movement towards Manassas, in compliance with my letter of instructions of the 16th.

Jackson probably received information of this movement, and supposed that no force of any consequence was left in the vicinity of Winchester, and upon the falling back of Shields to that place, for the purpose of enticing Jackson in pursuit, the latter promptly followed, whereupon ensued a skirmish on the 22d, in which General Shields was wounded, and an affair at Winchester on the 23d, resulting in the defeat of Jackson, who was pursued as rapidly as the exhaustion of our troops and the difficulty of obtaining supplies permitted. It is presumed that the full reports of the battle of Winchester were forwarded direct to the War Department by General Banks.

It being now clear that the enemy had no intention of returning by the Manassas route, the following letter of April 1 was written to General Banks:

"HEADQUARTERS ARMY OF THE POTOMAC,
"*On board the Commodore, April* 1, 1862.

"GENERAL: The change in affairs in the valley of the Shenandoah has rendered necessary a corresponding departure, temporarily at least, from the plan we some days since agreed upon.

"In my arrangements I assume that you have with you a force amply sufficient to drive Jackson before you, provided he is not re-enforced largely. I also assume that you may find it impossible to detach anything towards Manassas for some days, probably not until the operations of the main army have drawn all the rebel force towards Richmond.

"You are aware that General Sumner has for some days been at Manassas Junction with two divisions of infantry, six batteries, and two regiments of cavalry, and that a reconnoissance to the Rappahannock forced the enemy to destroy the railway bridge at Rappahannock Station, on the Orange and Alexandria railroad. Since that time our cavalry have found nothing on this side the Rappahannock in that direction, and it seems clear that we have no reason to fear any return of the rebels in that quarter. Their movements near Fredericksburg also indicate a final abandonment of that neighborhood. I doubt whether Johnson will now re-enforce Jackson with a view of offensive operations. The time is probably passed when he could have gained anything by doing so. I have ordered in one of Sumner's divisions (that of Richardson, late Sumner's) to

Alexandria for embarcation. Blenker's has been detached from the army of the Potomac and ordered to report to General Frémont.

"Abercrombie is probably at Warrenton Junction to-day. Geary is at White Plains.

"Two regiments of cavalry have been ordered out, and are now on the way to relieve the two regiments of Sumner.

"Four thousand infantry and one battery leave Washington at once for Manassas. Some three thousand more will move in one or two days, and soon after some three thousand additional.

"I will order Blenker to march on Strasburg and to report to you for temporary duty, so that should you find a large force in your front you can avail yourself of his aid as soon as possible. Please direct him to Winchester, thence to report to the Adjutant General of the army for orders; but keep him until you are sure what you have in front.

"In regard to your own movements, the most important thing at present is to throw Jackson well back, and then to assume such a position as to enable you to prevent his return. As soon as the railway communications are re-established it will be probably important and advisable to move on Staunton, but this would require secure communications, and a force of from twenty-five thousand to thirty thousand for active operations. It should also be nearly coincident with my own move on Richmond, at all events not so long before it as to enable the rebels to concentrate on you, and then return on me. I fear that you cannot be ready in time, although it may come in very well with a force less than that I have mentioned, after the main battle near Richmond. When General Sumner leaves Warrenton Junction, General Abercrombie will be placed in immediate command of Manassas and Warrenton Junction, under your general orders Please inform me frequently by telegraph and otherwise as to the state of things in your front.

"I am very truly yours,

"GEORGE B. McCLELLAN,
"*Major General Commanding.*

Major General N. P. BANKS,
Commanding Fifth Corps.

"P. S.—From what I have just learned, it would seem that the regiments of cavalry intended for Warrenton Junction have gone to Harper's Ferry. Of the four additional regiments placed under your orders, two should as promptly as possible move by the shortest route on Warrenton Junction.

"I am, sir, very respectfully, your obedient servant,

"GEORGE B. McCLELLAN,
"*Major General Commanding.*"

This letter needs no further explanation than to say that it was my intention, had the operations in that quarter remained under my charge, either to have resumed the defensive position marked out in the letter of March 16, or to have advanced General Banks upon Staunton as might in the progress of events seem advisable.

It is to be remembered that when I wrote the preceding and following letters of April 1 I had no expectation of being relieved from the charge of the operations in the Shenandoah valley, the President's war order No. 3 giving no intimation of such an intention, and that so far as reference was made to final operations after driving Jackson back and taking such a position as to prevent his return, no positive orders were given in the letter, the matter being left for future consideration, when the proper time arrived for a decision.

From the following letter to the Adjutant General, dated April 1, 1862, it will be seen that I left for the defence of the national capital and its approaches, when I sailed for the Peninsula, 73,456 men, with 109 pieces of light artillery, including the 32 pieces in Washington alluded to, but not enumerated in my letter to the Adjutant General. It will also be seen that I recommended other available troops in New York (more than 4,000) to be at once ordered forward to re-enforce them.

"HEADQUARTERS ARMY OF THE POTOMAC,
"*Steamer Commodore, April* 1, 1862.

"GENERAL: I have to request that you will lay the following communication before the Hon. Secretary of War.

"The approximate numbers and positions of the troops left near and in rear of the Potomac are as follows:

"General Dix has, after guarding the railroads under his charge, sufficient to give him 5,000 for the defence of Baltimore, and 1,988 available for the Eastern Shore, Annapolis, &c. Fort Delaware is very well garrisoned by about 400 men.

"The garrisons of the forts around Washington amount to 10,600 men; other disposable troops now with General Wadsworth about 11,400 men.

"The troops employed in guarding the various railways in Maryland amount to some 3,359 men. These it is designed to relieve, being old regiments, by dismounted cavalry, and to send forward to Manassas.

"General Abercrombie occupies Warrenton with a force, which, including Colonel Geary, at White Plains, and the cavalry to be at his disposal, will amount to some 7,780 men, with 12 pieces of artillery.

"I have the honor to request that all the troops organized for service in Pennsylvania and New York, and in any of the eastern States, may be ordered to Washington. I learn from Governor Curtin that there are some 3,500 men now ready in Pennsylvania. This force I should be glad to have sent to Manassas. Four thousand men from General Wadsworth I desire to be ordered to Manassas. These troops, with the railroad guards above alluded to, will make up a force under the command of General Abercrombie of something like 18,639 men.

"It is my design to push General Blenker's division from Warrenton upon Strasburg. He should remain at Strasburg long enough to allow matters to assume a definite form in that region before proceeding to his ultimate destination.

"The troops in the valley of the Shenandoah will thus, including Blenker's division, 10,028 strong, with 24 pieces of artillery; Banks's 5th corps, which embraces the command of General Shields, 19,687 strong, with 41 guns, some 3,652 disposable cavalry, and the railroad guards, about 2,100 men, amount to about 35,467 men.

"It is designed to relieve General Hooker by one regiment, say 850 men, being, with some 500 cavalry, 1,350 men on the lower Potomac.

"To recapitulate: At Warrenton there is to be..........	7,780	men
"At Manassas, say..................................	10,859	"
"In the valley of the Shenandoah.....................	35,467	"
"On the lower Potomac............................	1,350	"
"In all..................................	55,456	"

"There would thus be left for the garrisons and the front of Washington, under General Wadsworth, some 18,000, inclusive of the batteries under instruction. The troops organizing or ready for service in New York, I learn, will probably number more than four thousand. These should be assembled at Washington, subject to disposition where their services may be most required.

"I am, very respectfully, your obedient servant,

"GEORGE B. McCLELLAN,
"*Major General Commanding.*

"Brig. Gen. L. THOMAS,
"*Adjutant General United States Army.*"

The following letter from General Barry shows thatt hirty-two (32) field guns, with men, horses, and equipments, were also left in Washington city when the army sailed. These were the batteries under instruction referred to above:

"HEADQUARTERS INSPECTOR OF ARTILLERY,
"*Washington, December* 16, 1862.

"GENERAL: It having been stated in various public prints, and in a speech of Senator Chandler, of Michigan, in his place in the United States Senate, quoting what he stated to be a portion of the testimony of Brigadier General Wadsworth, military governor of Washington, before the joint Senate and House committee on the conduct of the war, that Major General McClellan had left an insufficient force for the defence of Washington, and *not a gun on wheels.*—

"I have to contradict this charge as follows:

"From official reports made at the time to me, (the chief of artillery of the army of the Potomac,) and now in my possession, by the commanding officer of the light artillery troops left in camp in the city of Washington by your orders, it appears that the following named field batteries were left:

"Battery C, 1st New York artillery, Captain Barnes, 2 guns; battery K, 1st New York artillery, Captain Crounse, 6 guns; battery L, 2d New York artillery, Captain Robinson, 6 guns: 9th New York independent battery, Captain Monzordi, 6 guns; 16th New York independent battery, Captain Locke; battery A, 2d battalion New York artillery, Captain Hogan, 6 guns; battery B, 2d battalion New York artillery, Captain McMahon, 6 guns; total of batteries, 32 guns.

"With the exception of a few horses which could have been procured from the quartermaster's department in a few hours, the batteries were all fit for immediate service, excepting the 16th New York battery, which having been previously ordered, on General Wadsworth's application, to report to him for special service, was unequipped with either guns or horses.

"I am, general, very respectfully, your obedient servant,
"W. F. BARRY,
"*Brig. Gen, Inspector of Artillery United States Army.*

"Maj. Gen. MCCLELLAN,
"*United States Army.*"

It is true that Blenker's division, which is included in the force enumerated by me, was under orders to re-enforce General Frémont, but the following despatch from the Secretary of War, dated March 31, 1862, will show that I was authorized to detain him at Strasburg until matters assumed a definite form in that region, before proceeding to his ultimate destination; in other words, until Jackson was disposed of. And had he been detained there, instead of moving on to Harper's Ferry and Franklin, under other orders, it is probable that General Banks would have defeated Jackson, instead of being himself obliged subsequently to retreat to Williamsport.

"WAR DEPARTMENT,
"*Washington, D. C., March* 31, 1862.

"The order in respect to Blenker is not designed to hinder or delay the movement of Richardson, or any other force. He can remain wherever you desire him as long as required for your movements, and in any position you desire. The order is simply to place him in position for re-enforcing Frémont, as soon as your dispositions will permit, and he may go to Harper's Ferry by such route and at such time as you shall direct. State your own wishes as to the movement, when and how it shall be made.

"EDWIN M. STANTON,
"*Secretary of War.*

"Maj. Gen. MCCLELLAN."

Without including General Blenker's division, there were left 67,428 men and 85 pieces of light artillery, which, under existing circumstances, I deemed more than adequate to insure the perfect security of Washington against any force the enemy could bring against it, for the following reasons:

The light troops I had thrown forward under General Stoneman in pursuit of the rebel army, after the evacuation of Manassas and Centreville, had driven their rear guard across Cedar run, and subsequent expeditions from Sumner's corps had forced them beyond the Rappahannock. They had destroyed all the railroad bridges behind them, thereby indicating that they did not intend to return over that route. Indeed, if they had attempted such a movement, their progress must have been slow and difficult, as it would have involved the reconstruction of the bridges; and if my orders for keeping numerous cavalry patrols well out to the front, to give timely notice of any approach of the enemy, had been strictly enforced (and I left seven regiments of cavalry for this express purpose) they could not by any possibility have reached Washington before there would have been ample time to concentrate the entire forces left for its defence, as well as those at Baltimore, at any necessary point.

It was clear to my mind, as I reiterated to the authorities, that the movement of the army of the Potomac would have the effect to draw off the hostile army from Manassas to the defence of their capital, and thus free Washington from menace. This opinion was confirmed the moment the movement commenced, or rather as soon as the enemy became aware of our intentions; for with the exception of Jackson's force of some 15,000, which his instructions show to have been intended to operate in such a way as to prevent McDowell's corps from being sent to re-enforce me, no rebel force of any magnitude made its appearance in front of Washington during the progress of our operations on the Peninsula; nor until the order was given for my return from Harrison's landing was Washington again threatened.

Surrounded, as Washington was, with numerous and strong fortifications, well garrisoned, it was manifest that the enemy could not afford to detach from his main army a force sufficient to assail them.

It is proper to remark, that just previous to my departure for Fort Monroe, I sent my chief of staff to General Hitchcock, who at that time held staff relations with his excellency the President and the Secretary of War, to submit to him a list of the troops I proposed to leave for the defence of Washington, and the positions in which I designed posting them. General Hitchcock, after glancing his eye over the list, observed that he was not the judge of what was required for defending the capital; that General McClellan's position was such as to enable him to understand the subject much better than he did, and he presumed that if the force designated was, in his judgment, sufficient, nothing more would be required. He was then told by the chief of staff that I would be glad to have his opinion, as an old and experienced officer; to this he replied, that as I had had the entire control of the defences for a long time, I was the best judge of what was needed, and he declined to give any other expression of opinion at that time.

On the 2d of April, the day following my departure for Fort Monroe, Generals Hitchcock and Thomas were directed by the Secretary of War to examine and report whether the President's instructions to me, of March 8 and 13 had been complied with; on the same day their report was submitted, and their decision was—

"That the requirement of the President, that this city (Washington) shall be left entirely secure, has not been fully complied with."

The President, in his letter to me on the 9th of April, says: "And now allow me to ask, do you really think I should permit the line from Richmond, *via* Manassas Junction, to this city, to be entirely open, except what resistance could be presented by less than twenty thousand unorganized troops."

In the report of Generals Hitchcock and Thomas, alluded to, it is acknowledged that there was no danger of an attack from the direction of Manassas, in these words: "In regard to occupying Manassas Junction, as the enemy have destroyed the railroads leading to it, it may be fair to assume that they have no intention of returning for the reoccupation of their late position, and therefore no large force would be necessary to hold that position."

That, as remarked before, was precisely the view I took of it, and this was enforced by the subsequent movements of the enemy.

In another paragraph of the report it is stated that fifty-five thousand men was the number considered adequate for the defence of the capital. That General McClellan, in his enumeration of the forces left, had included Banks's army corps, operating in the Shenandoah valley, but whether this corps should be regarded as available for the protection of Washington, they decline to express an opinion.

At the time this report was made, the only enemy on any approach to Washington was Jackson's force, in front of Banks in the Shenandoah valley, with the Manassas Gap railroad leading from this valley to Washington; and it will be admitted, I presume, that Banks, occupying the Shenandoah valley, was in the best position to defend not only that approach to Washington, but the roads to Harper's Ferry and above.

The number of troops left by me for the defence of Washington, as given in my letter to the Adjutant General, were taken from the latest official returns of that date, and these, of course, constituted the most trustworthy and authentic source from which such information could be obtained.

Another statement made by General Hitchcock before the "Committee on the Conduct of the War," in reference to this same order, should be noticed. He was asked the following question: "Do you understand now that the movement made by General McClellan to Fort Monroe, and up the York river, was in compliance with the recommendation of the council of generals commanding corps, and held at Fairfax Court-house on the 13th of March last, or in violation of it?"

To which he replied as follows: "I have considered, and do now consider, that it was in violation of the recommendation of that council in two important particulars; one particular being that portion of this report which represents the council as agreeing to the expedition by way of the Peninsula, *provided* the rebel steamer Merrimac could first be neutralized. That important provision General McClellan disregarded."

* * * * * * * * * *

The second particular alluded to by General Hitchcock was in reference to the troops left for the defence of Washington, which has been disposed of above.

In regard to the steamer Merrimac, I have also stated that, so far as our operations on York river were concerned, the power of this vessel was neutralized. I now proceed to give some of the evidence which influenced me in coming to that conclusion.

Previous to our departure for the Peninsula, Mr. Watson, Assistant Secretary of War, was sent by the President to Fort Monroe to consult with Flag-officer Goldsborough upon this subject. The result of that consultation is contained in the following extract from the evidence of Admiral Goldsborough before the "Committee on the Conduct of the War," viz: "I told Mr. Watson, Assistant Secretary of War, that the President might make his mind perfectly easy about the Merrimac going up York river; that she could never get there, for I had ample means to prevent that."

Captain G. V. Fox, Assistant Secretary of the Navy, testifies before the committee as follows:

"General McClellan expected the navy to neutralize the Merrimac, and I promised that it should be done."

General Keyes, commanding 4th army corps, testifies as follows before the committee:

"During the time that the subject of the change of base was discussed, I had refused to consent to the Peninsula line of operations until I had sent word to the Navy Department and asked two questions: First, whether the Merrimac was certainly neutralized, or not? Second, whether the navy was in a condition to co-operate efficiently with the army to break through between Yorktown and Gloucester point? To both of these, answers were returned in the affirmative; that is, the Merrimac was neutralized, and the navy was in a condition to co-operate efficiently to break through between Yorktown and Gloucester point."

Before starting for the Peninsula, I instructed Lieutenant Colonel B. S. Alexander, of the United States corps of engineers, to visit Manassas Junction and its vicinity for the purpose of determining upon the defensive works necessary to enable us to hold that place with a small force. The accompanying letters from Colonel Alexander will show what steps were taken by him to carry into effect this important order.

I regret to say that those who succeeded me in command of the region in front of Washington, whatever were the fears for its safety did not deem it necessary to carry out my plans and instructions to them. Had Manassas been placed in condition for a strong defence, and its communications secured as recommended by Colonel Alexander, the result of General Pope's campaign would probably have been different.

"WASHINGTON, D. C., *April* 2, 1862.

"SIR: You will proceed to Manassas at as early a moment as practicable and mark on the ground the works for the defence of that place, on the positions which I indicated to you yesterday. You will find two carpenters, experienced in this kind of work, ready to accompany you, by calling on Mr. Dougherty, the master carpenter of the Treasury extension.

"The general idea of the defence of this position is, to occupy the fringe of elevation which lies about half way between Manassas depot and the junction of the railroad, with a series of works open to the rear, so that they may be commanded by the work hereafter to be described.

"There will be at least four of these works, three of them being on the left of the railroad leading from Alexandria, at the positions occupied by the enemy's works. The other on the right of this road, on the position we examined yesterday. The works of the enemy to the north of this latter position, numbered 1 and 2 on Lieutenant Comstock's sketch, may also form a part of the front line of our defence; but the sides of these works looking towards Manassas station should be levelled, so that the interior of the works may be seen from the latter position.

"Embrasures should be arranged in all these works for *field* artillery. The approaches should be such that a battery can drive into the works. The number of embrasures in each battery will depend upon its size and the ground to be commanded. It is supposed there will be from four to eight embrasures in each battery.

"The other works of the enemy looking towards the east and south may be stengthened so as to afford sufficient defence in these directions. The work No. 3 in Lieutenant Comstock's sketch may be also strengthened and arranged for field artillery, when time will permit. This work is in a good position to cover a retreat, which would be made down the valley in which the railroad runs towards Bull run.

"At Manassas station there should be a fort constructed. The railroad will pass through this fort, and the depot, if there should be one built, should be placed in its rear. This latter work should be regarded as the key to the position. It should be as large as the nature of the ground will permit.

"By going down the slopes, which are not steep, it may be made large enough to accommodate 2,000 or 3,000 men. The top of the position need not be cut away; it will be better to throw up the earth into a large traverse, which may also be a bomb-proof. Its profile should be strong, and its ditches should be flanked. It should receive a heavy armament of 24 or 32 pounders, with some rifled (Parrott) 20 or 30 pounders. Its guns should command all the exterior works, so that these works could be of no use to the enemy, should he take them. In accommodating the fort to the ground this consideration should not be lost sight of.

"After tracing these works on the ground, you will make a sketch embracing the whole of them, showing their relative positions and size. This sketch should embrace the junction of the railroads and the ground for some distance around the main work. It need not be made with extreme accuracy. The distances may be paced, or measured, with a tape line. The bearings may be taken by compass.

"Having located the works and prepared your sketch, you will report to Captain Frederick E. Prime, of the corps of engineers, who will furnish you the means of construction.

"It is important that these works should be built with the least possible delay. You will, therefore, expedite matters as fast as possible.

"Very respectfully, your obedient servant,

"B. S. ALEXANDER,

"*Lieutenant Colonel, Aide-de-Camp.*

"Captain FRED. R. MUNTHER, *Present.*"

"WASHINGTON, *April* 6, 1862.

"SIR: I enclose you herewith a copy of the instructions which I gave to Captain Munther, in reference to the defences of Manassas.

"As there has been a new department created, (that of the Rappahannock,) it is possible that you and I, as well as General McClellan, are relieved from the further consideration of this subject at the present time.

"I will, however, state for your information, should the subject ever come before you again, that in my opinion the communication with Manassas by land should be secured.

"To effect this in the best manner, so far as my observations extended, I think the bridge over Bull run, near Union mills and just above the railroad bridge, should be rebuilt or thoroughly repaired, and that a small work, or two or three open batteries, should be erected on the adjacent heights to protect it as well as the railroad bridge.

"The communication by land would then be through or near Centreville, over the road used by the enemy.

"I write this for fear something should detain me here; but I hope to leave here to join you to-morrow. My health is much improved.

"Very respectfully, your obedient servant,

"B. S. ALEXANDER,

"*Lieutenant Colonel, Aide-de-Camp.*

"Brigadier General J. G. BARNARD,
"*Chief Engineer, Army of the Potomac.*"

I may be permitted also to mention that the plans (also unexecuted by my successor) indicated in my letter of instructions to General Banks, dated March 16, 1862, for intrenching Chester gap and the point where the Manassas railroad crosses the Shenandoah, were for the purpose of preventing even the attempt of such a raid as that of Jackson in the month of May following.

MILITARY INCIDENTS OF THE FIRST PERIOD.

Before taking up the history of the embarcation and Peninsula campaign, I should remark that during the fall and winter of 1861–'62, while the army of the Potomac was in position in front of Washington, reconnoissances were made from time to time, and skirmishes frequently occurred, which were of great importance in the education of the troops, accustoming them to the presence of the enemy, and giving them confidence under fire. There were many instances of individual gallantry displayed in these affairs; the reports of them will be found among the documents which accompany this report.

One of the most brilliant of these affairs was that which took place at Drainsville on December 20, 1861, when the 3d brigade of McCall's division, under Brigadier General E. O. C. Ord, with Easton's battery, routed and pursued four regiments of infantry, one of cavalry, and a battery of six pieces.

The operations of Brigadier General F. W. Lander on the upper Potomac, during the months of January and February, 1862, frustrated the attempts of General Jackson against the Baltimore and Ohio railroad, Cumberland, &c., and obliged him to fall back to Winchester. His constitution was impaired by the hardships he had experienced, and on the 2d March the fearless General Lander expired, a victim to the excessive fatigue of the campaign.

SECOND PERIOD.

CHAPTER I.

The council composed of the four corps commanders, organized by the President of the United States, at its meeting on the 13th of March, adopted Fort Monroe as the base of operations for the movement of the army of the Potomac upon Richmond. For the prompt and successful execution of the projected operation, it was regarded by all as necessary that the whole of the four corps should be employed, with at least the addition of ten thousand men drawn from the forces in the vicinity of Fortress Monroe, that position and its dependencies being regarded as amply protected by the naval force in its neighborhood, and the advance of the main army up the Peninsula, so that it could be safely left with a small garrison.

In addition to the land forces, the co-operation of the navy was desired in the projected attack upon the batteries at Yorktown and Gloucester, as well as in controlling the York and James rivers for the protection of our flanks, and the use of the transports bringing supplies to the army. With these expectations, and for reasons stated elsewhere in this report, my original plan of moving by Urbana and West Point was abandoned, and the line with Fort Monroe as a base adopted. In the arrangements for the transportation of the army to the Peninsula by water, the vessels were originally ordered to rendezvous mainly at Annapolis; but upon the evacuation of Manassas and the batteries of the lower Potomac by the enemy, it became more convenient to embark the troops and material at Alexandria, and orders to that effect were at once given.

In making the preliminary arrangements for the movement it was determined that the first corps, General McDowell's, should move as a unit first, and effect a landing either at the Sand-box, some four miles south of Yorktown, in order to turn all the enemy's defences at Ship point, Howard's bridge, Big Bethel, &c., or else, should existing circumstances render it preferable, land on the Gloucester side of York river and move on West Point.

The transports, however, arrived slowly and few at a time. In order, therefore, to expedite matters, I decided to embark the army by divisions, as transports arrived, keeping army corps together as much as possible, and to collect the troops at Fort Monroe. In determining the order of embarcation, convenience and expedition were especially consulted, except that the first corps was to be embarked last, as I intended to move it in mass to its point of disembarcation, and to land it on either bank of the York, as might then be determined.

On the 17th of March Hamilton's division, of the 3d corps, embarked at Alexandria and proceeded to Fort Monroe, with the following orders:

"WASHINGTON, D. C., *March* 17, 1862.

"You will, on your arrival at Fort Monroe, report to General Wool and request him to assign you ground for encamping your division. You will remain at Fort Monroe until further orders from General McClellan. Should General Wool require the services of your division in repelling an attack, you will obey his orders and use every effort to carry out his views.

"R. B. MARCY,
"*Chief of Staff.*

"General C. S. HAMILTON,
"*Commanding Division.*"

On the 22d of March, as soon as transportation was ready, General Fitz John Porter's division, of the same corps, embarked. General Heintzelman was ordered to accompany it, under the following instructions:

"HEADQUARTERS ARMY OF THE POTOMAC,
"*Seminary, March* 22, 1862.

"GENERAL: Upon the disembarcation of Porter's division at Fort Monroe, I have to request that you will move your two divisions, Porter's and Hamilton's, some three or four miles out from the fort to find good camping places, where wood and water can be readily obtained, and where your positions will be good in a defensive point of view. You may find it advisable to place one division on or near the road leading to Yorktown from Newport News—the other upon that leading to Yorktown direct from Fort Monroe. If you find that the nature of the country will permit easy communication and mutual support between the two divisions, it will be best to place one on each road. It will be best to remain pretty near the fort for the present, in order to give the impression that our object is to attack Norfolk rather than Yorktown. You will do well, however, to push strong reconnoissances well to the front to ascertain the position of the enemy and his pickets. I will, as soon as possible, re-enforce you by the 3d division of your corps, and it is probable that a part or the whole of the 4th corps will also move from Fort Monroe. This will probably be determined before your disembarcation is completed, and you will be informed accordingly.

"My desire would be to make no important move in advance until we are fully prepared to follow it up and give the enemy no time to recover.

"The quartermaster of your corps will receive detailed instructions in regard to land transportation from General Van Vliet.

"It will be advisable to mobilize your corps with the least possible delay, and have it prepared for an advance. I have directed extra clothing, ammunition, &c., to be sent to Fort Monroe, so that all deficiencies may be supplied without delay.

"Please report to me frequently and fully the condition of things on the new field of operations, and whatever intelligence you gain as to the enemy.

"Engage guides in sufficient numbers at once, and endeavor to send out spies.

"I am very truly yours,

"GEO. B. McCLELLAN,
"*Major General, Commanding.*

"Brigadier General S. P. HEINTZELMAN,
"*Commanding 3d Corps.*"

The remaining divisions embarked as rapidly as transports could be supplied.

On the 1st of April I embarked with the headquarters on the steamer Commodore, and reached Fort Monroe on the afternoon of the 2d.

In consequence of the delay in the arrival of the horse transports at Alexandria, but a small portion of the cavalry had arrived, and the artillery reserve had not yet completed its disembarcation.

I found there the 3d Pennsylvania cavalry and the 5th regular cavalry; the 2d regular cavalry and a portion of the 1st had arrived, but not disembarked. So few wagons had arrived that it was not possible to move Casey's division at all for several days, while the other divisions were obliged to move with scant supplies.

As to the force and position of the enemy the information then in our possession was vague and untrustworthy. Much of it was obtained from the staff officers of General Wool, and was simply to the effect that Yorktown was surrounded by a continuous line of earthworks, with strong water batteries on the York river, and garrisoned by not less than 15,000 troops, under command of General J. B. Magruder. Maps, which had been prepared by the topographical engineers under General Wool's command, were furnished me, in which the Warwick river was represented as flowing parallel to, but not crossing, the road from Newport News to Williamsburg, making the so-called Mulberry island a real island; and we had no information as to the true course of the Warwick *across* the Peninsula, nor of the formidable line of works which it covered.

Information which I had collected during the winter placed General Magruder's command at from 15,000 to 20,000 men, independently of General Huger's force at Norfolk, estimated at about 15,000.

It was also known that there were strong defensive works at or near Williamsburg.

Knowing that General Huger could easily spare some troops to re-enforce Yorktown, that he had indeed done so, and that Johnston's army of Manassas could be brought rapidly by the James and York rivers to the same point, I proposed to invest that town without delay.

The accompanying map of Colonel Cram, U. S. topographical engineers, attached to General Wool's staff, given to me as the result of several months' labor, indicated the feasibility of the design. It was also an object of primary importance to reach the vicinity of Yorktown before the enemy was re-enforced sufficiently to enable him to hold in force his works at Big Bethel, Howard's bridge, Ship point, &c., on the direct road to Yorktown and Young's mills, on the road from Newport News. This was the more urgent, as it was now evident that some days must elapse before the first corps could arrive.

Everything possible was done to hasten the disembarcation of the cavalry, artillery and wagons in the harbor; and on the 3d the orders of march were given for the following day.

There were at Fort Monroe and in its vicinity on the 3d, ready to move, two divisions of the 3d corps, two divisions of the 4th corps, and one division of the 2d corps, and Sykes's brigade of regular infantry, together with Hunt's artillery reserve and the regiments of cavalry before named, in all about 58,000 men and 100 guns, besides the division of artillery.

Richardson's and Hooker's divisions of the 2d and 3d corps had not arrived, and Casey's division of the 4th corps was unable to move for want of wagons.

Before I left Washington an order had been issued by the War Department placing Fort Monroe and its dependencies under my control, and authorizing me to draw from the troops under General Wool a division of about 10,000 men, which was to be assigned to the 1st corps.

During the night of the 3d I received a telegram from the Adjutant General of the army, stating that, by the President's order, I was deprived of all control over General Wool and the troops under his command, and forbidden to detach any of his troops without his sanction.

This order left me without any base of operations under my own control, and to this day I am ignorant of the causes which led to it.

On my arrival at Fort Monroe the James river was declared by the naval authorities closed to the operations of their vessels by the combined influence of the enemy's batteries on its banks and the confederate steamers Merrimac, Yorktown, Jamestown, and Teazer. Flag-Officer Goldsborough, then in command of the United States squadron in Hampton roads, regarded it (and no doubt justly) as his highest and most imperative duty to watch and neutralize the Merrimac; and as he designed using his most powerful vessels in a contest with her, he did not feel able to detach to the assistance of the army a suitable force to attack the water batteries at Yorktown and Gloucester. All this was contrary to what had been previously stated to me, and materially affected my plans.

At no time during the operations against Yorktown was the navy prepared to lend us any material assistance in its reduction until after our land batteries had partially silenced the works.

I had hoped, let me say, by rapid movements, to drive before me or capture the enemy on the Peninsula, open the James river, and press on to Richmond before he should be materially re-enforced from other portions of the territory. As the narrative proceeds the causes will be developed which frustrated these apparently well-grounded expectations.

I determined then to move the two divisions of the 4th corps by the Newport News and Williamsburg road, to take up a position between Yorktown and Williamsburg, while the two divisions of the 3d corps moved direct from Fort Monroe upon Yorktown; the reserves moving so as to support either corps as might prove necessary. I designed, should the works at Yorktown and Williamsburg offer a serious resistance, to land the 1st corps, re-enforced if necessary, on the left bank of the York or on the Severn, to move it on Gloucester and West Point, in order to take in reverse whatever force the enemy might have on the Peninsula, and compel him to abandon his positions.

In the commencement of the movement from Fort Monroe, serious difficulties were encountered from the want of precise topographical information as to the country in advance. Correct local maps were not to be found, and the country, though known in its general feature, we found to be inaccurately described in essential particulars in the only maps and geographical memoirs or papers to which access could be had. Erroneous courses to streams and roads were frequently given, and no dependence could be placed on the information thus derived. This difficulty has been found to exist with respect to most portions of the State of Virginia, through which my military operations have extended. Reconnoissances, frequently under fire, proved the only trustworthy sources of information. Negroes, however truthful their reports, possessed or were able to communicate very little accurate and no comprehensive topographical information.

On the 3d the following orders were given for the movement of the 4th:

"Porter's and Hamilton's divisions and Averill's cavalry of the 3d corps, and Sedgwick's division of the 2d corps, under Brigadier General Heintzelman, commanding 3d corps, will move to-morrow in the following order: Porter's division with Averill's cavalry at 6 a. m., over the Newmarket and New bridges to Big Bethel and Howard's bridge. This division will send forward to the batteries where the Ship Point road intersects the main Yorktown road a sufficient force to hold that point, and cut off the garrison of the Ship Point batteries. The whole division may be used for this purpose if necessary, and if possible the batteries should be occupied by our troops to-morrow. The portion of the division not necessary for this purpose will encamp at Howard's bridge.

"Hamilton's division will march at 7 a. m. by the New bridge road to Big Bethel, and will encamp on Howard's creek.

"Sedgwick's division will march at 8 a. m. by the Newmarket bridge, taking the direct road to Big Bethel, and will also encamp at Howard's bridge.

"Brigadier General Keyes, commanding 4th corps, will move with Smith's and Couch's division at 6 a. m., (Smith's division in advance,) by the James river road. The 5th regular cavalry, temporarily assigned to this corps, will move with Smith's division, which will encamp at Young's mills, throwing forward at least one brigade to the road from Big Bethel to Warwick. Couch's division will encamp at Fisher's creek.

"The reserve cavalry, artillery and infantry will move at 8.30 a. m., by the Newmarket bridge, to Big Bethel, where it will encamp. On the march it will keep in rear of Sedgwick's division."

The following is an extract from the order issued on the 4th for the march of the 5th:

"The following movements of the army will be carried out to-morrow (5th:)

"General Keyes will move forward Smith's division at 6 a. m., *via* Warwick Court House and the road leading near the old ship yard, to the 'Half-way House' on the Yorktown and Williamsburg road.

"General Couch's division will march at 6 a. m., to close up on General Smith's division at the 'Half-way House.'

"General Keyes's command will occupy and hold the narrow dividing ridge near the 'Half-way House,' so as to prevent the escape of the garrison at Yorktown by land, and prevent re-enforcements being thrown in.

"General Heintzelman will move forward General Porter's two rear brigades at 6 a. m., upon the advanced guard, when the entire division will advance to a point about two and three quarters miles from Yorktown, where the road turns abruptly to the north, and where a road comes in from Warwick Court House.

"General Hamilton's division will move at 6 a. m., and follow General Porter's division, camping as near it as possible.

"General Sedgwick's division will march at 5 a. m., as far as the Warwick road, which enters the main Yorktown road near Doctor Powers's house, and will await further orders.

"The reserve will march at 6 a. m., upon the main Yorktown road, halting for further orders at Doctor Powers's house; the infantry leading, the artillery following next, and the cavalry in rear.

"General Sedgwick's division will, for the present, act with the reserve, and he will receive orders from headquarters."

In giving these orders of march for the 4th and 5th, it was expected that there would be no serious opposition at Big Bethel, and that the advance of the 3d corps beyond that point would force the enemy to evacuate the works at Young's mills, while our possession of the latter would make it necessary for him to abandon those at Howard's bridge, and the advance thence on Yorktown would place Ship point in our possession, together with its garrison, unless they abandoned it promptly. The result answered the expectation.

During the afternoon of the 4th, General Keyes obtained infomation of the presence of some 5,000 to 8,000 of the enemy in a strong position at Lee's mills. The nature of that position in relation to the Warwick not being at that time understood, I instructed General Keyes to attack and carry this position upon coming in front of it.

Early in the afternoon of the 5th the advance of each column was brought to a halt, that of Heintzelman (Porter's division) in front of Yorktown, after overcoming some resistance at Big Bethel and Howard's bridge; that of Keyes (Smith's division) unexpectedly before the enemy's works at Lee's mills, where the road from Newport News to Williamsburg crosses Warwick river.

The progress of each column had been retarded by heavy rains on that day, which had made the roads almost impassable to the infantry of Keyes's column, and impassable to all but a small portion of the artillery, while the ammunition, provisions and forage could not be brought up at all.

When General Keyes approached Lee's mills his left flank was exposed to a sharp artillery fire from the further bank of the Warwick, and upon reaching the vicinity of the mill he found it altogether stronger than was expected, unapproachable by reason of the Warwick river, and incapable of being carried by assault.

The troops composing the advance of each column were, during the afternoon, under a warm artillery fire, the sharpshooters even of the right column being engaged when covering reconnoissances.

It was at this stage and moment of the campaign that the following telegram was sent to me:

"ADJUTANT GENERAL'S OFFICE,
"*April* 4, 1862.

"By direction of the President, General McDowell's army corps has been detached from the force under your immediate command, and the general is ordered to report to the Secretary of War. Letter by mail.

"L. THOMAS,
"*Adjutant General.*

"General MCCLELLAN."

The President having promised, in an interview following his order of March 31, withdrawing Blenker's division of 10,000 men from my command, that nothing of the sort should be repeated—that I might rest assured that the campaign should proceed, with no further deductions from the force upon which its operations had been planned—I may confess to having been shocked at this order, which, with that of the 31st ultimo and that of the 3d, removed nearly 60,000 men from my command, and reduced my force by more than one-third, after its task had been assigned; its operations planned; its fighting begun. To me the blow was most discouraging. It frustrated all my plans for impending operations. It fell when I was too deeply committed to withdraw. It left me incapable of continuing operations which had been begun. It compelled the adoption of another, a different and a less effective plan of campaign. It made rapid and brilliant operations impossible. It was a fatal error.

It was now, of course, out of my power to turn Yorktown by West Point. I had, therefore, no choice left but to attack it directly in front, as I best could with the force at my command.

Reconnoissances made under fire on that and the following day determined that the sources of the Warwick river were near Yorktown, commanded by its guns, while that stream, for some distance from its mouth on the James river, was controlled by the confederate gunboats; that the fords had been destroyed by dams, the approaches to which were generally through dense forests and deep swamps, and defended by extensive and formidable works; that timber felled for defensive purposes and the flooding of the roads, caused by the dams, had made these works apparently inaccessible and impossible to turn; that Yorktown was strongly fortified, armed and garrisoned, and connected with the defences of the Warwick by forts and intrenchments, the ground in front of which was swept by the guns of Yorktown. It was also ascertained that the garrisons had been, and were daily being re-enforced by troops from Norfolk and the army under General J. E. Johnston. Heavy rains made the roads to Fort Monroe impassable, and delayed the arrival of troops, ammunition and supplies, while storms prevented for several days the sailing of transports from Hampton roads, and the establishment of depots on the creeks of York river, near the army.

The ground bordering the Warwick river is covered by very dense and extensive forests, the clearings being small and few. This, with the comparative flatness of the country, and the alertness of the enemy, everywhere in force, rendered thorough reconnoissances slow, dangerous and difficult, yet it was impossible otherwise to determine whether an assault was anywhere practicable, or whether the more tedious but sure operations of a siege must be resorted to.

I made, on the 6th and 7th, close personal reconnoissances of the right and left of the enemy's positions, which, with information acquired already, convinced me that it was best to prepare for an assault by the preliminary employment of heavy guns, and some siege operations. Instant assault would have been simple folly. On the 7th I telegraphed to the President as follows:

"Headquarters Army of the Potomac,
"*April* 7, 1862.

"Your telegram of yesterday is received. In reply, I have the honor to state that my entire force for duty amounts to only about (85,000) eighty-five thousand men. General Wool's command, as you will observe from the accompanying order, has been taken out of my control, although he has most cheerfully co-operated with me. The only use that can be made of his command is to protect my communications in rear of this point. At this time only fifty-three thousand men have joined me, but they are coming up as rapidly as my means of transportation will permit.

"Please refer to my despatch to the Secretary of War to-night, for the details of our present situation.

"GEO. B. McCLELLAN,
"*Major General.*

"To the President, *Washington, D. C.*"

On the same day I sent the following:

"Headquarters Army of the Potomac,
"In front of Yorktown,
"*April* 7, 1862—7 *p. m.*

"Your telegram of yesterday arrived here while I was absent, examining the enemy's right, which I did pretty closely.

"The whole line of the Warwick, which really heads within a mile of Yorktown, is strongly defended by detached redoubts and other fortifications, armed with heavy and light guns. The approaches, except at Yorktown, are covered by the Warwick, over which there is but one, or, at most, two passages, both of which are covered by strong batteries. It will be necessary to resort to the use of heavy guns, and some siege operations, before we assault. All the prisoners state that General J. E. Johnston arrived at Yorktown yesterday with strong re-enforcements. It seems clear that I shall have the whole force of the enemy on my hands—probably not less than (100,000) one hundred thousand men, and probably more. In consequence of the loss of Blenker's division and the 1st corps, my force is possibly less than that of the enemy, while they have all the advantage of position.

"I am under great obligations to you for the offer that the whole force and material of the government will be as fully and as speedily under my command as heretofore, or as if the new departments had not been created.

"Since my arrangements were made for this campaign, at least (50,000) fifty thousand men have been taken from my command. Since my despatch of the 5th inst., five divisions have been in close observation of the enemy, and frequently exchanging shots. When my present command all joins, I shall have about (85,000) eighty-five thousand men for duty, from which a large force must be taken for guards, scouts, &c. With this army I could assault the enemy's works, and perhaps carry them; but were I in possession of their intrenchments, and assailed by double my numbers, I should have no fears as to the result.

"Under the circumstances that have been developed since we arrived here, I feel fully impressed with the conviction that here is to be fought the great battle that is to decide the existing contest. I shall, of course, commence the attack as soon as I can get up my siege train, and shall do all in my power to carry the enemy's works, but to do this with a reasonable degree of certainty requires, in my judgment, that I should, if possible, have at least the whole of the 1st corps to land upon the Severn river and attack Gloucester in the rear.

"My present strength will not admit of a detachment sufficient for this purpose, without materially impairing the efficiency of this column. Flag-Officer Goldsborough thinks the works too strong for his available vessels, unless I can turn Gloucester. I send, by mail, copies of his letter and one of the commander of the gunboats here.

"GEO. B. McCLELLAN,
"*Major General.*

"Hon. E. M. Stanton,
"*Secretary of War.*"

I had provided a small siege train and moderate supplies of intrenching tools for such a contingency as the present. Immediate steps were taken to secure the necessary additions. While the engineer officers were engaged in ascertaining the character and strength of all the defences, and the configuration of the ground in front of Yorktown, in order to determine the point of attack and to develop the approaches, the troops were occupied in opening roads to the depots established at the nearest available points, on branches of York river. Troops were brought to the front as rapidly as possible, and on the 10th of April the army was posted as follows:

Heintzelman's corps, composed of Porter's, Hooker's, and Hamilton's divisions, in front of Yorktown, extending in the order named, from the mouth of Wormley's creek to the Warwick road, opposite Winn's mills. Sumner's corps—Sedgwick's division only having arrived—on the left of Hamilton, extending down to Warwick and opposite to Winn's mills works. Keyes's corps (Smith's, Couch's, and Casey's divisions,) on the left of Sedgwick, facing the works at the one-gun battery, Lee's mills, &c., on the west bank of the Warwick. Sumner, after the 6th of April, commanded the left wing, composed of his own and Keyes's corps.

Throughout the preparations for, and during the siege of Yorktown, I kept the corps under General Keyes, and afterwards the left wing, under General Sumner, engaged in ascertaining the character of the obstacles presented by the Warwick, and the enemy intrenched upon the right bank, with the intention, if possible, of overcoming them and breaking that line of defence, so as to gain possession of the road to Williamsburg, and cut off Yorktown from its supports and supplies. The forces under General Heintzelman were engaged in similar efforts upon the works between Winn's mills and Yorktown. General Keyes's report of the 16th of April, enclosing reports of brigade commanders engaged in reconnoissances up to that day, said, "that no part of his (the enemy's line opposite his own) line, so far as discovered, can be taken by assault without an enormous waste of life."

Reconnoissances on the right flank demonstrated the fact that the Warwick was not passable in that direction, except over a narrow dam, the approaches to which were swept by several batteries, and intrenchments which could be filled quickly with supports sheltered by the timber immediately in rear.

General Barnard, chief engineer of the army of the Potomac, whose position entitled his opinions to the highest consideration, expressed the judgment that those formidable works could not, with any reasonable degree of certainty, be carried by assault. General Keyes, commanding 4th army corps, after the examination of the enemy's defences on the left, before alluded to, addressed the following letter to the Hon. Ira Harris, United States Senate, and gave me a copy. Although not strictly official, it describes the situation at that time in some respects so well, that I have taken the liberty of introducing it here:

"Headquarters 4th Corps,
"*Warwick Court-House, Va., April* 7, 1862.

"My Dear Senator: The plan of campaign on this line was made with the distinct understanding that *four* army corps should be employed, and that the navy should co-operate in the taking of Yorktown, and also (as I understood it) support us on our left by moving gunboats up James river.

"To-day I have learned that the 1st corps, which by the President's order was to embrace four divisions, and one division (Blenker's) of the 2d corps, have been withdrawn altogether from this line of operations, and from the army of the Potomac. At the same time, as I am informed, the navy has not the means to attack Yorktown, and is afraid to send gunboats up James river, for fear of the Merrimac.

"The above plan of campaign was adopted unanimously by Major General McDowell and Brigadier Generals Sumner, Heintzelman, and Keyes, and was concurred in by Major General McClellan, who first proposed Urbanna as our base.

"This army being reduced by forty-five thousand troops, some of them among the best in the service, and without the support of the navy, the plan to which we are reduced bears scarcely any resemblance to the one I voted for.

"I command the James river column, and I left my camp near Newport News the morning of the 4th instant. I only succeeded in getting my artillery ashore the afternoon of the day before, and one of my divisions had not all arrived in camp the day I left, and for the want of transportation has not yet joined me. So you will observe that not a day was lost in the advance, and in fact we marched so quickly, and so rapidly, that many of our animals were twenty-four and forty-eight hours without a ration of forage. But notwithstanding the rapidity of our advance, we were stopped by a line of defence nine or ten miles long, strongly fortified by breast-works, erected nearly the whole distance behind a stream, or succession of ponds, nowhere fordable, one terminus being Yorktown, and the other ending in the James river, which is commanded by the enemy's gunboats. Yorktown is fortified all around with bastioned works, and on the water side it and Gloucester are so strong that the navy are afraid to attack either.

"The approaches on one side are generally through low, swampy, or thickly wooded ground, over roads which we are obliged to repair or to make before we can get forward our carriages. The enemy is in great force, and is constantly receiving re-enforcements from the two rivers. The line in front of us is therefore one of the strongest ever opposed to an invading force in any country.

"You will, then, ask why I advocated such a line for our operations? My reasons are few, but I think good.

"With proper assistance from the navy we could take Yorktown, and then with gunboats on both rivers we could beat any force opposed to us on Warwick river, because the shot and shell from the gunboats would nearly overlap across the Peninsula; so that if the enemy should retreat—and retreat he must—he would have a long way to go without rail or steam transportation, and every soul of his army must fall into our hands or be destroyed.

"Another reason for my supporting the new base and plan was, that this line, it was expected, would furnish water transportation nearly to Richmond.

"Now, supposing we succeed in breaking through the line in front of us, what can we do next? The roads are very bad, and if the enemy retains command of James river, and we do not first reduce Yorktown, it would be impossible for us to subsist this army three marches beyond where it is now. As the roads are at present, it is with the utmost difficulty that we can subsist it in the position it now occupies.

"You will see, therefore, by what I have said, that the force originally intended for the capture of Richmond should be all sent forward. If I thought the four army corps necessary when I supposed the navy would co-operate, and when I judged of the obstacles to be encountered by what I learned from maps and the opinions of officers long stationed at Fort Monroe, and from all other sources, how much more should I think the full complement of troops requisite now that the navy cannot co-operate, and now that the strength of the enemy's lines and the number of his guns and men prove to be almost immeasurably greater than I had been led to expect. The line in front of us, in the opinion of all the military men here, who are at all competent to judge, is one of the strongest in the world, and the force of the enemy capable of being increased beyond the numbers we now have to oppose to him. Independently of the strength of the lines in front of us, and of the force of the enemy behind them, we cannot advance until we get command of either York river or James river. The efficient co-operation of the navy is, therefore, absolutely essential, and so I considered it when I voted to change our base from the Potomac to Fort Monroe.

"An iron-clad boat must attack Yorktown; and if several strong gunboats could be sent up James river also, our success will be certain and complete, and the rebellion will soon be put down.

"On the other hand, we must butt against the enemy's works with heavy artillery, and a great waste of time, life, and material.

"If we break through and advance, both our flanks will be assailed from two great water-courses in the hands of the enemy; our supplies would give out, and the enemy, equal if not superior in numbers, would, with the other advantages, beat and destroy this army.

"The greatest master of the art of war has said, 'that if you would invade a country successfully you must have *one* line of operations, and *one* army, under *one* general.' But what is our condition? The State of Virginia is made to constitute the command, in part or wholly, of some six generals, viz: Frémont, Banks, McDowell, Wool, Burnside, and McClellan, besides the scrap over the Chesapeake, in the care of Dix.

"The great battle of the war is to come off here. If we win it, the rebellion will be crushed—if we lose it, the consequences will be more horrible than I care to tell. The plan of campaign I voted for, if carried out with the means proposed, will certainly succeed. If any part of the means proposed are withheld or diverted, I deem it due to myself to say that our success will be uncertain.

"It is no doubt agreeable to the commander of the 1st corps to have a separate department, and as this letter advocates his return to General McClellan's command, it is proper to state that I am not at all influenced by personal regard or dislike to any of my seniors in rank. If I were to credit all the opinions which have been poured into my ears, I must believe that, in regard to my present fine command, I owe much to General McDowell and nothing to General McClellan. But I have disregarded all such officiousness, and I have from last July to the present day supported General McClellan, and obeyed all his orders with as hearty a good will as though he had been my brother or the friend to whom I owed most. I shall continue to do so to the last, and so long as he is my commander. And I am not desirous to displace him, and would not if I could He left Washington with the understanding that he was to execute a definite plan of campaign with certain prescribed means. The plan was good and the means sufficient, and without modification the enterprise was certain of success. But with the reduction of force and means, the plan is entirely changed, and is now a bad plan, with means insufficient for certain success.

"Do not look upon this communication as the offspring of despondency. I never despond; and when you see me working the hardest, you may be sure that fortune is frowning upon me. I am working now to my utmost.

"Please show this letter to the President, and I should like also that Mr. Stanton should know its contents. Do me the honor to write to me as soon as you can, and believe me, with perfect respect,

"Your most obedient servant,

"E. D. KEYES,

"*Brigadier General, Commanding 4th Army Corps.*

"Hon. IRA HARRIS, *U. S. Senate.*"

On the 7th of April, and before the arrival of the divisions of Generals Hooker, Richardson and Casey, I received the following despatches from the President and Secretary of War:

"WASHINGTON, *April* 6, 1862—8 *p. m.*

"Yours of 11 a. m. to-day received. Secretary of War informs me that the forwarding of transportation, ammunition, and Woodbury's brigade, under your orders, is not, and will not be, interfered with. You now have over one hundred thousand troops with you, independent of General Wool's command. I think you better break the enemy's line from Yorktown to Warwick river at once. This will probably use time as advantageously as you can.

"A. LINCOLN, *President.*

"General G. B. McCLELLAN."

"WASHINGTON, *April* 6, 1862—2 *p. m.*

"The President directs me to say that your despatch to him has been received. General Sumner's corps is on the road to join you, and will go forward as fast as possible. Franklin's division is now on the advance towards Manassas. There is no means of transportation here to send it forward in time to be of service in your present operations. Telegraph frequently, and all in the power of the government shall be done to sustain you as occasion may require.

"E. M. STANTON,
"*Secretary of War.*

"General G. B. McCLELLAN."

By the 9th of April I had acquired a pretty good knowledge of the position and strength of the enemy's works, and the obstacles to be overcome. On that day I received the following letter from the President:

"WASHINGTON, *April* 9, 1862.

"MY DEAR SIR: Your despatches complaining that you are not properly sustained, while they do not offend me, do pain me very much.

"Blenker's division was withdrawn from you before you left here, and you know the pressure under which I did it, and, as I thought, acquiesced in it—certainly not without reluctance.

"After you left I ascertained that less than 20,000 unorganized men, without a single field battery, were all you designed to be left for the defence of Washington and Manassas Junction, and part of this even was to go to General Hooker's old position. General Banks's corps, once designed for Manassas Junction, was diverted and tied up on the line of Winchester and Strasburg, and could not leave it without again exposing the upper Potomac and the Baltimore and Ohio railroad. This presented, or would present, when McDowell and Sumner should be gone, a great temptation to the enemy to turn back from the Rappahannock and sack Washington. My implicit order that Washington should, by the judgment of all the commanders of army corps, be left entirely secure, had been neglected. It was precisely this that drove me to detain McDowell.

"I do not forget that I was satisfied with your arrangement to leave Banks at Manassas Junction; but when that arrangement was broken up, and nothing was substituted for it, of course I was constrained to substitute something for it myself. And allow me to ask, do you really think I should permit the line from Richmond, via Manassas Junction, to this city, to be entirely open, except what resistance could be presented by less than 20,000 unorganized troops? This is a question which the country will not allow me to evade.

"There is a curious mystery about the number of troops now with you. When I telegraphed you on the 6th, saying you had over a hundred thousand with you, I had just obtained from the Secretary of War a statement taken, as he said, from your own returns, making 108,000 then with you and *en route* to you. You now say you will have but 85,000 when all *en route* to you shall have reached you. How can the discrepancy of 23,000 be accounted for?

"As to General Wool's command, I understand it is doing for you precisely what a like number of your own would have to do if that command was away.

"I suppose the whole force which has gone forward for you is with you by this time. And if so, I think it is the precise time for you to strike a blow. By delay the enemy will relatively gain upon you—that is, he will gain faster by fortifications and re-enforcements than you can by re-enforcements alone. And once more let me tell you, it is indispensable to you that you strike a blow. I am powerless to help this. You will do me the justice to remember I always insisted that going down the bay in search of a field, instead of fighting at or near Manassas, was only shifting, and not surmounting, a difficulty; that we would find the same enemy, and the same or equal intrenchments, at either place. The country will not fail to note, is now noting, that the present hesitation to move upon an intrenched enemy is but the story of Manassas repeated.

"I beg to assure you that I have never written you or spoken to you in greater kindness of feeling than now, nor with a fuller purpose to sustain you, so far as, in my most anxious judgment, I consistently can. But you must act.

"Yours, very truly,

"A. LINCOLN.

"Major General McClellan."

With great deference to the opinions and wishes of his excellency the President, I most respectfully beg leave to refer to the facts which I have presented and those contained in the accompanying letter of General Keyes, with the reports of General Barnard and other officers, as furnishing a reply to the above letter. His excellency could not judge of the formidable character of the works before us as well as if he had been on the ground; and whatever might have been his desire for prompt action, (certainly no greater than mine,) I feel confident if he could have made a personal inspection of the enemy's defences, he would have forbidden me risking the safety of the army and the possible successes of the campaign on a sanguinary assault of an advantageous and formidable position, which, even if successful, could not have been followed up to any other or better result than would have been reached by the regular operations of a siege. Still less could I forego the conclusions of my most instructed judgment for the mere sake of avoiding the personal consequences intimated in the President's despatch.

The following extracts from the report of the chief engineer (Brigadier General J. G. Barnard) embody the result of our reconnoissances, and give, with some degree of detail, the character and strength of the defences of Yorktown and the Warwick, and some of the obstacles which the army contended against and overcame.

Extracts from General Barnard's report.

"The accompanying drawing (map No. 2) gives with accuracy the outline and armament of the fortifications of Yorktown proper, with the detached works immediately connected with it.

"The three bastioned fronts, looking towards our approaches, appear to have been earliest built, and have about fifteen feet thickness of parapet and eight feet to ten feet depth of ditch, the width varying much, but never being less at top of scarp than fifteen feet—I think generally much more.

"The works extending around the town, from the western salient of fronts just mentioned, appear to have been finished during the past winter and spring. They have formidable profiles, eighteen feet thickness of parapet, and generally ten feet depth of ditch.

"The water batteries had generally eighteen feet parapet, the guns in barbette.

"They were (as well as all the works mentioned) carefully constructed with well-made sod revetments.

"There were numerous traverses between the guns, and ample magazines; how sufficient in bomb-proof qualities I am unable to say.

"The two first guns of the work on the heights bear upon the water as well as the land, and were of heavy calibre.

"The list herewith gives all the guns in position, or for which there were emplacements. The vacant emplacements were all occupied before the evacuation by siege guns, rifled 4½-inch 24-pounders, and 18-pounders.

"In Fort Magruder (the first exterior work) there were found one 8-inch columbiad, one 42-pounder, and one 8-inch siege howitzer; the two former in barbette. The sketch will show the emplacements for guns on field and siege carriages; making, I think, with the foregoing, twenty-two. Two of these were placed behind traverses, with embrasures covered by blindages.

"The two external redoubts, with the connecting parapets, formed a re-entrant with the fronts of attack, and all the guns bore on our approaches.

"It will be seen, therefore, that our approaches were swept by the fire of at least forty-nine guns, nearly all of which were heavy, and many of them the most formidable guns known. Besides that, two-thirds of the guns of the water batteries and all the guns of Gloucester bore on our right batteries, though under disadvantageous circumstances.

"The ravine behind which the left of the Yorktown fronts of attack was placed was not very difficult, as the heads formed depressions in front of their left, imperfectly seen by their fire, and from which access could be had to the ditches; but we could not be sure of the fact before the evacuation. The enemy held, by means of a slight breastwork and rifle trenches, a position in advance of the heads of these ravines as far forward as the burnt house.

"The ravines which head between the Yorktown fortifications and the exterior works are deep and intricate. They were tolerably well seen, however, by the works which run westwardly from the Yorktown works, and which were too numerous and complicated to be traced on paper.

"Fort Magruder, the first lunette on our left, appears to have been built at an early period.

"The external connexion between this work was first a rifle trench, probably afterwards enlarged into a parapet, with external ditch and an emplacement for four guns in or near the small redan in the centre.

"Behind this they had constructed numerous epaulments, with connecting boyaus not fully arranged for infantry fires, and mainly intended probably to protect their camps and reserves against the destructive effects of our artillery.

"From the 'red redoubt' these trenches and epaulments ran to the woods and rivulet which forms one head of the Warwick, and continue almost without break to connect with the works at Wynn's mill. This stream, just mentioned, whatever be its name, (the term 'Warwick,' according to some, applying only to the tidal channel from the James river up as high as Lee's mill,) was inundated by a number of dams from near where its head is crossed by the epaulments mentioned down to Lee's mill.

"Below Lee's mill the Warwick follows a tortuous course through salt marshes of two hundred yards or three hundred yards in width, from which the land rises up boldly to a height of thirty or forty feet.

"The first group of works is at Wynn's mill, where there is a dam and bridge. The next is to guard another dam between Wynn's and Lee's mills; (this is the point attacked by General Smith on the 16th ultimo, and where Lieutenant Merrill was wounded; the object of the attack was merely to prevent the further construction of works and feel the strength of the position.) A work, of what strength is not known, was at the sharp angle of the stream just above Lee's mill, and a formidable group of works was at Lee's mill, where there was also a dam and bridge.

"From Lee's mill a line of works extends across Mulberry island, or is supposed to do so.

"At Southal's landing is another formidable group of works, and from here, too, they extend apparently across to the James river.

"These groups of field-works were connected by rifle trenches or parapets for nearly the whole distance.

"They are far more extensive than may be supposed from the mention of of them I make, and every kind of obstruction which the country affords, such as abattis, marsh, inundation, &c., was skilfully used. The line is certainly one of the most extensive known to modern times.

"The country on both sides of the Warwick, from near Yorktown down, is a dense forest with few clearings. It was swampy, and the roads impassable during the heavy rains we have constantly had, except where our own labors had corduroyed them.

"If we could have broken the enemy's line across the isthmus we could have invested Yorktown, and it must, with its garrison, have soon fallen into our hands. It was not deemed practicable, considering the strength of that line and the difficulty of handling our forces, (owing to the impracticable character of the country,) to do so.

"If we could take Yorktown, or drive the enemy out of that place, the enemy's line was no longer tenable. This we could do by siege operations. It was deemed too hazardous to attempt the reduction of the place by assault."

The plan of the approaches and their defences as determined upon and finally executed is exhibited on the accompanying map, (No. —.) It was, in words, to open the first parallel as near as possible to the works of the enemy, and under its protection to establish almost simultaneously batteries along the whole front, extending from York river on the right to the Warwick on the left, a cord of about one mile in length. The principal approaches were directed against the east end of the main work, which was most heavily armed and bore both on the water and land, and lay between Wormley's creek and York river. There also were placed the most of the batteries designed to act against the land front to enfilade the water batteries, and to act upon Gloucester.

I designed at the earliest moment to open simultaneously with several batteries, and as soon as the enemy's guns, which swept the neck of land between Wormley's creek and the Warwick, were crippled and their fire kept down, to push the trenches as far forward as necessary and to assault Yorktown and the adjacent works.

The approaches to the batteries, the necessary bridges, and the roads to the depots, had been vigorously pushed to completion by the troops under Generals Heintzelman and Sumner, and were available for infantry, and in some instances for artillery, on the 17th of April, when the batteries and their connexions were commenced, and labor upon them kept up night and day until finished. Some of the batteries on easy ground and concealed from the view of the enemy were early completed and armed, and held ready for any emergency, but not permitted to open, as the return fire of the enemy would interfere too much with the labor on other and more important works. The completion of the more exposed and heaviest batteries was delayed by storms, preventing the landing of guns and ammunition.

It having been discovered that the enemy were receiving artillery stores at the wharf in Yorktown, on May 1 battery No. 1 was opened with effect upon the wharf and town.

On the 22d of April General Franklin, with his division from General

McDowell's corps, had arrived and reported to me. The garrison of Gloucester point had been re-enforced and the works strengthened; but as this division was too small to detach to the Severn, and no more troops could be spared, I determined to act on Gloucester by disembarking it on the north bank of the York river, under the protection of the gunboats. The troops were mainly kept on board ship while the necessary preparations were made for landing them, and supporting them in case of necessity. For a full account of this labor I refer to the report of Lieutenant Colonel B. S. Alexander, of the engineer corps, detailed for this expedition.

While the siege works were being rapidly completed, the roads on the left wing necessary for communication and advance were opened and corduroyed over the marshes, batteries were erected to silence the enemy's guns, and drive him from his works at Wynn's and Lee's mills, preparatory to the general attack. Active reconnoissances were continually going on, and attempts in force made to drive the enemy from the banks.

The result of various reconnoissances made under the immediate direction of General W. F. Smith, commanding second division fourth corps, led to the belief that the weakest point of that part of the enemy's lines was opposite a field where it was ascertained that there was a dam covered by a battery known to contain at least one gun.

It was determined to push a strong reconnoissance on this point to silence the enemy's fire, and ascertain the actual strength of the position. Being prepared to sustain the reconnoitring party by a real attack, if found expedient, General W. F. Smith was directed to undertake the operation on the 16th of April. He silenced the fire of the enemy's guns, discovered the existence of other works previously concealed and unknown, and sent a strong party across the stream, which was finally forced to retire with some loss. Smith intrenched himself in a position immediately overlooking the dam and the enemy's works, so as to keep them under control, and prevent the enemy from using the dam as a means of crossing the Warwick to annoy us.

Many times towards the end of the month the enemy attempted to drive in our pickets, and take our rifle-pits near Yorktown, but always without success.

As the siege progressed, it was with great difficulty that the rifle-pits on the right could be excavated and held, so little covering could be made against the hot fire of the enemy's artillery and infantry. Their guns continued firing up to a late hour of the night of the 3d of May.

Our batteries would have been ready to open on the morning of the 6th May at latest; but on the morning of the 4th it was discovered that the enemy had already been compelled to evacuate his position during the night, leaving behind him all his heavy guns, uninjured, and a large amount of ammunition and supplies. For the details of the labor of the siege I refer to the accompanying reports and journals of Brigadier General J. G. Barnard, chief engineer, charged with the selections, laying out, and completion of the approaches and batteries; of Brigadier General Wm. F. Barry, chief of artillery, charged with arming and supplying with ammunition all the siege and field batteries; and of Brigadier General Fitz-John Porter, director of the siege, to whom were assigned the guarding of the trenches, the assembling and distribution of the working parties, &c., &c.

Early in the morning of the 4th, on the enemy's abandoning his lines at Yorktown, I ordered all the available cavalry force, with four batteries of horse artillery, under Brigadier General Stoneman, chief of cavalry, in immediate pursuit by the Yorktown and Williamsburg road, with orders to harass the enemy's rear, and try to cut off such of his forces as had taken the Lee's mill and Williamsburg road.

General Heintzelman was directed to send Hooker's division forward on the Yorktown and Williamsburg road to support General Stoneman; and Smith was ordered to proceed with his division upon the Lee's mill and Williamsburg road for the same purpose. Afterwards, the divisions of Generals Kearney, Couch, and Casey, were put en route—the first on the Yorktown road, and the others on the Lee's mill road. These roads unite about a quarter of a mile south of Fort Magruder, and are connected by cross-roads at several points between Yorktown and Williamsburg. After these directions had been given, General Sumner (the officer second in rank in the army of the Potomac) was ordered to proceed to the front and take immediate charge of operations until my arrival.

General Stoneman moved forward promptly with his command, consisting of four batteries of horse artillery under Lieutenant Colonel Hays, the 1st and 6th United States cavalry, the 3d Pennsylvania and 8th Illinois, and Barker's squadron, meeting with but little opposition until he arrived in front of the enemy's works about two miles east of Williamsburg.

At a point about eight miles from Yorktown, in accordance with my instructions, he detached General Emory with Benson's battery, the 3d Pennsylvania cavalry, (Colonel Averill,) and Barker's squadron, to gain the Lee's mill road, and endeavor, with the assistance of General Smith, to cut off the portion of the enemy's rear guard which had taken that route. General Emory had some sharp skirmishes with a regiment of cavalry and a battery under General Stuart, and drove them in the direction of Lee's mill.

General Smith having met with obstructions in his front, had transferred his column, by a cross-road, to the Yorktown and Williamsburg road, so that General Emory, finding no force to co-operate with him, was unable to cut off the rear guard, and they succeeded in escaping by a circuitous route along the bank of the James river.

The position in which General Stoneman encountered the enemy is about four miles in extent, the right resting on College creek, and the left on Queen's creek; nearly three-fourths of its front being covered by tributaries of these two creeks, upon which there are ponds.

The ground between the heads of the boundary streams is a cultivated plain, across which a line of detached works had been constructed, consisting of Fort Magruder, a large work in the centre with a bastion front, and twelve other redoubts and epaulments for field guns.

The parapet of Fort Magruder is about six feet high and nine feet thick; the ditch nine feet wide and nine feet deep, filled with water. The length of the interior crest is about 600 yards. The redoubts have strong profiles, but are of small dimensions, having faces of about forty yards. The woods is front of the position were felled, and the open ground in front of the works was dotted with numerous rifle-pits.

The roads leading from the lower part of the Peninsula to Williamsburg, one along the York river, (the Yorktown road,) and the other along the James, (the Lee's mill road,) unite between the heads of the tributary streams a short distance in front of Fort Magruder, by which they are commanded, and debouch from the woods just before uniting. A branch from the James river road leaves it about one and three-fourths of a mile below Fort Magruder and unites with the road from Allen's landing to Williamsburg, which crosses the tributary of College creek over a dam at the outlet of the pond, and passes just in rear of the line of works, being commanded by the three redoubts on the right of the line, at about the same distance from Fort Magruder. A branch leaves the York river road and crosses the tributary of Queen's creek on a dam, and passing over the position and through the works in its rear, finally enters Williamsburg; this road is commanded by redoubts on the left of the line of the works.

General Stoneman debouched from the woods with his advance guard, (consisting of a part of the 1st United States cavalry, and one section of Gibson's battery, under the command of General Cooke,) and the enemy immediately opened on him with several field-pieces from Fort Magruder, having the correct range, and doing some execution. Gibson's battery was brought into position as rapidly as the deep mud would permit, and returned the fire; while the 6th United States cavalry was sent to feel the enemy's left. This regiment passed one redoubt, which it found unoccupied, and appeared in the rear of a second, when a strong cavalry force, with infantry and artillery, came down upon it, whereupon the regiment was withdrawn. The rear squadron, under command of Captain Saunders, repelled a charge of the enemy's cavalry in the most gallant manner. In the mean time the enemy was being re-enforced by infantry, and the artillery fire becoming very hot. General Stoneman, having no infantry to carry the works, ordered the withdrawal of the battery. This was accomplished, with the exception of one piece, which could not be extricated from the mud. The enemy attempted to prevent the movement, but their charges were met by the 1st United States cavalry, under command of Lieutenant Colonel Grier, and they were driven back, losing several officers and one stand of colors. General Stoneman then took a defensive position a short distance in the rear of the first, to await the arrival of the infantry.

The advance of General Smith's column reached Skiff's creek about 11½ o'clock, and found the bridge over that stream in flames, and the road impassable. A practicable route to the Yorktown road having been discovered, the division, by order of General Sumner, moved on by that road, and reached General Stoneman's position about 5½ o'clock. General Sumner, arriving with it, assumed command.

Generals Heintzelman and Keyes also arrived. During the afternoon of the 4th, near the Halfway House, the head of General Hooker's column encountered Smith's division filing into the road, and was obliged to halt between three and four hours until it had passed. General Hooker then followed on, and at Cheesecake church turned off, by General Heintzelman's direction, taking a cross-road, and moved out on the Lee's mill road, thus changing places with General Smith. Marching part of the night, he came in sight of Fort Magruder early in the morning of the 5th.

General Smith's division having been deployed, General Sumner ordered an attack on the works in his front; but the lines having been thrown into confusion while moving through the dense forest, and darkness coming on, the attempt for that night was abandoned. The troops bivouacked in the woods, and a heavy rain began, which continued until the morning of the 6th, making the roads, already in very bad condition, almost impassable.

During the morning of the 5th General Sumner reconnoitred the position in his front, and at 11 o'clock ordered Hancock's brigade, of Smith's division, to take possession of a work on the enemy's left, which had been found to be unoccupied. The remainder of Smith's division occupied the woods in front without being actually engaged.

The divisions of Couch and Casey had received orders during the night to march at daylight; but on account of the terrible condition of the roads, and other impediments, were not able to reach the field until after 1 o'clock p. m., at which time the first brigade of Couch's division arrived, and was posted in the centre, on Hooker's right. The other two brigades came up during the afternoon, followed by Casey's division.

In the mean time General Hooker, having reconnoitred the enemy's position, began the attack at 7½ a. m., and for a while silenced the guns of

Fort Magruder, and cleared the ground in his front; but the enemy being continually re-enforced, until their strength greatly exceeded his, made attack after attack, endeavoring to turn his left.

For several hours his division struggled gallantly against the superior numbers of the enemy. Five guns of Webber's battery were lost, and between three and four o'clock his ammunition began to give out. The loss had been heavy, and the exhaustion of the troops was very great. At this time the division of General Kearney came up, who, at 9 a. m., had received orders to re-enforce Hooker, and who had succeeded, by the greatest exertions, in passing Casey's troops, and pushing on to the front through the deep mud. General Kearney at once gallantly attacked, and thereby prevented the loss of another battery, and drove the enemy back at every point, enabling General Hooker to extricate himself from his position, and withdraw his wearied troops. Peck's brigade, of Couch's division, as has been mentioned before, was, immediately on its arrival, ordered by General Sumner to deploy on Hooker's right. This was promptly done, and the attacks of the enemy at that point were repulsed. General Peck held his position until late in the afternoon, when he was relieved by the other two brigades of Couch's division, and they were in quiet possession of the ground when night closed the contest. The vigorous action of these troops relieved General Hooker considerably. General Emory had been left with his command, on the night of the 4th, to guard the branch of the Lee's mill road which leads to Allen's farm; and on the morning of the 5th it was ascertained that by this route the enemy's right could be turned. A request for infantry for this purpose was made to General Heintzelman, who, late in the afternoon, sent four regiments and two batteries of Kearney's division—the first disposable troops he had—and directed General Emory to make the attack. With these re-enforcements his force amounted to about 3,000 men and three batteries. General Emory, on account of want of knowledge of the ground, and the lateness of the hour, did not succeed in this movement. It involved some risks, but, if successful, might have produced important results.

At 11 a. m., as before mentioned, General Smith received orders from General Sumner to send one brigade across a dam on our right, to occupy a redoubt on the left of the enemy's line. Hancock's brigade was selected for this purpose. He crossed the dam, took possession of the first redoubt, and afterwards, finding the second one vacated, he occupied that also, and sent for re-enforcements to enable him to advance further and take the next redoubt, which commanded the plain between his position and Fort Magruder, and would have enabled him to take in reverse and cut the communication of the troops engaged with Generals Hooker and Kearney.

The enemy soon began to show himself in strength before him, and as his rear and right flank were somewhat exposed, he repeated his request for re-enforcements General Smith was twice ordered to join him, with the rest of his division, but each time the order was countermanded at the moment of execution, General Sumner not being willing to weaken the centre. At length, in reply to General Hancock's repeated messages for more troops, General Sumner sent him an order to fall back to his first position, the execution of which General Hancock deferred as long as possible, being unwilling to give up the advantage already gained, and fearing to expose his command by such a movement.

During the progress of these events, I had remained at Yorktown to complete the preparations for the departure of General Franklin's and other troops to West Point by water, and to make the necessary arrangements with the naval commander for his co-operation.

By pushing General Franklin, well supported by water, to the right bank of the Pamunkey, opposite West Point, it was hoped to force the enemy to abandon whatever works he might have on the Peninsula below that point, or be cut off. It was of paramount importance that the arrangements to this end should be promptly made at an early hour of the morning. I had sent two of my aids (Lieutenant Colonel Sweitzer and Major Hammerstein) to observe the operations in front, with instructions to report to me everything of importance that might occur. I received no information from them leading me to suppose that there was anything occurring of more importance than a simple affair of a rear-guard, until about one o'clock p. m., when a despatch arrived from one of them that everything was not progressing favorably. This was confirmed a few minutes later by the reports of Governor Sprague and Major Hammerstein, who came directly from the scene of action.

Completing the necessary arrangements, I returned to my camp without delay, rode rapidly to the front, a distance of some fourteen miles, through roads much obstructed by troops and wagons, and reached the field between four and five p. m., in time to take a rapid survey of the ground. I soon learned that there was no direct communication between our centre and the left under General Heintzelman; the centre was chiefly in the nearer edge of the woods, situated between us and the enemy. As heavy firing was heard in the direction of General Hancock's command, I immediately ordered General Smith to proceed with his two remaining brigades to support that part of the line. General Naglee, with his brigade, received similar orders. I then directed our centre to advance to the further edge of the woods mentioned above, which was done, and I attempted to open direct communication with General Heintzelman, but was prevented by the marshy state of the ground in the direction in which the attempt was made.

Before Generals Smith and Naglee could reach the field of General Hancock's operations, although they moved with great rapidity, he had been confronted by a superior force. Feigning to retreat slowly, he awaited their onset, and then turned upon them, and after some terrific volleys of musketry, he charged them with the bayonet, routing and dispersing their whole force, killing, wounding, and capturing from 500 to 600 men, he himself losing only 31 men.

This was one of the most brilliant engagements of the war, and General Hancock merits the highest praise for the soldierly qualities displayed, and his perfect appreciation of the vital importance of his position.

Night put an end to the operations here, and all the troops who had been engaged in this contest slept on the muddy field, without shelter, and many without food.

Notwithstanding the report I received from General Heintzelman, during the night, that General Hooker's division had suffered so much that it could not be relied on next day, and that Kearney's could not do more than hold its own without re-enforcements—being satisfied that the result of Hancock's engagement was to give us possession of the decisive point of the battle-field during the night, I countermanded the order for the advance of the divisions of Sedgwick and Richardson, and directed them to return to Yorktown, to proceed to West Point by water.

Our loss during the day, the greater part of which was sustained by Hooker's division, was as follows:

Killed, 456; wounded, 1,400; missing, 372; total, 2,228.

On the next morning we found the enemy's position abandoned, and occupied Fort Magruder and the town of Williamsburg, which was filled with the enemy's wounded, to whose assistance eighteen of their surgeons were sent by General J. E. Johnston, the officer in command. Several guns and caissons, which the enemy could not carry off on account of the mud, were secured. Colonel Averill was sent forward at once with a strong cavalry force to endeavor to overtake the enemy's rear-guard. He found several guns abandoned, and picked up a large number of stragglers, but the condition of the roads and the state of the supplies forced him to return, after advancing a few miles.

It is my opinion that the enemy opposed us here with only a portion of his army. When our cavalry first appeared there was nothing but the enemy's rear-guard in Williamsburg. Other troops were brought back during the night and the next day to hold the works as long as possible, in order to gain time for the trains, &c., already well on the way to Richmond, to make their escape. Our troops were greatly exhausted by the laborious march through the mud from their positions in front of Yorktown, and by the protracted battle through which they had just passed. Many of them were out of rations and ammunition, and one division, in its anxiety to make a prompt movement, had marched with empty haversacks. The supply trains had been forced out of the roads on the fourth and fifth to allow the troops and artillery to pass to the front, and the roads were now in such a state, after thirty-six hours' continuous rain, that it was almost impossible to pass even empty wagons over them. General Hooker's division had suffered so severely that it was in no condition to follow the enemy, even if the roads had been good. Under these circumstances, an immediate pursuit was impossible.

Steps were at once taken to care for and remove the wounded, and to bring up provisions, ammunition, and forage.

The condition of the roads, as has been said, rendered it next to impossible to accomplish this by land from Yorktown. A temporary depot was therefore promptly established on Queen's creek, and supplies drawn, and the wounded shipped from that place.

The divisions of Franklin, Sedgwick, Porter, and Richardson were sent from Yorktown by water to the right bank of the Pamunkey, in the vicinity of West Point. The remaining divisions, the trains, and the reserve artillery moved subsequently by land.

Early on the morning of the 7th General Franklin had completed the disembarcation of his division, and had placed it in a good position to cover the landing place, both his flanks and a large portion of his front being protected by water.

Dana's brigade of Sedgwick's division arrived during the morning.

At about 9 a. m. a large force of the enemy appeared, consisting of Whiting's division and other troops, and between 10 and 11 they attacked the part of the line held by Newton's brigade.

The action continued until 3 p. m., when the enemy retired, all his attacks having been repulsed. This affair, the most important in which the division had yet been engaged, was highly creditable to General Franklin and his command. For the details I refer to his report, which is herewith submitted. Our loss was 49 killed, 104 wounded, and 41 missing. Total, 194, which includes a large proportion of officers.

Cavalry reconnoissances were sent out from Williamsburg on the 6th and 7th, and on the 8th General Stoneman moved with an advance guard of cavalry, artillery, and infantry to open communication with General Franklin.

As soon as our supplies had been received and the condition of the roads had become a little better, though still very bad, the advance of the remaining troops was begun, Smith's division moving on the 8th. On the 10th headquarters were at Roper's church, 19 miles from Williamsburg, all the divisions which had moved by land, except Hooker's, being in the vicinity of that place.

We were now in direct communication with the portion of the army which had gone by water, and we began to draw supplies from them.

On account of the small number and narrowness of the roads in this neighborhood, movements were difficult and slow.

On the 15th, headquarters and the divisions of Franklin, Porter, Sykes, and Smith reached Cumberland, which was made a temporary depot. Couch and Casey were then near New Kent Court House, Hooker and Kearney near Roper's church and Richardson and Sedgwick near Eltham.

On the 14th and 15th much rain fell.

On the 15th and 16th the divisions of Franklin, Smith, and Porter were with great difficulty moved to White House, five miles in advance. So bad was the road that the train of one of these divisions required thirty-six hours to pass over this short distance. General Stoneman had occupied this place some days before, after several successful skirmishes, in which our cavalry proved superior to that of the enemy. The reports of these affairs are appended.

About this time, with the consent of the President, two additional corps were organized, viz: the 5th provisional corps, consisting of the divisions of Porter and Sykes, and the reserve artillery, under the command of General F. J. Porter, and the 6th provisional corps, consisting of the divisions of Franklin and Smith, under the command of General W. B Franklin.

Headquarters reached White House on the 16th, and a permanent depot was at once organized there.

On the 19th, headquarters and the corps of Porter and Franklin moved to Tunstall's station, five miles from White House.

On the 20th more rain fell.

On the 21st the position of the troops was as follows: Stoneman's advance guard, one mile from New bridge; Franklin's corps three miles from New bridge, with Porter's corps at supporting distance in its rear; Sumner's corps, on the railroad about three miles from the Chickahominy, connecting the right with the left; Keyes's corps, on New Kent road near Bottom's bridge, with Heintzelman's corps at supporting distance in the rear.

The ford at Bottom's bridge was in our possession, and the rebuilding of the bridge, which had been destroyed by the enemy, was commenced.

On the 22d, headquarters moved to Coal Harbor.

On the 26th the railroad was in operation as far as the Chickahominy, and the railroad bridge across that stream nearly completed.

CHAPTER II.

When, on the 20th of May, our advanced light troops reached the banks of the Chickahominy river, at Bottom's bridge, they found that this as well as the railroad bridge, about a mile above, had been destroyed by the enemy.

The Chickahominy in this vicinity is about forty feet wide, fringed with a dense growth of heavy forest trees, and bordered by low marshy bottom lands, varying from half a mile to a mile in width.

Our operations embraced that part of the river between Bottom's and Meadow bridges, which covered the principal approaches to Richmond from the east.

Within these limits the firm ground lying above high-water mark seldom approaches near the river on either bank, and no locality was found within this section where the high ground came near the stream on both sides. It was subject to frequent, sudden, and great variations in the volume of water, and a rise of a few feet overflowed the bottom lands on both sides.

At low water it could be forded at almost any point; but during high water it was above a fording stage, and could then be crossed only at the few points where bridges had been constructed. These bridges had all been destroyed by the enemy on our approach, and it was necessary not only to reconstruct these, but to build several others.

The west bank of the river opposite the New and Mechanicsville bridges was bordered by elevated bluffs, which afforded the enemy commanding positions to fortify, establish his batteries, enfilading the approaches upon the two principal roads to Richmond on our right, and resist the reconstruction of the important bridges. This obliged us to select other less exposed points for our crossings.

As the enemy was not in great force opposite Bottom's bridge on the arrival of our left at that point, and as it was important to secure a lodgment upon the right bank before he should have time to concentrate his forces and contest the passage, I forthwith ordered Casey's division to ford the river and occupy the opposite heights. This was promptly done on the 20th, and reconnoissances were at once pushed out in advance.

These troops were directed to throw up defences in an advantageous position to secure our left flank. General Heintzelman's corps was thrown forward in support, and Bottom's bridge immediately rebuilt.

In the mean time our centre and right were advanced to the river above, and on the 24th we carried the village of Mechanicsville, driving the enemy out with our artillery, and forcing them across the bridge, which they destroyed. General Naglee on the same day dislodged a force of the enemy from the vicinity of the "Seven Pines," on the Bottom's bridge road, and our advance on the left secured a strong position near that place.

All the information obtained from deserters, negroes, and spies, indicated that the enemy occupied in force all the approaches to Richmond from the east, and that he intended to dispute every step of our advance beyond the Chickahominy, and the passage of the stream opposite our right. That their army was superior to ours in numbers, did not admit of a doubt. Strong defences had been constructed around Richmond.

Impressed by these facts with the necessity of strengthening the army for the struggle, I did not fail to urge repeatedly upon my superiors the importance of re-enforcing the army of the Potomac with every disposable man, in order to insure the success of our attack upon the rebel capital.

On the 10th of May I telegraphed as follows:

"CAMP AT EWELL'S FARM, THREE MILES BEYOND WILLIAMSBURG,
"*May* 10, 1862—5 *a. m.*

"From the information reaching me from every source, I regard it as certain that the enemy will meet us with all his force on or near the Chickahominy. They can concentrate many more men than I have, and are collecting troops from all quarters, especially well disciplined troops from the south. Casualties, sickness, garrisons, and guards have much reduced our numbers, and will continue to do so. I shall fight the rebel army with whatever force I may have, but duty requires me to urge that every effort be made to re-enforce me without delay with all the disposable troops in Eastern Virginia, and that we concentrate all our forces, as far as possible, to fight the great battle now impending, and to make it decisive.

"It is possible that the enemy may abandon Richmond without a serious struggle; but I do not believe he will, and it would be unwise to count upon anything but a stubborn and desperate defence—a life and death contest. I see no other hope for him than to fight this battle, and we must win it. I shall fight them whatever their force may be, but I ask for every man that the department can send me. No troops should now be left unemployed. Those who entertain the opinion that the rebels will abandon Richmond without a struggle, are, in my judgment, badly advised, and do not comprehend their situation, which is one requiring desperate measures.

"I beg that the President and Secretary will maturely weigh what I say, and leave nothing undone to comply with my request. If I am not re-enforced, it is probable that I will be obliged to fight nearly double my numbers strongly intrenched. I do not think it will be at all possible for me to bring more than (70,000) seventy thousand men upon the field of battle.

"GEORGE B. McCLELLAN,
"*Major General Commanding.*

"Hon. EDWIN M. STANTON,
"*Secretary of War.*"

On the 14th of May I sent the following telegram to the President:

"CAMP AT CUMBERLAND, *May* 14, 1862.

"I have more than twice telegraphed to the Secretary of War, stating that, in my opinion, the enemy were concentrating all their available force to fight this army in front of Richmond, and that such ought to be their policy. I have received no reply whatever to any of these telegraphs. I beg leave to repeat their substance to your excellency, and to ask that kind consideration which you have ever accorded to my representations and views. All my information from every source accessible to me establishes the fixed purpose of the rebels to defend Richmond against this army by offering us battle with all the troops they can collect from east, west, and south, and my own opinion is confirmed by that of all my commanders whom I have been able to consult.

"Casualties, sickness, garrisons, and guards have much weakened my force, and will continue to do so. I cannot bring into actual battle against the enemy more than eighty thousand men at the utmost, and with them I must attack in position, probably intrenched, a much larger force, perhaps double my numbers. It is possible that Richmond may be abandoned without a serious struggle; but the enemy are actually in great strength between here and there, and it would be unwise, and even insane, for me to calculate upon anything but a stubborn and desperate resistance. If they should abandon Richmond, it may well be that it is done with the purpose of making the stand at some place in Virginia south or west of there, and we should be in condition to press them without delay. The confederate leaders must employ their utmost efforts against this army in Virginia, and they will be supported by the whole body of their military officers, among whom there may be said to be no Union feeling, as there is also very little among the higher class of citizens in the seceding States.

"I have found no fighting men left in this Peninsula. All are in the ranks of the opposing foe.

"Even if more troops than I now have should prove unnecessary for purposes of military occupation, our greatest display of imposing force in the capital of the rebel government will have the best moral effect. I most respectfully and earnestly urge upon your excellency that the opportunity has come for striking a fatal blow at the enemies of the Constitution, and I beg that you will cause this army to be re-enforced without delay by all the disposable troops of the government. I ask for every man that the War Department can send me. Any commander of the re-enforcements whom your excellency may designate will be acceptable to me, whatever expression I may have heretofore addressed to you on that subject.

"I will fight the enemy whatever their force may be, with whatever force I may have; and I firmly believe that we shall beat them, but our triumph should be made decisive and complete. The soldiers of this army love their government, and will fight well in its support. You may rely upon them. They have confidence in me as their general, and in you as their President. Strong re-enforcements will at least save the lives of many of them. The greater our force the more perfect will be our combinations, and the less our loss.

"For obvious reasons I beg you to give immediate consideration to this communication, and to inform me fully at the earliest moment of your final determination.

"GEORGE B. McCLELLAN,
"*Major General.*

"His Excellency ABRAHAM LINCOLN,
"*President of the United States.*"

To which, on the 18th of May, I received this reply:

"WASHINGTON, *May* 18—2 *p. m.*

"GENERAL: Your despatch to the President, asking re-enforcements, has been received and carefully considered.

"The President is not willing to uncover the capital entirely; and it is believed that even if this were prudent, it would require more time to effect a junction between your army and that of the Rappahannock by the way of the Potomac and York river, than by a land march. In order, therefore, to increase the strength of the attack upon Richmond at the earliest moment, General McDowell has been ordered to march upon that city by the shortest route. He is ordered, keeping himself always in position to save the capital from all possible attack, so to operate as to put his left wing in communication with your right wing, and you are instructed to co-operate so as to establish this communication as soon as possible by extending your right wing to the north of Richmond.

"It is believed that this communication can be safely established either north or south of the Pamunkey river.

"In any event, you will be able to prevent the main body of the enemy's forces from leaving Richmond, and falling in overwhelming force upon General McDowell. He will move with between thirty-five (35) and forty thousand (40,000) men.

"A copy of the instructions to General McDowell are with this. The specific task assigned to his command has been to provide against any danger to the capital of the nation.

"At your earnest call for re-enforcements, he is sent forward to co-operate in the reduction of Richmond, but charged, in attempting this, not to uncover the city of Washington, and you will give no order, either before or after your junction, which can put him out of position to cover this city. You and he will communicate with each other by telegraph or otherwise, as frequently as may be necessary for sufficient co-operation. When General McDowell is in position on your right, his supplies must be drawn from West Point, and you will instruct your staff officers to be prepared to supply him by that route.

"The President desires that General McDowell retain the command of the department of the Rappahannock, and of the forces with which he moves forward.

"By order of the President.

"EDWIN M. STANTON,
"*Secretary of War.*

"Major General GEORGE B. McCLELLAN,
"*Commanding Army of the Potomac, before Richmond.*"

It will be observed that this order rendered it impossible for me to use the James river as a line of operations, and forced me to establish our depots on the Pamunkey, and to approach Richmond from the north.

I had advised, and preferred, that re-enforcements should be sent by water, for the reasons that their arrival would be more safe and certain, and that I would be left free to rest the army on the James river whenever the navigation of that stream should be opened.

The land movement obliged me to expose my right in order to secure the junction; and as the order for General McDowell's march was soon countermanded, I incurred great risk, of which the enemy finally took advantage, and frustrated the plan of campaign. Had General McDowell joined me by water, I could have approached Richmond by the James, and thus avoided the delays and losses incurred in bridging the Chickahominy, and would have had the army massed in one body instead of being necessarily divided by that stream.

The following is a copy of the instructions to General McDowell:

"WAR DEPARTMENT,
"*Washington, May* 17, 1862.

"GENERAL: Upon being joined by General Shields's division, you will move upon Richmond by the general route of the Richmond and Fredericksburg railroad, co-operating with the forces under General McClellan, now threatening Richmond from the line of the Pamunkey and York rivers.

"While seeking to establish as soon as possible a communication between your left wing and the right wing of General McClellan, you will hold yourself always in such position as to cover the capital of the nation against a sudden dash of any large body of the rebel forces.

"General McClellan will be furnished with a copy of these instructions, and will be directed to hold himself in readiness to establish communication with your left wing, and to prevent the main body of the enemy's army from leaving Richmond, and throwing itself upon your column, before a junction of the two armies is effected.

"A copy of his instructions in regard to the employment of your force is annexed.

"By order of the President.

"EDWIN M. STANTON,
"*Secretary of War.*

"General MCDOWELL,
"*Commanding Department of Rappahannock.*"

Having some doubts, from the wording of the foregoing orders, as to the extent of my authority over the troops of General McDowell, and as to the time when I might anticipate his arrival, on the 21st of May I sent this despatch:

"HEADQUARTERS ARMY OF THE POTOMAC,
"*Camp near Tunstall's Station, Virginia, May* 21, 1862—11 *p. m.*

"Your despatch of yesterday, respecting our situation and the batteries of Fort Darling, was received while I was absent with the advance, where I have been all this day. I have communicated personally with Captain Goldsborough, and by letter with Captain Smith. The vessels can do nothing without co-operation on land, which I will not be in condition to afford for several days. Circumstances must determine the propriety of a land attack.

"It rained again last night, and rain on this soil soon makes the roads incredibly bad for army transportation. I personally crossed the Chickahominy to-day at Bottom's bridge ford, and went a mile beyond, the enemy being about half a mile in front. I have three regiments on the other bank guarding the re-building of the bridge. Keyes's corps is on the New Kent road, near Bottom's bridge. Heintzelman is on the same road, within supporting distance. Sumner is on the railroad, connecting right with left. Stoneman, with advanced guard, is within one mile of New bridge. Franklin, with two divisions, is about two miles this side of Stoneman. Porter's division, with the reserves of infantry and artillery, is within supporting distance. Headquarters will probably be at Coal Harbor to-morrow, one mile this side of Franklin. All the bridges over the Chickahominy are destroyed. The enemy are in force on every road leading to Richmond, within a mile or two west of the stream. Their main body is on the road from New bridge, encamped along it for four or five miles, spreading over the open ground on both sides. Johnston's headquarters are about two miles beyond the bridge.

"All accounts report their numbers as greatly exceeding our own. The position of the rebel forces, the declaration of the confederate authorities, the resolutions of the Virginia legislature, the action of the city government, the conduct of the citizens, and all other sources of information accessible to me give positive assurance that our approach to Richmond involves a desperate battle between the opposing armies.

"All our divisions are moving towards the foe. I shall advance steadily and carefully, and attack them according to my best judgment, and in such manner as to employ my greatest force.

"I regret the state of things as to General McDowell's command. We must beat the enemy in front of Richmond. One division added to this army for that effort would do more to protect Washington than his whole force can possibly do anywhere else in the field. The rebels are concentrating from all points for the two battles at Richmond and Corinth. I would still, most respectfully, suggest the policy of our concentrating here by movements on water. I have heard nothing as to the probabilities of the contemplated junction of McDowell's force with mine. I have no idea when he can start, what are his means of transportation, or when he may be expected to reach this vicinity. I fear there is little hope that he can join me over land in time for the coming battle. Delays on my part will be dangerous. I f ar sickness and demoralization. This region is unhealthy for northern men, and unless kept moving, I fear that our soldiers may become discouraged. At present our numbers are weakening from disease, but our men remain in good heart.

"I regret also the configuration of the department of the Rappahannock. It includes a portion even of the city of Richmond. I think that my own department should embrace the entire field of military operations designed for the capture and occupation of that city.

"Again, I agree with your excellency that one bad general is better than two good ones.

"I am not sure that I fully comprehend your orders of the 17th instant addressed to myself and General McDowell. If a junction is effected before we occupy Richmond, it must necessarily be east of the railroad to Fredericksburg and within my department. This fact, my superior rank, and the express language of the 62d article of war, will place his command under my orders, unless it is otherwise specially directed by your excellency; and I consider that he will be under my command, except that I am not to detach any portion of his forces, or give any orders which can put him out of position to cover Washington. If I err in my construction, I desire to be at once set right. Frankness compels me to say, anxious as I am for an increase of force, that the march of McDowell's column upon Richmond by the shortest route will, in my opinion, uncover Washington, as to any interposition by it, as completely as its movement by water. The enemy cannot advance by Fredericksburg on Washington.

"Should they attempt a movement, which to me seems utterly improbable, their route would be by Gordonsville and Manassas. I desire that the extent of my authority over McDowell may be clearly defined, lest misunderstandings and conflicting views may produce some of those injurious results which a divided command has so often caused. I would respectfully suggest that this danger can only be surely guarded against by explicitly placing General McDowell under my orders in the ordinary way, and holding me strictly responsible for the closest observance of your instructions. I hope, Mr. President, that it is not necessary for me to assure you that your instructions would be observed in the utmost good faith, and that I have no personal feelings which could influence me to disregard them in any particular.

"I believe that there is a great struggle before this army, but I am neither dismayed nor discouraged. I wish to strengthen its force as much as I can, but in any event I shall fight it with all the skill, caution, and determination that I possess, and I trust that the result may either obtain for me the permanent confidence of my government, or that it may close my career.

"GEORGE B. McCLELLAN,
"*Major General Commanding.*

"His Excellency ABRAHAM LINCOLN,
"*President of the United States.*"

On the 24th I received the following reply:

"MAY 24, 1862.—(*From Washington, 24th.*)

"I left General McDowell's camp at dark last evening. Shields's command is there, but it is so worn that he cannot move before Monday morning, the twenty-sixth, (26th.) We have so thinned our line to get troops for other places that it was broken yesterday at Front Royal, with a probable loss to us of one (1) regiment infantry, two (2) companies cavalry, putting General Banks in some peril.

"The enemy's forces, under General Anderson, now opposing General McDowell's advance, have, as their line of supply and retreat, the road to Richmond.

"If, in conjunction with McDowell's movement against Anderson, you could send a force from your right to cut off the enemy's supplies from Richmond, preserve the railroad bridges across the two (2) forks of the Pamunkey and intercept the enemy's retreat, you will prevent the army now opposed to you from receiving an accession of numbers of nearly fifteen thousand (15,000) men; and if you succeed in saving the bridges, you will secure a line of railroad for supplies in addition to the one you now have. Can you not do this almost as well as not, while you are building the Chickahominy bridges? McDowell and Shields both say they can, and positively will, move Monday morning. *I wish you to move cautiously and safely.*

"You will have command of McDowell, after he joins you, precisely as you indicated in your long despatch to us of the twenty-first, (21st.)

"A. LINCOLN, *President.*

"Major General G. B. McCLELLAN."

This information that McDowell's corps would march for Fredericksburg on the following Monday, (the 26th,) and that he would be under my command, as indicated in my telegram of the 21st, was cheering news, and I now felt confident that we would on his arrival be sufficiently strong to overpower the large army confronting us.

At a later hour on the same day I received the following:

"MAY 24, 1862.—(*from Washington, 4 p. m.*)

"In consequence of General Banks's critical position, I have been compelled to suspend General McDowell's movements to join you. The enemy are making a desperate push upon Harper's Ferry, and we are trying to throw General Frémont's force, and part of General McDowell's, in their rear.

"A. LINCOLN, *President.*

"Major General GEO. B. McCLELLAN."

From which it will be seen that I could not expect General McDowell to join me in time to participate in immediate operations in front of Richmond, and on the same evening I replied to the President that I would make my calculations accordingly.

It then only remained for me to make the best use of the forces at my disposal, and to avail myself of all artificial auxiliaries to compensate as much as possible for the inadequacy of men. I concurred fully with the President in the injunction contained in his telegram of the 24th, that it was necessary with my limited force to move "cautiously and safely." In view of the peculiar character of the Chickahominy, and the liability of its bottom land to sudden inundation, it became necessary to construct between Bottom's bridge and Mechanicsville eleven (11) new bridges, all long and difficult, with extensive log-way approaches.

The entire army could probably have been thrown across the Chickahominy immediately after our arrival, but this would have left no force on the left bank to guard our communications or to protect our right and rear. If the communication with our supply depot had been cut by the enemy, with our army concentrated upon the right bank of the Chickahominy, and the stage of water as it was for many days after our arrival, the bridges carried away, and our means of transportation not furnishing a single day's supplies in advance, the troops must have gone without rations, and the animals without forage, and the army would have been paralyzed.

It is true I might have abandoned my communications and pushed forward towards Richmond, trusting to the speedy defeat of the enemy and the consequent fall of the city for a renewal of supplies; but the approaches were fortified, and the town itself was surrounded with a strong line of intrenchments, requiring a greater length of time to reduce than our troops could have dispensed with rations.

Under these circumstances, I decided to retain a portion of the army on the left bank of the river until our bridges were completed.

It will be remembered that the order for the co-operation of General McDowell was simply suspended, not revoked, and therefore I was not at liberty to abandon the northern approach.

A very dashing and successful reconnoissance was made near New bridge, on the 24th of May, by Lieutenant Bowen, topographical engineers, escorted by the 4th Michigan volunteers and a squadron of the United States cavalry, commanded, respectively, by Colonel Woodbury and Captain Gordon.

Our troops encountered a Louisiana regiment, and with little loss drove it back upon its brigade, killing a large number and capturing several prisoners. Great credit is due to the staff officers, as well as to Colonel Woodbury, Captain Gordon, and their commands, for their conduct on this occasion.

The work upon the bridges was commenced at once, and pushed forward with great vigor; but the rains, which from day to day continued to fall, flooded the valley, and raised the water to a greater height than had been known for twenty years.

This demolished a great amount of our labor, and our first bridges, with their approaches, which were not made with reference to such extreme high water, were carried off or rendered impassable. We were obliged, with immense labor, to construct others, much longer, more elevated, and stable; our men worked in the water, exposed to the enemy's fire from the opposite bank.

On the 25th of May I received the following telegram.

"WASHINGTON, *May* 25, 1862.

"Your despatch received. General Banks was at Sharpsburg with about six thousand (6,000) men, Shields having been taken from him to swell a column for McDowell to aid you at Richmond, and the rest of his force scattered at various places. On the twenty-third (23d) a rebel force of seven (7) to ten thousand (10,000) fell upon one regiment and two companies guarding the bridge at Port Royal, destroying it entirely; crossed the Shenandoah, and on the twenty-fourth, (24th,) yesterday, pushed on to get north of Banks on the road to Winchester. General Banks ran a race with them, beating them into Winchester yesterday evening. This morning a battle ensued between the two forces, in which General Banks was beaten back into full retreat towards Martinsburg, and probably is broken up into a total rout. Geary, on the Manassas Gap railroad, just now reports that Jackson is now near Front Royal with ten thousand (10,000) troops, following up and supporting, as I understand, the force now pursuing Banks. Also, that another force of ten thousand is near Orleans, following on in the same direction. Stripped bare, as we are here, I will do all we can to prevent them crossing the Potomac at Harper's Ferry or above. McDowell has about twenty thousand of his forces moving back to the vicinity of Port Royal; and Frémont, who was at Franklin, is moving to Harrisonburg; both these movements intended to get in the enemy's rear.

"One more of McDowell's brigades is ordered through here to Harper's Ferry; the rest of his forces remain for the present at Fredericksburg. We are sending such regiments and dribs from here and Baltimore as we can spare to Harper's Ferry, supplying their places in some sort, calling in militia from the adjacent States. We also have eighteen cannon on the road to Harper's Ferry, of which arm there is not a single one at that point. This is now our situation.

"If McDowell's force was now beyond our reach, we should be entirely helpless. Apprehensions of something like this, and no unwillingness to sustain you, has always been my reason for withholding McDowell's forces from you.

"Please understand this, and do the best you can with the forces you have.

"A. LINCOLN, *President.*

"Major General McClellan."

On the 25th the following was also received:

"Washington, *May* 25, 1862—2 *p. m.*

"The enemy is moving north in sufficient force to drive General Banks before him; precisely in what force we cannot tell. He is also threatening Leesburg, and Geary on the Manassas Gap railroad, from both north and south; in precisely what force we cannot tell. I think the movement is a general and concerted one, such as would not be if he was acting upon the purpose of a very desperate defence of Richmond. I think the time is near when you must either attack Richmond or give up the job, and come to the defence of Washington. Let me hear from you instantly.

"A. LINCOLN, *President.*

"Major General McClellan."

To which I replied as follows:

"Coal Harbor, *May* 25, 1862.

"Telegram received. Independently of it, the time is very near when I shall attack Richmond. The object of the movement is probably to prevent re-enforcements being sent to me. All the information obtained from balloons, deserters, prisoners, and contrabands, agrees in the statement that the mass of the rebel troops are still in the immediate vicinity of Richmond, ready to defend it. I have no knowledge of Banks's position and force, nor what there is at Manassas; therefore cannot form a definite opinion as to the force against him.

"I have two corps across Chickahominy, within six miles of Richmond; the others on this side at other crossings within same distance, and ready to cross when bridges are completed.

"G. B. McCLELLAN,
"*Major General, Commanding.*

"His Excellency A. Lincoln, *President.*"

2029.

On the 26th I received the following:

"WASHINGTON, *May* 26, 1862—12.40 *a. m.*

"We have General Banks's official report. He has saved his army and baggage, and has made a safe retreat to the river, and is probably safe at Williamsport. He reports the attacking force at fifteen thousand (15,000.)

"A. LINCOLN, *President.*

"Major General McCLELLAN."

On the 26th I received the following:

"WASHINGTON, *May* 26, 1862.

"Can you not cut the Aquia Creek railroad. Also, what impression have you as to intrenched works for you to contend with in front of Richmond? Can you get near enough to throw shells into the city?

"A. LINCOLN, *President.*

"Major General G. B. McCLELLAN."

On the same day I sent the following:

"COAL HARBOR, *May* 26, 1862.

"Have cut the Virginia Central road in three places between Hanover Court House and the Chickahominy. Will try to cut the other. I do not think Richmond intrenchments formidable; but am not certain. Hope very soon to be within shelling distance. Have railroad in operation from White House to Chickahominy. Hope to have Chickahominy bridge repaired to night. Nothing of interest to-day.

"G. B. McCLELLAN,
"*Major General, Commanding.*

"His Excellency A. LINCOLN, *President.*"

The interruption of the railroad, here referred to, was effected by the command of Brigadier General Stoneman, and was intended to prevent the enemy from drawing supplies by that route, or from sending re-enforcements to Anderson or Jackson.

At 10 a. m. I sent also the following despatch:

"Telegrams of last night received. I am glad to know affairs are not so bad as might have been. I would earnestly call your attention to my instructions to General Banks of March 16, to General Wadsworth of same date, and to my letter of April 1 to the Adjutant General. I cannot but think that a prompt return to the principles there laid down would relieve all probability of danger. I will forward copies by mail. I beg to urge the importance of Manassas and Front Royal in contradistinction to Fredericksburg.

"G. B. McCLELLAN,
"*Major General.*

"His Excellency A. LINCOLN, *President.*"

Later on the 26th I sent the following:

"CAMP NEAR NEW BRIDGE,
"*May* 26, 1862—7.30 *p. m.*

"Have arranged to carry out your last orders. We are quietly closing in upon the enemy, preparatory to the last struggle. Situated as I am, I feel forced to take every possible precaution against disaster, and to secure my flanks against the probably superior force in front of me. My arrangements for to-morrow are very important, and if successful, will leave me free to strike on the return of the force detached.

"G. B. McCLELLAN,
"*Major General.*

"His Excellency A. LINCOLN, *President.*"

On the same day I received intelligence that a very considerable force of the enemy was in the vicinity of Hanover Court House, to the right and rear of our army, thus threatening our communications, and in a position either to re-enforce Jackson, or to impede McDowell's junction, should he finally move to unite with us. On the same day I also received information from General McDowell, through the Secretary of War, that the enemy had fallen back from Fredericksburg towards Richmond, and that General McDowell's advance was eight miles south of the Rappahannock. It was thus imperative to dislodge or defeat this force, independently even of the wishes of the President, as expressed in his telegram of the 26th. I intrusted this task to Brigadier General Fitz-John Porter, commanding the fifth corps, with orders to move at daybreak on the 27th.

Through a heavy rain, and over bad roads, that officer moved his command as follows:

Brigadier General W. H. Emory led the advance, with the 5th and 6th regiments United States cavalry and Benson's horse battery of the 2d United States artillery, taking the road from New bridge *via* Mechanicsville, to Hanover Court House.

General Morell's division, composed of the brigades of Martindale, Butterfield and McQuade, with Berdan's regiment of sharpshooters, and three batteries, under Captain Charles Griffin, 5th United States artillery, followed on the same road.

Colonel G. K. Warren, commanding a provisional brigade, composed of the 5th and 13th New York, the 1st Connecticut artillery, acting as infantry, the 6th Pennsylvania cavalry, and Weeden's Rhode Island battery, moved from his station at Old Church by a road running to Hanover Court House, parallel to the Pamunkey.

After a fatiguing march of fourteen miles through the mud and rain, General Emory, at noon, reached a point about two miles from Hanover Court House where the road forks to Ashland, and found a portion of the enemy formed in line across the Hanover Court House road.

General Emory had, before this, been joined by the 25th New York, (of Martindale's brigade,) and Berdan's sharpshooters; these regiments were deployed with a section of Benson's battery, and advanced slowly towards the enemy until re-enforced by General Butterfield with four regiments of his brigade, when the enemy was charged and quickly routed, one of his guns being captured by the 17th New York, under Colonel Lansing, after having been disabled by the fire of Benson's battery. The firing here lasted about an hour. The cavalry and Benson's battery were immediately ordered in pursuit, followed by Morell's infantry and artillery, with the exception of Martindale's brigade. Warren's brigade having been delayed by repairing bridges, &c., now arrived, too late to participate in this affair; a portion of this command was sent to the Pamunkey to destroy bridges, and captured quite a number of prisoners; the remainder followed Morell's division. In the meantime General Martindale, with the few remaining regiments of his brigade and a section of artillery, advanced on the Ashland road, and found a force of the enemy's infantry, cavalry, and artillery, in position near Beake's station, on the Virginia Central railroad; he soon forced them to retire towards Ashland.

The 25th New York having been ordered to rejoin him, General Martindale was directed to form his brigade and move up the railroad to rejoin the rest of the command at Hanover Court House

He sent one regiment up the railroad, but remained with the 2d Maine, afterwards joined by the 25th New York, to guard the rear of the main column.

The enemy soon returned to attack General Martindale, who at once formed the 2d Maine, 25th New York, and a portion of the 44th New York, with one section of Martin's battery, on the New bridge road, facing his own position of the morning, and then held his ground for an hour against large odds until re-enforced.

General Porter was at Hanover Court House, near the head of his column, when he learned that the rear had been attacked by a large force. He at once faced the whole column about, recalled the cavalry sent in pursuit towards Ashland, moved the 13th and 14th New York and Griffin's battery direct to Martindale's assistance, pushed the 9th Massachusetts and 62d Pennsylvania, of McQuade's brigade, through the woods on the right, (our original left,) and attacked the flank of the enemy, while Butterfield, with the 83d Pennsylvania and 16th Michigan, hastened towards the scene of action by the railroad, and through the woods, further to the right, and completed the rout of the enemy. During the remainder of this and the following day our cavalry was active in the pursuit, taking a number of prisoners.

Captain Harrison, of the 5th United States cavalry, with a single company, brought in as prisoners two entire companies of infantry with their arms and ammunition. A part of Rush's lancers also captured an entire company with their arms.

The immediate results of these affairs were, some two hundred of the enemy's dead buried by our troops, seven hundred and thirty prisoners sent to the rear, one 12-pound howitzer, one caisson, a large number of small arms, and two railroad trains, captured.

Our loss amounted to 53 killed, 344 wounded and missing.

The force encountered and defeated was General Branch's division, of North Carolina and Georgia troops, supposed to have been some 9,000 strong.

Their camp at Hanover Court House was taken and destroyed.

Having reason to believe that General Anderson, with a strong force, was still at Ashland, I ordered General Syke's division of regulars to move on the 28th from New bridge toward Hanover Court House, to be in position to support General Porter. They reached a point within three miles of Hanover Court House, and remained there until the evening of the 29th, when they returned to their original camp.

On the 28th General Stoneman's command of cavalry, horse artillery, and two regiments of infantry, were also placed under General Porter's orders.

On the same day I visited Hanover Court House, whence I sent the following despatch:

"HANOVER COURT HOUSE,
"*May 28—2 p. m.*

"Porter's action of yesterday was truly a glorious victory; too much credit cannot be given to his magnificent division and its accomplished leader. The rout of the rebels was complete; not a defeat, but a complete rout. Prisoners are constantly coming in; two companies have this moment arrived with excellent arms.

"There is no doubt that the enemy are concentrating everything on Richmond. I will do my best to cut off Jackson, but am doubtful whether I can.

"It is the policy and duty of the government to send me by water all the well-drilled troops available. I am confident that Washington is in no danger. Engines and cars in large numbers have been sent up to bring down Jackson's command.

"I may not be able to cut them off, but will try; we have cut all but the Fredericksburg and Richmond railroad. The real issue is in the battle about to be fought in front of Richmond. All our available troops should be collected here, not raw regiments, but the well-drilled troops. It cannot be ignored that a desperate battle is before us; if any regiments of good troops remain unemployed, it will be an irreparable fault committed.

"G. B. McCLELLAN,
"*Major General.*

"Hon. E. M. STANTON, *Secretary of War.*"

Having ascertained the state of affairs, instructions were given for the operations of the following day.

On the 28th a party under Major Williams, 6th United States cavalry, destroyed the common road bridges over the Pamunkey, and Virginia Central railroad bridge over the South Ann.

On the 29th he destroyed the Fredericksburg and Richmond railroad bridge over the South Ann, and the turnpike bridge over the same stream.

On the same day, and mainly to cover the movement of Major Williams, General Emory moved a column of cavalry towards Ashland, from Hanover Court House. The advance of this column under Captain Chambliss, 5th United States cavalry, entered Ashland, driving out a party of the enemy, destroyed the railroad bridge over Stoney creek, broke up the railroad and telegraph.

Another column of all arms, under Colonel Warren, was sent on the same day by the direct road to Ashland, and entered it shortly after General Emory's column had retired, capturing a small party there.

General Stoneman on the same day moved on Ashland by Leach's station, covering well the movements of the other columns.

The objects of the expedition having been accomplished, and it being certain that the 1st corps would not join us at once, General Porter withdrew his command to their camps with the main army on the evening of the 29th.

On the night of the 27th and 28th I sent the following despatch to the Secretary of War:

"HEADQUARTERS ARMY OF THE POTOMAC,
"*Camp near New Bridge, May* 28, 1862—12.30 *a. m.*

"Porter has gained two complete victories over superior forces, yet I feel obliged to move in the morning with re-enforcements to secure the complete destruction of the rebels in that quarter. In doing so, I run some risk here, but I cannot help it. The enemy are even in greater force than I had supposed. I will do all that quick movements can accomplish, but you must send me all the troops you can, and leave to me full latitude as to choice of commanders. It is absolutely necessary to destroy the rebels near Hanover Court House before I can advance.

"G. B. McCLELLAN,
"*Major General.*

"Hon. E. M. STANTON,
"*Secretary of War.*"

In reply to which, I received the following from the President:

"WASHINGTON, *May* 28, 1862.

"I am very glad of General F. J. Porter's victory; still, if it was a total rout of the enemy, I am puzzled to know why the Richmond and Fredericksburg railroad was not seized again, as you say you have all the railroads but the Richmond and Fredericksburg. I am puzzled to see how, lacking that, you can have any, except the scrap from Richmond to West Point. The scrap of the Virginia Central, from Richmond to Hanover Junction, without more, is simply nothing. That the whole of the enemy is concentrating on Richmond, I think, cannot be certainly known to you or me. Saxton, at Harper's Ferry, informs us that large forces, supposed to be Jackson's and Ewell's, forced his advance from Charlestown to-day. General King telegraphs us from Fredericksburg that contrabands give certain information that fifteen thousand left Hanover Junction Monday morning to re-enforce Jackson. I am painfully impressed with the importance of the struggle before you, and shall aid you all I can consistently with my view of due regard to all points.

"A. LINCOLN.

"Major General McClellan."

At 6 p. m. of the 29th I sent the Secretary of War the following despatch:

"Headquarters Army of the Potomac,
"*May* 29, 1862—6 *p. m.*

"General Porter has gained information that General Anderson left his position in vicinity of Fredericksburg at 4 a. m. Sunday with the following troops: 1st South Carolina, Colonel Hamilton; one battalion South Carolina rifles; 34th and 38th North Carolina; 45th Georgia; 12th, 13th, and 14th South Carolina; 3d Louisiana; two batteries of four guns each, namely, Letcher's Virginia and McIntosh's South Carolina batteries. General Anderson and his command passed Ashland yesterday evening en route for Richmond, leaving men behind to destroy bridges over the telegraph road which they travelled. This information is reliable. It is also positively certain that Branch's command was from Gordonsville, bound for Richmond, whither they have now gone.

"It may be regarded as positive, I think, that there is no rebel force between Fredericksburg and Junction.

"G. B. McCLELLAN,
"*Major General.*

"Hon. E. M. Stanton,
"*Secretary of War.*"

The following was also sent on the same day:

"Headquarters Army of the Potomac,
"*May* 29, 1862.

"A detachment from General F. J. Porter's command, under Major Williams, 6th cavalry, destroyed the South Ann railroad bridge at about 9 a. m to-day; a large quantity of confederate public property was also destroyed at Ashland this morning.

"R. B. MARCY,
"*Chief of Staff.*

"Hon. E. M. Stanton,
"*Secretary of War.*"

In reply to which, the following was received:

"Washington, *May* 29, 1862.

"Your despatch as to the South Ann and Ashland being seized by our forces this morning is received. Understanding these points to be on the Richmond and Fredericksburg railroad, I heartily congratulate the country, and thank General McClellan and his army for their seizure.

"A. LINCOLN.

"General R. B. Marcy."

On the 30th I sent the following:

"Headquarters Army of the Potomac,
"*May* 30, 1862.

"From the tone of your despatches, and the President's, I do not think that you at all appreciate the value and magnitude of Porter's victory. It has entirely relieved my right flank, which was seriously threatened; routed and demoralized a considerable portion of the rebel forces; taken over seven hundred and fifty prisoners; killed and wounded large numbers; one gun, many small arms, and much baggage taken. It was one of the handsomest things in the war, both in itself and in its results. Porter has returned, and my army is again well in hand. Another day will make the probable field of battle passable for artillery. It is quite certain that there is nothing in front of McDowell at Fredericksburg. I regard the burning of South Anna bridges as the least important result of Porter's movement.

"G. B. McCLELLAN,
"*Major General.*

"Hon. E. M. STANTON,
"*Secretary of War.*"

The results of this brilliant operation of General Porter were the dispersal of General Branch's division, and the clearing of our right flank and rear. It was rendered impossible for the enemy to communicate by rail with Fredericksburg, or with Jackson *via* Gordonsville, except by the very circuitous route of Lynchburg, and the road was left entirely open for the advance of McDowell had he been permitted to join the army of the Potomac. His withdrawal towards Front Royal was, in my judgment, a serious and fatal error; he could do no good in that direction, while, had he been permitted to carry out the orders of May 17, the united forces would have driven the enemy withint he immediate intrenchments of Richmond before Jackson could have returned to its succor, and probably would have gained possession promptly of that place. I respectfully refer to the reports of General Porter and his subordinate commanders for the names of the officers who deserve especial mention for the parts they took in these affairs, but I cannot omit here my testimony to the energy and ability here displayed by General Porter on this occasion, since to him is mainly due the successes there gained.

On the 20th of May a reconnoissance was ordered on the south side of the Chickahominy towards James river. This was accomplished by Brigadier General H. M. Naglee, who crossed his brigade near Bottom's bridge, and pushed forward to within two miles of James river without serious resistance, or finding the enemy in force. The rest of the 4th corps, commanded by General E. D. Keyes, crossed the Chickahominy on the 23d of May.

On the 24th, 25th, and 26th, a very gallant reconnoissance was pushed by General Naglee, with his brigade, beyond the Seven Pines, and on the 25th the 4th corps was ordered to take up and fortify a position in the vicinity of the Seven Pines. The order was at once obeyed; a strong line of rifle-pits opened, and an abatis constructed a little in the rear of the point where the nine-mile road comes into the Williamsburg road.

On the same day General Heintzelman was ordered to cross with his corps, (the 3d,) and take a position two miles in advance of Bottom's bridge, watching the crossing of White Oak swamp, and covering the left and the rear of the left wing of the army. Being the senior officer on that side of the river, he was placed in command of both corps, and ordered to hold the Seven Pines at all hazards, but not to withdraw the troops from the crossings of White Oak swamp unless in an emergency.

On the 28th General Keyes was ordered to advance Casey's division to Fair Oaks, on the Williamsburg road, some three-quarters of a mile in front of the Seven Pines, leaving General Couch's division at the line of rifle-pits. A new line of rifle-pits and a small redoubt for six field guns were commenced, and much of the timber in front of this line was felled on the two days following. The picket line was established, reaching from the Chickahominy to White Oak swamp.

On the 30th General Heintzelman, representing that the advance had met with sharp opposition in taking up their position, and that he considered the point a critical one, requested and obtained authority to make such dispositions of his troops as he saw fit to meet the emergency. He immediately advanced two brigades of Kearney's division about the fourth of a mile in front of Savage's station, thus placing them within supporting distance of Casey's division, which held the advance of the 4th corps.

On the 30th the troops on the south side of the Chickahominy were in position as follows: Casey's division on the right of the Williamsburg road, at right angles to it, the centre at Fair Oaks; Couch's division at the Seven Pines; Kearney's division on the railroad, from near Savage's station towards the bridge; Hooker's division on the borders of White Oak swamp. Constant skirmishing had been kept up between our pickets and those of the enemy; while these lines were being taken up and strengthened, large bodies of confederate troops were seen immediately to the front and right of Casey's position.

During the day and night of the 30th of May a very violent storm occurred, the rain falling in torrents rendered work on the rifle-pits and bridges impracticable; made the roads almost impassable, and threatened the destruction of the bridges over the Chickahominy.

The enemy perceiving the unfavorable position in which we were placed, and the possibility of destroying that part of our army which was apparently cut off from the main body by the rapidly rising stream, threw an overwhelming force, (grand divisions of Generals D. H. Hill, Huger, Longstreet, and G. W. Smith,) upon the position occupied by Casey's division.

It appears from the official reports of General Keyes and his subordinate commanders that at ten o'clock a. m. on the 31st of May an aide-de-camp of General J. E. Johnston was captured by General Naglee's pickets. But little information as to the movements of the enemy was obtained from him, but his presence so near our lines excited suspicion and caused increased vigilance, and the troops were ordered by General Keyes to be under arms at eleven o'clock. Between eleven and twelve o'clock it was reported to General Casey that the enemy were approaching in considerable force on the Williamsburg road. At this time Casey's division was disposed as follows: Naglee's brigade extending from the Williamsburg road to the Garnett field, having one regiment across the railroad; General Wessel's brigade in the rifle-pits, and General Palmer's in the rear of General Wessel's; one battery of artillery in advance with General Naglee; one battery in rear of rifle-pits to the right of the redoubt; one battery in rear of the redoubt, and another battery unharnessed in the redoubt. General Couch's division, holding the second line, had General Abercrombie's brigade on the right, along the nine-mile road, with two regiments and one battery across the railroad near Fair Oaks station; General Peck's brigade on the right, and General Devins's in the centre.

On the approach of the enemy, General Casey sent forward one of General Palmer's regiments to support the picket line, but this regiment gave way without making much, if any, resistance. Heavy firing at once commenced, and the pickets were driven in. General Keyes ordered General Couch to move General Peck's brigade to occupy the ground on the left of the Williamsburg road, which had not before been occupied by our forces, and thus to support General Casey's left, where the first attack was the most severe. The enemy now came on in heavy force, attacking General Casey simultaneously in front and on both flanks. General Keyes sent to General Heintzelman for re-enforcements, but the messenger was delayed, so that orders were not sent to Generals Kearney and Hooker until nearly 3 o'clock, and it was nearly 5 p. m. when Generals Jameson and Perry's brigades of General Kearney's division arrived on the field. General Birney was ordered up the railroad, but by General Kearney's order halted his brigade before arriving at the scene of action. Orders were also despatched for

General Hooker to move up from White Oak swamp, and he arrived after dark at Savage's station.

As soon as the firing was heard at headquarters, orders were sent to General Sumner to get his command under arms and be ready to move at a moment's warning. His corps, consisting of Generals Richardson's and Sedgwick's divisions, was encamped on the north side of the Chickahominy, some six miles above Bottom's bridge; each division had thrown a bridge over the stream opposite to its own position.

At one o'clock General Sumner moved the two divisions to their respective bridges, with instructions to halt and await further orders. At two o'clock orders were sent from headquarters to cross these divisions without delay, and push them rapidly to General Heintzelman's support. This order was received and communicated at half past two, and the passage was immediately commenced. In the mean time General Naglee's brigade, with the batteries of General Casey's division, which General Naglee directed, struggled gallantly to maintain the redoubt and rifle-pits against the overwhelming masses of the enemy. They were re-enforced by a regiment from General Peck's brigade. The artillery under command of Colonel G. D. Bailey, 1st New York artillery, and afterwards of General Naglee, did good execution on the advancing column. The left of this position was, however, soon turned, and a sharp cross-fire opened upon the gunners and men in the rifle-pits. Colonel Bailey, Major Van Valkenberg, and Adjutant Ramsey, of the same regiment, were killed; some of the guns in the redoubt were taken, and the whole line was driven back upon the position occupied by General Couch. The brigades of Generals Wessel and Palmer, with the re-enforcements which had been sent them from General Couch, had also been driven from the field with heavy loss, and the whole position occupied by General Casey's division was taken by the enemy.

Previous to this time General Keyes ordered General Couch to advance two regiments to relieve the pressure upon General Casey's right flank. In making this movement, General Couch discovered large masses of the enemy pushing towards our right, and crossing the railroad, as well as a heavy column which had been held in reserve, and which was now making its way towards Fair Oaks station. General Couch at once engaged this column with two regiments; but, though re-enforced by two additional regiments, he was overpowered, and the enemy pushed between him and the main body of his division. With these four regiments and one battery General Couch fell back about half a mile towards the Grapevine bridge, where, hearing that General Sumner had crossed, he formed line of battle facing Fair Oaks station, and prepared to hold the position.

Generals Berry and Jameson's brigades had by this time arrived in front of the Seven Pines. General Berry was ordered to take possession of the woods on the left, and push forward so as to have a flank fire on the enemy's lines. This movement was executed brilliantly, General Berry pushing his regiments forward through the woods until their rifles commanded the left of the camp and works occupied by General Casey's division in the morning. Their fire on the pursuing columns of the enemy was very destructive, and assisted materially in checking the pursuit in that part of the field. He held his position in these woods against several attacks of superior numbers, and after dark, being cut off by the enemy from the main body, he fell back towards White Oak swamp, and by a circuit brought his men into our lines in good order.

General Jameson, with two regiments, (the other two of his brigade having been detached—one to General Peck and one to General Birney,) moved rapidly to the front on the left of the Williamsburg road, and succeeded for a time in keeping the abatis clear of the enemy. But large numbers of the enemy pressing past the right of his line, he, too, was forced to retreat through the woods towards White Oak swamp, and in that way gained camp under cover of night.

Brigadier General Devens, who had held the centre of General Couch's division, had made repeated and gallant efforts to regain portions of the ground lost in front, but each time was driven back, and finally withdrew behind the rifle-pits near Seven Pines.

Meantime General Sumner had arrived with the advance of his corps, General Sedgwick's division, at the point held by General Couch with four regiments and one battery. The roads leading from the bridge were so miry that it was only by the greatest exertion General Sedgwick had been able to get one of his batteries to the front.

The leading regiment (1st Minnesota, Colonel Sully) was immediately deployed to the right of Couch, to protect the flank, and the rest of the division formed in line of battle, Kirby's battery near the centre, in an angle of the woods. One of General Couch's regiments was sent to open communication with General Heintzelman. No sooner were these dispositions made than the enemy came in strong force and opened a heavy fire along the line. He made several charges, but was each time repulsed with great loss by the steady fire of the infantry and the splendid practice of the battery. After sustaining the enemy's fire for a considerable time, General Sumner ordered five regiments (the 34th New York, Colonel Sinter; 82d New York, Lieutenant Colonel Hudson; 15th Massachusetts, Lieutenant Colonel Kimball; 20th Massachusetts, Colonel Lee; 7th Michigan, Major Richardson—the three former of General Gorman's brigade, the two latter of General Dana's brigade,) to advance and charge with the bayonet. This charge was executed in the most brilliant manner. Our troops springing over two fences which were between them and the enemy, rushed upon his lines, and drove him in confusion from that part of the field. Darkness now ended the battle for that day.

During the night dispositions were made for its early renewal. General Couch's division, and so much of General Casey's as could be collected together, with General Kearney's, occupied the rifle-pits near Seven Pines. General Peck, in falling back on the left, had succeeded late in the afternoon in rallying a considerable number of stragglers, and was taking them once more into the action, when he was ordered back to the intrenched camp by General Kearney. General Hooker brought up his division about dark, having been delayed by the heaviness of the roads and the throng of fugitives from the field, through whom the colonel of the leading regiment (Starr) reports he "was obliged to force his way with the bayonet." This division bivouacked for the night in rear of the right of the rifle-pits, on the other side of the railroad. General Richardson's division also came upon the field about sunset. He had attempted the passage of the Chickahominy by the bridge opposite his own camp, but it was so far destroyed that he was forced to move Generals Howard and Meagher's brigades, with all his artillery, around by General Sedgwick's bridge, while General French's brigade, with the utmost difficulty, crossed by the other. General Sedgwick's division, with the regiments under General Couch, held about the same position as when the fight ceased, and General Richardson on his arrival was ordered to place his division on the left to connect with General Kearney; General French's brigade was posted along the railroad, and Generals Howard and Meagher's brigades in second and third lines. All his artillery had been left behind, it being impossible to move it forward through the deep mud as rapidly as the infantry pushed towards the field, but during the night the three batteries of the division were brought to the front.

About five o'clock on the morning of the first of June skirmishers and some cavalry of the enemy were discovered in front of General Richardson's division. Captain Pettit's battery, (B, 1st New York,) having come upon the ground, threw a few shells among them, when they dispersed. There was a wide interval between General Richardson and General Kearney. To close this, General Richardson's line was extended to the left and his first line moved over the railroad. Scarcely had they gained the position, when the enemy appearing in large force from the woods in front, opened a heavy fire of musketry at short range along the whole line. He approached very rapidly with columns of attack formed on two roads which crossed the railroad. These columns were supported by infantry in line of battle on each side, cutting General French's line. He threw out no skirmishers, but appeared determined to carry all before him by one crushing blow. For nearly an hour the first line of General Richardson's division stood and returned the fire, the lines of the enemy being re-enforced and relieved time after time, till finally General Howard was ordered with his brigade to go to General French's assistance. He led his men gallantly to the front, and in a few minutes the fire of the enemy ceased and his whole line fell back on that part of the field. On the opening of the firing in the morning General Hooker pushed forward on the railroad with two regiments (5th and 6th New Jersey,) followed by General Sickles's brigade. It was found impossible to move the artillery of this division from its position on account of the mud. On coming near the woods, which were held by the enemy in force, General Hooker found General Birney's brigade, Colonel J. Hobart Ward in command, in line of battle. He sent back to hasten General Sickles's brigade, but ascertained that it had been turned off to the left by General Heintzelman to meet a column advancing in that direction. He at once made the attack with the two New Jersey regiments, calling upon Colonel Ward to support him with General Birney's brigade. This was well done, our troops advancing into the woods under a heavy fire, and pushing the enemy before them for more than an hour of hard fighting. A charge with the bayonet was then ordered by General Hooker with the 5th and 6th New Jersey, 3d Maine, and 38th and 40th New York, and the enemy fled in confusion, throwing down arms and even clothing in his flight. General Sickles, having been ordered to the left, formed line of battle on both sides of the Williamsburg road and advanced under a sharp fire from the enemy, deployed in the woods in front of him; after a brisk interchange of musketry fire while crossing the open ground, the Excelsior brigade dashed into the timber with the bayonet and put the enemy to flight.

On the right the enemy opened fire after half an hour's cessation, which was promptly responded to by General Richardson's division. Again the most vigorous efforts were made to break our line, and again they were frustrated by the steady courage of our troops. In about an hour General Richardson's whole line advanced, pouring in their fire at close range, which threw the line of the enemy back in some confusion. This was followed up by a bayonet charge led by General French in person, with the 57th and 66th New York, supported by two regiments sent by General Heintzelman, the 71st and 73d New York, which turned the confusion of the enemy into precipitated flight. One gun captured the previous day was retaken.

Our troops pushed forward as far as the lines held by them on the 31st before the attack. On the battle-field there were found many of our own and the confederate wounded, arms, caissons, wagons, subsistence stores, and forage, abandoned by the enemy in his rout. The state of the roads and impossibility of manœuvring artillery prevented further pursuit. On the next morning a reconnoissance was sent forward, which pressed back the pickets of the enemy to within five miles of Richmond; but again the impossibility of forcing even a few batteries forward precluded our holding permanently this position. The lines held previous to the battle were therefore resumed. General J. E. Johnston reports loss of the enemy in Longstreet's and J. W. Smith's divisions at 4,283; General D. H. Hill, who had taken the advance in the attack, estimates his loss at 2,500; which would give the enemy's loss 6,783. Our loss was, in General Sumner's corps, 1,223; General Heintzelman's corps, 1,394; General Keyes's corps, 3,120—total, 5,737.

Previous to the arrival of General Sumner upon the field of battle, on the 31st of May, General Heintzelman, the senior corps commander present, was in the immediate command of the forces engaged. The first information I received that the battle was in progress was a despatch from him stating that Casey's division had given way. During the night of the 31st I received a despatch from him, dated 8.45 p. m., in which he says: "I am just in. When I got to the front the most of General Casey's division had dispersed. * * * The rout of General Casey's men had a most dispiriting effect on the troops as they came up. I saw no reason why we should have been driven back."

This official statement, together with other accounts received previous to my arrival upon the battle-field, to the effect that Casey's division had given way without making a proper resistance, caused me to state, in a telegram to the Secretary of War on the first, that this division "gave way unaccountably and discreditably." Subsequent investigations, however, greatly modified the impressions first received, and I accordingly advised the Secretary of War of this in a d.spatch on the 5th of June.

The official reports of Generals Keyes, Casey, and Naglee show that a very considerable portion of this division fought well, and that the brigade of General Naglee is entitled to credit for its gallantry. This division, among the regiments of which were eight of comparatively new troops, was attacked by superior numbers; yet, according to the reports alluded to, it stood the attack "for three hours before it was re-enforced." A portion of the division was thrown into great confusion upon the first onslaught of the enemy; but the personal efforts of General Naglee, Colonel Bailey, and other officers, who boldly went to the front and encouraged the men by their presence and example, at this critical juncture, rallied a great part of the division, and thereby enabled it to act a prominent part in this severely contested battle. It therefore affords me great satisfaction to withdraw the expression contained in my first despatch, and I cordially give my indorsement to the conclusion of the division commander, "that those parts of his command which behaved discreditably were exceptional cases."

On the 31st, when the battle of Fair Oaks commenced, we had two of our bridges nearly completed; but the rising waters flooded the log-way approaches and made them almost impassable, so that it was only by the greatest efforts that General Sumner crossed his corps and participated in that hard-fought engagement. The bridges became totally useless after this corps had passed, and others on a more permanent plan were commenced.

On my way to headquarters, after the battle of Fair Oaks, I attempted to cross the bridge where General Sumner had taken over his corps on the day previous. At the time General Sumner crossed this was the only available bridge above Bottom's bridge. I found the approach from the right bank for some 400 yards submerged to the depth of several feet, and on reaching the place where the bridge had been, I found a great part of it carried away, so that I could not get my horse over, and was obliged to send him to Bottom's bridge, six miles below, as the only practicable crossing.

The approaches to New and Mechanicsville bridges were also overflowed, and both of them were enfiladed by the enemy's batteries established upon commanding heights on the opposite side. These batteries were supported by strong forces of the enemy, having numerous rifle-pits in their front, which would have made it necessary, even had the approaches been in the best possible condition, to have fought a sanguinary battle, with but little prospect of success, before a passage could have been secured.

The only available means, therefore, of uniting our forces at Fair Oaks for an advance on Richmond soon after the battle, was to march the troops from Mechanicsville, and other points, on the left banks of the Chickahominy down to Bottom's bridge, and thence over the Williamsburg road to the position near Fair Oaks, a distance of about twenty-three (23) miles. In the condition of the roads at that time this march could not have been made with artillery in less than two days, by which time the enemy would have been secure within his intrenchments around Richmond. In short, the idea of uniting the two wings of the army in time to make a vigorous pursuit of the enemy, with the prospect of overtaking him before he reached Richmond, only five miles distant from the field of battle, is simply absurd, and was, I presume, never for a moment seriously entertained by any one connected with the army of the Potomac. An advance, involving the separation of the two wings by the impassable Chickahominy, would have exposed each to defeat in detail. Therefore I held the position already gained, and completed our crossings as rapidly as possible.

In the mean time, the troops at Fair Oaks were directed to strengthen their positions by a strong line of intrenchments, which protected them while the bridges were being built, gave security to the trains, liberated a larger fighting force, and offered a safer retreat in the event of disaster.

On the 2d of June, I sent the following despatch:

"HEADQUARTERS ARMY OF THE POTOMAC,
"*New Bridge, June 2, 1862—10.30 a. m.*

"Our left is everywhere advanced considerably beyond the positions it occupied before the battle. I am in strong hopes that the Chickahominy will fall sufficiently to enable me to cross the right. We have had a terrible time with our communications—bridges and causeways, built with great care, having been washed away by the sudden freshets, leaving us almost cut off from communication. All that human labor can do is being done to accomplish our purpose.

"Please regard the portion of this relating to condition of Chickahominy as confidential, as it would be serious if the enemy were aware of it. I do not yet know our loss; it has been very heavy on both sides, as the fighting was desperate. Our victory complete. I expect still more fighting before we reach Richmond.

"G. B. McCLELLAN,
"*Major General.*

"Hon. E. M. STANTON,
"*Secretary of War.*"

On the same day I received the following from the Secretary of War:

"WASHINGTON, *June 2, 1862.*

"Your telegram has been received, and we are greatly rejoiced at your success—not only in itself, but because of the dauntless spirit and courage it displays in your troops. You have received, of course, the order made yesterday in respect to Fortress Monroe. The object was to place at your command the disposable force of that department. The indications are that Frémont or McDowell will fight Jackson to-day, and as soon as he is disposed of another large body of troops will be at your service.

"The intelligence from Halleck shows that the rebels are fleeing, and pursued in force, from Corinth. All interest now centres in your operations, and full confidence is entertained of your brilliant and glorious success.

"EDWIN M. STANTON,
"*Secretary of War.*

"Major General McCLELLAN."

On the 3d I received the following from the President:

"WASHINGTON, *June 3, 1862.*

"With these continuous rains, I am very anxious about the Chickahominy—so close in your rear, and crossing your line of communication. Please look to it.

"ABRAHAM LINCOLN, *President.*

"Major General McCLELLAN."

To which I replied as follows:

"HEADQUARTERS ARMY OF THE POTOMAC,
"*New Bridge, June* 3, 1862.

"Your despatch of 5 p.m. just received. As the Chickahominy has been almost the only obstacle in my way for several days, your excellency may rest assured that it has not been overlooked. Every effort has been made, and will continue to be, to perfect the communications across it. Nothing of importance, except that it is again raining.

"G. B. McCLELLAN,
"*Major General, Commanding.*

"A. LINCOLN, *President, Washington.*"

My views of the condition of our army on the 4th are explained in the following despatch to the President:

"HEADQUARTERS ARMY OF THE POTOMAC,
"*New Bridge, June* 4, 1862.

"Terrible rain, storm during the night and morning—not yet cleared off. Chickahominy flooded, bridges in bad condition. Are still hard at work at them. I have taken every possible step to insure the security of the corps on the right bank, but I cannot re-enforce them here until my bridges are all safe, as my force is too small to insure my right and rear, should the enemy attack in that direction, as they may probably attempt. I have to be very cautious now. Our loss in the late battle will probably exceed (5,000) five thousand. I have not yet full returns. On account of the effect it might have on our own men and the enemy, I request that you will regard this information as confidential for a few days. I am satisfied that the loss of the enemy was very considerably greater; they were terribly punished. I mention these facts now merely to show you that the army of the Potomac has had serious work, and that no child's play is before it.

"You must make your calculations on the supposition that I have been correct from the beginning in asserting that the serious opposition was to be made here.

"G. B. McCLELLAN,
"*Major General, Commanding.*

"A. LINCOLN, *President.*"

And in the following to the Secretary of War, on the same day:

"HEADQUARTERS ARMY OF THE POTOMAC,
"*New Bridge, June* 4, 1862.

"Please inform me at once what re-enforcements, if any, I can count upon having at Fortress Monroe or White House within the next three days, and when each regiment may be expected to arrive. It is of the utmost importance that I should know this immediately. The losses in the battle of the 31st and 1st will amount to (7, 000) seven thousand. Regard this as confidential for the present.

"If I can have (5) five new regiments for Fort Monroe and its dependencies, I can draw (3) three more old regiments from there safely. I can well dispose of four more raw regiments on my communications. I can well dispose of from (15) fifteen to (20) twenty well drilled regiments among the old brigades in bringing them up to their original effective strength. Recruits are especially necessary for the regular and volunteer batteries of artillery, as well as for the regular and volunteer regiments of infantry. After the losses in our last battle,

I trust that I will no longer be regarded as an alarmist. I believe we have at least one more desperate battle to fight.

"G. B. McCLELLAN,
"*Major General, Commanding.*

"Hon. E. M. STANTON,
"*Secretary of War.*"

Also in my despatch to the Secretary of War, on the 5th:

"HEADQUARTERS ARMY OF THE POTOMAC,
"*New Bridge, June 5*, 1862.

"Rained most of the night; has now ceased, but is not clear. The river still very high and troublesome. Enemy opened with several batteries on our bridges near here this morning; our batteries seem to have pretty much silenced them, though some firing still kept up. The rain forces us to remain in statu quo. With great difficulty a division of infantry has been crossed this morning to support the troops on the other side, should the enemy renew attack. I felt obliged to do this, although it leaves us rather weak here.

"G. B. McCLELLAN,
"*Major General, Commanding.*

"Hon. E. M. STANTON,
"*Secretary of War.*"

On the 5th the Secretary telegraphed me as follows:

"WASHINGTON, *June* 5, 1862—8.30 *p. m.*

"I will send you five (5) new regiments as fast as transportation can take them; the first to start to-morrow from Baltimore. I intend sending you a part of McDowell's force as soon as it can return from its trip to Front Royal, probably as many as you want. The order to ship the new regiments to Fort Monroe has already been given. I suppose that they may be sent directly to the fort. Please advise me if this be as you desire.

"EDWIN M. STANTON,
"*Secretary of War.*

"Major General McCLELLAN."

On the 7th of June I telegraphed as follows:

"HEADQUARTERS ARMY OF THE POTOMAC,
"*June* 7, 1862—4.40 *p. m.*

"In reply to your despatch of 2 p. m. to day, I have the honor to state that the Chickahominy river has risen so as to flood the entire bottoms to the depth of three and four feet. I am pushing forward the bridges in spite of this, and the men are working night and day, up to their waists in water, to complete them.

"The whole face of the country is a perfect bog, entirely impassable for artillery, or even cavalry, except directly in the narrow roads, which renders any general movement, either of this or the rebel army, entirely out of the question until we have more favorable weather.

"I am glad to learn that you are pressing forward re-enforcements so vigorously.

"I shall be in perfect readiness to move forward and take Richmond the moment McCall reaches here and the ground will admit the passage of artillery. I have advanced my pickets about a mile to-day, driving off the rebel pickets and securing a very advantageous position.

"The rebels have several batteries established, commanding the debouches from two of our bridges, and fire upon our working parties continually, but as yet they have killed but very few of our men.

"G. B. McCLELLAN,
"*Major General, Commanding.*

"Hon. E. M. STANTON,
"*Secretary of War.*"

As I did not think it probable that any re-enforcements would be sent me in time for the advance on Richmond, I stated in the foregoing despatch that I should be ready to move when General McCall's division joined me; but I did not intend to be understood by this that no more re-enforcements were wanted, as will be seen from the following dispatch.

"JUNE 10, 1862—3.30 *p. m.*

"I have again information that Beauregard has arrived, and that some of his troops are to follow him. No great reliance—perhaps none whatever—can be attached to this; but it is possible, and ought to be their policy.

"I am completely checked by the weather. The roads and fields are literally impassable for artillery, almost so for infantry. The Chickahominy is in a dreadful state; we have another rain-storm on our hands.

"I shall attack as soon as the weather and ground will permit; but there will be a delay, the extent of which no one can foresee, for the season is altogether abnormal.

"In view of these circumstances, I present for your consideration the propriety of detaching largely from Halleck's army to strengthen this; for it would seem that Halleck has now no large organized force in front of him, while we have. If this cannot be done, or even in connexion with it, allow me to suggest the movement of a heavy column from Dalton upon Atlanta. If but the one can be done, it would better conform to military principles to strengthen this army. And even although the re-enforcements might not arrive in season to take part in the attack upon Richmond, the moral effect would be great, and they would furnish valuable assistance in ulterior movements.

"I wish to be distinctly understood that, whenever the weather permits, I will attack with whatever force I may have, although a larger force would enable me to gain much more decisive results.

"I would be glad to have McCall's infantry sent forward by water at once, without waiting for his artillery and cavalry.

"If General Prim returns *via* Washington, please converse with him as to the condition of affairs here.

"GEO. B. McCLELLAN,
"*Major General, Commanding.*

"Hon. E. M. STANTON,
"*Secretary of War.*"

Our work upon the bridges continued to be pushed forward vigorously until the 20th, during which time it rained almost every day, and the exposure of the men caused much sickness.

On the 11th the following was received from the Secretary of War:

"WASHINGTON, *June* 11, 1862.

"Your despatch of three thirty, (3.30,) yesterday, has been received. I am fully impressed with the difficulties mentioned, and which no art or skill can avoid, but only endure, and am striving to the uttermost to render you every aid in the power of the government. Your suggestions will be immediately communicated to General Halleck, with a request that he shall conform to them. At last advice he contemplated sending a column to operate with Mitchell against Chattanooga, and thence upon East Tennessee. Buel reports Kentucky and Tennessee to be in a critical condition, demanding immediate attention. Halleck says the main body of Beauregard's force is with him at Okolona. McCall's force was reported yesterday as having embarked, and on its way to join you. It is intended to send the residue of McDowell's force also to join you as speedily as possible.

"Frémont had a hard fight, day before yesterday, with Jackson's force at Union church, eight miles from Harrisonburg. He claims the victory, but was pretty badly handled. It is clear that a strong force is operating with Jackson for the purpose of detaining the forces here from you. I am urging, as fast as possible, the new levies.

"Be assured, general, that there never has been a moment when my desire has been otherwise than to aid you with my whole heart, mind, and strength, since the hour we first met; and whatever others may say for their own purposes, you have never had, and never can have, any one more truly your friend, or more anxious to support you, or more joyful than I shall be at the success which I have no doubt will soon be achieved by your arms.

"EDWIN M. STANTON,
"*Secretary of War.*

"Major General G. B. McCLELLAN."

On the 12th and 13th General McCall's division arrived.

On the 13th of June two squadrons of the 5th United States cavalry, under the command of Captain Royall, stationed near Hanover old church, were attacked and overpowered by a force of the enemy's cavalry, numbering about fifteen hundred men, with four guns. They pushed on towards our depots, but at some distance from our main body, and, though pursued very cleverly, made the circuit of the army, repassing the Chickahominy at Long bridge. The burning of two schooners laden with forage, and fourteen government wagons, the destruction of some sutlers' stores, the killing of several of the guard and teamsters at Garlick's landing, some little damage done at Tunstall's station, and a little eclat, were the precise results of this expedition.

On the 14th I sent the following to the Secretary of War:

"HEADQUARTERS ARMY OF THE POTOMAC,
"*Camp Lincoln, June 14, 1862—midnight.*

"All quiet in every direction. The stampede of last night has passed away. Weather now very favorable. I hope two days more will make the ground practicable. I shall advance as soon as the bridges are completed and the ground fit for artillery to move. At the same time I would be glad to have whatever troops can be sent to me. I can use several new regiments to advantage.

"It ought to be distinctly understood that McDowell and his troops are completely under my control. I received a telegram from him requesting that McCall's division might be placed so as to join him immediately on his arrival.

"That request does not breathe the proper spirit. Whatever troops come to me must be disposed of so as to do the most good. I do not feel that, in such circumstances as those in which I am now placed, General McDowell should wish the general interests to be sacrificed for the purpose of increasing his command.

"If I cannot fully control all his troops, I want none of them, but would prefer to fight the battle with what I have, and let others be responsible for the results.

"The department lines should not be allowed to interfere with me; but General McD., and all other troops sent to me, should be placed completely at my disposal, to do with them as I think best. In no other way can they be of assistance to me. I therefore request that I may have entire and full control. The stake at issue is too great to allow personal considerations to be entertained; you know that I have none.

"The indications are, from our balloon reconnoissances and from all other sources, that the enemy are intrenching, daily increasing in numbers, and determined to fight desperately.

"G. B. McCLELLAN,
"*Major General, Commanding.*

"Hon. E. M. STANTON,
"*Secretary of War.*"

On the 20th the following was communicated to the President:

"HEADQUARTERS ARMY OF THE POTOMAC,
"*Camp Lincoln, June* 20, 1862—2 *p. m.*

"Your excellency's despatch of (11) eleven a. m. received, also that of General Sigel.

"I have no doubt that Jackson has been re-enforced from here. There is reason to believe that General R. S. Ripley has recently joined Lee's army, with a brigade or division from Charleston. Troops have arrived recently from Goldsboro'. There is not the slightest reason to suppose that the enemy intends evacuating Richmond; he is daily increasing his defences. I find him everywhere in force, and every reconnoissance costs many lives, yet I am obliged to feel my way, foot by foot, at whatever cost, so great are the difficulties of the country; by to-morrow night the defensive works, covering our position on this side of the Chickahominy, should be completed. I am forced to this by my inferiority in numbers, so that I may bring the greatest possible numbers into action, and secure the army against the consequences of unforeseen disaster. I would be glad to have permission to lay before your excellency, by letter or telegraph, my views as to the present state of military affairs throughout the whole country. In the mean time I would be pleased to learn the disposition, as to numbers and position, of the troops not under my command, in Virginia and elsewhere.

"GEORGE B. McCLELLAN,
"*Major General, Commanding.*

"His Excellency A. LINCOLN, *President.*"

To which I received this reply:

"WASHINGTON, *June* 21, 1862—6 *p. m.*

"Your despatch of yesterday, two (2) p. m., was received this morning. If it would not divert too much of your time and attention from the army under your immediate command, I would be glad to have your views as to the present state of military affairs throughout the whole country, as you say you would be glad to give them. I would rather it should be by letter than by telegraph, because of the better chance of secrecy. As to the numbers and positions of the troops not under your command, in Virginia and elsewhere, even if I could do it with accuracy, which I cannot, I would rather not transmit either by telegraph or letter, because of the chances of its reaching the enemy. I would be very glad to talk with you, but you cannot leave your camp, and I cannot well leave here.

"A. LINCOLN, *President.*

"Major General GEORGE B. McCLELLAN."

To which I sent the following reply:

"CAMP LINCOLN, *June* 22—1 *p. m.*

"I have the honor to acknowledge the receipt of your telegram of 8 p. m. yesterday. Under the circumstances, as stated in your despatch, I perceive that it will be better at least to defer, for the present, the communication I desired to make.

"G. B. McCLELLAN,
"*Major General, Commanding.*

"His Excellency the PRESIDENT."

All the information I could obtain, previous to the 24th of June, regarding the movements of General Jackson, led to the belief that he was at Gordonsville, where he was receiving re-enforcements from Richmond *via* Lynchburg and Stanton; but what his purposes were did not appear until the date specified, when a young man, very intelligent, but of suspicious appearance, was brought in by our scouts from the direction of Hanover Court House. He at first stated that he was an escaped prisoner, from Colonel Kenley's Maryland regiment, captured at Front Royal, but finally confessed himself to be a deserter from Jackson's command, which he left near Gordonsville on the 21st. Jackson's troops were then, as he said, moving to Frederickshall, along the Virginia Central railroad, for the purpose of attacking my rear on the 28th. I immediately despatched two trusty negroes to proceed along the railroad and ascertain the truth of the statement. They were unable, however, to get beyond Hanover Court House, where they encountered the enemy's pickets, and were forced to turn back without obtaining the desired information. On that day I sent the following despatch:

"HEADQUARTERS ARMY OF THE POTOMAC,
"*June* 24, 1862—12 *p. m.*

"A very peculiar case of desertion has just occurred from the enemy. The party states that he left Jackson, Whiting and Ewell, (fifteen brigades,) at Gordonsville on the 21st; that they were moving to Frederickshall, and that it was intended to attack my rear on the 28th. I would be glad to learn, at your earliest convenience, the most exact information you have as to the position and movements of Jackson, as well as the sources from which your information is derived, that I may the better compare it with what I have.

"G. B. McCLELLAN,
"*Major General.*"

The following is his reply:

"WASHINGTON, *June* 25, 1862.

"We have no definite information as to the numbers or position of Jackson's force. General King yesterday reported a deserter's statement that Jackson's force was, nine days ago, forty thousand men. Some reports place ten thousand rebels under Jackson, at Gordonsville; others, that his force is at Port Republic, Harrisonburg, and Luray. Frémont yesterday reported rumors that Western Virginia was threatened; and General Kelly, that Ewell was advancing to New creek, where Frémont has his depots. The last telegram from Frémont contradicts this rumor. The last telegram from Banks says the enemy's pickets are strong in advance at Luray; the people decline to give any information of his whereabouts. Within the last two (2) days the evidence is strong that for some purpose the enemy is circulating rumors of Jackson's advance in various directions, with a view to conceal the real point of attack. Neither McDowell, who is at Manassas, nor Banks and Frémont, who are at Middletown, appear to have any accurate knowledge of the subject. A letter transmitted to the department yesterday, purported to be dated Gordonsville on the fourteenth (14th) instant, stated that the actual attack was designed for Washington and Baltimore as soon as you attacked Richmond, but that the report was to be circulated that Jackson had gone to Richmond, in order to mislead. This letter looked very much like a blind, and induces me to suspect that Jackson's real movement now is towards Richmond. It came from Alexandria, and is certainly designed, like the numerous rumors put afloat, to mislead. I think, therefore, that while the warning of the deserter to you may also be a blind, that it could not safely be disregarded. I will transmit to you any further information on this subject that may be received here.

"EDWIN M. STANTON,
"*Secretary of War.*

"Major General McCLELLAN."

On the 25th, our bridges and intrenchments being at last completed, an advance of our picket line of the left was ordered, preparatory to a general forward movement.

Immediately in front of the most advanced redoubt on the Williamsburg road was a large open field; beyond that, a swampy belt of timber, some five hundred yards wide, which had been disputed ground for many days. Further in advance was an open field, crossed by the Williamsburg road and the railroad, and commanded by a redoubt and rifle-pits of the enemy.

It was decided to push our lines to the other side of these woods, in order to enable us to ascertain the nature of the ground, and to place Generals Heintzelman and Sumner in position to support the attack intended to be made on the Old Tavern, on the 26th or 27th, by General Franklin, by assailing that position in the rear.

Between 8 and 9 o'clock, on the morning of the 25th, the advance was begun by General Heintzelman's corps. The enemy were found to be in strong force all along the line, and contested the advance stubbornly, but by sunset our object was accomplished. The troops engaged in this affair were the whole of Heintzelman's corps, Palmer's brigade of Couch's division of Keyes's corps, and a part of Richardson's division of Sumner's corps. For the details I refer to the report of General Heintzelman.

The casualties (not including those in Palmer's brigade, which have not been reported) were as follows: officers killed, 1; wounded, 14; missing, 1; enlisted men killed, 50; wounded, 387; missing, 63; total, 516.

The following telegrams were sent to the Secretary of War, during the day, from the field of operations:

"REDOUBT No. 3, *June* 25, 1862—1.30 *p. m.*

"We have advanced our pickets on the left considerably, under sharp resistance. Our men behaved very handsomely. Some firing still continues.

"G. B. McCLELLAN,
"*Major General, Commanding.*

"Hon. E. M. STANTON."

"REDOUBT No. 3, *June* 25, 1862—3.15 *p. m.*

"The enemy are making a desperate resistance to the advance of our picket's lines. Kearney's and one-half of Hooker's are where I want them.

"I have this moment re-enforced Hooker's right with a brigade and a couple of guns, and hope in a few minutes to finish the work intended for to-day. Our men are behaving splendidly. The enemy are fighting well also. This is not a battle; merely an affair of Heintzelman's corps, supported by Keyes, and thus far all goes well. We hold every foot we have gained.

"If we succeed in what we have undertaken, it will be a very important advantage gained. Loss not large thus far. The fighting up to this time has been done by General Hooker's division, which has behaved as usual—that is, most splendidly.

"On our right, Porter has silenced the enemy's batteries in his front.

"G. B. McCLELLAN,
"*Major General, Commanding.*

"Hon. E. M. Stanton,
"*Secretary of War.*"

"Redoubt No. 3, *June* 25, 1862—5 *p. m.*

"The affair is over, and we have gained our point fully, and with but little loss, notwithstanding the strong opposition. Our men have done all that could be desired. The affair was partially decided by two guns that Captain De Russey brought gallantly into action under very difficult circumstances. The enemy was driven from the camps in front of this place, and is now quiet.

"G. B. McCLELLAN,
"*Major General, Commanding.*

"Hon. E. M. Stanton,
"*Secretary of War.*"

Also, on the same day, the following:

"Headquarters Army of the Potomac,
"*Camp Lincoln, June* 25, 1862—6.15 *p. m.*

"I have just returned from the field, and find your despatch in regard to Jackson.

"Several contrabands, just in, give information confirming the supposition that Jackson's advance is at or near Hanover Court House, and that Beauregard arrived, with strong re-enforcements, in Richmond, yesterday.

"I incline to think that Jackson will attack my right and rear. The rebel force is stated at two hundred thousand (200,000,) including Jackson and Beauregard. I shall have to contend against vastly superior odds if these reports be true. But this army will do all in the power of men to hold their position, and repulse any attack.

"I regret my great inferiority in numbers, but feel that I am in no way responsible for it, as I have not failed to represent repeatedly the necessity of re-enforcements, that this was the decisive point, and that all the available means of the government should be concentrated here. I will do all that a general can do with the splendid army I have the honor to command, and, if it is destroyed by overwhelming numbers, can at least die with it and share its fate. But if the result of the action which will probably occur to-morrow, or within a short time, is a disaster, the responsibility cannot be thrown on my shoulders; it must rest where it belongs.

"Since I commenced this I have received additional intelligence confirming the supposition in regard to Jackson's movements and Beauregard's arrival. I shall probably be attacked to-morrow, and now go to the other side of the Chickahominy to arrange for the defence on that side. I feel that there is no use in again asking for re-enforcements.

"G. B. McCLELLAN,
"*Major General.*

"Hon. E. M. Stanton,
"*Secretary of War.*"

The report of the chief of the "secret service corps," herewith forwarded, and dated the 26th of June, shows the estimated strength of the enemy, at the time of the evacuation of Yorktown, to have been from 100,000 to 120,000. The same report puts his numbers, on the 26th of June, at about 180,000, and the specific information obtained regarding their organization warrants the belief that this estimate did not exceed his actual strength. It will be observed that the evidence contained in the report shows the following organizations, viz: two hundred regiments of infantry and cavalry, including the forces of Jackson and Ewell, just arrived; eight battalions of independent troops; five battalions of artillery; twelve companies of infantry and independent cavalry, besides forty-six companies of artillery; amounting, in all, to from forty to fifty brigades. There were undoubtedly many others whose designations we did not learn.

The report also shows that numerous and heavy earthworks had been completed for the defence of Richmond, and that in thirty-six of these were mounted some two hundred guns.

On the 26th, the day upon which I had decided as the time for our final advance, the enemy attacked our right in strong force, and turned my attention to the protection of our communications and depots of supply.

The event was a bitter confirmation of the military judgment which had been reiterated to my superiors from the inception and through the progress of the Peninsula campaign.

I notified the Secretary of War in the following despatch:

"HEADQUARTERS ARMY OF THE POTOMAC,
"*Camp Lincoln, June* 26, 1862—12 *m.*

"I have just heard that our advanced cavalry pickets on the left bank of Chickahominy are being driven in. It is probably Jackson's advanced guard. If this be true, you may not hear from me for some days, as my communications will probably be cut off. The case is perhaps a difficult one, but I shall resort to desperate measures, and will do my best to out-manœuvre, out-wit, and out-fight the enemy. Do not believe reports of disaster, and do not be discouraged if you learn that my communications are cut off, and even Yorktown in possession of the enemy. Hope for the best, and I will not deceive the hopes you formerly placed in me.

"G. B. McCLELLAN,
"*Major General.*

"Hon. E. M. STANTON,
"*Secretary of War.*"

"HEADQUARTERS ARMY OF THE POTOMAC,
"*Camp Lincoln, June* 26, 1862—2.30 *p. m.*

"Your despatch and that of the President received. Jackson is driving in my pickets, &c., on the other side of the Chickahominy. It is impossible to tell where re-enforcements ought to go, as I am yet unable to predict result of approaching battle. It will probably be better that they should go to Fort Monroe, and thence according to state of affairs when they arrive.

"It is not probable that I can maintain telegraphic communication more than an hour or two longer.

"G. B. McCLELLAN,
"*Major General.*

"Hon. E. M. STANTON,
"*Secretary of War.*"

On the same day I received the following despatches from the Secretary of War:

"WASHINGTON, *June* 25, 1862—11.20 *p. m.*

"Your telegram of 6.15 has just been received. The circumstances that have hitherto rendered it impossible for the government to send you any more re-enforcements than has been done, have been so distinctly stated to you by the President that it is needless for me to repeat them.

"Every effort has been made by the President and myself to strengthen you. King's division has reached Falmouth, Shields's division and Ricketts's division are at Manassas. The President designs to send a part of that force to aid you as speedily as it can be done.

"E. M. STANTON,
"*Secretary of War.*

"Major General G. B. McCLELLAN."

"WASHINGTON, *June* 26, 1862—6 *p. m.*

"Arrangements are being made as rapidly as possible to send you five thousand (5,000) men as fast as they can be brought from Manassas to Alexandria and embarked, which can be done sooner than to wait for transportation at Fredericksburg. They will be followed by more, if needed. McDowell, Banks, and Frémont's force will be consolidated as the army of Virginia, and will operate promptly in your aid by land. Nothing will be spared to sustain you, and I have undoubting faith in your success. Keep me advised fully of your condition.

"EDWIN M. STANTON,
"*Secretary of War.*

"Major General G. B. McCLELLAN."

But 5,000 of the re enforcements spoken of in these communications came to the army of the Potomac, and these reached us at Harrison's bar, after the seven days.

In anticipation of a speedy advance on Richmond, to provide for the contingency of our communications with the depot at the White House being severed by the enemy, and at the same time to be prepared for a change of the base of our operations to James river, if circumstances should render it advisable, I had made arrangements more than a week previous (on the 18th) to have transports with supplies of provisions and forage, under a convoy of gunboats, sent up James river. They reached Harrison's landing in time to be available for the army on its arrival at that point. Events soon proved this change of base to be, though most hazardous and difficult, the only prudent course.

In order to relieve the troops of the 6th corps, on the 19th of June General Reynolds's and General Seymour's brigades, of General McCall's division, (Pennsylvania reserves,) were moved from Gaines's farm to a position on Beaver Dam creek, General Meade's brigade being held in reserve in front of Gaines's farm. One regiment and a battery were thrown forward to the heights overlooking Mechanicsville, and a line of pickets extended along the Chickahominy river between the Mechanicsville and Meadow bridges. As has been already stated, I received, while engaged on the 25th in directing the operations of Heintzelman's corps, information which strengthened my suspicions that Jackson was advancing with a large force upon our right and rear. On this day General Casey, at the White House, was instructed to prepare for a vigorous resistance, and defensive works were ordered at Tunstall's station. Early on the 25th General Porter was instructed to send out reconnoitring parties towards Hanover Court House to discover the position and force of the enemy, and to destroy the bridges on the Tolopotamoy as far as possible.

Up to the 26th of June the operations against Richmond had been conducted along the roads leading to it from the east and northeast. The reasons (the President's anxiety about covering Washington from Fredericksburg, McDowell's promised co-operation, partial advance, and immediate withdrawal) which compelled the choice of this line of approach, and our continuance upon it, have been attended to above.

The superiority of the James river route, as a line of attack and supply, is too obvious to need exposition. My own opinion on that subject had been early given, and need not be repeated here. The dissipation of all hope of the co-operation by land of General McDowell's forces, deemed to be occupied in the defence of Washington, their inability to hold or defeat Jackson, disclosed an opportunity to the enemy, and a new danger to my right, and to the long line of supplies from the White House to the Chickahominy, and forced an immediate change of base across the Peninsula. To that end, from the evening of the 26th, every energy of the army was bent. Such a change of base, in the presence of a powerful enemy, is one of the most difficult undertakings in war. I was confident of the valor and discipline of my brave army, and knew that it could be trusted equally to retreat or advance, and to fight the series of battles now inevitable, whether retreating from victories or marching through defeats; and, in short, I had no doubt whatever of its ability, even against superior numbers, to fight its way through to the James river, and get a position whence a successful advance upon Richmond would be again possible. Their superb conduct through the next seven days justified my faith.

On the same day General Van Vliet, chief quartermaster of the army of the Potomac, by my orders, telegraphed to Colonel Ingalls, quartermaster at the White House, as follows: "Run the cars to the last moment, and load them with provisions and ammunition. Load every wagon you have with subsistence, and send them to Savage's station, by way of Bottom's bridge. If you are obliged to abandon White House, burn everything that you cannot get off. You must throw all our supplies up the James river as soon as possible, and accompany them yourself with all your force. It will be of vast importance to establish our depots on James river without delay if we abandon White House. I will keep you advised of every movement so long as the wires work; after that you must exercise your own judgment."

All these commands were obeyed. So excellent were the dispositions of the different officers in command of the troops, depots, and gunboats, and so timely the warning of the approach of the enemy, that almost everything was saved, and but a small amount of stores destroyed to prevent their falling into the hands of the enemy.

General Stoneman's communications with the main army being cut off, he fell back upon the White House, and thence to Yorktown, when the White House was evacuated.

On the 26th orders were sent to all the corps commanders on the right bank of the Chickahominy to be prepared to send as many troops as they could spare on the following day to the left bank of the river, as will be seen by the appended telegrams. General Franklin received instructions to hold General Slocum's division in readiness by daybreak of the 27th, and if heavy firing should at that time be heard in the direction of General Porter, to move at once to his assistance without further orders.

At noon on the 26th the approach of the enemy, who had crossed above Meadow bridge, was discovered by the advanced pickets at that point, and at 12.30 p. m. they were attacked and driven in. All the pickets were now called in, and the regiment and battery at Mechanicsville withdrawn.

Meade's brigade was ordered up as a reserve in rear of the line, and shortly after Martindale's and Griffin's brigades, of Morell's division, were moved forward and deployed on the right of McCall's division, towards Shady Grove church, to cover that flank. Neither of these three brigades, however, were warmly engaged, though two of Griffin's regiments relieved a portion of Reynolds's line just at the close of the action.

The position of our troops was a strong one, extending along the left bank of Beaver Dam creek, the left resting on the Chickahominy, and the righ in thick woods beyond the upper road from Mechanicsville to Coal Harbor. The lower or river road crossed the creek at Ellison's mills. Seymour's brigade held the left of the line from the Chickahominy to beyond the mill, partly in woods and partly in clear ground, and Reynolds's the right, principally in the woods and covering the upper road. The artillery occupied positions commanding the roads and the open ground across the creek.

Timber had been felled, rifle-pits dug, and the position generally prepared with a care that greatly contributed to the success of the day. The passage of the creek was difficult along the whole front, and impracticable for artillery, except by the two roads where the main efforts of the enemy were directed.

At 3 p. m. he formed his line of battle, rapidly advanced his skirmishers, and soon attacked our whole line, making at the same time a determined attempt to force the passage of the upper road, which was successfully resisted by General Reynolds. After a severe struggle he was forced to retire with very heavy loss.

A rapid artillery fire, with desultory skirmishing, was maintained along the whole front, while the enemy massed his troops for another effort at the lower road about two hours later, which was likewise repulsed by General Seymour with heavy slaughter.

The firing ceased, and the enemy retired about 9 p. m., the action having lasted six hours, with entire success to our arms. But few, if any, of Jackson's troops were engaged on this day. The portion of the enemy encountered were chiefly from the troops on the right bank of the river, who crossed near Meadow bridge and at Mechanicsville.

The information in my possession soon after the close of this action convinced me that Jackson was really approaching in large force. The position on Beaver Dam creek, although so successfully defended, had its right flank too much in the air, and was too far from the main army to make it available to retain it longer. I therefore determined to send the heavy guns at Hogan's and Gaines's houses over the Chickahominy during the night, with as many of the wagons of the 5th corps as possible, and to withdraw the corps itself to a position stretching around the bridges, where its flanks would be reasonably secure, and it would be within supporting distance of the main army. General Porter carried out my orders to that effect.

It was not advisable at that time, even had it been practicable, to withdraw the 5th corps to the right bank of the Chickahominy. Such a movement would have exposed the rear of the army, placed as between two fires, and enabled Jackson's fresh troops to interrupt the movement to James river, by crossing the Chickahominy in the vicinity of Jones's bridge before we could reach Malvern hill with our trains. I determined then to resist Jackson with the 5th corps, re-enforced by all our disposable troops in the new position near the bridge heads, in order to cover the withdrawal of the trains and heavy guns, and to give time for the arrangements to secure the adoption of the James river as our line of supplies in lieu of the Pamunkey.

The greater part of the heavy guns and wagons having been removed to the right bank of the Chickahominy, the delicate operation of withdrawing the troops from Beaver Dam creek was commenced shortly before daylight, and successfully executed.

Meade's and Griffin's brigades were the first to leave the ground; Seymour's brigade covered the rear with the horse batteries of Captains Robertson and Tidball, but the withdrawal was so skilful and gradual, and the repulse of the preceding day so complete, that although the enemy followed the retreat closely, and some skirmishing occurred, he did not appear in front of the new line in force till about noon of the 27th, when we were prepared to receive him.

About this time General Porter, believing that General Stoneman would be cut off from him, sent him orders to fall back on the White House, and afterwards rejoin the army as best he could.

On the morning of the 27th of June, during the withdrawal of his troops from Mechanicsville to the selected position already mentioned, General Porter telegraphed as follows:

"I hope to do without aid, though I request that Franklin, or some other command, be held ready to re-enforce me. The enemy are so close that I expect to be hard pressed in front. I hope to have a portion in position to cover the retreat. This is a delicate movement, but relying on the good qualities of the commanders of divisions and brigades, I expect to get back and hold the new line."

This shows how closely Porter's retreat was followed.

Notwithstanding all the efforts used during the entire night to remove the heavy guns and wagons, some of the siege guns were still in position at Gaines's house after sunrise, and were finally hauled off by hand. The new position of the 5th corps was about an arc of a circle, covering the approaches to the bridges which connected our right wing with the troops on the opposite side of the river.

Morell's division held the left of the line in a strip of woods on the left bank of the Gaines's mill stream, resting its left flank on the descent to the Chickahominy, which was swept by our artillery on both sides of the river, and extending into open ground on the right towards New Coal Harbor. In this line General Butterfield's brigade held the extreme left, General Martindale's joined his right, and General Griffin, still further to the right, joined the left of General Sykes's division, which, partly in woods and partly in open ground, extended in the rear of Coal Harbor.

Each brigade had in reserve two of its own regiments. McCall's division having been engaged on the day before, was formed in a second line in the rear of the first, Meade's brigade on the left near the Chickahominy, Reynolds's brigade on the right, covering the approaches from Coal Harbor and Despatch station to Sumner's bridge, and Seymour's in reserve to the second line, still further in rear. General P. St. George Cooke, with five companies of the 5th regular cavalry, two squadrons of the 1st regular and three squadrons of the 6th Pennsylvania cavalry, (lancers,) was posted behind a hill in rear of the position, and near the Chickahominy, to aid in watching the left flank and defending the slope to the river.

The troops were all in position by noon, with the artillery on the commanding ground, and in the intervals between the divisions and brigades. Besides the division batteries, there were Robertson's and Tidball's horse batteries, from the artillery reserve; the latter posted on the right of Sykes's division, and the former on the extreme left of the line, in the valley of the Chickahominy. Shortly after noon the enemy were discovered approaching in force, and it soon became evident that the entire position was to be attacked. His skirmishers advanced rapidly, and soon the firing became heavy along our whole front. At 2 p. m., General Porter asked for re-enforcements. Slocum's division of the 6th corps was ordered to cross to the left bank of the river, by Alexander's bridge, and proceed to his support.

General Porter's first call for reinforcements, through General Barnard, did not reach me, nor his demand for more axes, through the same officer.

By 3 p. m. the engagement had become so severe, and the enemy were so greatly superior in numbers, that the entire second line and reserves had been moved forward to sustain the first line against repeated and desperate assaults along our whole front.

At 3.30 p. m. Slocum's division reached the field and was immediately brought into action at the weak points of our line.

On the left the contest was for the strip of woods running almost at right angles to the Chickahominy, in front of Adams's house, or between that and Gaines's house. The enemy several times charged up to this wood, but were each time driven back with heavy loss. The regulars, of Sykes's division, on the right, also repulsed several strong attacks.

But our own loss under the tremendous fire of such greatly superior numbers was very severe, and the troops, most of whom had been under arms more than two days, were rapidly becoming exhausted by the masses of fresh men constantly brought against them.

When General Slocum's division arrived on the ground it increased General Porter's force to some 35,000, who were probably contending against about 70,000 of the enemy. The line was severely pressed in several points, and as its being pierced at any one would have been fatal, it was unavoidable for General Porter, who was required to hold his position until night, to divide Slocum's division, and send parts of it, even single regiments, to the points most threatened.

About 5 p. m., General Porter having reported his position as critical, French's and Meagher's brigades, of Richardson's division, (3d corps,) were ordered to cross to his support. The enemy attacked again in great force at 6 p. m., but failed to break our lines, though our loss was very heavy.

About 7 p. m. they threw fresh troops against General Porter with still greater fury, and finally gained the woods held by our left. This reverse, aided by the confusion that followed an unsuccessful charge by five companies of the 5th cavalry, and followed as it was by more determined assaults on the remainder of our lines, now outflanked, caused a general retreat from our position to the hill in rear overlooking the bridge.

French's and Meagher's brigades now appeared, driving before them the stragglers who were thronging towards the bridge.

These brigades advanced boldly to the front, and by their example, as well as by the steadiness of their bearings reanimated our own troops and warned the enemy that re-enforcements had arrived. It was now dusk. The enemy, already repulsed several times with terrible slaughter, and hearing the shouts of the fresh troops, failed to follow up their advantage. This gave an opportunity to rally our men behind the brigades of Generals French and Meagher, and they again advanced up the hill ready to repulse another attack. During the night our thin and exhausted regiments were all withdrawn in safety, and by the following morning all had reached the other side of the stream. The regular infantry formed the rear guard, and about 6 o'clock on the morning of the 28th crossed the river, destroying the bridge behind them.

Our loss in this battle in killed, wounded, and missing, was very heavy, especially in officers, many of whom were killed, wounded, or, taken prisoners while gallantly leading on their men or rallying them to renewed exertions.

It is impossible to arrive at the exact numbers lost in this desperate engagement, owing to the series of battles which followed each other in quick succession, and in which the whole army was engaged. No general returns were made until after we had arrived at Harrison's landing, when the losses during the whole seven days were estimated together.

Although we were finally forced from our first line after the enemy had been repeatedly driven back, yet the objects sought for had been obtained. The enemy was held at bay. Our siege guns and material were saved, and the right wing had now joined the main body of the army.

The number of guns captured by the enemy at this battle was 22, three of which were lost by being run off the bridge during the final withdrawal.

Great credit is due for the efficiency and bravery with which this important arm of the service (the artillery) was fought, and it was not until the last successful charge of the enemy that the cannoneers were driven from their pieces or struck down, and the guns captured. Deidrich's, Knierim's, and Grimm's batteries took position during the engagement in the front of General Smith's line on the right bank of the stream, and with a battery of siege guns, served by the 1st Connecticut artillery, helped to drive back the enemy in front of General Porter.

So threatening were the movements of the enemy on both banks of the Chickahominy, that it was impossible to decide until the afternoon where the real attack would be made. Large forces of infantry were seen during the day near the old tavern, on Franklin's right, and threatening demonstrations were frequently made along the entire line on this side of the river, which rendered it necessary to hold a considerable force in position to meet them.

On the 26th a circular was sent to the corps commanders, on the right bank of the river, asking them how many of their troops could be spared to re-enforce General Porter, after retaining sufficient to hold their positions for twenty-four hours.

To this the following replies were received:

"HEADQUARTERS THIRD CORPS,
"*June 26—4 p. m.*

"I think I can hold the intrenchments with four brigades for twenty-four hours. That would leave two brigades disposable for service on the other side of the river, but the men are so tired and worn out that I fear they would not be in a condition to fight after making a march of any distance. * * *

"S. P. HEINTZELMAN,
"*Brigadier General.*

"General R. B. MARCY."

Telegrams from General Heintzelman, on the 25th and 26th, had indicated that the enemy was in large force in front of Generals Hooker and Kearney, and on the Charles City road, (Longstreet, Hill, and Huger,) and General Heintzelman expressed the opinion, on the night of the 25th, that he could not hold his advanced position without re-enforcements.

General Keyes telegraphed:

"As to how many men will be able to hold this position for twenty-four hours, I must answer, all I have, if the enemy is as strong as ever in front, it having at all times appeared to me that our forces on this flank are small enough."

On the morning of the 27th, the following despatch was sent to General Sumner:

"HEADQUARTERS ARMY OF THE POTOMAC,
"*June 27—8.45 a. m.*

"General Smith just reports that six or eight regiments have moved down to the woods in front of General Sumner.

"R. B. MARCY,
"*Chief of Staff.*

"General E. V. SUMNER,
"*Comd'g Second Army Corps.*"

At 11 o'clock a. m. General Sumner telegraphed, as follows:

"The enemy threaten an attack on my right, near Smith."

At 12.30 p. m. he telegraphed:

"Sharp shelling on both sides."

At 2.45 p. m.:

"Sharp musketry firing in front of Burns; we are replying with artillery and infantry. The man on the lookout reports some troops drawn up in line of battle about opposite my right and Smith's left; the number cannot be made out."

In accordance with orders given on the night of the 26th, General Slocum's division commenced crossing the river to support General Porter soon after daybreak on the morning of the 27th; but as the firing in front of General Porter ceased, the movement was suspended. At 2 p. m. General Porter called for re-enforcements. I ordered them at once, and at 3.25 p. m. sent him the following:

"Slocum is now crossing Alexander's bridge with his whole command; enemy has commenced an infantry attack on Smith's left; I have ordered down Sumner's and Heintzelman's reserves, and you can count on the whole of Slocum's. Go on as you have begun."

During the day the following despatches were received, which will show the condition of affairs on the right bank of the Chickahominy:

"JUNE 27, 1862.

"General Smith thinks the enemy are massing heavy columns in the clearings to the right of James Garnett's house, and on the other side of the river opposite it. Three regiments are reported to be moving from Sumner's to Smith's front. The arrangements are very good, made by Smith.

"W. B. FRANKLIN,
"*Brigadier General.*

"Colonel A. V. COLBURN,
"*Assistant Adjutant General.*"

Afterwards he telegraphed:

"The enemy has begun an attack on Smith's left with infantry. I know no details."

Afterwards the following:

"The enemy has opened on Smith from a battery of three pieces to the right of the White House. Our shells are bursting well, and Smith thinks Sumner will soon have a cross fire upon them that will silence them."

Afterwards (at 5.50 p. m.) the following was sent to General Keyes:

"Please send one brigade of Couch's division to these headquarters, without a moment's delay. A staff officer will be here to direct the brigade where to go."

Subsequently the following was sent to Generals Sumner and Franklin:

"Is there any sign of the enemy being in force in your front? Can you spare any more force to be sent to General Porter? Answer at once."

At 5.15 p. m. the following was received from General Franklin:

"I do not think it prudent to take any more troops from here at present."

General Sumner replied as follows:

"If the general desires to trust the defence of my position to my front line alone, I can send French with three regiments, and Meagher with his brigade. to the right; everything is so uncertain, that I think it would be hazardous to do it."

These two brigades were sent to re-enforce General Porter, as has been observed.

At 5.25 p. m. I sent the following to General Franklin:

"Porter is hard pressed; it is not a question of prudence, but of possibilities. Can you possibly maintain your position until dark with two brigades? I have ordered eight regiments of Sumner's to support Porter; one brigade of Couch's to this place.

"Heintzelman's reserve to go in rear of Sumner. If possible, send a brigade to support Porter. It should follow the regiments ordered from Sumner."

At 7.35 p. m. the following was sent to General Sumner:

"If it is possible, send another brigade to re-enforce General Smith; it is said three heavy columns of infantry are moving on him."

From the foregoing despatches it will be seen that all disposable troops were sent from the right bank of the river to re-enforce General Porter, and that the corps commanders were left with smaller forces to hold their positions than they deemed adequate. To have done more, even though Porter's reverse had been prevented, would have had the still more disastrous result of imperilling the whole movement across the Peninsula.

The operations of this day proved the numerical superiority of the enemy, and made it evident that while he had a large army on the left bank of the Chickahominy, which had already turned our right, and was in position to intercept the communications with our depot at the White House, he was also in large force between our army and Richmond; I therefore effected a junction of our forces.

This might probably have been executed on either side of the Chickahominy; and if the concentration had been effected on the left bank, it is possible we might, with our entire force, have defeated the enemy there; but at that time they held the roads leading to the White House, so that it would have been impossible to have sent forward supply trains in advance of the army in that direction, and the guarding of those trains would have seriously embarrassed our operations in the battle; we would have been compelled to fight, if concentrated on that bank of the river. Moreover, we would at once have been followed by the enemy's forces upon the Richmond side of the river operating upon our rear, and if, in the chances of war, we had been ourselves defeated in the effort, we would have been forced to fall back to the White House, and probably to Fort Monroe; and, as both our flanks and rear would then have been entirely exposed, our entire supply train, if not the greater part of the army itself, might have been lost.

The movements of the enemy showed that they expected this, and, as they themselves acknowledged, they were prepared to cut off our retreat in that direction.

I therefore concentrated all our forces on the right bank of the river.

During the night of the 26th and morning of the 27th, all our wagons, heavy guns, &c., were gathered there.

It may be asked, why, after the concentration of our forces on the right bank of the Chickahominy, with a large part of the enemy drawn away from Richmond upon the opposite side, I did not, instead of striking for James river, fifteen miles below that place, at once march directly on Richmond.

It will be remembered that at this juncture the enemy was on our rear, and there was every reason to believe that he would sever our communications with the supply depot at the White House.

We had on hand but a limited amount of rations, and if we had advanced directly on Richmond, it would have required considerable time to carry the strong works around that place, during which our men would have been destitute of food; and even if Richmond had fallen before our arms, the enemy could still have occupied our supply communications between that place and the gunboats, and turned the disaster into victory. If, on the other hand, the enemy had concentrated all his forces at Richmond during the progress of our attack, and we had been defeated, we must in all probability have lost our trains before reaching the flotilla.

The battles which continued day after day in the progress of our flank movement to the James river, with the exception of the one at Gaines's mill, were successes to our arms, and the closing engagement at Malvern hill was the most decisive of all.

On the evening of the 27th of June I assembled the corps commanders at my headquarters, and informed them of my plan, its reasons, and my choice of route and method of execution.

General Keyes was directed to move his corps, with its artillery and baggage, across the White Oak swamp bridge, and to seize strong positions on the opposite side of the swamp, to cover the passage of the other troops and trains. This was executed on the 28th by noon. Before daybreak on the 28th I went to Savage's station, and remained there during the day and night, directing the withdrawal of the trains and supplies of the army.

Orders were given to the different commanders to load their wagons with ammunition and provisions, and the necessary baggage of the officers and men, and to destroy all property which could not be transported with the army.

Orders were also given to leave with those of the sick and wounded who could not be transported, a proper complement of surgeons and attendants, with a bountiful supply of rations and medical stores.

The large herd of 2,500 beef-cattle was, by the chief commissary, Colonel Clarke, transferred to the James river without loss.

On the morning of the 28th, while General Franklin was withdrawing his command from Golding's farm, the enemy opened upon General Smith's division from Garnett's hill, from the valley above, and from Gaines's hill on the opposite side of the Chickahominy; and shortly afterwards two Georgia regiments attempted to carry the works about to be vacated, but this attack was repulsed by the 23d New York and the 49th Pennsylvania volunteers on picket, and a section of Mott's battery.

Porter's corps was moved across White Oak swamp during the day and night, and took up positions covering the roads leading from Richmond towards White Oak swamp and Long bridge. McCall's division was ordered, on the night of the 28th, to move across the swamp and take a proper position to assist in covering the remaining troops and trains.

During the same night the corps of Sumner and Heintzelman, and the division of Smith, were ordered to an interior line, the left resting on Keyes's old intrenchments, and curving to the right, so as to cover Savage's station.

General Slocum's division, of Franklin's corps, was ordered to Savage's station, in reserve.

They were ordered to hold this position until dark of the 29th, in order to cover the withdrawal of the trains, and then to fall back across the swamp and unite with the remainder of the army.

On the 28th I sent the following to the Secretary of War:

"HEADQUARTERS ARMY OF THE POTOMAC,
"*Savage's Station, June 28, 1862—12.20 a. m.*

"I now know the full history of the day. On this side of the river (the right bank) we repulsed several strong attacks. On the left bank our men did all that men could do, all that soldiers could accomplish, but they were overwhelmed by vastly superior numbers, even after I brought my last reserves into action. The loss on both sides is terrible. I believe it will prove to be the most desperate battle of the war. The sad remnants of my men behave as men. Those battalions who fought most bravely, and suffered most, are still in the best order. My regulars were superb; and I count upon what are left to turn another battle, in company with their gallant comrades of the volunteers. Had I twenty thousand (20,000,) or even ten thousand, (10,000,) fresh troops to use to-morrow, I could take Richmond; but I have not a man in reserve, and shall be glad to cover my retreat and save the material and personnel of the army.

"If we have lost the day, we have yet preserved our honor, and no one need blush for the army of the Potomac. I have lost this battle because my force was too small.

"I again repeat that I am not responsible for this, and I say it with the earnestness of a general who feels in his heart the loss of every brave man who has been needlessly sacrificed to-day. I still hope to retrieve our fortunes; but to do this the government must view the matter in the same earnest light that I do. You must send me very large re-enforcements, and send them at once. I shall draw back to this side of the Chickahominy, and think I can withdraw all our material. Please understand that in this battle we have lost nothing but men, and those the best we have.

"In addition to what I have already said, I only wish to say to the President that I think he is wrong in regarding me as ungenerous when I said that my force was too weak. I merely intimated a truth which to-day has been too plainly proved. If, at this instant, I could dispose of ten thousand (10,000) fresh men, I could gain the victory to-morrow.

"I know that a few thousand more men would have changed this battle from a defeat to a victory. As it is, the government must not and cannot hold me responsible for the result.

"I feel too earnestly to-night. I have seen too many dead and wounded comrades to feel otherwise than that the government has not sustained this army. If you do not do so now, the game is lost.

"If I save this army now, I tell you plainly that I owe no thanks to you, or to any other persons in Washington.

"You have done your best to sacrifice this army.

"G. B. McCLELLAN.

"Hon. E. M. STANTON."

The headquarters camp at Savage's station was broken up early on the morning of the 29th, and moved across White Oak swamp. As the essential part of this day's operation was the passage of the trains across the swamp, and their protection against attack from the direction of New Market and Richmond, as well as the immediate and secure establishment of our communications with the gunboats, I passed the day in examining the ground, directing the posting of troops, and securing the uninterrupted movement of the trains.

In the afternoon I instructed General Keyes to move during the night to James river, and occupy a defensive position near Malvern hill, to secure our extreme left flank.

General F. J. Porter was ordered to follow him, and prolong the line towards the right. The trains were to be pushed on towards James river in rear of these corps, and placed under the protection of the gunboats as they arrived.

A sharp skirmish with the enemy's cavalry early this day on the Quaker road showed that his efforts were about to be directed towards impeding our progress to the river, and rendered my presence in that quarter necessary.

BATTLE OF ALLEN'S FARM.

General Sumner vacated his works at Fair Oaks on June 29, at daylight, and marched his command to Orchard station, halting at Allen's field, between Orchard and Savage's station. The divisions of Richardson and Sedgwick were formed on the right of the railroad, facing towards Richmond, Richardson holding the right, and Sedgwick joining the right of Heintzelman's corps. The first line of Richardson's division was held by General French, General Caldwell supporting in the second. A log building in front of Richardson's division was held by Colonel Brooks with one regiment, (53d Pennsylvania volunteers,) with Hazzard's battery on an elevated piece of ground, a little in rear of Colonel Brooks's command.

At nine a. m. the enemy commenced a furious attack on the right of General Sedgwick, but were repulsed. The left of General Richardson was next attacked, the enemy attempting in vain to carry the position of Colonel Brooks. Captain Hazzard's battery, and Pettet's battery, which afterwards replaced it, were served with great effect, while the 53d Pennsylvania kept up a steady fire on the advancing enemy, compelling them at last to retire in disorder. The enemy renewed the attack three times, but were as often repulsed.

BATTLE OF SAVAGE'S STATION.

General Slocum arrived at Savage's station at an early hour on the 29th, and was ordered to cross White Oak swamp and relieve General Keyes's corps. As soon as General Keyes was thus relieved, he moved towards James river, which he reached in safety, with all his artillery and baggage, early on the morning of the 30th, and took up a position below Turkey creek bridge.

During the morning General Franklin heard that the enemy, after having repaired the bridges, was crossing the Chickahominy in large force, and advancing towards Savage's station. He communicated this information to General Sumner, at Allen's farm, and moved Smith's division to Savage's station. A little after noon General Sumner united his forces with those of General Franklin, and assumed command.

I had ordered General Heintzelman, with his corps, to hold the Williamsburg road until dark, at a point where were several field-works, and a skirt of timber between these works and the railroad; but he fell back before night, and crossed White Oak swamp at Brackett's ford.

General Sumner in his report of the battle of Savage's station says:

"When the enemy appeared on the Williamsburg road I could not imagine why General Heintzelman did not attack him, and not till some time afterwards did I learn, to my utter amazement, that General Heintzelman had left the field, and retreated with his whole corps (about 15,000 men) before the action commenced. This defection might have been attended with the most disastrous consequences; and although we beat the enemy signally and drove him from the field, we should certainly have given him a more crushing blow if General Heintzelman had been there with his corps."

General Heintzelman in his report of the operations of his corps says:

"On the night of the 28th of June I received orders to withdraw the troops of my corps from the advanced position they had taken on the 25th of June, and to occupy the intrenched lines about a mile in rear. A map was sent me, showing the positions General Sumner's and General Franklin's corps would occupy.

"About sunrise the next day our troops slowly fell back to the new position, cautiously followed by the enemy, taking possession of our camps as soon as we left them.

"From some misapprehension General Sumner held a more advanced position than was indicated on the map furnished me, thus leaving a space of about three-fourths of a mile between the right of his corps and General Smith's division of General Franklin's corps.

* * * * * * * *

"At 11 a. m. on the 29th the enemy commenced an attack on General Sumner's troops, a few shells falling within my lines. Late in the forenoon reports reached me that the rebels were in possession of Dr. Trent's house, only a mile and a half from Savage's station. I sent several cavalry reconnoissances, and finally was satisfied of the fact. General Franklin came to my headquarters, when I learned of the interval between his left and General Sumner's right, in which space Dr. Trent's house is; also that the rebels had repaired one of the bridges across the Chickahominy, and were advancing.

* * * * * * * *

"I rode forward to see General Sumner, and met his troops falling back on the Williamsburg road through my lines. General Sumner informed me that he intended to make a stand at Savage's station, and for me to join him to determine upon the position.

"This movement of General Sumner's uncovering my right flank, it became necessary for me to at once withdraw my troops. * * * *

"I rode back to find General Sumner. After some delay, from the mass of troops in the field, I found him, and learned that the course of action had been determined on; so I returned to give the necessary orders for the destruction of the railroad cars, ammunition, and provisions still remaining on the ground.

* * * * * * * * * *

"The whole open space near Savage's station was crowded with troops—more than I supposed could be brought into action judiciously. An aid from the commanding general had in the morning reported to me to point out a road across the White Oak swamp, starting from the left of General Kearney's position and leading by Brackett's ford. * * * * * *

"The advance of the column reached the Charles City road at 6½ p. m., and the rear at 10 p. m., without accident."

The orders given by me to Generals Sumner, Heintzelman, and Franklin were to hold the positions assigned them until dark. As stated by General Heintzelman, General Sumner did not occupy the designated position; but, as he was the senior officer present on that side of the White Oak swamp, he may have thought that the movements of the enemy justified a deviation from the letter of the orders. It appears from his report that he assumed command of all the troops near Savage's station, and determined to resist the enemy there; and that he gave General Heintzelman orders to hold the same position as I had assigned him.

The aid sent by me to General Heintzelman to point out the road across the swamp was to guide him in retiring after dark.

On reaching Savage's station, Sumner's and Franklin's commands were drawn up in line of battle in the large open field to the left of the railroad, the left resting on the edge of the woods, and the right extending down to the railroad. General Brooks, with his brigade, held the wood to the left of the field, where he did excellent service, receiving a wound, but retaining his command.

General Hancock's brigade was thrown into the woods on the right and front. At 4 p. m. the enemy commenced his attack in large force by the Williamsburg road. It was gallantly met by General Burns's brigade, supported and re-enforced by two lines in reserve, and finally by the New York 69th, Hazzard's and Pettet's batteries again doing good service. Osborn's and Bramhall's batteries also took part effectively in this action, which was continued with great obstinacy until between 8 and 9 p. m., when the enemy were driven from the field.

Immediately after the battle the orders were repeated for all the troops to fall back and cross White Oak swamp, which was accomplished during the night in good order. By midnight all the troops were on the road to White

Oak swamp bridge, General French, with his brigade, acting as rear guard, and at 5 a. m. on the 30th all had crossed and the bridge was destroyed.

On the afternoon of the 29th I gave to the corps commanders their instructions for the operations of the following day. As stated before, Porter's corps was to move forward to James river, and, with the corps of General Keyes, to occupy a position at or near Turkey Bend, on a line perpendicular to the river, thus covering the Charles City road to Richmond, opening communication with the gunboats, and covering the passage of the supply trains, which were pushed forward as rapidly as possible upon Haxall's plantation. The remaining corps were pressed onward, and posted so as to guard the approaches from Richmond, as well as the crossings of the White Oak swamp, over which the army had passed. General Franklin was ordered to hold the passage of White Oak swamp bridge, and cover the withdrawal of the trains from that point. His command consisted of his own corps, with General Richardson's division and General Naglee's brigade placed under his orders for the occasion. General Slocum's division was on the right of the Charles City road.

On the morning of the 30th I again gave to the corps commanders within reach instructions for posting their troops. I found that, notwithstanding all the efforts of my personal staff and other officers, the roads were blocked by wagons, and there was great difficulty in keeping the trains in motion.

The engineer officers whom I had sent forward on the 28th to reconnoitre the roads had neither returned nor sent me any reports or guides. Generals Keyes and Porter had been delayed—one by losing the road, and the other by repairing an old road—and had not been able to send any information. We then knew of but one road for the movement of the troops and our immense trains.

It was therefore necessary to post the troops in advance of this road as well as our limited knowledge of the ground permitted, so as to cover the movement of the trains in the rear.

I then examined the whole line from the swamp to the left, giving final instructions for the posting of the troops and the obstructions of the roads toward Richmond, and all corps commanders were directed to hold their positions until the trains had passed, after which a more concentrated position was to be taken up near James river.

Our force was too small to occupy and hold the entire line from the White Oak swamp to the river, exposed as it was to be taken in reverse by a movement across the lower part of the swamp, or across the Chickahominy, below the swamp. Moreover, the troops were then greatly exhausted, and required rest in a more secure position.

I extended my examinations of the country as far as Haxall's, looking at all the approaches to Malvern, which position I perceived to be the key to our operations in this quarter, and was thus enabled to expedite very considerably the passage of the trains, and to rectify the positions of the troops.

Everything being then quiet, I sent aids to the different corps commanders to inform them what I had done on the left, and to bring me information of the condition of affairs on the right. I returned from Malvern to Haxall's, and having made arrangements for instant communication from Malvern by signals, went on board of Captain Rodgers's gunboat, lying near, to confer with him in reference to the condition of our supply vessels, and the state of things on the river. It was his opinion that it would be necessary for the army to fall back to a position below City Point, as the channel there was so near the southern shore that it would not be possible to bring up the transports, should the enemy occupy it. Harrison's landing was, in his opinion, the nearest suitable point. Upon the termination of this interview I returned to Malvern hill, and remained there until shortly before daylight.

BATTLE OF "NELSON'S FARM," OR "GLENDALE."

On the morning of the 30th General Sumner was ordered to march with Sedgwick's division to Glendale ("Nelson's farm.") General McCall's division (Pennsylvania reserves) was halted during the morning on the New Market road, just in advance of the point where the road turns off to Quaker church. This line was formed perpendicularly to the New Market road, with Meade's brigade on the right, Seymour's on the left, and Reynolds's brigade, commanded by Colonel S. G. Simmons, of the 5th Pennsylvania, in reserve; Randall's regular battery on the right, Kern's and Cooper's batterries opposite the centre, and Dietrich's and Kanerhun's batteries of the artillery reserve on the left—all in front of the infantry line. The country in General McCall's front was an open field, intersected towards the right by the New Market road, and a small strip of timber parallel to it; the open front was about 800 yards, its depth about 1,000 yards.

On the morning of the 30th General Heintzelman ordered the bridge at Brackett's ford to be destroyed, and trees to be felled across that road and the Charles City road. General Slocum's division was to extend to the Charles City road. General Kearney's left to connect with General Slocum's left. General McCall's position was to the left of the Long bridge road, in connexion with General Kearney's left. General Hooker was on the left of General McCall. Between 12 and 1 o'clock the enemy opened a fierce cannonade upon the divisions of Smith and Richardson, and Naglee's brigade, at White Oak swamp bridge. This artillery fire was continued by the enemy through the day, and he crossed some infantry below our position. Richardson's division suffered severely. Captain Ayres directed our artillery with great effect. Captain Hazzard's battery, after losing many cannoneers, and Captain Hazzard being mortally wounded, was compelled to retire. It was replaced by Pettit's battery, which partially silenced the enemy's guns.

General Franklin held his position until after dark, repeatedly driving back the enemy in their attempts to cross the White Oak swamp.

At two o'clock in the day the enemy were reported advancing in force by the Charles City road, and at half past two o'clock the attack was made down the road on General Slocum's left, but was checked by his artillery. After this the enemy, in large force, comprising the divisions of Longstreet and A. P. Hill, attacked General McCall, whose division, after severe fighting, was compelled to retire.

General McCall, in his report of the battle, says:

* * * * * * *

"About half past two my pickets were driven in by a strong advance, after some skirmishing, without loss on our part.

"At three o'clock the enemy sent forward a regiment on the left centre and another on the right centre to feel for a weak point. They were under cover of a shower of shells, and boldly advanced, but were both driven back—on the left by the 12th regiment, and on the right by the 7th regiment.

"For nearly two hours the battle raged hotly here." * * * "At last the enemy was compelled to retire before the well-directed musketry fire of the reserves. The German batteries were driven to the rear, but I rode up and sent them back. It was, however, of little avail, and they were soon after abandoned by the cannoneers." * * * * * * *

"The batteries in front of the centre were boldly charged upon, but the enemy was speedily forced back." * * * * * * *

"Soon after this a most determined charge was made on Randall's battery by a full brigade, advancing in wedge shape, without order, but in perfect recklessness. Somewhat similar charges had, I have stated, been previously made on

Cooper's and Kern's batteries by single regiments without success, they having recoiled before the storm of cannister hurled against them. A like result was anticipated by Randall's battery, and the 4th regiment was requested not to fire until the battery had done with them.

"Its gallant commander did not doubt his ability to repel the attack, and his guns did, indeed, mow down the advancing host, but still the gaps were closed, and the enemy came in upon a run to the very muzzle of his guns.

"It was a perfect torrent of men, and they were in his battery before the guns could be removed. Two guns that were, indeed, successfully limbered, had their horses killed and wounded and were overturned on the spot, and the enemy, dashing past, drove the greater part of the 4th regiment before them.

"The left company, (B,) nevertheless, stood its ground, with its captain, Fred. A. Conrad, as did, likewise, certain men of other companies. I had ridden into the regiment and endeavored to check them, but with only partial success."

* * * * * * *

"There was no running. But my division, reduced by the previous battles to less than six thousand, (6,000,) had to contend with the divisions of Longstreet and A. P. Hill, considered two of the strongest and best among many of the confederate army, numbering that day 18,000 or 20,000 men, and it was reluctantly compelled to give way before heavier force accumulated upon them."

* * * * * * *

General Heintzelman states that about 5 o'clock p. m. General McCall's division was attacked in large force, evidently the principal attack; that in less than an hour the division gave way, and adds: "General Hooker being on his left, by moving to his right, repulsed the rebels in the handsomest manner with great slaughter. General Sumner, who was with General Sedgwick in McCall's rear, also greatly aided with his artillery and infantry in driving back the enemy. They now renewed their attack with vigor on General Kearney's left, and were again repulsed with heavy loss."

* * * * * * *

"This attack commenced about 4 p. m., and was pushed by heavy masses with the utmost determination and vigor. Captain Thompson's battery, directed with great precision, firing double charges, swept them back. The whole open space, two hundred paces wide, was filled with the enemy; each repulse brought fresh troops. The third attack was only repulsed by the rapid volleys and determined charge of the 63d Pennsylvania, Colonel Hays, and half of the 37th New York volunteers."

General McCall's troops soon began to emerge from the woods into the open field. Several batteries were in position and began to fire into the woods over the heads of our men in front. Captain DeRussy's battery was placed on the right of General Sumner's artillery with orders to shell the woods. General Burns's brigade was then advanced to meet the enemy, and soon drove him back; other troops began to return from the White Oak swamp. Late in the day, at the call of General Kearney, General Taylor's first New Jersey brigade, Slocum's division, was sent to occupy a portion of General McCall's deserted position, a battery accompanying the brigade. They soon drove back the enemy, who shortly after gave up the attack, contenting themselves with keeping up a desultory firing till late at night. Between 12 and 1 o'clock at night General Heintzelman commenced to withdraw his corps, and soon after daylight both of his divisions, with General Slocum's division and a portion of General Sumner's command, reached Malvern hill.

On the morning of the 30th General Sumner, in obedience to orders, had moved promptly to Glendale, and upon a call from General Franklin for re-enforcements, sent him two brigades, which returned in time to participate and render good service in the battle near Glendale. General Sumner says of this battle:

"The battle of Glendale was the most severe action since the battle of Fair Oaks. About 3 o'clock p. m. the action commenced, and after a furious contest, lasting till after dark, the enemy was routed at all points and driven from the field."

The rear of the supply trains and the reserve artillery of the army reached Malvern hill about 4 p. m. At about this time the enemy began to appear in General Porter's front, and at 5 o'clock advanced in large force against his left flank, posting artillery under cover of a skirt of timber, with a view to engage our force on Malvern hill, while with his infantry and some artillery he attacked Colonel Warren's brigade. A concentrated fire of about thirty guns was brought to bear on the enemy, which, with the infantry fire of Colonel Warren's command, compelled him to retreat, leaving two guns in the hands of Colonel Warren. The gunboats rendered most efficient aid at this time, and helped to drive back the enemy.

It was very late at night before my aids returned to give me the results of the day's fighting along the whole line, and the true position of affairs. While waiting to hear from General Franklin, before sending orders to Generals Sumner and Heintzelman, I received a message from the latter that General Franklin was falling back; whereupon I sent Colonel Colburn, of my staff, with orders to verify this, and if it were true, to order in Generals Sumner and Heintzelman at once. He had not gone far when he met two officers sent from General Franklin's headquarters with the information that he was falling back. Orders were then sent to General Sumner and Heintzelman to fall back also, and definite instructions were given as to the movement which was to commence on the right. The orders met these troops already en route to Malvern. Instructions were also sent to General Franklin as to the route he was to follow.

General Barnard then received full instructions for posting the troops as they arrived.

I then returned to Haxall's, and again left for Malvern soon after daybreak. Accompanied by several general officers, I once more made the entire circuit of the position, and then returned to Haxall's, whence I went with Captain Rodgers to select the final location for the army and its depots. I returned to Malvern before the serious fighting commenced, and after riding along the lines, and seeing most cause to feel anxious about the right, remained in that vicinity.

BATTLE OF MALVERN HILL.

The position selected for resisting the further advance of the enemy on the 1st of July was with the left and centre of our lines resting on Malvern hill, while the right curved backwards through a wooded country towards a point below Haxall's, on James river. Malvern hill is an elevated plateau about a mile and a half by three-fourths of a mile in area, well cleared of timber, and with several converging roads running over it. In front are numerous defensible ravines, and the ground slopes gradually toward the north and east to the woodland, giving clear ranges for artillery in those directions. Towards the northwest the plateau falls off more abruptly into a ravine which extends to James river. From the position of the enemy his most obvious lines of attack would come from the direction of Richmond and White Oak swamp, and would almost of necessity strike us upon our left wing. Here, therefore, the lines were strengthened by massing the troops and collecting the principal part of the artillery. Porter's corps held the left of the line, (Sykes's division on the left, Morell's on the right,) with the artillery of his two divisions advantageously posted, and the artillery of the reserve so disposed on the high ground that a concentrated fire of some sixty guns could be brought to bear on any point in his front or left. Colonel Tyler also had, with great exertion, succeeded in getting ten of his siege guns in position on the highest point of the hill.

Couch's division was placed on the right of Porter; next came Kearney and Hooker; next Sedgwick and Richardson; next Smith and Slocum; then the remainder of Keyes's corps, extending by a backwood curve nearly to the river. The Pennsylvania reserve corps was held in reserve, and stationed behind Porter's and Couch's position. One brigade of Porter's was thrown to the left on the low ground to protect that flank from any movement direct from the Richmond road. The line was very strong along the whole front of the open plateau, but from thence to the extreme right the troops were more deployed. This formation was imperative, as an attack would probably be made upon our left. The right was rendered as secure as possible by slashing the timber and by barricading the roads. Commodore Rodgers, commanding the flotilla on James river, placed his gunboats so as to protect our flank, and to command the approaches from Richmond.

Between 9 and 10 a. m. the enemy commenced feeling along our whole left wing, with his artillery and skirmishers, as far to the right as Hooker's division.

About 2 o'clock a column of the enemy was observed moving towards our right, within the skirt of woods in front of Heintzelman's corps, but beyond the range of our artillery. Arrangements were at once made to meet the anticipated attack in that quarter, but, though the column was long, occupying more than two hours in passing, it disappeared, and was not again heard of. The presumption is, that it retired by the rear, and participated in the attack afterwards made on our left.

About 3 p. m. a heavy fire of artillery opened on Kearney's left and Couch's division, speedily followed up by a brisk attack of infantry on Couch's front. The artillery was replied to with good effect by our own, and the infantry of Couch's division remained lying on the ground until the advancing column was within short musket range, when they sprang to their feet and poured in a deadly volley which entirely broke the attacking force and drove them in disorder back over their own ground. This advantage was followed up until we had advanced the right of our line some seven or eight hundred yards, and rested upon a thick clump of trees, giving us a stronger position and a better fire.

Shortly after four o'clock the firing ceased along the whole front, but no disposition was evinced on the part of the enemy to withdraw from the field. Caldwell's brigade, having been detached from Richardson's division, was stationed upon Couch's right by General Porter, to whom he had been ordered to report. The whole line was surveyed by the general, and everything held in readiness to meet the coming attack. At six o'clock the enemy suddenly opened upon Couch and Porter with the whole strength of his artillery, and at once began pushing forward his columns of attack to carry the hill. Brigade after brigade, formed under cover of the woods, started at a run to cross the open space and charge our batteries, but the heavy fire of our guns, with the cool and steady volleys of our infantry, in every case sent them reeling back to shelter, and covered the ground with their dead and wounded. In several instances our infantry withheld their fire until the attacking column, which rushed through the storm of canister and shell from our artillery, had reached within a few yards of our lines. They then poured in a single volley and dashed forward with the bayonet, capturing prisoners and colors, and driving the routed columns in confusion from the field.

About 7 o'clock, as fresh troops were accumulating in front of Porter and Couch, Meagher and Sickles were sent with their brigades, as soon as it was considered prudent to withdraw any portion of Sumner's and Heintzelman's troops, to re-enforce that part of the line and hold the position. These brigades relieved such regiments of Porter's corps and Couch's division as had expended their ammunition, and batteries from the reserve were pushed forward to replace those whose boxes were empty. Until dark the enemy persisted in his efforts to take the position so tenaciously defended; but, despite his vastly superior numbers, his repeated and desperate attacks were repulsed with fearful loss, and darkness ended the battle of Malvern hill, though it was not until after 9 o'clock that the artillery ceased its fire.

During the whole battle Commodore Rodgers added greatly to the discomfiture of the enemy, by throwing shell among his reserves and advancing columns.

As the army in its movement from the Chickahominy to Harrison's landing was continually occupied in marching by night and fighting by day, its commanders found no time or opportunity for collecting data which would enable them to give exact returns of casualties in each engagement. The aggregate of our entire losses from the 26th of June to the 1st of July, inclusive, was ascertained, after arriving at Harrison's landing, to be as follows:

List of the killed, wounded, and missing in the army of the Potomac from the 26th of June to the 1st of July, 1862, *inclusive.*

Corps.	Killed.	Wounded.	Missing.	Aggregate.
1st. McCall's division*	253	1,240	1,581	3,074
2d. Sumner's	187	1,076	848	2,111
3d. Heintzelman's	189	1,051	833	2,073
4th. Keyes's	69	507	201	777
5th. Porter's	620	2,460	1,198	4,278
6th. Franklin's	245	1,313	1,179	2,737
Engineers	....	2	21	23
Cavalry	19	60	97	176
Total	1,582	7,709	5,958	15,249

* Pennsylvania reserves.

Although the result of the battle of Malvern was a complete victory, it was, nevertheless, necessary to fall back still further, in order to reach a point where our supplies could be brought to us with certainty. As before stated, in the opinion of Captain Rodgers, commanding the gunboat flotilla, this could only be done below City Point; concurring in his opinion, I selected Harrison's bar as the new position of the army. The exhaustion of our supplies of food, forage, and ammunition, made it imperative to reach the transports immediately.

The greater portion of the transportion of the army having been started for Harrison's landing during the night of the 30th of June and 1st of July, the order for the movement of the troops was at once issued upon the final repulse of the enemy at Malvern hill. The order prescribed a movement by the left and rear, General Keyes's corps to cover the manœuvre. It was not carried out in detail as regards the divisions on the left, the roads being somewhat blocked by the rear of our trains. Porter and Couch were not able to move out as early as had been anticipated, and Porter found it necessary to place a rear guard between his command and the enemy. Colonel Averill, of the 3d Pennsylvania cavalry, was intrusted with this delicate duty. He had under his command his own regiment and Lieutenant Colonel Buchanan's brigade of regular infantry and one battery. By a judicious use of the resources at his command he deceived the enemy so as to cover the withdrawal of the left wing without being attacked, remaining himself on the previous day's battle-field until about 7 o'clock of the 2d of July. Meantime General Keyes, having received his orders, commenced vigorous preparations for covering the movement of the entire army and protecting the trains. It being evident that the immense number of wagons and artillery carriages pertaining to the army could not move with celerity along a single road, General Keyes took advantage of every accident of the ground to open new avenues and to facilitate the movement. He made preparations for obstructing the roads, after the army had passed, so as to prevent any rapid pursuit, destroying effectually Turkey bridge, on the main road, and rendering other roads and approaches temporarily impassable by felling trees across them. He kept the trains well closed up, and directed the march so that the troops could move on each side of the roads, not obstructing the passage, but being in good position to repel an attack from any quarter. His dispositions were so successful that, to use his own words, "I do not think more vehicles or more public property were abandoned on the march from Turkey bridge than would have been left, in the same state of the roads, if the army had been moving toward the enemy instead of away from him. And when it is understood that the carriages and teams belonging to this army, stretched out in one line, would extend not far from forty miles, the energy and caution necessary for their safe withdrawal from the presence of an enemy, vastly superior in numbers, will be appreciated." The last of the wagons did not reach the site selected at Harrison's bar until after dark on the 3d of July, and the rear guard did not move into their camp until everything was secure. The enemy followed up with a small force, and on the 3d threw a few shells at the rear guard, but were quickly dispersed by our batteries and the fire of the gunboats.

Great credit must be awarded to General Keyes for the skill and energy which characterized his performance of the important and delicate duties intrusted to his charge.

High praise is also due to the officers and men of the 1st Connecticut artillery, Colonel Tyler, for the manner in which they withdrew all the heavy guns during the seven days, and from Malvern hill. Owing to the crowded state of the roads the teams could not be brought within a couple of miles of the position, but these energetic soldiers removed the guns by hand for that distance, leaving nothing behind.

THIRD PERIOD.

On the 1st July I received the following from the President:

"WASHINGTON, *July* 1, 1862—3.30 *p. m.*

"It is impossible to re-enforce you for your present emergency. If we had a million of men we could not get them to you in time. We have not the men to send. If you are not strong enough to face the enemy, you must find a place of security, and wait, rest and repair. Maintain your ground if you can, but save the army at all events, even if you fall back to Fort Monroe. We still have strength enough in the country, and will bring it out.

"A. LINCOLN.

"Major General G. B. McCLELLAN."

In a despatch from the President to me, on the 2d of July, he says:

"If you think you are not strong enough to take Richmond just now, I do not ask you to. Try just now to save the army, material and personnel, and I will strengthen it for the offensive again as fast as I can. The governors of eighteen States offer me a new levy of three hundred thousand, which I accept."

On the 3d of July the following kind despatch was received from the President:

[Extract.]

"WASHINGTON, *July* 3, 1862—3 *p. m.*

"Yours of 5.30 yesterday is just received. I am satisfied that yourself, officers and men, have done the best you could. All accounts say better fighting was never done. Ten thousand thanks for it.

* * * * * *

"A. LINCOLN.

"Major General G. B. McCLELLAN."

On the 4th I sent the following to the President:

"HEADQUARTERS ARMY OF THE POTOMAC,
"*Harrison's Bar, James River, July* 4, 1862.

"I have the honor to acknowledge the receipt of your despatch of the 2d instant.

"I shall make a stand at this place, and endeavor to give my men the repose they so much require.

"After sending my communication on Tuesday, the enemy attacked the left of our lines, and a fierce battle ensued, lasting until night; they were repulsed with great slaughter. Had their attack succeeded, the consequences would have been disastrous in the extreme. This closed the hard fighting which had continued from the afternoon of the 26th ultimo, in a daily series of engagements wholly unparalleled on this continent for determination and slaughter on both sides.

"The mutual loss in killed and wounded is enormous. That of the enemy certainly greatest. On Tuesday morning, the 1st, our army commenced its movement from Haxall's to this point, our line of defence there being too extended to be maintained by our weakened forces. Our train was immense, and about 4 p. m. on the 2d a heavy storm of rain began, which continued during the entire day and until the forenoon of yesterday.

"The roads became horrible. Troops, artillery, and wagons moved on steadily, and our whole army, men and material, was finally brought safe into this camp.

"The last of the wagons reached here at noon yesterday. The exhaustion was very great, but the army preserved its morale, and would have repelled any attack which the enemy was in condition to make.

"We now occupy a line of heights, about two miles from the James, a plain extending from there to the river; our front is about three miles long; these heights command our whole position, and must be maintained. The gunboats can render valuable support upon both flanks. If the enemy attack us in front we must hold our ground as we best may, and at whatever cost.

"Our positions can be carried only by overwhelming numbers. The spirit of the army is excellent; stragglers are finding their regiments, and the soldiers exhibit the best results of discipline. Our position is by no means impregnable, especially as a morass extends on this side of the high ground from our centre to the James on our right. The enemy may attack in vast numbers, and if so, our front will be the scene of a desperate battle, which, if lost, will be decisive. Our army is fearfully weakened by killed, wounded and prisoners.

"I cannot now approximate to any statement of our losses, but we were not beaten in any conflict.

"The enemy were unable, by their utmost efforts, to drive us from any field. Never did such a change of base, involving a retrograde movement, and under incessant attacks from a most determined and vastly more numerous foe, partake so little of disorder. We have lost no guns except 25 on the field of battle, 21 of which were lost by the giving way of McCall's division, under the onset of superior numbers.

"Our communications by the James river are not secure. There are points where the enemy can establish themselves with cannon or musketry and command the river, and where it is not certain that our gunboats can drive them out. In case of this, or in case our front is broken, I will still make every effort to preserve, at least, the personnel of the army, and the events of the last few days leave no question that the troops will do all that their country can ask. Send such re-enforcements as you can; I will do what I can. We are shipping our wounded and sick and landing supplies. The Navy Department should co-operate with us to the extent of its resources. Captain Rogers is doing all in his power in the kindest and most efficient manner.

"When all the circumstances of the case are known, it will be acknowledged by all competent judges that the movement just completed by this army is unparalleled in the annals of war. Under the most difficult circumstances we have preserved our trains, our guns, our material, and, above all, our honor.

"G. B. McCLELLAN,
"*Major General.*

"The PRESIDENT."

To which I received the following reply:

"WASHINGTON, *July* 5, 1862—9 *a. m.*

"A thousand thanks for the relief your two despatches, of twelve and one p. m. yesterday, gave me. Be assured the heroism and skill of yourself and officers and men is, and forever will be, appreciated.

"If you can hold your present position we shall hive the enemy yet.

"A. LINCOLN.

"Maj. Gen. G. B. McCLELLAN,
"*Commanding Army of the Potomac.*"

The following letters were received from his excellency the President:

"WAR DEPARTMENT,
"*Washington City, D. C., July* 4, 1862.

"I understand your position as stated in your letter, and by General Marcy. To re-enforce you so as to enable you to resume the offensive within a month, or even six weeks, is impossible. In addition to that arrived and now arriving from the Potomac, (about ten thousand men, I suppose,) and about ten thousand, I hope, you will have from Burnside very soon, and about five thousand from Hunter a little later, I do not see how I can send you another man within a month. Under these circumstances, the defensive, for the present, must be your only care. Save the army, first, where you are, if you *can*, and, secondly, by removal, if you must. You, on the ground, must be the judge as to which you will attempt, and of the means for effecting it. I but give it as my opinion, that with the aid of the gunboats and the re-enforcements mentioned above, you can hold your present position; provided, and so long as you can keep the James river open below you. If you are not tolerably confident you can keep the James river open, you had better remove as soon as possible. I do not remember that you have expressed any apprehension as to the danger of having your communication cut on the river below you, yet I do not suppose it can have escaped your attention.

"Yours, very truly,

"A. LINCOLN.

"Major General McCLELLAN."

"P. S.—If at any time you feel able to take the offensive, you are not restrained from doing so.

"A. L."

The following telegram was sent on the 7th:

"HEADQUARTERS ARMY OF THE POTOMAC,
"*Berkeley, July* 7, 1862—8.30 *a. m.*

"As boat is starting, I have only time to acknowledge receipt of despatch by General Marcy. Enemy have not attacked. My position is very strong, and daily becoming more so. If not attacked to-day, I shall laugh at them. I have been anxious about my communications. Had long consultation about it with Flag-Officer Goldsborough last night; he is confident he can keep river open. He should have all gunboats possible. Will see him again this morning. My men in splendid spirits and anxious to try it again.

"Alarm yourself as little as possible about me, and don't lose confidence in this army.

"G. B. McCLELLAN,
"*Major General.*

"A. LINCOLN, *President.*"

While general-in-chief, and directing the operations of all our armies in the field, I had become deeply impressed with the importance of adopting and carrying out certain views regarding the conduct of the war, which, in my judgment, were essential to its objects and its success.

During an active campaign of three months in the enemy's country, these were so fully confirmed that I conceived it a duty, in the critical position we then occupied, not to withhold a candid expression of the more important of these views from the commander-in-chief, whom the Constitution places at the head of the armies and navies, as well as of the government of the nation.

The following is a copy of my letter to Mr. Lincoln:

"HEADQUARTERS ARMY OF THE POTOMAC,
"*Camp near Harrison's Landing, Va., July* 7, 1862.

"MR. PRESIDENT: You have been fully informed that the rebel army is in the front, with the purpose of overwhelming us by attacking our positions or reducing us by blocking our river communications. I cannot but regard our condition as critical, and I earnestly desire, in view of possible contingencies, to lay before your excellency, for your private consideration, my general views concerning the existing state of the rebellion, although they do not strictly relate to the situation of this army, or strictly come within the scope of my official duties. These views amount to convictions, and are deeply impressed upon my mind and heart. Our cause must never be abandoned; it is the cause of free institutions and self-government. The Constitution and the Union must be preserved, whatever may be the cost in time, treasure, and blood. If secession is successful, other dissolutions are clearly to be seen in the future. Let neither military disaster, political faction, nor foreign war shake your settled purpose to enforce the equal operation of the laws of the United States upon the people of every State.

"The time has come when the government must determine upon a civil and military policy, covering the whole ground of our national trouble.

"The responsibility of determining, declaring, and supporting such civil and military policy, and of directing the whole course of national affairs in regard to the rebellion, must now be assumed and exercised by you, or our cause will be lost. The Constitution gives you power, even for the present terrible exigency.

"This rebellion has assumed the character of a war; as such it should be regarded, and it should be conducted upon the highest principles known to christian civilization. It should not be a war looking to the subjugation of the people of any State, in any event. It should not be at all a war upon population, but against armed forces and political organizations. Neither confiscation of property, political executions of persons, territorial organization of States, or forcible abolition of slavery should be contemplated for a moment.

"In prosecuting the war, all private property and unarmed persons should be strictly protected, subject only to the necessity of military operations; all private property taken for military use should be paid or receipted for; pillage and waste should be treated as high crimes; all unnecessary trespass sternly prohibited, and offensive demeanor by the military towards citizens promptly rebuked. Military arrests should not be tolerated, except in places where active hostilities exist; and oaths, not required by enactments, constitutionally made, should be neither demanded nor received.

"Military government should be confined to the preservation of public order and the protection of political right. Military power should not be allowed to interfere with the relations of servitude, either by supporting or impairing the authority of the master, except for repressing disorder, as in other cases. Slaves, contraband, under the act of Congress, seeking military protection, should receive it. The right of the government to appropriate permanently to its own service claims to slave labor should be asserted, and the right of the owner to compensation therefor should be recognized. This principle might be extended, upon grounds of military necessity and security, to all the slaves of a particular State, thus working manumission in such State; and in Missouri, perhaps in Western Virginia also, and possibly even in Maryland, the expediency of such a measure is only a question of time. A system of policy thus constitutional, and pervaded by the influences of Christianity and freedom, would receive the support of almost all truly loyal men, would deeply impress the rebel masses and all foreign nations, and it might be humbly hoped that it would commend itself to the favor of the Almighty.

"Unless the principles governing the future conduct of our struggle shall be made known and approved, the effort to obtain requisite forces will be almost hopeless. A declaration of radical views, especially upon slavery, will rapidly disintegrate our present armies. The policy of the government must be supported by concentrations of military power. The national forces should not be dispersed in expeditions, posts of occupation, and numerous armies, but should be mainly collected into masses, and brought to bear upon the armies of the Confederate States. Those armies thoroughly defeated, the political structure which they support would soon cease to exist.

"In carrying out any system of policy which you may form, you will require a commander-in-chief of the army, one who possesses your confidence, understands your views, and who is competent to execute your orders, by directing the military forces of the nation to the accomplishment of the objects by you proposed. I do not ask that place for myself. I am willing to serve you in such position as you may assign me, and I will do so as faithfully as ever subordinate served superior.

"I may be on the brink of eternity; and as I hope forgiveness from my Maker, I have written this letter with sincerity towards you and from love for my country.

"Very respectfully, your obedient servant,

"GEORGE B. McCLELLAN,

"*Major General, Commanding.*

"His Excellency A. LINCOLN, *President.*"

I telegraphed the President on the 11th as follows:

"HEADQUARTERS ARMY OF THE POTOMAC,
"*Berkeley, July* 11, 1862—3 *p. m.*

* * * * * *

"We are very strong here now, so far as defensive is concerned. Hope you will soon make us strong enough to advance and try it again. All in fine spirits.

"GEORGE B. McCLELLAN,
"*Major General, Commanding.*

"A. LINCOLN, *President.*"

These telegrams were sent on the 12th, 17th, and 18th, to his excellency the President:

"HEADQUARTERS ARMY OF THE POTOMAC,
"*Berkeley, July* 12, 1862—7.15 *a. m.*

"Hill and Longstreet crossed into New Kent county, *via* Long bridge. I am still ignorant what road they afterwards took, but will know shortly.

"Nothing else of interest since last despatch. Rain ceased, and everything quiet. Men resting well, but beginning to be impatient for another fight.

"I am more and more convinced that this army ought not to be withdrawn from here, but promptly re-enforced and thrown again upon Richmond. If we have a little more than half a chance we can take it.

"I dread the effects of any retreat upon the morale of the men.

"GEORGE B. McCLELLAN,
"*Major General, Commanding.*

"A. LINCOLN, *President.*"

"HEADQUARTERS ARMY OF THE POTOMAC,
"*Berkeley, July* 17, 1862—8 *a. m.*

"I have consulted fully with General Burnside, and would commend to your favorable consideration the general's plan for bringing (7) seven additional regiments from North Carolina by leaving Newburn to the care of the gunboats. It appears manifestly to be our policy to concentrate here everything we can possibly spare from less important points, to make sure of crushing the enemy at Richmond, which seems clearly to be the most important point in rebeldom. Nothing should be left to chance here. I would recommend that General Burnside, with all his troops, be ordered to this army, to enable it to assume the offensive as soon as possible.

"GEORGE B. McCLELLAN,
"*Major General, Commanding.*

"A. LINCOLN, *President.*"

"HEADQUARTERS ARMY OF THE POTOMAC,
"*Berkeley, July* 18, 1862—8 *a. m.*

"No change worth reporting in the state of affairs. Some (20,000) twenty thousand to (25,000) twenty-five thousand of the enemy at Petersburg, and others thence to Richmond.

"Those at Petersburg say they are part of Beauregard's army. New troops arriving *via* Petersburg. Am anxious to have determination of government that no time may be lost in preparing for it. Hours are very precious now, and perfect unity of action necessary.

"GEORGE B. McCLELLAN,
"*Major General, Commanding.*

"A. LINCOLN, *President.*"

The following was telegraphed to General Halleck on the 28th:

"HEADQUARTERS ARMY OF THE POTOMAC,
"*Berkeley, July* 28, 1862—8 *a. m.*

"Nothing especially new except corroboration of reports that re-enforcements reaching Richmond from south. It is not confirmed that any of Bragg's troops are yet here. My opinion is more and more firm that here is the defence of Washington, and that I should be at once re-enforced by all available troops to enable me to advance. Retreat would be disastrous to the army and the cause. I am confident of that.

"GEORGE B. McCLELLAN,
"*Major General.*

"Major General H. W. HALLECK,
"*Commanding U. S. Army, Washington, D. C.*"

On the 30th I sent the following to the general-in-chief.

"HEADQUARTERS ARMY OF THE POTOMAC,
"*Berkeley, July* 30, 1862—7 *a. m.*

*   *   *   *   *   *

"I hope that it may soon be decided what is to be done by this army, and that the decision may be to re-enforce it at once. We are losing much valuable time, and that at a moment when energy and decision are sadly needed.

"GEORGE B. McCLELLAN,
"*Major General.*

"Major General H. W. HALLECK,
"*Commanding U. S. Army, Washington, D. C.*"

About half an hour after midnight, on the morning of August 1, the enemy brought some light batteries to Coggin's point and the Coles house, on the right bank of James river, directly opposite Harrison's landing, and opened a heavy fire upon our shipping and encampments. It was continued rapidly for about thirty minutes, when they were driven back by the fire of our guns; this affair was reported in the following despatch:

"HEADQUARTERS ARMY OF THE POTOMAC,
"*Berkeley, August* 2, 1862—8 *a. m.*

"Firing of night before last killed some ten (10) men and wounded about (15) fifteen.

"No harm of the slightest consequence done to the shipping, although several were struck. Sent party across river yesterday to the Coles house, destroyed it and cut down the timber; will complete work to-day, and also send party to Coggin's point, which I will probably occupy. I will attend to your telegraph about pressing at once; will send Hooker out. Give me Burnside, and I will stir these people up. I need more cavalry; have only (3,700) thirty-seven hundred for duty in cavalry division.

"Adjutant General's office forgot to send Sykes's commission as major general, with those of other division commanders; do me the favor to hurry it on.

"G. B. McCLELLAN,
"*Major General, Commanding.*

"Major General H. W. HALLECK,
"*Washington, D. C.*"

To prevent another demonstration of this charac er, and to insure a debouche on the south bank of the James, it became neces ary to oc upy Coggin's point, which was done on the 3d, and the enemy, as vill be se n from the following despatch, driven back towards Petersburg:

"HEADQUARTERS ARMY OF THE POTOMAC,
"*Berkeley, August* 3, 1862—10 *p. m.*

"Coggin's point was occupied to-day, and timber felled so as to make it quiet defensible. I went over the ground myself, and found that Duane had, as usual, selected an admirable position, which can be intrenched with a small amount of labor, so as to make it a formidable tête de pont, covering the landing of a large force.

"I shall begin intrenching it by the labor of contrabands to-morrow. The position covers the Coles house, which is directly in front of Westover. We have now a safe debouche on the south bank, and are secure against midnight cannonading. A few thousand more men would place us in condition at least to annoy and disconcert the enemy very much.

"I sent Colonel Averill this morning with three hundred (300) cavalry to examine the country on the south side of the James, and try to catch some cavalry at Sycamore church, which is on the main road from Petersburg to Suffolk, and some five (5) miles from Coles house. He found a cavalry force of five hundred and fifty (550) men, attacked them at once, drove in their advance guards to their camp, where we had a sharp skirmish, and drove them off in disorder.

"He burned their entire camp, with their commissary and quartermaster's stores, and then returned and re-crossed the river. He took but (2) two prisoners, had one man wounded by a ball, and one by a sabre cut.

"Captain McIntosh made a handsome charge. The troops engaged were of the (5th) fifth regulars, and the (3d) third Pennsylvania cavalry.

"Colonel Averill conducted this affair, as he does everything he undertakes, to my entire satisfaction.

"G. B. McCLELLAN,
"*Major General, Commanding.*

"Maj. Gen. H. W. HALLECK,
"*Commanding United States Army, Washington, D. C.*"

On the 1st of August I received the following despatches:

"WASHINGTON, *July* 30, 1862—8 *p. m.*

"A despatch just received from General Pope says that deserters report that the enemy is moving south of James river, and that the force in Richmond is very small. I suggest he be pressed in that direction, so as to ascertain the facts of the case.

"H. W. HALLECK,
"*Majov General.*

"Maj. Gen. G. B. MCCLELLAN."

"WASHINGTON, *July* 30, 1862—8 *p. m.*

"In order to enable you to move in any direction, it is necessary to relieve you of your sick. The Surgeon General has, therefore, been directed to make arrangements for them at other places, and the Quartermaster General to provide transportation. I hope you will send them away as quickly as possible, and advise me of their removal.

"H. W. HALLECK,
"*Major General.*

"Maj. Gen. G. B. MCCLELLAN."

It is clear that the general-in-chief attached some weight to the report received from General Pope, and I was justified in supposing that the order in regard to the removing the sick contemplated an offensive movement rather than a retreat, as I had no other data than the telegrams just given, from which to form an opinion as to the intentions of the government.

The following telegram strengthened me in that belief:

"WASHINGTON, *July* 31, 1862—10 *a. m.*

"General Pope again telegraphs that the enemy is reported to be evacuating Richmond, and falling back on Danville and Lynchburg.

"H. W. HALLECK,
"*Major General.*

"Maj. Gen. G. B. McCLELLAN."

In occupying Coggin's point, as already described, I was influenced by the necessity of possessing a secure debouche on the south of the James, in order to enable me to move on the communications of Richmond in that direction, as well as to prevent a repetition of midnight cannonades.

To carry out General Halleck's first order, of July 30, it was necessary first to gain possession of Malvern hill, which was occupied by the enemy, apparently in some little force, and controlled the direct approach to Richmond. Its temporary occupation, at least, was equally necessary in the event of a movement upon Petersburg, or even the abandonment of the Peninsula. General Hooker, with his own division, and Pleasonton's cavalry, was therefore directed to gain possession of Malvern hill on the night of the 2d of August.

He failed to do so, as the following despatch recites:

"HEADQUARTERS ARMY OF THE POTOMAC,
"*Berkeley, August* 3, 1862—10.20 *p. m.*

"The movement undertaken up the river last night failed on account of the incompetency of guides.

"The proper steps have been taken to-day to remedy this evil, and I hope to be ready to-morrow night to carry out your suggestions as to pressing, at least to accomplish the first indispensable step.

"G. B. McCLELLAN,
"*Major General, Commanding.*

"Maj. Gen. HALLECK,
"*Commanding United States Army.*"

On the 4th General Hooker was re-enforced by General Sedgwick's division, and having obtained a knowledge of the roads, he succeeded in turning Malvern hill, and driving the enemy back towards Richmond.

The following is my report of this affair at the time:

"MALVERN HILL, *August* 5, 1862—1 *p. m.*

"General Hooker, at 5.30 this morning, attacked a very considerable force of infantry and artillery stationed at this place, and carried it handsomely, driving the enemy towards Newmarket, which is four miles distant, and where it is said they have a large force. We have captured 100 prisoners, killed and wounded several, with a loss on our part of only three killed and eleven wounded; among the latter, two officers.

"I shall probably remain here to-night, ready to act as circumstances may require, after the return of my cavalry reconnoissances.

"The mass of the enemy escaped under the cover of a dense fog; but our cavalry are still in pursuit, and I trust may succeed in capturing many more.

"This is a very advantageous position to cover an advance on Richmond, and only 14¾ miles distant; and I feel confident that with re-enforcements I would march this army there in five days.

"I this instant learn that several brigades of the enemy are four miles from here on the Quaker road, and I have taken steps to prepare to meet them.

"General Hooker's dispositions were admirable, and his officers and men displayed their usual gallantry.

"GEORGE B. McCLELLAN,
"*Major General, Commanding.*

"Major General H. W. HALLECK,
"*Commanding United States Army.*"

"MALVERN HILL, *August* 5, 1862—8 *p. m.*

"Since my last despatch Colonel Averill has returned from a reconnoissance, in the direction of Savage's station, towards Richmond. He encountered the 18th Virginia cavalry near White Oak swamp bridge, charged and drove them some distance towards Richmond, capturing 28 men and horses, killing and wounding several.

"Our troops have advanced (12) twelve miles in one direction, and (17) seventeen in another, towards Richmond to-day.

"We have secured a strong position at Coggin's point, opposite our quartermaster's depot, which will effectually prevent the rebels from using artillery hereafter against our camps.

"I learn this evening that there is a force of 20,000 men about six miles back from this point, on the south bank of the river. What their object is I do not know, but will keep a sharp lookout on their movements.

"I am sending off sick as rapidly as our transports will take them. I am also doing everything in my power to carry out your orders, to push reconnoissances towards the rebel capital, and hope soon to find out whether the reports regarding the abandonment of that place are true.

"GEORGE B. McCLELLAN,
"*Major General.*

"Major General H. W. HALLECK,
"*Commanding United States Army.*"

To the despatch of 1 p. m., August 5, the following answer was received:

"WASHINGTON, *August* 6, 1862—3 *a. m.*

"I have no re-enforcements to send you.

"H. W. HALLECK,
"*Major General.*

"Major General G. B. McCLELLAN."

And soon after the following:

"WASHINGTON, *August* 6, 1862.

"You will immediately send a regiment of cavalry and several batteries of artillery to Burnside's command at Aquia creek. It is reported that Jackson is moving north with a very large force.

"H. W. HALLECK,
"*Major General.*

"Major General G. B. McCLELLAN."

On the 4th I had received General Halleck's order of the 3d, (which appears below,) directing me to withdraw the army to Aquia, and on the same day sent an earnest protest against it. A few hours before this, General Hooker had informed me that his cavalry pickets reported large bodies of the enemy advancing and driving them in, and that he would probably be attacked at daybreak.

Under these circumstances I had determined to support him; but as I could not get the whole army in position until the next afternoon, I concluded, upon the receipt of the above telegram from the general-in-chief, to withdraw General

Hooker, that there might be the least possible delay in conforming to General Halleck's orders. I therefore sent to General Hooker the following letter:

"HEADQUARTERS ARMY OF THE POTOMAC,
"*Berkeley, August 6, 1862—10 p. m.*

"MY DEAR GENERAL: I find it will not be possible to get the whole army into position before some time to-morrow afternoon, which will be too late to support you, and hold the entire position, should the enemy attack in large force at daybreak, which there is strong reasons to suppose he intends doing.

"Should we fight a general battle at Malvern, it will be necessary to abandon the whole of our works here, and run the risk of getting back here.

"Under advices I have received from Washington, I think it necessary for you to abandon the position to night, getting everything away before daylight.

"Please leave cavalry pickets at Malvern, with orders to destroy the Turkey creek bridge when they are forced back.

"The roads leading into Haxall's from the right should be strongly watched, and Haxall's at least held by strong cavalry force and some light batteries as long as possible.

"I leave the manner of the withdrawal entirely to your discretion.

"Please signal to the fleet when the withdrawal is about completed.

"Report frequently to these headquarters.

"General Sumner was ordered up to support you, but will halt where this passes him, and will inform you where he is.

"GEORGE B. McCLELLAN,
"*Major General.*

"General J. HOOKER,
"*Commanding at Malvern Hill.*"

And the following reply was sent to General Halleck:

"HEADQUARTERS ARMY OF THE POTOMAC,
"*Berkeley, August 6, 1862—11.30 p. m.*

"Despatch of to-day received. I have not quite (4,000) four thousand cavalry for duty in cavalry division, so that I cannot possibly spare any more.

"I really need many more than I now have to carry out your instructions.

"The enemy are moving a large force on Malvern hill. In view of your despatches, and the fact that I cannot place the whole army in position before daybreak, I have ordered Hooker to withdraw during the night if it is possible; if he cannot do so, I must support him.

"Until this matter is developed I cannot send any batteries; I hope I can do so to-morrow if transportation is on hand.

"I will obey the order as soon as circumstances permit. My artillery is none too numerous now. I have only been able to send off some (1,200) twelve hundred sick. No transportation. There shall be no delay that I can avoid.

"GEORGE B. McCLELLAN,
"*Major General, Commanding.*

"Major General H. W. HALLECK,
"*Commanding U. S. Army.*"

Five batteries, with their horses and equipments complete, were embarked on the 7th and 8th, simultaneously with General Hooker's operations upon Malvern.

I despatched a calvary force under Colonel Averill towards Savage's station, to ascertain if the enemy were making any movements towards our right flank.

He found a rebel cavalry regiment near the White Oak swamp bridge, and completely routed it, pursuing well towards Savage's station.

These important preliminary operations assisted my preparations for the removal of the army to Aquia creek; and the sending off our sick and supplies was pushed both day and night as rapidly as the means of transportation permitted.

On the subject of the withdrawal of the army from Harrison's landing, the following correspondence passed between the general-in-chief and myself, while the reconnoissances towards Richmond were in progress.

On the 2d of August I received the following:

"WASHINGTON, *August* 2, 1862—3.45 *p. m.*

"You have not answered my telegram of July 30, 8 p. m., about the removal of your sick. Remove them as rapidly as possible, and telegraph me when they will be out of your way. The President wishes an answer as early as possible.

"H. W. HALLECK,
"*Major General.*"

"Major General G. B. McCLELLAN."

To which this reply was sent:

"HEADQUARTERS ARMY OF THE POTOMAC,
"*Berkeley, August* 3—11 *p. m.*

"Your telegram of (2) second is received. The answer (to despatch of July 30) was sent this morning.

"We have about (12,500) twelve thousand five hundred sick, of whom perhaps (4,000) four thousand might make easy marches. We have here the means to transport (1,200) twelve hundred, and will embark to-morrow that number of the worst cases, with all the means at the disposal of the medical director; the remainder could be shipped in from (7) seven to (10) ten days.

"It is impossible for me to decide what cases to send off, unless I know what is to be done with this army.

"Were the disastrous measures of a retreat adopted, all the sick who cannot march and fight should be despatched by water.

"Should the army advance, many of the sick could be of service at the depots. If it is to remain here any length of time, the question assumes still a different phase.

"Until I am informed what is to be done, I cannot act understandingly or for the good of the service. If I am kept longer in ignorance of what is to be effected, I cannot be expected to accomplish the object in view.

"In the mean time I will do all in my power to carry out what I conceive to be your wishes.

"GEO. B. McCLELLAN,
"*Major General, Commanding.*

"Major General H. W. HALLECK,
"*Commanding United States Army, Washington, D. C.*"

The moment I received the instructions for removing the sick, I at once gave the necessary directions for carrying them out.

With the small amount of transportation at hand, the removal of the severe cases alone would necessarily take several days, and, in the mean time, I desired information to determine what I should do with the others.

The order required me to send them away as quickly as possible, and to notify the general-in-chief *when they were removed.*

Previous to the receipt of the despatch of the 2d of August, not having been advised of what the army under my command was expected to do, or which way it was to move, if it moved at all, I sent the following despatch:

"HEADQUARTERS ARMY OF THE POTOMAC,
"*Berkeley, August* 3, 1862.

"I hear of sea steamers at Fort Monroe; are they for removing my sick? If so, to what extent am I required to go in sending them off? There are not many who need go.

"As I am not in any way informed of the intentions of the government in regard to this army, I am unable to judge what proportion of the sick should leave here, and must ask for specific orders.

"G. B. McCLELLAN,
"*Major General, Commanding.*

"Major General H. W. HALLECK,
"*Commanding United States Army, Washington.*"

If the army was to retreat to Fort Monroe, it was important that it should be unencumbered with any sick, wounded, or other men who might at all interfere with its mobility; but if the object was to operate directly on Richmond, from the position we then occupied, there were many cases of slight sickness which would speedily be cured, and the patients returned to duty.

As the service of every man would be important in the event of a forward offensive movement, I considered it to be of the utmost consequence that I should know what was to be done. It was to ascertain this that I sent the despatch of 11 p. m. on the 3d, before receiving the following telegram:

"WASHINGTON, *August* 3, 1862—7.45 *p. m.*

"I have waited most anxiously to learn the result of your forced reconnoissance towards Richmond, and also whether all your sick have been sent away, and I can get no answer to my telegram.

"It is determined to withdraw your army from the Peninsula to Aquia creek. You will take immediate measures to effect this, covering the movement the best you can.

"Its real object and withdrawal should be concealed even from your own officers.

"Your material and transportation should be removed first. You will assume control of all the means of transportation within your reach, and apply to the naval forces for all the assistance they can render you. You will consult freely with the commander of these forces. The entire execution of the movement is left to your discretion and judgment.

"You will leave such forces as you may deem proper at Fort Monroe, Norfolk, and other places, which we must occupy.

"H. W. HALLECK,
"*Major General, Commanding United States Army.*

"Major General GEO. B. McCLELLAN."

I proceeded to obey this order with all possible rapidity, firmly impressed, however, with the conviction that the withdrawal of the army of the Potomac from Harrison's landing, where its communications had by the co-operation of the gunboats been rendered perfectly secure, would, at that time, have the most disastrous effect upon our cause.

I did not, as the commander of that army, allow the occasion to pass without distinctly setting forth my views upon the subject to the authorities in the following telegram:

"HEADQUARTERS ARMY OF THE POTOMAC,
"*Berkeley, August 4, 1862—12 m.*

"Your telegram of last evening is received. I must confess that it has caused me the greatest pain I ever experienced, for I am convinced that the order to withdraw this army to Aquia creek will prove disastrous to our cause. I fear it will be a fatal blow. Several days are necessary to complete the preparations for so important a movement as this, and while they are in progress, I beg that careful consideration may be given to my statements.

"This army is now in excellent discipline and condition. We hold a debouche on both banks of the James river, so that we are free to act in any direction; and with the assistance of the gunboats, I consider our communications as now secure

"We are twenty-five (25) miles from Richmond, and are not likely to meet the enemy in force sufficient to fight a battle until we have marched fifteen (15) to eighteen (18) miles, which brings us practically within ten (10) miles of Richmond. Our longest line of land transportation would be from this point twenty-five (25) miles, but with the aid of the gunboats we can supply the army by water during its advance, certainly to within twelve (12) miles of Richmond.

"At Aquia creek we would be seventy-five (75) miles from Richmond, with land transportation all the way.

"From here to Fort Monroe is a march of about seventy (70) miles, for I regard it as impracticable to withdraw this army and its material, except by land.

"The result of the movement would thus be a march of one hundred and forty-five (145) miles to reach a point now only twenty-five (25) miles distant, and to deprive ourselves entirely of the powerful aid of the gunboats and water transportation.

"Add to this the certain demoralization of this army which would ensue, the terribly depressing effect upon the people of the north, and the strong probability that it would influence foreign powers to recognize our adversaries; and these appear to me sufficient reasons to make it my imperative duty to urge in the strongest terms afforded by our language that this order may be rescinded, and that far from recalling this army, it may be promptly re-enforced to enable it to resume the offensive.

"It may be said that there are no re-enforcements available. I point to Burnside's force; to that of Pope, not necessary to maintain a strict defensive in front of Washington and Harper's Ferry; to those portions of the army of the west not required for a strict defensive there. Here, directly in front of this army, is the heart of the rebellion; it is here that all our resources should be collected to strike the blow which will determine the fate of the nation.

"All points of secondary importance elsewhere should be abandoned, and every available man brought here; a decided victory here, and the military strength of the rebellion is crushed. It matters not what partial reverses we may meet with elsewhere; here is the true defence of Washington; it is here, on the banks of the James, that the fate of the Union should be decided.

"Clear in my convictions of right, strong in the consciousness that I have ever been, and still am, actuated solely by the love of my country, knowing that no ambitious or selfish motives have influenced me from the commencement of this war, I do now, what I never did in my life before, I entreat that this order may be rescinded.

"If my counsel does not prevail, I will with a sad heart obey your orders to the utmost of my power, directing to the movements, which I clearly foresee will be one of the utmost delicacy and difficulty, whatever skill I may possess. Whatever the result may be—and may God grant that I am mistaken in my forebodings—I shall at least have the internal satisfaction that I have written and spoken frankly, and have sought to do the best in my power to avert disaster from my country.

"G. B. McCLELLAN,
"*Major General, Commanding.*

"Major General H. W. HALLECK,
"*Commanding United States Army.*"

Soon after sending this telegram, I received the following, in reply to mine of 11 p. m. of the 3d.

"WASHINGTON, *August* 4, 1862—12.45 *p. m.*

"My telegram to you of yesterday will satisfy you in regard to future operations; it was expected that you would have sent off your sick, as directed, without waiting to know what were or would be the intentions of the government respecting future movements.

"The President expects that the instructions which were sent you yesterday, with his approval, will be carried out with all possible despatch and caution. The Quartermaster General is sending to Fort Monroe all the transportation he can collect.

"H. W. HALLECK,
"*Major General.*

"Major General G. B. McCLELLAN."

To which the following is my reply:

"HEADQUARTERS ARMY OF THE POTOMAC,
"*Berkeley, August* 5, 1862—7 *a. m.*

"Your telegram of yesterday received, and is being carried out as promptly as possible. With the means at my command, no human power could have moved the sick in the time you say you expected them to be moved.

* * * * * * * * *

"GEO. B. McCLELLAN,
"*Major General.*

"Major General H. W. HALLECK,
"*Commanding United States Army.*"

My efforts for bringing about a change of policy were unsuccessful, as will be seen from the following telegram and letter received by me in reply to mine of 12 m. of the 4th.

"WASHINGTON, *August* 5, 1862—12 *m.*

"You cannot regret the order of the withdrawal more than I did the necessity of giving it. It will not be rescinded, and you will be expected to execute it with all possible promptness. It is believed that it can be done now without serious danger. This may not be so, if there should be any delay. I will write you my views more fully by mail.

"H. W. HALLECK,
"*Major General, Commanding United States Army.*

"Major General G. B. McCLELLAN."

The letter was as follows:

"HEADQUARTERS OF THE ARMY,
"*Washington, August* 6, 1862.

"GENERAL: Your telegram of yesterday was received this morning, and I immediately telegraphed a brief reply, promising to write you more fully by mail.

"You, general, certainly could not have been more pained at receiving my order, than I was at the necessity of issuing it. I was advised by high officers, in whose judgment I had great confidence, to make the order immediately on my arrival here, but I determined not to do so until I could learn your wishes from a personal interview. And even after that interview I tried every means in my power to avoid withdrawing your army, and delayed my decision as long as I dared to delay it.

"I assure you, general, it was not a hasty and inconsiderate act, but one that caused me more anxious thoughts than any other of my life. But after full and mature consideration of all the *pros* and *cons*, I was reluctantly forced to the conclusion that the order must be issued—there was to my mind no alternative.

"Allow me to allude to a few of the facts in the case.

"You and your officers at one interview estimated the enemy's forces in and around Richmond at two hundred thousand men. Since then, you and others report that they have received and are receiving large re-enforcements from the south. General Pope's army, covering Washington, is only about forty thousand. Your effective force is only about ninety thousand. You are thirty miles from Richmond, and General Pope eighty or ninety, with the enemy directly between you ready to fall with his superior numbers upon one or the other as he may elect; neither can re-enforce the other in case of such an attack.

"If General Pope's army be diminished to re-enforce you, Washington, Maryland, and Pennsylvania would be left uncovered and exposed. If your force be reduced to strengthen Pope, you would be too weak to even hold the position you now occupy, should the enemy turn round and attack you in full force. In other words, the old army of the Potomac is split into two parts, with the entire force of the enemy directly between them. They cannot be united by land without exposing both to destruction, and yet they must be united. To send Pope's forces by water to the Peninsula is, under present circumstances, a military impossibility. The only alternative is to send the forces on the Peninsula to some point by water, say Fredericksburg, where the two armies can be united.

"Let me now allude to some of the objections which you have urged: you say that the withdrawal from the present position will cause the certain demoralization of the army 'which is now in excellent discipline and condition.'

"I cannot understand why a simple change of position to a new and by no means distant base will demoralize an army in excellent discipline, unless the officers themselves assist in that demoralization, which I am satisfied they will not.

"Your change of front from your extreme right at Hanover Court House to your present condition was over thirty miles, but I have not heard that it demoralized your troops, notwithstanding the severe losses they sustained in effecting it.

"A new base on the Rappahannock at Fredericksburg brings you within about sixty miles of Richmond, and secures a re-enforcement of forty or fifty thousand fresh and disciplined troops.

"The change with such advantages will, I think, if properly represented to your army, encourage rather than demoralize your troops. Moreover you yourself suggested that a junction might be effected at Yorktown, but that a flank march across the isthmus would be more hazardous than to retire to Fort Monroe.

"You will remember that Yorktown is two or three miles further than Fredericksburg is. Besides, the latter is between Richmond and Washington, and covers Washington from any attack of the enemy.

"The political effect of the withdrawal may at first be unfavorable; but I think the public are beginning to understand its necessity, and that they will have much more confidence in a united army than in its separated fragments.

"But you will reply, why not re-enforce me here, so that I can strike Richmond from my present position? To do this, you said, at our interview, that you required thirty thousand additional troops. I told you that it was impossible to give you so many. You finally thought that you would have 'some chance' of success with twenty thousand. But you afterwards telegraphed me that you would require thirty-five thousand, as the enemy was being largely re-enforced.

"If your estimate of the enemy's strength was correct, your requisition was perfectly reasonable; but it was utterly impossible to fill it until new troop could be enlisted and organized, which would require several weeks.

"To keep your army in its present position until it could it be so re-enforced would almost destroy it in that climate.

"The months of August and September are almost fatal to whites who live on that part of James river; and even after you received the re-enforcements asked for, you admitted that you must reduce Fort Darling and the river batteries before you could advance on Richmond.

"It is by no means certain that the reduction of these fortifications would not require considerable time—perhaps as much as those at Yorktown.

"This delay might not only be fatal to the health of your army, but in the mean time General Pope's forces would be exposed to the heavy blows of the enemy without the slightest hope of assistance from you.

"In regard to the demoralizing effect of a withdrawal from the Peninsula to the Rappahannock, I must remark that a large number of your highest officers, indeed a majority of those whose opinions have been reported to me, are decidedly in favor of the movement. Even several of those who originally advocated the line of the Peninsula now advise its abandonment.

"I have not inquired, and do not wish to know, by whose advice or for what reasons the army of the Potomac was separated into two parts with the enemy between them. I must take things as I find them.

"I find the forces divided, and I wish to unite them. Only one feasible plan has been presented for doing this. If you, or any one else, had presented a better plan, I certainly should have adopted it. But all of your plans require re-enforcements which it is impossible to give you. It is very easy to *ask* for re-enforcements, but it is not so easy to give them when you have no disposable troops at your command.

"I have written very plainly as I understand the case, and I hope you will give me credit for having fully considered the matter, although I may have arrived at very different conclusions from your own.

"Very respectfully, your obedient servant,

"H. W. HALLECK,
"*General-in-Chief.*

"Major General G. B. McCLELLAN,
"*Commanding, &c., Berkeley, Virginia.*"

On the 7th I received the following telegram:

"WASHINGTON, *August* 7, 1862—10 *a. m.*

"You will immediately report the number of sick sent off since you received my order, the number still to be shipped, and the amount of transportation at your disposal—that is, the number of persons that can be carried on all the vessels which by my order you were authorized to control.

"H. W. HALLECK,
"*Major General.*

"Major General G. B. McCLELLAN."

To which I made this reply:

"HEADQUARTERS ARMY OF THE POTOMAC,
"*August* 7, 1862—10.40 *p. m*

"In reply to your despatch of 10 a. m. to-day, I report the number of sick sent off since I received your order as follows: Three thousand seven hundred and forty, including some that are embarked to-night and will leave in the morning. The number still to be shipped is, as nearly as can be ascertained, five thousand seven hundred.

"The embarcation of five batteries of artillery, with their horses, wagons, &c., required most of our available boats except the ferry-boats. All the transports that can ascend to this place have been ordered up; they will be here to-morrow evening. Colonel Ingalls reports to me that there are no transports now available for cavalry, and will not be for two or three days. As soon as they can be obtained I shall send off the first New York cavalry.

"After the transports with sick and wounded have returned, including some heavy-draft steamers at Fort Monroe that cannot come to this point, we can transport twenty-five thousand men at a time. We have some propellers here, but they are laden with commissary supplies and are not available.

"The transports now employed in transporting sick and wounded will carry 12,000 well infantry soldiers. Those at Fort Monroe, and of too heavy draft to come here, will carry 8,000 or 10,000 infantry. Several of the largest steamers have been used for transporting prisoners of war, and have only become available for the sick to-day.

"GEORGE B. McCLELLAN,
"*Major General.*

"Major General H. W. HALLECK,
"*Commanding United States Army.*"

The report of my chief quartermaster upon the subject is as follows:

"HEADQUARTERS ARMY OF THE POTOMAC,
"*Office of Chief Quartermaster, Harrison's Landing, August* 7, 1862.

"GENERAL: I have the honor to return the papers herewith which you sent me, with the following remarks:

"We are embarking five batteries of artillery, with their horses, baggage, &c., which requires the detailing of most of our available boats, except the ferry-boats. The medical department has ten or twelve of our largest transport vessels, which, if disposable, could carry 12,000 men. Besides, there are some heavy-draft steamers at Fort Monroe that cannot come to this point, but which can carry 8,000 or 10,000 infantry.

"I have ordered all up here that can ascend to this depot. They will be here to-morrow evening. As it now is, after the details already made, we cannot transport from this place more than 5,000 infantry.

"There are no transports now available for cavalry. From and after to-morrow, if the vessels arrive, I could transport 10,000 infantry. In two or three days a regiment of cavalry can be sent if required. If you wait, and ship from Yorktown or Fort Monroe after the sick and wounded transports are at my disposal, we can transport 25,000 at a time. The number that can be transported is contingent on circumstances referred to.

"Most of the propellers here are laden with commissary or other supplies, and most of the tugs are necessary to tow off sail craft also laden with supplies.

"I am, very respectfully, your most obedient servant,
"RUFUS INGALLS,
"*Chief Quartermaster.*

"General R. B. MARCY,
"*Chief of Staff.*"

On the 9th I received this despatch:

"WASHINGTON, *August* 9, 1862—12.45 *p. m.*

"I am of the opinion that the enemy is massing his forces in front of Generals Pope and Burnside, and that he expects to crush them and move forward to the Potomac.

"You must send re-enforcements instantly to Aquia creek.

"Considering the amount of transportation at your disposal, your delay is not satisfactory. You must move with all possible celerity.

"H. W. HALLECK,
"*Major General.*

"Major General G. B. McCLELLAN."

To which I sent the following reply:

"HEADQUARTERS ARMY OF THE POTOMAC,
"*Berkeley, August* 10, 1862—8 *a. m.*

"Telegram of yesterday received. The batteries sent to Burnside took the last available transport yesterday morning. Enough have since arrived to ship one regiment of cavalry to-day. The sick are being embarked as rapidly as possible. There has been no unnecessary delay, as you assert—not an hour's—but everything has been and is being pushed as rapidly as possible to carry out your orders.

"G. B. McCLELLAN,
"*Major General Commanding.*

"Major General H. W. HALLECK,
"*Commanding United States Army.*"

The following report, made on the same day by the officer then in charge of the transports, exposes the injustice of the remark in the despatch of the gen, eral-in-chief, that, "considering the amount of transportation at your disposal your delay is not satisfactory."

"ASSISTANT QUARTERMASTER'S OFFICE, ARMY OF THE POTOMAC,
"*Harrison's Landing, Virginia, August* 10, 1862.

"Colonel Ingalls, being himself ill, has requested me to telegraph to you concerning the state and capacity of the transports now here. On the night of the 8th I despatched eleven steamers, principally small ones, and six schooners, with five batteries of heavy horse artillery, none of which have yet returned.

"Requisition is made this morning for transportation of one thousand cavalry to Aquia creek. All the schooners that had been chartered for carrying horses have been long since discharged, or changed into freight vessels.

"A large proportion of the steamers now here are still loaded with stores, or are in the floating hospital service engaged in removing the sick. To transport the one thousand cavalry to-day will take all the available steamers now here not engaged in the service of the harbor. These steamers could take a large number of infantry, but are not well adapted to the carrying of horses, and much space is thus lost. Several steamers are expected here to-day, and we are unloading schooners rapidly; most of these are not chartered, but are being taken for the service required, at same rates of pay as other chartered schooners. If you could cause a more speedy return of the steamers sent away from here, it would facilitate matters.

"C. G. SAWTELLE,
"*Captain and Assistant Quartermaster, commanding Depot.*

"General M. C. MEIGS,
"*Quartermaster General United States Army, Washington.*"

Our wharf facilities at Harrison's landing were very limited, admitting but few vessels at one time. These were continually in use as long as there were disposable vessels, and the officers of the medical and quartermaster's departments, with all their available forces, were incessantly occupied day and night in embarking and sending off the sick men, troops, and material.

Notwithstanding the repeated representations I made to the general-in-chief that such were the facts, on the 10th I received the following:

"WASHINGTON, *August* 10, 1862—12 *p. m.*

"The enemy is crossing the Rapidan in large force. They are fighting General Pope to-day; there must be no further delay in your movements; that which has already occurred was entirely unexpected, and must be satisfactorily explained. Let not a moment's time be lost, and telegraph me daily what progress you have made in executing the order to transfer your troops.

"H. W. HALLECK,
"*Major General.*

"Major General G. B. McCLELLAN."

To which I sent this reply:

"HEADQUARTERS ARMY OF THE POTOMAC,
"*Berkeley, August* 10, 1862—11.30 *p. m.*

"Your despatch of to-day is received. I assure you again that there has not been any unnecessary delay in carrying out your orders.

"You are probably laboring under some great mistake as to the amount of transportation available here.

"I have pushed matters to the utmost in getting off our sick, and the troops you ordered to Burnside.

"Colonel Ingalls has more than once informed the Quartermaster General of the condition of our water transportation. From the fact that you directed me to keep the order secret, I took it for granted that you would take the steps necessary to provide the requisite transportation.

"A large number of transports for all arms of service, and for wagons, should at once be sent to Yorktown and Fort Monroe.

"I shall be ready to move the whole army by land the moment the sick are disposed of. You may be sure that not an hour's delay will occur that can be avoided. I fear you do not realize the difficulty of the operation proposed.

"The regiment of cavalry for Burnside has been in course of embarcation to-day and to-night; (10) ten steamers were required for the purpose; (1,258) twelve hundred and fifty-eight sick loaded to-day and to-night.

"Our means exhausted, except one vessel returning to Fort Monroe in the morning, which will take some (500) five hundred cases of slight sickness.

"The present moment is probably not the proper one for me to refer to the unnecessary, harsh, and unjust tone of your telegrams of late. It will, however, make no difference to my official action.

"G. B. McCLELLAN,
"*Major General Commanding.*

"Major General H. W. HALLECK,
"*Commanding United States Army.*"

On the eleventh this report was made:

"HEADQUARTERS ARMY OF THE POTOMAC,
"*Berkeley, August* 11, 1862—11.30 *p. m.*

"The embarcation of (850) eight hundred and fifty cavalry, and (1) one brigade of infantry will be completed by (2) two o'clock in the morning; (500) five hundred sick were embarked to-day. Another vessel arrived to-night, and

(600) six hundred more sick are now being embarked I still have some (4000) four thousand sick to dispose of. You have been greatly misled as to the amount of transportation at my disposal.

"Vessels loaded to their utmost capacity with stores, and others indispensable for service here, have been reported to you as available for carrying sick and well. I am sending off all that can be unloaded at Fort Monroe to have them return here. I repeat that I have lost no time in carrying out your orders.

"G. B. McCLELLAN,
"*Major General Commanding.*

"Major General H. W. HALLECK,
"*Commanding United States Army.*"

On the same day I received the following from the quartermaster in charge of the depot:

"ASSISTANT QUARTERMASTER'S OFFICE, ARMY OF THE POTOMAC
"*Harrison's Landing, August* 11, 1862.

"COLONEL: In reply to the communication from General Marcy, which was referred to me by you, I have to state that there are now in this harbor no disposable transports not already detailed, either for the use of the hospital department, for the transportation of the 1st N. Y. cavalry, or for the necessary service of the harbor. I think the steamers loading and to be loaded with cavalry could take in addition three thousand infantry. These boats are, however, directed to leave as fast as they are loaded; some have already started. The embarcation of this cavalry regiment is going on very slowly, and it is not in my power to hurry the matter, although I have had several agents of the department and one commissioned officer at the wharf, to render all the assistance possible. The entire army is this morning turning in, to be stored on vessels, knapsacks, officers' baggage, and other surplus property, and with our limited wharf facilities it is impossible, unless the regular issues of forage, &c., are suspended, to avoid great confusion and delay with what is already ordered to be done. Of course, if any infantry is ordered to embark on these cavalry transports, the confusion and difficulties will be increased.

"I know of no boats that may be expected here to-day, except the South America and Fanny Cadwallader, a propeller which was ordered to be sent back from Fort Monroe.

"The transports with the artillery left for Aquia creek on the night of the 8th and the morning of the 9th. They were ordered to return immediately.

"I am, very respectfully, your obedient servant,

"C. G. SAWTELLE,
"*Captain and A. Q. M., commanding Depot.*

"Lieut. Colonel RUFUS INGALLS,
"*A. D. C. and Chief Quartermaster, Army of the Potomac.*"

On the 12th I received the following:

"WASHINGTON, *August* 12, 1862—12 *m.*

"The Quartermaster General informs me that nearly every available steam vessel in the country is now under your control. To send more from Philadelphia, Baltimore and New York, would interfere with the transportation of army supplies and break up the channels of travel by which we are to bring forward the new troops. Burnside moved nearly thirteen thousand (13,000) troops to Aquia creek in less than two (2) days, and his transports were immediately sent back to you. All vessels in the James river and the Chesapeake bay were placed at your disposal, and it was supposed that (8) eight or (10) ten thousand of your men could be transported daily.

"In addition to steamers, there is a large fleet of sailing vessels which could be used as transports.

"The bulk of your material on shore it was thought could be sent to Fort Monroe, covered by that part of the army which could not get water transportation. Such were the views of the government here; perhaps we were misinformed as to the facts. If so, the delay could be explained. Nothing in my telegram was intentionally harsh or unjust, but the delay was so unexpected that an explanation was required. There has been, and is, the most urgent necessity for despatch, and not a single moment must be lost in getting additional troops in front of Washington.

"H. W. HALLECK,
"*Major General.*

"Major General G. B. McClellan."

I telegraphed the following reply:

"Headquarters Army of the Potomac,
"*Berkeley, August* 12, 1862—11 *p. m.*

"Your despatch of noon to-day received. It is positively the fact that no more men could have been embarked hence than have gone, and that no unnecessary delay has occurred. Before your orders were received, Colonel Ingalls directed all available vessels to come from Monroe. Officers have been sent to take personal direction. Have heard nothing here of Burnside's fleet.

"There are some vessels at Monroe, such as Atlantic and Baltic, which draw too much to come here. Hospital accommodations exhausted this side New York. Propose filling Atlantic and Baltic with serious cases, for New York, and to encamp slight cases for the present at Monroe. In this way can probably get off the (3,400) thirty-four hundred sick, still on hand, by day after tomorrow night.

"I am sure that you have been misinformed as to the availability of vessels on hand. We cannot use heavily loaded supply vessels for troops or animals; and such constitute the mass of those here, which have been represented to you as capable of transporting this army.

"I fear you will find very great delay in embarking troops and material at Yorktown and Monroe, both from want of vessels and of facilities of embarcation; at least two additional wharves should at once be built at each place. I ordered two at the latter some (2) two weeks ago, but you countermanded the order.

"I learn that wharf accommodations at Aquia are altogether inadequate for landing troops and supplies to any large extent. Not an hour should be lost in remedying this.

"Great delay will ensue there from shallow water. You will find a vast deficiency in horse transports. We had nearly two hundred when we came here; I learn of only (20) twenty provided now; they carry about (50) fifty horses each. More hospital accommodations should be provided. We are much impeded here because our wharves are used night and day to land current supplies. At Monroe a similar difficulty will occur.

"With all the facilities at Alexandria and Washington, (6) six weeks about were occupied in embarking this army and its material.

"Burnside's troops are not a fair criterion for rate of embarcation. All his means were in hand, his outfit specially prepared for the purpose, and his men habituated to the movement.

"There shall be no unnecessary delay, but I cannot manufacture vessels. I state these difficulties from experience, and because it appears to me that we have been lately working at cross purposes, because you have not been properly informed by those around you, who ought to know the inherent difficulties of such an undertaking. It is not possible for any one to place this army where you wish it, ready to move, in less than a month.

"If Washington is in danger now, this army can scarcely arrive in time to save it; it is in much better position to do so from here than from Aquia.

"Our material can only be saved by using the whole army to cover it, if we are pressed. If sensibly weakened by detachments, the result might be the loss of much material and many men. I will be at the telegraph office to-morrow morning.

"G. B. McCLELLAN,
"*Major General.*

"Major General H. W. HALLECK,
"*Washington, D. C.*"

To the reasons given in the foregoing despatch, to show why General Burnside's movement from Fort Monroe was not a fair criterion for our operations, the following may be added:

He was not encumbered by either sick or wounded men.

He had no cavalry, artillery, wagons, or teams. His force consisted of infantry alone, with a few ambulances and officers' horses.

His baggage was already on the transports, where it had remained since his arrival from North Carolina, and his men had only to resume their places on board.

The cavalry and artillery mentioned in my despatches of the 7th, 10th and 11th, were sent to supply his total deficiency in those arms.

I may also repeat that the vessels used by General Burnside had not returned from Aquia creek when the army left Harrison's bar.

It will be seen by the concluding paragraph of the foregoing despatch that in order to have a more direct, speedy, and full explanation of the condition of affairs in the army than I could by sending a single despatch by steamer to the nearest telegraph office at Jamestown island, some seventy miles distant, and waiting ten hours for a reply, I proposed to go in person to the office. This I did.

On my arrival at Jamestown island there was an interruption in the electric current, which rendered it necessary for me to continue on to Fort Monroe, and across the Chesapeake bay to Cherry Stone inlet, on the "eastern shore," where I arrived late in the evening, and immediately sent the annexed despatches:

"CHERRY STONE, *August* 13, 1862—11.30 *p. m.*

"Please come to office; wish to talk to you. What news from Pope?

"G. B. McCLELLAN,
"*Major General.*

"Major General H. W. HALLECK, *Washington.*"

"CHERRY STONE INLET, *August* 14, 1862—12.30 *a. m.*

"Started to Jamestown island to talk with you; found cable broken and came here. Please read my long telegram. (See above despatch of August 12, 11 p. m.) All quiet at camp. Enemy burned wharves at City Point yesterday. No rebel pickets within eight (8) miles of Coggin's point yesterday.

"Richmond prisoners state that large force with guns left Richmond northward on Sunday.

"G. B. McCLELLAN,
"*Major General.*

"Major General H. W. HALLECK, *Washington.*"

To which the following reply was received:

"WASHINGTON, *August* 14, 1862—1.40 *a. m.*

"I have read your despatch. There is no change of plans. You will send up your troops as rapidly as possible. There is no difficulty in landing them. According to your own accounts, there is now no difficulty in withdrawing your forces. Do so with all possible rapidity.

"H. W. HALLECK,
"*Major General.*

"Major General G. B. McCLELLAN."

Before I had time to decipher and reply to this despatch, the telegraph operator in Washington informed me that General Halleck had gone out of the office immediately after writing this despatch, without leaving any intimation of the fact for me, or waiting for any further information as to the object of my journey across the bay. As there was no possibility of other communication with him at that time, I sent the following despatch, and returned to Harrison's landing:

"CHERRY STONE INLET, *August* 14, 1862—1.40 *a. m.*

"Your orders will be obeyed. I return at once. I had hoped to have had a longer and fuller conversation with you, after travelling so far for the purpose.

"G. B. McCLELLAN,
"*Major General.*

"Major General H. W. HALLECK, *Washington, D. C.*"

On the 14th and 15th, and before we had been able to embark all our sick men, two army corps were put in motion towards Fort Monroe. This was reported in the annexed despatch:

"HEADQUARTERS ARMY OF THE POTOMAC,
"*Berkeley, August* 14, 1862—11 *p. m.*

"Movement has commenced by land and water. All sick will be away to-morrow night. Everything being done to carry out your orders. I don't like Jackson's movements; he will suddenly appear when least expected. Will telegraph fully and understandingly in the morning.

"G. B. McCLELLAN,
"*Major General.*

"Major General H. W. HALLECK, *Washington, D. C.*"

The phrase "movement has commenced," it need not be remarked, referred obviously to the movement of the main army, after completing the necessary preliminary movements of the sick, &c., &c.

The perversion of the term, to which the general-in-chief saw fit to give currency in a letter to the Secretary of War, should have been here rendered impossible by the despatches which precede this of the 14th, which show that the movement really begun immediately after the receipt of the order of August 4th.

The progress made in the movement on the 15th was reported in the following despatches:

"HEADQUARTERS ARMY OF THE POTOMAC,
"*August* 15, 1862—12 *m.*

"Colonel Ingalls this moment reports that after embarking the remaining brigade of McCall's division, with the sick, who are constantly accumulating, the transports now disposable will be all consumed.

"Two of my army corps marched last night and this morning en route for

Yorktown—one *via* Jones's bridge, and the other *via* Barrett's Ferry, where we have a pontoon bridge. The other corps will be pushed forward as fast as the roads are clear; and I hope before to-morrow morning to have the entire army in motion.

"A report has just been received from my pickets that the enemy in force is advancing on us from the Chickahominy, but I do not credit it; shall know soon. Should any more transports arrive here before my departure, and the enemy do not show such a force in our front as to require all the troops I have remaining to insure the safety of the land movement with its immense train, I shall send every man by water that transports will carry.

"G. B. McCLELLAN,
"*Major General.*

"Major General H. W. HALLECK,
"*Commanding U. S. A.*"

"HEADQUARTERS ARMY OF THE POTOMAC,
"*Berkeley, August* 15, 1862—1.30 *p. m.*

"The advanced corps and trains are fairly started. I learn nothing more in relation to reported advance of rebels *via* Jones's bridge. Shall push the movement as rapidly as possible.

"G. B. McCLELLAN,
"*Major General.*

"Major General H. W. HALLECK,
"*Washington, D. C.*"

"HEADQUARTERS ARMY OF THE POTOMAC,
"*Berkeley, August* 15, 1862—10 *p. m.*

"Coggin's point is abandoned. The whole of McCall's division, with its artillery, is now en route for Burnside. We have not yet transportation sufficient for our sick. I hope we will get it to-morrow.

"Porter is across the Chickahominy, near its mouth, with his wagons and reserve artillery. Heintzelman at Jones's bridge with a portion of his corps. They will all be up by morning.

"Averell's cavalry on the other side. All quiet thus far. I cannot get the last of the wagons as far as Charles City Court House before some time to-morrow afternoon.

"I am hurrying matters with the utmost rapidity possible. Wagons will move all night.

"G. B. McCLELLAN,
"*Major General.*

"Major General H. W. HALLECK,
"*Washington, D. C.*"

After the commencement of the movement, it was continued with the utmost rapidity, until all the troops and material were en route both by land and water, on the morning of the 16th.

Late in the afternoon of that day, when the last man had disappeared from the deserted camps, I followed with my personal staff in the track of the grand army of the Potomac; bidding farewell to the scenes still covered with the marks of its presence, and to be forever memorable in history as the vicinity of its most brilliant exploits.

Previous to the departure of the troops, I had directed Captain Duane, of the engineer corps, to proceed to Barrett's ferry, near the mouth of the Chickahominy, and throw across the river at that point a pontoon bridge. This was executed promptly and satisfactorily under the cover of gunboats; and an excellent bridge of about two thousand feet in length was ready for the first arrival of troops.

The greater part of the army, with its artillery, wagon trains, &c., crossed it rapidly, and in perfect order and safety, so that on the night of the 17th everything was across the Chickahominy, except the rear guard, which crossed early on the morning of the 18th, when the pontoon bridge was immediately removed.

General Porter's corps, which was the first to march from Harrison's landing, had been pushed forward rapidly, and on the 16th reached Williamsburg, where I had directed him to halt until the entire army was across the Chickahominy.

On his arrival at Williamsburg, however, he received an intercepted letter, which led to the belief that General Pope would have to contend against a very heavy force then in his front. General Porter, therefore, very properly took the responsibility of continuing his march directly on to Newport News, which place he reached on the morning of the 18th of August, having marched his corps sixty miles in the short period of three days and one night, halting one day at the crossing of the Chickahominy.

The embarcation of this corps commenced as soon as transports were ready, and on the 20th it had all sailed for Aquia creek. I made the following report from Barrett's ferry:

"HEADQUARTERS ARMY OF THE POTOMAC,
"*Barrett's Ferry, Chickahominy, August* 17, 1862—11 *a. m.*

"Everything is removed from our camp at Harrison's bar. No property nor men left behind.

"The (5th) fifth corps is at Williamsburg with all its wagons and the reserve artillery. The (3d) third corps is on the march from Jones's bridge to Williamsburg, *via* Diascund bridge, and has probably passed the latter before this hour. Averell's cavalry watches everything in that direction.

"The mass of the wagons have passed the pontoon bridge here, and are parked on the other side. Peck's wagons are now crossing; his division will soon be over. Headquarters wagons follow Peck's. I hope to have everything over to-night, and the bridge removed by daylight. May be delayed beyond that time. Came here to see Burnside, otherwise should have remained with the rear guard. Thus far all is quiet, and not a shot that I know of since we began the march.

"I shall not feel entirely secure until I have the whole army beyond the Chickahominy. I will then begin to forward troops by water as fast as transportation permits.

"G. B. McCLELLAN,
"*Major General, Commanding.*

"Major General H. W. HALLECK,
"*Commanding United States Army, Washington, D. C.*"

On the 18th and 19th our march was continued to Williamsburg and Yorktown, and on the 20th the remainder of the army was ready to embark at Yorktown, Fortress Monroe, and Newport News.

The movement of the main body of the army on this march was covered by General Pleasonton with his cavalry and horse artillery. That officer remained at Haxall's until the army had passed Charles City Court House, when he gradually fell back, picking up the stragglers as he proceeded, and crossed the bridge over the Chickahominy, after the main body had marched towards Williamsburg. His troops were the last to cross the bridge, and he deserves great credit for the manner in which he performed this duty.

General Averell did a similar service, in the same satisfactory way, in covering the march of the 3d corps.

As the campaign on the Peninsula terminated here, I cannot close this part of my report without giving an expression of my sincere thanks and gratitude to the officers and men whom I had the honor to command.

From the commencement to the termination of this most arduous campaign, the army of the Potomac always evinced the most perfect subordination, zeal, and alacrity in the performance of all the duties required of it.

The amount of severe labor accomplished by this army in the construction of intrenchments, roads, bridges, &c. was enormous; yet all the work was performed with the most gratifying cheerfulness and devotion to the interests of the service.

During the campaign ten severely contested and sanguinary battles had been fought, besides numerous smaller engagements, in which the troops exhibited the most determined enthusiasm and bravery. They submitted to exposure, sickness, and even death, without a murmur. Indeed, they had become veterans in their country's cause, and richly deserved the warm commendation of the government.

It was in view of these facts that this seemed to me an appropriate occasion for the general-in-chief to give, in general orders, some appreciative expression of the services of the army while upon the Peninsula. Accordingly, on the 18th I sent him the following despatch:

"HEADQUARTERS ARMY OF THE POTOMAC,
"*August* 18, 1862—11 *p. m.*

"Please say a kind word to my army that I can repeat to them in general orders in regard to their conduct at Yorktown, Williamsburg, West Point, Hanover Court House, and on the Chickahominy, as well as in regard to the (7) seven days and the recent retreat.

"No one has ever said anything to cheer them but myself. Say nothing about me. Merely give my men and officers credit for what they have done. It will do you much good, and will strengthen you much with them if you issue a handsome order to them in regard to what they have accomplished. They deserve it.

"G. B. McCLELLAN,
"*Major General.*

"Major General HALLECK,
"*Washington, D. C.*"

As no reply was received to this communication, and no order was issued by the general-in-chief, I conclude that suggestion did not meet with his approbation.

All the personnel and material of the army had been transferred from Harrison's landing to the different points of embarcation in the very brief period of five days without the slightest loss or damage. Porter's troops sailed from Newport News on the 19th and 20th. Heintzelman's corps sailed from Yorktown on the 21st. On that day I received the following telegram from the general-in-chief:

"WASHINGTON, *August* 21, 1862—6 *p. m.*

"Leave such garrisons in Fortress Monroe, Yorktown, &c., as you may deem proper. They will be replaced by new troops as rapidly as possible.

"The forces of Burnside and Pope are hard pushed, and require aid as rapidly as you can send it. Come yourself as soon as you can.

"By all means see that the troops sent have plenty of ammunition. We have no time here to supply them. Moreover, they may have to fight as soon as they land.

"H. W. HALLECK,
"*Major General, Commanding United States Army.*

"General McCLELLAN."

To which the following are replies:

"HEADQUARTERS ARMY OF THE POTOMAC,
"*Fortress Monroe, August* 21, 1862—7.30 *p. m.*

"Your despatch of (6) six p. m. received. I have not lost an hour in sending troops, nor will I. Franklin is here, and I will try to get some of his troops on board to-night. I had already ordered all the ammunition forward.

"I will put headquarters on board ship early to-morrow morning, so that I can leave at a moment's notice. I hope that I can get off to-morrow. Shall I go in person to Aquia, or do you wish to see me first at Washington? If you wish it I can probably ship quite an amount of ammunition for other troops than this army.

"G. B. McCLELLAN,
"*Major General.*

"Major General HALLECK,
"*Washington, D. C.*"

"HEADQUARTERS ARMY OF THE POTOMAC,
"*Fort Monroe, August* 21, 1862—10.25 *p. m.*

"I have ample supplies of ammunition for infantry and artillery, and will have it up in time. I can supply any deficiency that may exist in General Pope's army. Quite a number of rifled field guns are on hand here.

"The forage is the only question for you to attend to; please have that ready for me at Aquia. I want many more schooners for cavalry horses; they should have water on hand when they come here.

"If you have leisure, and there is no objection, please communicate to me fully the state of affairs, and your plans. I will then be enabled to arrange details understandingly.

"G. B. McCLELLAN,
"*Major General.*

"Major General HALLECK, *Washington.*"

Immediately on reaching Fort Monroe, I gave directions for strengthening the defences of Yorktown, to resist any attack from the direction of Richmond, and left General Keyes, with his corps, to perform the work, and temporarily garrison the place.

I telegraphed as follows on the 22d:

"HEADQUARTERS ARMY OF THE POTOMAC,
"*Fort Monroe, August* 22, 1862—2.15 *p. m.*

"Despatch of to-day received. Franklin's corps is embarking as rapidly as possible. Sumner's corps is at Newport News, ready to embark as fast as transportation arrives. Keyes is still at Yorktown, putting it in a proper state of defence. I think that all of Franklin's corps will get off to-day, and hope to commence with Sumner to-morrow. I shall then push off the cavalry and wagons.

"G. B. McCLELLAN,
"*Major General.*

"Major General H. W. HALLECK,
"*Washington, D. C.*"

"HEADQUARTERS ARMY OF THE POTOMAC,
"*Fort Monroe, August* 22, 1862—3.40 *p. m.*

"Two (2) good ordnance sergeants are needed immediately at Yorktown and Gloucester. The new defences are arranged and commenced.

"I recommend that (5,000) five thousand new troops be sent immediately to garrison York and Gloucester. They should be commanded by an experienced general officer, who can discipline and instruct them. About (900) nine hundred should be artillery. I recommend that a new regiment, whose colonel is an artillery officer, or graduate, be designated as heavy artillery, and sent there. A similar regiment is absolutely necessary here.

"G. B. McCLELLAN, *Major General.*

"Major General H. W. HALLECK,
"*Commanding United States Army.*"

On the 23d Franklin's corps sailed. I reported this in the following despatch:

"HEADQUARTERS ARMY OF THE POTOMAC,
"*Fort Monroe, August* 23, 1862—1.30 *p. m.*

"Franklin's corps has started. I shall start for Aquia in about half an hour. No transports yet for Sumner's corps.

"G. B. McCLELLAN,
"*Major General.*

"Major General H. W. HALLECK,
"*Commanding United States Army.*"

On that evening I sailed with my staff for Aquia creek, where I arrived at daylight on the following morning, reporting as follows:

"HEADQUARTERS ARMY OF THE POTOMAC,
"*Aquia Creek, August* 24, 1862.

"I have reached here, and respectfully report for orders.

"G. B. McCLELLAN,
"*Major General.*

"Major General HALLECK,
"*Commanding United States Army.*"

I also telegraphed as follows:

"HEADQUARTERS ARMY OF THE POTOMAC,
"*Aquia Creek, August* 24, 1862—2 *p. m.*

"Your telegram received. Morell's scouts report Rappahannock station burned and abandoned by Pope, without any notice to Morell or Sykes. This was telegraphed you some hours ago. Reynolds, Reno, and Stevens are supposed to be with Pope, as nothing can be heard of them to-day. Morell and Sykes are near Morrisville Post Office, watching the lower fords of Rappahannock, with no troops between there and Rappahannock station, which is reported abandoned by Pope.

"Please inform me immediately exactly where Pope is, and what doing; until I know that I cannot regulate Porter's movements; he is much exposed now, and decided measures should be taken at once. Until I know what my command and position are to be, and whether you still intend to place me in the command indicated in your first letter to me, and orally through General Burnside, at the Chickahominy, I cannot decide where I can be of most use. If your determination is unchanged, I ought to go to Alexandria at once. Please define my position and duties.

"G. B. McCLELLAN,
"*Major General.*

"Major General H. W. HALLECK,
"*Commanding United States Army.*"

[illegible] which I received the following reply:

"WASHINGTON, August 26, 1862.

"[illegible]

"H. W. HALLECK,
"General-in-Chief.

"Major General McCLELLAN."

On the 27th I received the following:

"WASHINGTON, August 27, 1862—11 a. m.

"There is [illegible] the enemy is [illegible] Manassas [illegible] as very great irregularities are reported there. General Franklin's corps will march as soon as it receives transportation.

"H. W. HALLECK,
"General-in-Chief.

"Major General G. B. McCLELLAN."

On receipt of this I immediately started for Alexandria, and reported as follows:

"ALEXANDRIA, August 27, 1862—10 a. m.

"I arrived here last night, and have taken measures to ascertain the state of affairs here, and that proper [illegible] may be applied. Just received a report that railway bridge over Bull Run was burned last night.

"G. B. McCLELLAN,
"Major General.

"Major General H. W. HALLECK,
"Commanding United States Army."

"ALEXANDRIA, August 27, 1862—1? a. m.

"The town is quiet, although quite full of soldiers, who are said to be chiefly stragglers.

"The affairs of the quartermaster's department are reported as going on well.

"It is said that the Bull Run bridge will be repaired by to-morrow. The disembarkation of Sumner's corps commenced at Aquia yesterday afternoon. [illegible]

"G. B. McCLELLAN,
"Major General.

"Major General H. W. HALLECK,
"Commanding United States Army."

On the same day I received the following:

"WASHINGTON, August 27, 1862.

"Telegrams from General Porter to General Burnside, just received, say that Banks is at Fayetteville; McDowell, Sigel, and Ricketts near Warrenton; Reno on his right. Porter is marching on Warrenton Junction to reënforce

"ALEXANDRIA, *August* 27, 1862—10.30 *a. m.*

"Where are you, and what is state of affairs—what troops in your front, right, and left? Sumner is now landing at Aquia. Where is Pope's left, and what of enemy? Enemy burned Bull run bridge last night with cavalry force.

"G. B. McCLELLAN,
"*Major General.*

"Major General HEINTZELMAN, *Warrenton.*
"Major General PORTER, *Bealton.*

"P. S.—If these general officers are not at the places named, nearest operator will please have message forwarded."

I also telegraphed to the general-in-chief as follows:

"ALEXANDRIA, *August* 27, 1862—10.50 *a. m.*

"I have sent all the information I possess to Burnside, instructing him to look out well for his right flank, between the Rappahannock and Potomac, and to send no trains to Porter without an escort. I fear the cavalry who dashed at Bull run last night may trouble Burnside a little. I have sent to communicate with Porter and Heintzelman, *via* Falmouth, and hope to give you some definite information in a few hours. I shall land the next cavalry I get hold of here, and send it out to keep open the communication between Pope and Porter, also to watch vicinity of Manassas. Please send me a number of copies of the best maps of present field of operations. I can use fifty (50) to advantage.

"G. B. McCLELLAN,
"*Major General.*

"Major General HALLECK,
"*Commanding United States Army.*"

"ALEXANDRIA, *August* 27, 1862—12.50 *a. m.*

"In view of Burnside's despatch, just received, would it not be advisable to throw the mass of Sumner's corps here, to move out with Franklin to Centreville or vicinity? If a decisive battle is fought at Warrenton, a disaster would leave any troops on lower Rappahannock in a dangerous position.

"They would do better service in front of Washington.

"G. B. McCLELLAN,
"*Major General.*

"Major General HALLECK,
"*Washington, D. C.*"

"ALEXANDRIA, *August* 27, 1862—12.5 *p. m.*

"My aid has just returned from General Franklin's camp; reports that Generals Franklin, Smith, and Slocum are all in Washington. He gave the order to the next in rank to place the corps in readiness to move at once. I learn that heavy firing has been heard this morning at Centreville, and have sent to ascertain the truth. I can find no cavalry to send out on the roads. Are the works garrisoned and ready for defence?

"G. B. McCLELLAN,
"*Major General.*

Major General HALLECK, *Washington.*"

"ALEXANDRIA, *August* 27, 1862—12.20 *p. m.*

"What bridges exist over Bull run? Have steps been taken to construct bridges for the advance of troops to re-enforce Pope, or to enable him to retreat if in trouble?

"There should be two gunboats at Aquia creek at once. Shall I push the rest of Sumner's corps here, or is Pope so strong as to be reasonably certain of success? I have sent to inspect the works near here and their garrisons.

"As soon as I can find General Casey, or some other commanding officer, I will see to the railway, &c. It would be well to have them report to me, as I do not know where they are. I am trying to find them, and will lose no time in carrying out your orders. Would like to see Burnside.

"G. B. McCLELLAN,
"*Major General.*

"Major General H. W. HALLECK, *Washington.*"

"ALEXANDRIA, *August* 27, 1862—1.15 *p. m.*

"Franklin's artillery have no horses, except for (4) four guns without caissons. I can pick up no cavalry. In view of these facts, will it not be well to push Sumner's corps here by water as rapidly as possible, to make immediate arrangements for placing the works in front of Washington in an efficient condition of defence? I have no means of knowing the enemy's force between Pope and ourselves.

"Can Franklin, without his artillery or cavalry, effect any useful purpose in front?

"Should not Burnside take steps at once to evacuate Falmouth and Aquia, at the same time covering the retreat of any of Pope's troops who may fall back in that direction?

"I do not see that we have force enough in hand to form a connexion with Pope, whose exact position we do not know. Are we safe in the direction of the valley?

"G. B. McCLELLAN,
"*Major General.*

"Major General HALLECK, *Washington.*"

"ALEXANDRIA, *August* 27, 1862—1.35 *p. m.*

"I learn that Taylor's brigade, sent this morning to Bull run bridge, is either cut to pieces or captured.

"That the force against them had many guns, and about (5,000) five thousand infantry, receiving re-enforcements every minute; also, that Gainesville is in possession of the enemy. Please send some cavalry out towards Drainsville, *via* Chain bridge, to watch Lewinsville and Drainsville, and go as far as they can. If you will give me even one squadron of good cavalry here I will ascertain the state of the case. I think our policy now is to make these works perfectly safe, and mobilize a couple of corps as soon as possible, but not to advance them until they can have their artillery and cavalry. I have sent for Colonel Tyler to place his artillerymen in the works.

"Is Fort Marcy securely held?

"G. B. McCLELLAN,
"*Major General.*

"General HALLECK."

"ALEXANDRIA, *August* 27, 1862—2.30 *p. m.*

"Sumner has been ordered to send here all of his corps that are within reach. Orders have been sent to Couch to come here from Yorktown with the least possible delay. But one squadron of my cavalry has arrived; that will be disembarked at once and sent to the front.

"If there is any cavalry in Washington it should be ordered to report to me at once.

"I still think that we should first provide for the immediate defence of Washington on both sides of the Potomac.

"I am not responsible for the past, and cannot be for the future, unless I receive authority to dispose of the available troops according to my judgment. Please inform me at once what my position is. I do not wish to act in the dark.

"G. B. McCLELLAN,
"*Major General.*

"Major General H. W. HALLECK,
"*Commanding United States Army.*"

"ALEXANDRIA, *August* 27, 1863—6 *p.m.*

"I have just received the copy of a despatch from General Pope to you' dated 10 a. m. this morning, in which he says: 'All forces now sent forward should be sent to my right at Gainesville.'

"I now have at my disposal here about (10,000) ten thousand men of Franklin's corps, about (2,800) twenty-eight hundred of General Tyler's brigade and Colonel Tyler's first Connecticut artillery, which I recommend should be held in hand for the defence of Washington.

"If you wish me to order any part of this force to the front, it is in readiness to march at a moment's notice to any point you may indicate.

"In view of the existing state of things in our front, I have deemed it best to order General Casey to hold his men for Yorktown in readiness to move, but not to send them off till further orders.

"G. B. McCLELLAN,
"*Major General.*

"Major General H. W. HALLECK,
"*Commanding United States Army.*"

On the 28th I telegraphed as follows:

"HEADQUARTERS CAMP NEAR ALEXANDRIA,
"*August* 28, 1862—4.10 *p.m.*

"General Franklin is with me here. I will know in a few minutes the condition of artillery and cavalry.

"We are not yet in condition to move; may be by to-morrow morning.

"Pope must cut through to-day, or adopt the plan I suggested. I have ordered troops to garrison the works at Upton's hill. They must be held at any cost. As soon as I can see the way to spare them, I will send a corps of good troops there. It is the key to Washington, which cannot be seriously menaced as long as it is held.

"G. B. McCLELLAN,
"*Major General.*

"Major General HALLECK,
"*Washington, D. C.*"

I received the following from the general-in-chief:

"WASHINGTON, *August* 28, 1862.

"I think you had better place Sumner's corps as it arrives near the guns, and particularly at the Chain bridge.

"The principal thing to be feared now is a cavalry raid into this city, especially in the night time.

"Use Cox's and Tyler's brigade, and the new troops for the same object, if you need them.

"Porter writes to Burnside from Bristow, 9.30 a. m. yesterday, that Pope's forces were then moving on Manassas, and that Burnside would soon hear of them by way of Alexandria.

"General Cullum has gone to Harper's Ferry, and I have only a single regular officer for duty in the office.

"Please send some of your officers to-day to see that every precaution is taken at the forts against a raid; also at the bridge. Please answer.

"H. W. HALLECK,
"*General-in-Chief.*

"Major General McCLELLAN."

On the 29th the following despatch was telegraphed:

"CAMP NEAR ALEXANDRIA,
"*August* 29, 1862—10.30 *a. m.*

"Franklin's corps is in motion; started about (6) six a.m. I can give him but two squadrons of cavalry. I propose moving General Cox to Upton's hill, to hold that important point with its works, and to push cavalry scouts to Vienna, *via* Freedom hill and Hunter's lane. Cox has (2) two squadrons of cavalry. Please answer at once whether this meets your approval. I have directed Woodbury, with the engineer brigade, to hold Fort Lyon. Sumner detached, last night, two regiments to vicinity of Forts Ethan Allen and Marcy. Meagher's brigade is still at Aquia. If he moves in support of Franklin it leaves us without any reliable troops in and near Washington. Yet Franklin is too weak alone. What shall be done? No more cavalry arrived; have but (3) three squadrons. Franklin has but (10) forty rounds of ammunition, and no wagons to move more. I do not think Franklin is in condition to accomplish much if he meets with serious resistance. I should not have moved him but for your pressing order of last night. What have you from Vienna and Drainsville?

"G. B. McCLELLAN,
"*Major General.*

"Major General HALLECK,
"*Washington, D. C.*"

To which the following is a reply:

"WASHINGTON, *August* 29, 1862—12 *m.*

"Upton's hill arrangement all right. We must send wagons and ammunition to Franklin as fast as they arrive.

"Meagher's brigade ordered up yesterday. Fitzhugh Lee was, it is said on good authority, in Alexandria on Sunday last for three hours. I have nothing from Drainesville.

"H. W. HALLECK,
"*General-in-Chief.*

"Major General McCLELLAN."

On the same day the following was received from his excellency the President:

"WASHINGTON, *August* 29, 1862—2.30 *p. m.*

"What news from direction of Manassas Junction? What generally?

"A. LINCOLN.

"Major General McCLELLAN."

To which I replied as follows:

"CAMP NEAR ALEXANDRIA,
"*August*, 29, 1862—2.45 *p. m.*

"The last news I received from the direction of Manassas was from stragglers, to the effect that the enemy were evacuating Centreville and retiring towards Thoroughfare gap. This by no means reliable.

"I am clear that one of two courses should be adopted: 1st, to concentrate all our available forces to open communications with Pope; 2d, to leave Pope to get out of his scrape, and at once use all our means to make the capital perfectly safe.

"No middle ground will now answer. Tell me what you wish me to do, and I will do all in my power to accomplish it. I wish to know what my orders and authority are. I ask for nothing, but will obey whatever orders you give. I only ask a prompt decision that I may at once give the necessary orders. It will not do to delay longer.

"G. B. McCLELLAN,
"*Major General.*

"A. LINCOLN, *President.*"
And copy to General Halleck.

To which the following is a reply:

"WASHINGTON, *August* 29, 1862—4.10 *p. m.*

"Yours of to-day just received. I think your first alternative, to wit, 'to concentrate all our available forces to open communication with Pope,' is the right one, but I wish not to control. That I now leave to General Halleck, aided by your counsels.

"A. LINCOLN.

"Major General McCLELLAN."

It had been officially reported to me from Washington that the enemy, in strong force, was moving through Vienna in the direction of the Chain bridge, and had a large force in Vienna. This report, in connexion with the despatch of the general-in-chief on the 28th, before noted, induced me to direct Franklin to halt his command near Anandale until it could be determined, by reconnoissances to Vienna and towards Manassas, whether these reports were true. General Cox was ordered to send his small cavalry force from Upton's hill towards Vienna and Drainsville in one direction, and towards Fairfax Court House in the other, and Franklin to push his two squadrons as far towards Manassas as possible, in order to ascertain the true position of the enemy.

With the enemy in force at Vienna, and towards Lewinsville, it would have been very injudicious to have pushed Franklin's small force beyond Anandale. It must be remembered that at that time we were cut off from direct communication with General Pope; that the enemy was, by the last accounts, at Manassas in strong force, and that Franklin had only from 10,000 to 11,000 men, with an entirely insufficient force of cavalry and artillery.

In order to represent this condition of affairs in its proper light to the general-in-chief, and to obtain definite instructions from him, I telegraphed as follows:

"CAMP NEAR ALEXANDRIA,
"*August* 29, 1862—12 *m.*

"Have ordered most of the (12th) twelfth Pennsylvania cavalry to report to General Barnard for scouting duty towards Rockville, Poolsville, &c.

"If you apprehended a raid of cavalry on your side of river, I had better send a brigade or two of Sumner's to near Tenallytown, where, with two or three old regiments in Forts Allen and Marcy, they can watch both Chain bridge and Tenallytown.

"Would it meet your views to post the rest of Sumner's corps between Arlington and Fort Corcoran, whence they can either support Cox, Franklin, or Chain bridge, and even Tenallytown?

"Franklin has only between (10,000) ten thousand and (11,000) eleven thousand for duty.

"How far do you wish this force to advance?

"G. B. McCLELLAN,
"*Major General.*

"Major General HALLECK, *Washington.*"

"CAMP NEAR ALEXANDRIA,
"*August* 29, 1862—1 *p. m.*

"I anxiously await reply to my last despatch in regard to Sumner. Wish to give the order at once.

"Please authorize me to attach new regiments permanently to my old brigades. I can do much good to old and new troops in that way. I shall endeavor to hold a line in advance of Forts Allen and Marcy, at least with strong advanced guards. I wish to hold the line through Prospect hill, Mackall's, Minor's, and Hall's hill. This will give us timely warning. Shall I do as seems best to me with all the troops in this vicinity, including Franklin, who I really think ought not, under present circumstances, to advance beyond Anandale?

"G. B. McCLELLAN,
"*Major General.*

"General HALLECK."

On the same day I received a despatch from the general-in-chief, in which he asks me why I halted Franklin in Anandale, to which I replied as follows:

"CAMP NEAR ALEXANDRIA,
"*August* 29, 1862—10.30 *a. m.*

"By referring to my telegrams of 10.30 a. m., 12 m., and 1 p. m., together with your reply of 2.48 p. m., you will see why Franklin's corps halted at Anandale. His small cavalry force, all I had to give him, was ordered to push on as far as possible towards Manassas.

"It was not safe for Franklin to move beyond Anandale, under the circumstances, until we knew what was at Vienna.

"General Franklin remained here until about 1 p. m., endeavoring to arrange for supplies for his command. I am responsible for both these circumstances, and do not see that either was in disobedience to your orders.

"Please give distinct orders in reference to Franklin's movements of to-morrow. I have sent to Colonel Haupt to push out construction and supply trains as soon as possible.

"General Tyler to furnish the necessary guards.

"I have directed General Banks's supply trains to start out to-night at least as far as Anandale, with an escort from General Tyler.

"In regard to to-morrow's movements I desire definite instructions, as it is not agreeable to me to be accused of disobeying orders, when I have simply exercised the discretion you committed to me.

"G. B. McCLELLAN,
"*Major General.*

"Major General HALLECK,
"*Washington, D. C.*"

On the same evening I sent the following despatches:

"CAMP NEAR ALEXANDRIA,
"*August* 29, 1862—10 *p. m.*

"Not hearing from you, I have sent orders to General Franklin to place himself in communication with General Pope as soon as possible, and at the same time cover the transit of Pope's supplies.

"Orders have been given for railway and wagon trains to move to Pope with least possible delay.

"I am having inspections made of all the forts around the city by members of my staff, with instructions to give all requisite orders.

"I inspected Worth and Ward myself this evening; found them in good order.

"Reports, so far as heard from, are favorable as to condition of works.

"G. B. McCLELLAN,
"*Major General.*

"Major General HALLECK, *Washington.*"

"CAMP NEAR ALEXANDRIA,
"*August* 29, 1862—10 *p. m.*

"Your despatch received. Franklin's corps has been ordered to march at 6 o'clock to-morrow morning. Sumner has about fourteen thousand infantry, without cavalry or artillery, here. Cox's brigade of four regiments is here, with two batteries of artillery. Men of two regiments, much fatigued, came in to-day. Tyler's brigade of three new regiments, but little drilled, is also here; all these troops will be ordered to hold themselves ready to march to-morrow morning, and all except Franklin's to await further orders.

"If you wish any of them to move towards Manassas, please inform me.

"Colonel Wagner, 2d New York artillery, has just come in from the front. He reports strong infantry and cavalry force of rebels near Fairfax Court House. Reports rumors from various sources that Lee and Stuart, with large forces, are at Manassas.

"That the enemy, with 120,000 men, intend advancing on the forts near Arlington and Chain bridge, with a view of attacking Washington and Baltimore.

"General Barnard telegraphs me to-night that the length of the line of fortifications on this side of the Potomac requires 2,000 additional artillerymen, and additional troops to defend intervals, according to circumstances; at all events, he says an old regiment should be added to the force at Chain bridge, and a few regiments distributed along the lines to give confidence to our new troops. I agree with him fully, and think our fortifications along the upper part of our line on this side the river very unsafe with their present garrisons, and the movements of the enemy seem to indicate an attack upon those works.

"G. B. McCLELLAN,
"*Major General.*

"General H. W. HALLECK,
General-in-Chief United States Army, Washington, D. C."

"CAMP NEAR ALEXANDRIA,
"*August* 30, 1862—11.30 *a. m.*

"Your telegram of 9 a. m. received. Ever since General Franklin received notice that he was to march from Alexandria, he has been endeavoring to get transportation from the quartermaster at Alexandria, but he has uniformly been told that there was none disposable, and his command marched without wagons.

After the departure of his corps he procured twenty wagons to carry some extra ammunition, by unloading Banks's supply train.

"General Sumner endeavored, by application upon the quartermaster's department, to get wagons to carry his reserve ammunition, but without success, and was obliged to march with what he could carry in his cartridge-boxes.

"I have this morning directed that all my headquarters wagons that are landed be at once loaded with ammunition for Sumner and Franklin; but they will not go far towards supplying the deficiency.

"Eighty-five wagons were got together by the quartermasters last night, loaded with subsistence, and sent forward at 1 a. m. with an escort via Anandale. Every effort has been made to carry out your orders promptly. The great difficulty seems to consist in the fact that the greater part of the transportation on hand at Alexandria and Washington has been needed for current supplies of the garrisons. Such is the state of the case as represented to me by the quartermasters, and it appears to be true.

"I take it for granted that this has not been properly explained to you.

"G. B. McCLELLAN,
"*Major General.*

"Major General HALLECK,
"*General-in-Chief.*"

On the morning of the 30th heavy artillery firing was heard in th direction of Fairfax Court House, which I reported to the general-in-chief.

At 11 a. m. the following telegram was sent:

"CAMP NEAR ALEXANDRIA,
"*August* 30, 1862—11 *a. m.*

"Have ordered Sumner to leave (1) one brigade in vicinity of Chain bridge, and to move the rest via Columbia pike on Anandale and Fairfax Court House

"Is this the route you wish them to take? He and Franklin are both instructed to join Pope as promptly as possible.

"Shall Couch move out also when he arrives?

"G. B. McCLELLAN,
"*Major General.*

"Major General HALLECK, *Washington.*"

On the same day I received the following:

"WASHINGTON, *August* 30, 1862—1.45 *p. m.*

"Ammunition, and particularly for artillery, must be immediately sent forward to Centreville for General Pope. It must be done with all possible despatch.

"H. W. HALLECK,
"*General-in-Chief.*

"General McCLELLAN."

To which this reply was made:

"CAMP NEAR ALEXANDRIA,
"*August* 30, 1862—2.10 *p. m.*

"I know nothing of the calibres of Pope's artillery. All I can do is to direct my ordnance officer to load up all the wagons sent to him. I have already sent all my headquarters wagons. You will have to see that wagons are sent from Washington. I can do nothing more than give the order that every available wagon in Alexandria shall be loaded at once.

"The order to the brigade of Sumner that I directed to remain near Chain bridge and Tenallytown should go from your headquarters to save time. I understand you to intend it also to move. I have no sharpshooters except the guard around my camp. I have sent off every man but those, and will now send them with the train as you direct. I will also send my only remaining squadron of cavalry with General Sumner. I can do no more. You now have every man of the army of the Potomac who is within my reach.

"G. B. McCLELLAN,
"*Major General.*

"Major General H. W. HALLECK."

At 10.30 p. m. the following telegram was sent:

"CAMP NEAR ALEXANDRIA,
"*August* 30, 1862—10.30 *p. m.*

"I have sent to the front all my troops with the exception of Couch's division, and have given the orders necessary to insure its being disposed of as you directed. I hourly expect the return of one of my aids, who will give authentic news from the field of battle.

"I cannot express to you the pain and mortification I have experienced to-day in listening to the distant sound of the firing of my men. As I can be of no further use here, I respectfully ask that, if there is a probability of the conflict being renewed to-morrow, I may be permitted to go to the scene of battle with my staff, merely to be with my own men, if nothing more; they will fight none the worse for my being with them. If it is not deemed best to intrust me with the command even of my own army, I simply ask to be permitted to share their fate on the field of battle.

"Please reply to this to-night.

"I have been engaged for the last few hours in doing what I can to make arrangements for the wounded. I have started out all the ambulances now landed. As I have sent my escort to the front, I would be glad to take some of Gregg's cavalry with me, if allowed to go.

"G. B. McCLELLAN,
"*Major General.*

"Major General H. W. HALLECK,
"*Commanding United States Army, Washington, D. C.*"

To which, on the following day, I received this answer:

"WASHINGTON, *August* 31, 1862—9.18 *a. m.*

"I have just seen your telegram of 11.5 last night. The substance was stated to me when received, but I did not know that you asked for a reply immediately. I cannot answer without seeing the President, as General Pope is in command, by his orders, of the department.

"I think Couch's division should go forward as rapidly as possible and find the battle-field.

"H. W. HALLECK,
"*General-in-Chief.*

"Major General McCLELLAN."

On the same day the following was received:

"WASHINGTON, *August* 31, 1862—12.45 *p. m.*

"The subsistence department are making Fairfax station their principal depot. It should be well guarded. The officer in charge should be directed to secure the depot by abatis against cavalry. As many as possible of the new regiments should be prepared to take the field. Perhaps some more should be sent to the vicinity of Chain bridge.

"H. W. HALLECK,
"*General-in-Chief.*

"Major General McCLELLAN."

At 2.30 p. m. the following despatch was telegraphed:

"CAMP NEAR ALEXANDRIA,
"*August* 31, 1862—2.30 *p. m.*

"Major Haller is at Fairfax station with my provost and headquarters guard and other troops. I have requested (4) four more companies to be sent at once, and the precautions you direct to be taken.

"Under the War Department order of yesterday I have no control over anything except my staff, some one hundred men in my camp here, and the few remaining near Fort Monroe. I have no control over the new regiments—do not know where they are, or anything about them, except those near here. Their commanding officers and those of the works are not under me.

"Where I have seen evils existing under my eye I have corrected them. I think it is the business of General Casey to prepare the new regiments for the field, and a matter between him and General Barnard to order others to the vicinity of Chain bridge. Neither of them is under my command, and by the War Department order I have no right to give them orders.

"G. B. McCLELLAN,
"*Major General.*

"General HALLECK, *Washington.*"

To which the following is an answer:

"WASHINGTON, *August* 31, 1862—10.7 *p. m.*

"Since receiving your despatch, relating to command, I have not been able to answer any not of absolute necessity. I have not seen the order as published, but will write to you in the morning. You will retain the command of everything in this vicinity not temporarily belonging to Pope's army in the field.

"I beg of you to assist me in this crisis with your ability and experience. I am entirely tired out.

"H. W. HALLECK,
"*General-in-Chief.*

"General McCLELLAN."

The order referred to in the preceding despatch was as follows:

"WAR DEPARTMENT, *August* 30, 1862.

"The following are the commanders of the armies operating in Virginia:

"General Burnside commands his own corps, except those that have been temporarily detached and assigned to General Pope.

"General McClellan commands that portion of the army of the Potomac that has not been sent forward to General Pope's command.

"General Pope commands the army of Virginia and all the forces temporarily attached to it. All the forces are under the command of Major General Halleck, general-in-chief.

"E. D. TOWNSEND,
"*Assistant Adjutant General.*"

I was informed by Colonel Townsend that the above was published by order of the Secretary of War.

At 11.30 p. m. I telegraphed the following:

"CAMP NEAR ALEXANDRIA,
"*August* 31, 1862—11.30 *p. m.*

"The squadron of 2d regular cavalry that I sent with General Sumner was captured to-day about 2 p. m., some three miles from Fairfax Court House, beyond it on the Little river pike, by Fitz Hugh Lee, with three thousand cavalry and three light batteries.

"I have conversed with the 1st sergeant, who says that when he last saw them they were within a mile of Fairfax. Pope had no troops on that road; this squadron getting there by mistake. There is nothing of ours on the right of Centreville but Sumner's corps. There was much artillery firing during the day. A rebel major told the sergeant that the rebels had driven in our entire left to-day. He says the road is filled with wagons and stragglers coming towards Alexandria.

"It is clear from the sergeant's account that we were badly beaten yesterday, and that Pope's right is entirely exposed.

"I recommend that no more of Couch's division be sent to the front, that Burnside be brought here as soon as practicable, and that everything available this side of Fairfax be drawn in at once, including the mass of the troops on the railroad. I apprehend that the enemy will, or have by this time occupied Fairfax Court House and cut off Pope entirely, unless he falls back to-night *via* Sangster's and Fairfax station.

"I think these orders should be sent at once. I have no confidence in the dispositions made as I gather them. To speak frankly—and the occasion requires it—there appears to be a total absence of brains, and I fear the total destruction of the army. I have some cavalry here that can carry out any orders you may have to send. The occasion is grave, and demands grave measures. The question is, the salvation of the country. I learn that our loss yesterday amounted to fifteen thousand. We cannot afford such losses without an object.

"It is my deliberate opinion that the interests of the nation demand that Pope should fall back to-night if possible, and not one moment is to be lost.

"I will use all the cavalry I have to watch our right. Please answer at once. I feel confident that you can rely upon the information I give you.

"I shall be up all night, and ready to obey any orders you give me.

"G. B. McCLELLAN,
"*Major General.*

"General HALLECK, *Washington.*"

To which this reply was received:

"WASHINGTON, *September* 1, 1862—1.30 *a. m.*

"Burnside was ordered up very early yesterday morning. Retain remainder of Couch's forces, and make arrangements to stop all retreating troops in line of works, or where you can best establish an entire line of defence. My news from Pope was up to 4 p. m.; he was then all right. I must wait for more definite information before I can order a retreat, as the falling back on the line of works must necessarily be directed in case of a serious disaster. Give me all additional news that is reliable.

"I shall be up all night, and ready to act as circumstances may require. I am fully aware of the gravity of the crisis, and have been for weeks.

"H. W. HALLECK,
"*General-in-Chief.*

"Major General McCLELLAN."

FOURTH PERIOD.

On the 1st of September I went into Washington, where I had an interview with the general-in-chief, who instructed me, verbally, to take command of its defences, expressly limiting my jurisdiction to the works and their garrisons, and prohibiting me from exercising any control over the troops actively engaged in front under General Pope. During this interview I suggested to the general-in-chief the necessity of his going in person, or sending one of his personal staff, to the army under General Pope, for the purpose of ascertaining the exact condition of affairs; he sent Colonel Kelton, his assistant adjutant general.

During the afternoon of the same day I received a message from the general-in-chief, to the effect that he desired me to go at once to his house to see the President.

The President informed me that he had reason to believe that the army of the Potomac was not cheerfully co-operating with and supporting General Pope; that he had "always been a friend of mine;" and now asked me, as a special favor, to use my influence in correcting this state of things. I replied, substantially, that I was confident that he was misinformed; that I was sure, whatever estimate the army of the Potomac might entertain of General Pope, that they would obey his orders, support him to the fullest extent, and do their whole duty. The President, who was much moved, asked me to telegraph to "Fitz-John Porter, or some other of my friends," and try to do away with any feeling that might exist; adding, that I could rectify the evil, and that no one else could.

I thereupon told him that I would cheerfully telegraph to General Porter, or do anything else in my power to gratify his wishes and relieve his anxiety; upon which he thanked me very warmly, assured me that he could never forget my action in the matter, &c., and left.

I then wrote the following telegram to General Porter, which was sent to him by the general-in-chief:

"WASHINGTON, *September* 1, 1862.

"I ask of you, for my sake, that of the country, and the old army of the Potomac, that you and all my friends will lend the fullest and most cordial co-operation to General Pope, in all the operations now going on. The destinies of our country, the honor of our arms, are at stake, and all depends now upon the cheerful co-operation of all in the field. This week is the crisis of our fate. Say the same thing to my friends in the army of the Potomac, and that the last request I have to make of them is, that, for their country's sake, they will extend to General Pope the same support they ever have to me.

"I am in charge of the defences of Washington, and am doing all I can to render your retreat safe, should that become necessary.

"GEO. B. McCLELLAN.

"Major General PORTER."

To which he sent the following reply:

"FAIRFAX COURT HOUSE, 10 a. m.,
"*September* 2, 1862.

"You may rest assured that all your friends, as well as every lover of his country, will ever give, as they have given, to General Pope their cordial co-operation and constant support in the execution of all orders and plans. Our killed, wounded, and enfeebled troops attest our devoted duty.

"F. J. PORTER.

"General GEORGE B. McCLELLAN,
"*Major General Commanding, Washington.*"

Neither at the time I wrote the telegram, nor at any other time, did I think for one moment that General Porter had been, or would be, in any manner derelict in the performance of his duty to the nation and its cause. Such an impression never entered my mind. The despatch in question was written purely at the request of the President.

On the morning of the 2d the President and General Halleck came to my house, when the President informed me that Colonel Kelton had returned from the front: that our affairs were in a bad condition; that the army was in full retreat upon the defences of Washington; the roads filled with stragglers, &c. He instructed me to take steps at once to stop and collect the stragglers; to place the works in a proper state of defence, and to go out to meet and take command of the army, when it approached the vicinity of the works, then to place the troops in the best position—committing everything to my hands.

I immediately took steps to carry out these orders, and sent an aid to General Pope with the following letter:

"HEADQUARTERS, WASHINGTON,
"*September* 2, 1862.

"GENERAL: General Halleck instructed me to report to you the order he sent this morning to withdraw your army to Washington, without unnecessary delay. He feared that his messenger might miss you, and desired to take this double precaution.

"In order to bring troops upon ground with which they are already familiar, it would be best to move Porter's corps upon Upton's hill, that it may occupy Hall's hill, &c.; McDowell's to Upton's hill; Franklin's to the works in front of Alexandria; Heintzelman's to the same vicinity; Couch to Fort Corcoran, or, if practicable, to the Chain bridge; Sumner either to Fort Albany or to Alexandria, as may be most convenient.

"In haste, general, very truly yours,

"GEO. B. McCLELLAN,
"*Major General United States Army.*

"Major General JOHN POPE,
"*Commanding Army of Virginia.*"

In the afternoon I crossed the Potomac and rode to the front, and at Upton's hill met the advance of McDowell's corps, and with it Generals Pope and McDowell. After getting what information I could from them, I sent the few aids at my disposal to the left to give instructions to the troops approaching in the direction of Alexandria: and hearing artillery firing in the direction of the Vienna and Langley road, by which the corps of Sumner, Porter, and Sigel were returning, and learning from General Pope that Sumner was probably engaged, I went, with a single aid and three orderlies, by the shortest line to meet that column. I reached the column after dark, and proceeded as far as Lewinsville, where I became satisfied that the rear corps (Sumner's) would be able to reach its intended position without any serious molestation.

I therefore indicated to Generals Porter and Sigel the positions they were to occupy, sent instructions to General Sumner, and at a late hour of the night returned to Washington.

Next day I rode to the front of Alexandria, and was engaged in rectifying the positions of the troops, and giving orders necessary to secure the issuing of the necessary supplies, &c.

I felt sure on this day that we could repulse any attack made by the enemy on the south side of the Potomac.

On the 3d the enemy had disappeared from the front of Washington, and the information which I received induced me to believe that he intended to cross the upper Potomac into Maryland. This materially changed the aspect of affairs, and enlarged the sphere of operations; for, in case of a crossing in force, an active campaign would be necessary to cover Baltimore, prevent the invasion of Pennsylvania, and clear Maryland.

I therefore, on the third, ordered the 2d and 12th corps to Tenallytown, and the 9th corps to a point on the Seventh street road near Washington, and sent such cavalry as was available to the fords near Poolsville, to watch and impede the enemy in any attempt to cross in that vicinity.

On September 5, the 2d and 12th corps were moved to Rockville, and Couch's division (the only one of the 4th corps that had been brought from the Peninsula) to Offut's cross-roads.

On the 6th the 1st and 9th corps were ordered to Leesburg; the 6th corps, and Sykes's division of the 5th corps, to Tenallytown.

On the 7th the 6th corps was advanced to Rockville, to which place my headquarters were moved on the same day.

All the necessary arrangements for the defence of the city, under the new condition of things, had been made, and General Banks was left in command, having received his instructions from me.

It will be seen from what has preceded that I lost no time that could be avoided in moving the army of the Potomac from the Peninsula to the support of the army of Virginia; that I spared no effort to hasten the embarcation of the troops at Fort Monroe, Newport News and Yorktown, remaining at Fort Monroe myself until the mass of the army had sailed; and that, after my arrival at Alexandria, I left nothing in my power undone to forward supplies and re-enforcements to General Pope. I sent, with the troops that moved, all the cavalry I could get hold of. Even my personal escort was sent out upon the line of the railway as a guard, with the provost and camp guards at headquarters, retaining less than one hundred men, many of whom were orderlies, invalids, members of bands, &c. All the headquarters teams that arrived were sent out with supplies and ammunition, none being retained even to move the headquarters camp. The squadron that habitually served as my personal escort was left at Falmouth with General Burnside, as he was deficient in cavalry.

I left Washington on the 7th of September. At this time it was known that the mass of the rebel army had passed up the south side of the Potomac in the direction of Leesburg, and that a portion of that army had crossed into Maryland; but whether it was their intention to cross their whole force with a view to turn Washington by a flank movement down the north bank of the Potomac, to move on Baltimore, or to invade Pennsylvania, were questions which, at that time, we had no means of determining. This uncertainty as to the intentions of the enemy obliged me, up to the 13th of September, to march cautiously and to advance the army in such order as continually to keep Washington and Baltimore covered, and at the same time to hold the troops well in hand so as to be able to concentrate and follow rapidly if the enemy took the direction of Pennsylvania; or to return to the defence of Washington, if, as was greatly feared by the authorities, the enemy should be merely making a feint with a small force to draw off our army, while with their main forces they stood ready to seize the first favorable opportunity to attack the capital.

In the mean time the process of re-organization, rendered necessary after the demoralizing effects of the disastrous campaign upon the other side of the Potomac, was rapidly progressing; the troops were regaining confidence, and their former soldierly appearance and discipline were fast returning. My cavalry was pushed out continually in all directions, and all possible steps were taken to learn the positions and movements of the enemy.

The following table shows the movements of the army, from day to day, up to the 14th of September:

	September 4.	September 6.	September 9.	September 10.
BURNSIDE.				
9th corps, Reno	Seventh street road.	Leesburg	Brookville	
1st corps, Hooker	Upton's hill	Leesburg	Brookville	
SUMNER.				
12th corps, Williams	Tenallytown	Rockville	Middleburg	Damascus
2d corps, Sumner	Tenallytown	Rockville	Middleburg	Clarksburg
FRANKLIN.				
6th corps, Franklin	Alex. Seminary	Tenallytown	Darnestown	Barnsville
Couch's division	Tenallytown	Offut's Cross Roads.	Mouth of Seneca	Poolsville
Sykes's division		Tenallytown	Rockville	Rockville

	September 11.	September 12.	September 13.	September 14.
BURNSIDE.				
9th corps, Reno	New Market	Frederick	Middleburg	South Mountain
1st corps, Hooker		Ridgeville, New Market, camp on the Monocacy.	Frederick	South Mountain
SUMNER.				
12th corps, Williams	Damascus	Ijamsville Cross Roads.	Frederick	South Mountain
2d corps, Sumner	Clarksburg	Urbana	Frederick	South Mountain
FRANKLIN.				
6th corps, Franklin	Barnsville	Lickenwell Cross Road.	Buckeystown	Burkettsville
Couch's division	Poolsville	Barnsville	Sicksville	Burkettsville
Sykes's division	Middleburg	Urbana	Frederick	Middletown

The right wing, consisting of the 1st and 9th corps, under the command of Major General Burnside, moved on Frederick; the 1st corps *via* Brooksville, Cooksville and Ridgeville, and the 9th corps *via* Damascus and New Market.

The 2d and 12th corps, forming the centre, under the command of General Sumner, moved on Frederick; the former *via* Clarksburg and Urbana, the 12th corps on a lateral road between Urbana and New Market, thus maintaining the communication with the right wing, and covering the direct road from Frederick to Washington. The 6th corps, under the command of General Franklin, moved to Buckeystown *via* Darnestown, Dawsonville and Barnesville, covering the road from the mouth of the Monocacy to Rockville, and being in a position to connect with and support the centre, should it have been necessary (as was supposed) to force the line of the Monocacy.

Couch's division moved by the "river road," covering that approach, watching the fords of the Potomac, and ultimately following and supporting the 6th corps.

The following extracts from telegrams, received by me after my departure from Washington, will show how little was known there about the enemy's movements, and the fears which were entertained for the safety of the capital. On the 9th of September, General Halleck telegraphed me as follows:

"Until we can get better advices about the numbers of the enemy at Drainsville, I think we must be very cautious about stripping, too much, the forts on the Virginia side. It may be the enemy's object to draw off the mass of our forces and then attempt to attack from the Virginia side of the Potomac. Think of this."

Again, on the 11th of September, General Halleck telegraphed me as follows:

"Why not order forward Keyes or Sigel? I think the main force of the enemy is in your front; more troops can be spared from here."

This despatch, as published by the Committee on the Conduct of the War, and furnished by the general-in-chief, reads as follows:

"Why not order forward Porter's corps or Sigel's? *If the main force of the enemy* is in your front, more troops can be spared from here."

I remark that the original despatch, as received by me from the telegraph operator, is in the words quoted above, "*I think the main force of the enemy*," &c.

In accordance with this suggestion I asked, on the same day, that all the troops that could be spared should at once be sent to re-enforce me, but none came.

On the 12th I received the following telegram from his excellency the President: "Governor Curtin telegraphs me, 'I have advices that Jackson is crossing the Potomac at Williamsport, and probably the whole rebel army will be drawn from Maryland.'" The President adds: "Receiving nothing from Harper's Ferry or Martinsburg to-day, and positive information from Wheeling that the line is cut, corroborates the idea that the enemy is re-crossing the Potomac. Please do not let him get off without being hurt."

On the 13th General Halleck telegraphed as follows: "Until you know more certainly the enemy's force south of the Potomac, you are wrong in thus uncovering the capital. I am of the opinion that the enemy will send a small column towards Pennsylvania to draw your forces in that direction, then suddenly move on Washington with the forces south of the Potomac and those he may cross over." Again, on the 14th, General Halleck telegraphed me that "scouts report a large force still on the Virginia side of the Potomac. If so, I fear you are exposing your left and rear."

Again, as late as the 16th, after we had the most positive evidence that Lee's entire army was in front of us, I received the following:

"WAR DEPARTMENT,
"*September* 16, 1862—12.3 *p. m.*

"Yours of 7 a. m. is this moment received. As you give me no information in regard to the position of your forces, except that at Sharpsburg, of course I cannot advise. I think, however, you will find that the whole force of the enemy in your front has crossed the river; I fear now more than ever that they will re-cross at Harper's Ferry, or below, and turn your left, thus cutting you off from Washington. This has appeared to me to be a part of their plan, and hence my anxiety on the subject; a heavy rain might prevent it.

"H. W. HALLECK,
"*General-in-Chief.*

"Major General McCLELLAN."

The importance of moving with all due caution, so as not to uncover the national capital until the enemy's position and plans were developed, was, I believe, fully appreciated by me; and as my troops extended from the Baltimore and Ohio railroad to the Potomac, with the extreme left flank moving along that stream, and with strong pickets left in rear to watch and guard all the available fords, I did not regard my left or rear as in any degree exposed. But it appears from the foregoing telegrams that the general-in-chief was of a different opinion, and that my movements were, in his judgment, too precipitate, not only for the safety of Washington, but also for the security of my left and rear.

The precise nature of these daily injunctions against a precipitate advance may now be perceived. The general-in-chief, in his testimony before the Committee on the Conduct of the War, says: "In respect to General McClellan going too fast or too slow from Washington, there can be found no such telegram from me to him. He had mistaken the meaning of the telegrams I sent him. I telegraphed him that he was going too far, not from Washington, but from the Potomac. leaving General Lee the opportunity to come down the Potomac and get between him and Washington. I thought General McClellan should keep more on the Potomac, and press forward his left rather than his right, so as the more readily to relieve Harper's Ferry."

As I can find no telegram from the general-in-chief recommending me to keep my left flank nearer the Potomac, I am compelled to believe that when he gave this testimony he had forgotten the purport of the telegrams above quoted, and had also ceased to remember the fact, well known to him at the time, that my left, from the time I left Washington, always rested on the Potomac, and my centre was continually in position to re-enforce the left or right, as occasion might require. Had I advanced my left flank along the Potomac more rapidly than the other columns marched upon the roads to the right, I should have thrown that flank out of supporting distance of the other troops, and greatly exposed it. And if I had marched the entire army in one column along the bank of the river instead of upon five different parallel roads, the column, with its trains, would have extended about fifty miles, and the enemy might have defeated the advance before the rear could have reached the scene of action. Moreover, such a movement would have uncovered the communications with Baltimore and Washington on our right, and exposed our right and rear. I presume it will be admitted by every military man that it was necessary to move the army in such order that it could at any time be concentrated for battle; and I am of opinion that this object could not have been accomplished in any other way than the one employed. Any other disposition of our forces would have subjected them to defeat in detached fragments.

On the 10th of September I received from my scouts information which rendered it quite probable that General Lee's army was in the vicinity of Frederick, but whether his intention was to move towards Baltimore or Pennsylvania was not then known. On the 11th I ordered General Burnside to push a strong reconnoissance across the National road and the Baltimore and Ohio railroad, towards New Market, and, if he learned that the enemy had moved towards Hagerstown, to press on rapidly to Frederick, keeping his troops constantly ready to meet the enemy in force. A corresponding movement of all the troops in the centre and on the left was ordered in the direction of Urbana and Poolsville.

On the 12th a portion of the right wing entered Frederick, after a brisk skirmish at the outskirts of the city and in the streets.

On the 13th the main bodies of the right wing and centre passed through Frederick. It was soon ascertained that the main body of the enemy's forces had marched out of the city on the two previous days, taking the roads to Boonsboro' and Harper's Ferry, thereby rendering it necessary to force the passes through the Catoctin and South Mountain ridges, and gain possession of Boonsboro' and Rohrersville before any relief could be extended to Colonel Miles at Harper's Ferry.

On the 13th an order fell into my hands, issued by General Lee, which fully disclosed his plans, and I immediately gave orders for a rapid and vigorous forward movement.

The following is a copy of the order referred to:

"SPECIAL ORDERS No. 191.

"HEADQUARTERS ARMY OF NORTHERN VIRGINIA,
"*September* 9, 1862.

"The army will resume its march to-morrow, taking the Hagerstown road. General Jackson's command will form the advance, and, after passing Middletown, with such portion as he may select, take the route towards Sharpsburg, cross the Potomac at the most convenient point, and, by Friday night, take possession of the Baltimore and Ohio railroad, capture such of the enemy as may be at Martinsburg, and intercept such as may attempt to escape from Harper's Ferry.

"General Longstreet's command will pursue the same road as far as Boonsboro', where it will halt with the reserve, supply and baggage trains of the army.

"General McLaws, with his own division and that of General R. H. Anderson, will follow General Longstreet: on reaching Middletown, he will take the route to Harper's Ferry, and, by Friday morning, possess himself of the Maryland heights, and endeavor to capture the enemy at Harper's Ferry and vicinity.

"General Walker, with his division, after accomplishing the object in which he is now engaged, will cross the Potomac at Cheek's ford, ascend its right bank to Lovettsville, take possession of Loudon heights, if practicable, by Friday morning; Keys's ford on his left, and the road between the end of the mountain and the Potomac on his right. He will, as far as practicable, co-operate with General McLaws and General Jackson in intercepting the retreat of the enemy.

"General D. H. Hill's division will form the rear guard of the army, pursuing the road taken by the main body. The reserve artillery, ordnance and supply trains, &c., will precede General Hill.

"General Stuart will detach a squadron of cavalry to accompany the commands of Generals Longstreet, Jackson and McLaws, and, with the main body of the cavalry, will cover the route of the army, and bring up all stragglers that may have been left behind.

"The commands of Generals Jackson, McLaws and Walker, after accomplishing the objects for which they have been detached, will join the main body of the army at Boonsboro' or Hagerstown.

"Each regiment on the march will habitually carry its axes in the regimental ordnance wagons, for use of the men at their encampments, to procure wood, &c.

"By command of General R. E. Lee.

"R. H. CHILTON,
"*Assistant Adjutant General.*

"Major General D. H. HILL,
"*Commanding Division.*"

In the report of a military commission, of which Major General D. Hunter was president, which convened at Washington for the purpose of investigating the conduct of certain officers in connexion with the surrender of Harper's Ferry, I find the following:

"The commission has remarked freely on Colonel Miles, an old officer, who has been killed in the service of his country, and it cannot, from any motives of delicacy, refrain from censuring those in high command when it thinks such censure deserved.

"The general-in-chief has testified that General McClellan, after having received orders to repel the enemy invading the State of Maryland, marched only six miles per day, on an average, when pursuing this invading army.

"The general-in-chief also testifies that, in his opinion, he could and should have relieved and protected Harper's Ferry, and in this opinion the commission fully concur."

I have been greatly surprised that this commission, in its investigations, never called upon me, nor upon any officer of my staff, nor, so far as I know, upon any officer of the army of the Potomac able to give an intelligent statement of the movements of that army. But another paragraph in the same report makes testimony from such sources quite superfluous. It is as follows:

"By a reference to the evidence it will be seen that, at the very moment Colonel Ford abandoned Maryland heights, his little army was in reality relieved by Generals Franklin's and Sumner's corps at Crampton's gap, within seven miles of his position."

The corps of Generals Franklin and Sumner were a part of the army which I at that time had the honor to command, and they were acting under my orders at Crampton's gap and elsewhere; and if, as the commission states, Colonel Ford's "little army was in reality relieved" by those officers, it was relieved by me.

I had, on the morning of the 10th, sent the following despatch in relation to the command at Harper's Ferry:

"CAMP NEAR ROCKVILLE,
"*September* 10, 1862—9.45 *a. m.*

"Colonel Miles is at or near Harper's Ferry, as I understand, with nine thousand troops. He can do nothing where he is, but could be of great service if ordered to join me. I suggest that he be ordered to join me by the most practicable route.

"GEORGE B. McCLELLAN,
"*Major General.*

"Major General HALLECK,
"*Washington, D. C.*"

To this I received the following reply:

"There is no way for Colonel Miles to join you at present; his only chance is to defend his works till you can open communication with him.

"H. W. HALLECK."

"GEORGE B. McCLELLAN, *Major General.*"

It seems necessary, for a distinct understanding of this matter, to state that I was directed on the 12th to assume command of the garrison of Harper's Ferry as soon as I should open communications with that place, and that when I received this order all communication from the direction in which I was approaching was cut off. Up to that time, however, Colonel Miles could, in my opinion, have marched his command into Pennsylvania, by crossing the Potomac at Williamsport or above; and this opinion was confirmed by the fact that Colonel Davis marched the cavalry part of Colonel Miles's command from Harper's Ferry on the 14th, taking the main road to Hagerstown, and he encountered no enemy except a small picket near the mouth of the Antietam.

Before I left Washington, and when there certainly could have been no enemy to prevent the withdrawal of the forces of Colonel Miles, I recommended to the proper authorities that the garrison of Harper's Ferry should be withdrawn via Hagerstown, to aid in covering the Cumberland valley; or that, taking up the pontoon bridge and obstructing the railroad bridge, it should fall back to the Maryland heights, and there hold out to the last.

In this position it ought to have maintained itself for many days. It was not deemed proper to adopt either of these suggestions, and when the matter was left to my discretion it was too late for me to do anything but endeavor to relieve the garrison. I accordingly directed artillery to be fired by our advance at frequent intervals as a signal that relief was at hand. This was done, and, as I afterwards learned, the reports of the cannon were distinctly heard at Harper's Ferry. It was confidently expected that Colonel Miles would hold out until we had carried the mountain passes, and were in condition to send a detachment to his relief. The left was therefore ordered to move through Crampton's pass in front of Burkettsville, while the centre and right marched upon Turner's pass in front of Middletown.

It may be asked by those who are not acquainted with the topography of the country in the vicinity of Harper's Ferry, why Franklin, instead of marching his column over the circuitous road from Jefferson via Burkettsville and Brownsville, was not ordered to move along the direct turnpike to Knoxville, and thence up the river to Harper's Ferry.

It was for the reason that I had received information that the enemy were anticipating our approach in that direction, and had established batteries on the south side of the Potomac which commanded all the approaches to Knoxville; moreover the road from that point winds directly along the river bank at the foot of a precipitous mountain, where there was no opportunity of forming in line of battle, and where the enemy could have placed batteries on both sides of the river to enfilade our narrow approaching columns.

The approach through Crampton's pass, which debouches into Pleasant valley in rear of Maryland heights, was the only one which afforded any reasonable prospect of carrying that formidable position; at the same time, the troops upon that road were in better relation to the main body of our forces.

On the morning of the 14th a verbal message reached me from Colonel Miles, which was the first authentic intelligence I had received as to the condition of things at Harper's Ferry. The messenger informed me that on the preceding afternoon Maryland heights had been abandoned by our troops after repelling an attack of the rebels, and that Colonel Miles's entire force was concentrated at Harper's Ferry, the Maryland, Loudon, and Bolivar heights having been abandoned by him, and occupied by the enemy. The messenger also stated that there was no apparent reason for the abandonment of the Maryland heights, and that Colonel Miles instructed him to say that he could hold out with certainty two days longer.

I directed him to make his way back, if possible, with the information that I was approaching rapidly, and felt confident I could relieve the place.

On the same afternoon I wrote the following letter to Colonel Miles, and despatched three copies by three different couriers on different routes. I did not, however, learn that any of these men succeeded in reaching Harper's Ferry:

"MIDDLETOWN, *September* 14, 1862.

"COLONEL: The army is being rapidly concentrated here. We are now attacking the pass on the Hagerstown road over the Blue ridge. A column is about attacking the Burkettsville and Boonsboro' pass. You may count on our making every effort to relieve you. You may rely upon my speedily accomplishing that object. Hold out to the last extremity. If it is possible, reoccupy the Maryland heights with your whole force. If you can do that, I will certainly be able to relieve you. As the Catoctin valley is in our possession, you can safely cross the river at Berlin or its vicinity, so far as opposition on this side of the river is concerned. Hold out to the last.

"GEORGE B. McCLELLAN,
"*Major General Commanding.*

"Colonel D. S. MILES."

On the previous day I had sent General Franklin the following instructions:

"HEADQUARTERS ARMY OF THE POTOMAC,
"*Camp near Frederick, September* 13, 1862—6.20 *p. m.*

"GENERAL: I have now full information as to movements and intentions of the enemy. Jackson has crossed the upper Potomac to capture the garrison at Martinsburg and cut off Miles's retreat towards the west. A division on the south side of the Potomac was to carry London heights and cut off his retreat in that direction. McLaws with his own command and the division of R. H. Anderson was to move by Boonsboro' and Rohrersville to carry the Maryland heights. The signal officers inform me that he is now in Pleasant valley. The firing shows that Miles still holds out. Longstreet was to move to Boonsboro', and there halt with the reserve corps; D. H. Hill to form the rear guard; Stuart's cavalry to bring up stragglers, &c. We have cleared out all the cavalry this side of the mountains and north of us. The last I heard from Pleasanton he occupied Middletown, after several sharp skirmishes. A division of Burnside's command started several hours ago to support him. The whole of Burnside's command, including Hooker's corps, march this evening and early to-morrow morning, followed by the corps of Sumner and Banks, and Sykes's division, upon Boonsboro' to carry that position. Couch has been ordered to concentrate his division and join you as rapidly as possible. Without waiting for the whole of that division to join, you will move at daybreak in the morning by Jefferson and Burkettsville upon the road to Rohrersville. I have reliable information that the mountain pass by this road is practicable for artillery and wagons. If this pass is not occupied by the enemy in force, seize it as soon as practicable, and debouch upon Rohrersville in order to cut off the retreat of or destroy McLaws's command. If you find this pass held by the enemy in large force, make all your dispositions for the attack and commence it about half an hour after you hear severe firing at the pass on the Hagerstown pike, where the main body will attack. Having gained the pass, your duty will be first to cut off, destroy, or capture McLaws's command and relieve Colonel Miles. If you effect this you will order him to join you at once with all his disposable troops, first destroying the bridges over the Potomac, if not already done, and, leaving a sufficient garrison to prevent the enemy from passing the ford, you will then return by Rohrersville on the direct road to Boonsboro', if the main column has not succeeded in its attack. If it has succeeded, take the road to Rohrersville, to Sharpsburg and Williamsport, in order either to cut off the retreat of Hill and Longstreet towards the Potomac, or prevent the repassage of Jackson. My general idea is to cut the enemy in two and beat him in detail. I believe I have sufficiently explained my intentions. I ask of you, at this important moment, all your intellect and the utmost activity that a general can exercise.

"GEORGE B. McCLELLAN,
"*Major General Commanding.*

"Major General W. B. FRANKLIN,
"*Commanding 6th Corps.*"

Again, on the 14th, I sent him the following:

"HEADQUARTERS ARMY OF THE POTOMAC,
"*Frederick, September* 14, 1862—2 *p. m.*

"Your despatch of 12.30 just received. Send back to hurry up Couch. Mass your troops and carry Burkettsville at any cost. We shall have strong opposition at both passes. As fast as the troops come up I will hold a reserve in readiness to support you. If you find the enemy in very great force at any of these passes let me know at once, and amuse them as best you can so as to retain them there. In that event I will probably throw the mass of the army on the pass in front of here. If I carry that it will clear the way for you, and you must follow the enemy as rapidly as possible.

"GEORGE B. McCLELLAN,
"*Major General Commanding.*

"Major General FRANKLIN."

General Franklin pushed his corps rapidly forward towards Crampton's pass, and at about 12 o'clock on the 14th arrived at Burkettsville, immediately in rear of which he found the enemy's infantry posted in force on both sides of the road, with artillery in strong positions to defend the approaches to the pass. Slocum's division was formed upon the right of the road leading through the gap, and Smith's upon the left. A line formed of Bartlett's and Torbett's brigades, supported by Newton, whose activity was conspicuous, advanced steadily upon the enemy at a charge on the right. The enemy were driven from their position at the base of the mountain, where they were protected by a stone wall, steadily forced back up the slope until they reached the position of their battery on the road, well up the mountain. There they made a stand. They were, however, driven back, retiring their artillery in echelon until, after an action of three hours, the crest was gained, and the enemy hastily fled down the mountain on the other side.

On the left of the road, Brooks's and Irvin's brigades, of Smith's division, formed for the protection of Slocum's flank, charged up the mountain in the same steady manner, driving the enemy before them until the crest was carried. Four hundred prisoners from seventeen different organizations, seven hundred stand of arms, one piece of artillery, and three colors, were captured by our troops in this brilliant action. It was conducted by General Franklin in all its details. These details are given in a report of General Franklin, herewith submitted, and due credit awarded to the gallant officers and men engaged.

The loss in General Franklin's corps was one hundred and fifteen killed, four hundred and sixteen wounded, and two missing. The enemy's loss was about the same. The enemy's position was such that our artillery could not be used with any effect. The close of the action found General Franklin's advance in Pleasant valley on the night of the 14th, within three and a half miles of the point on Maryland heights where he might, on the same night or on the morning of the 15th, have formed a junction with the garrison of Harper's Ferry had it not been previously withdrawn from Maryland heights, and within six miles of Harper's Ferry.

On the night of the 14th the following despatch was sent to General Franklin:

"BOLIVAR, *September* 15—1 *a. m.*

"GENERAL: * * * * * * * * *

"The commanding general directs that you occupy, with your command, the road from Rohrersville to Harper's Ferry, placing a sufficient force at Rohrersville to hold that position in case it should be attacked by the enemy from Boonsboro'. Endeavor to open communication with Colonel Miles at Harper's Ferry, attacking and destroying such of the enemy as you may find in Pleasant valley. Should you succeed in opening communication with Colonel Miles, direct him to join you with his whole command, with all the guns and public property that he can carry with him. The remainder of the guns will be spiked or destroyed; the rest of the public property will also be destroyed. You will then proceed to Boonsboro', which place the commanding general intends to attack to-morrow, and join the main body of the army at that place; should you find, however, that the enemy have retreated from Boonsboro' towards Sharpsburg, you will endeavor to fall upon him and cut off his retreat.

"By command of Major General McClellan.

"GEORGE D. RUGGLES.

"*Colonel and Aide-de-Camp.*

"General FRANKLIN."

On the 15th the following were received from General Franklin:

"AT THE FOOT OF MOUNT PLEASANT,
"*In Pleasant Valley, three miles from Rohrersville,*
"*September* 15—8.50 *a. m.*

"GENERAL: My command started at daylight this morning, and I am waiting to have it closed up here. General Couch arrived about 10 o'clock last night. I have ordered one of his brigades and one battery to Rohrersville or to the strongest point in its vicinity. The enemy is drawn up in line of battle about two miles to our front, one brigade in sight. As soon as I am sure that Rohrersville is occupied I shall move forward to attack the enemy. This may be two hours from now. If Harper's Ferry has fallen—and the cessation of firing makes me fear that it has—it is my opinion that I should be strongly re-enforced.

* * * * * * * *

"W. B. FRANKLIN,
"*Major General Commanding Corps.*

"General G. B. MCCLELLAN."

"SEPTEMBER 15—11 *a. m.*

"GENERAL: I have received your despatch by Captain O'Keefe. The enemy is in large force in my front, in two lines of battle stretching across the valley, and a large column of artillery and infantry on the right of the valley looking towards Harper's Ferry. They outnumber me two to one. It will of course not answer to pursue the enemy under these circumstances. I shall communicate with Burnside as soon as possible. In the mean time I shall wait here until I learn what is the prospect of re-enforcement. I have not the force to justify an attack on the force I see in front. I have had a very close view of it, and its position is very strong.

"Respectfully,

"W. B. FRANKLIN,
"*Major General.*

"General G. B. MCCLELLAN, *Commanding.*"

Colonel Miles surrendered Harper's Ferry at 8 a. m. on the 15th, as the cessation of the firing indicated, and General Franklin was ordered to remain where he was to watch the large force in front of him, and protect our left and rear until the night of the 16th, when he was ordered to join the main body of the army at Keedysville, after sending Couch's division to Maryland heights. While the events which have just been described were taking place at Crampton's gap the troops of the centre and right wing, which had united at Frederick on the 13th, were engaged in the contest for the possession of Turner's gap.

On the morning of the 13th General Pleasanton was ordered to send McReynolds's brigade and a section of artillery in the direction of Gettysburg, and Rush's regiment towards Jefferson to communicate with Franklin, to whom the 6th United States cavalry and a section of artillery had previously been sent, and to proceed with the remainder of his force in the direction of Middletown in pursuit of the enemy.

After skirmishing with the enemy all the morning, and driving them from several strong positions, he reached Turner's gap of the South mountain in the afternoon, and found the enemy in force and apparently determined to defend the pass. He sent back for infantry to General Burnside, who had been directed to support him, and proceeded to make a reconnoissance of the position.

The South mountain is at this point about one thousand feet in height, and its general direction is from northeast to southwest. The national road from Frederick to Hagerstown crosses it nearly at right angles through Turner's gap, a depression which is some four hundred feet in depth.

The mountain on the north side of the turnpike is divided into two crests, or ridges, by a narrow valley, which, though deep at the pass, becomes a slight depression at about a mile to the north. There are two country roads, one to the right of the turnpike and the other to the left, which give access to the crests overlooking the main road. The one on the left, called the "Old Sharpsburg road," is nearly parallel to and about half a mile distant from the turnpike, until it reaches the crest of the mountain, when it bends off to the left. The other road, called the "Old Hagerstown road," passes up a ravine in the mountains about a mile from the turnpike, and bending to the left over and along the first crest, enters the turnpike at the Mountain House, near the summit of the pass.

On the night of the 13th the positions of the different corps were as follows:

Reno's corps at Middletown, except Redman's division at Frederick.
Hooker's corps on the Monocacy, two miles from Frederick.
Sumner's corps near Frederick.
Banks's corps near Frederick.
Sykes's division near Frederick.
Franklin's corps at Buckeystown.
Couch's division at Licksville.

The orders from headquarters for the march on the 14th were as follows:

13th, 11.30 p. m.—Hooker to march at daylight to Middletown.

13th, 11.30 p. m.—Sykes to move at 6 a. m. after Hooker, on the Middletown and Hagerstown road.

14th, 1 a. m.—Artillery reserve to follow Sykes closely.

13th, 8.45 p. m.—Turner to move at 7 a. m.

14th, 9 a. m.—Sumner ordered to take the Shookstown road to Middletown.

13th, 6.45 p. m.—Couch ordered to move to Jefferson with his whole division.

On the 14th General Pleasanton continued his reconnoissance. Gibson's battery and afterwards Benjamin's battery (of Reno's corps) were placed on high ground to the left of the turnpike, and obtained a direct fire on the enemy's position in the gap.

General Cox's division, which had been ordered up to support General Pleasanton, left its bivouac, near Middletown, at 6 a. m. The 1st brigade reached the scene of action about 9 a. m., and was sent up the old Sharpsburg road by General Pleasanton to feel the enemy and ascertain if he held the crest on that side in strong force. This was soon found to be the case; and General Cox having arrived with the other brigade, and information having been received from General Reno that the column would be supported by the whole corps, the division was ordered to assault the position. Two 20-pounder Parrotts of Simmons's battery and two sections of McMullan's battery were left in the rear in position near the turnpike, where they did good service during the day against the enemy's batteries in the gap. Colonel Scammon's brigade was deployed, and, well covered by skirmishers, moved up the slope to the left of the road with the object of turning the enemy's right, if possible. It succeeded in gaining the crest and establishing itself there, in spite of the vigorous efforts of the enemy, who was posted behind stone walls and in the edges of timber, and the fire of a battery which poured in canister and case shot on the regiment on the right of the brigade. Colonel Crooke's brigade marched in columns at supporting distance. A section of McMullan's battery, under Lieutenant Croome, (killed while serving one of his guns,) was moved up with great difficulty, and opened with canister at very short range on the enemy's infantry, by whom (after having done considerable execution) it was soon silenced and forced to withdraw.

One regiment of Crook's brigade was now deployed on Scammon's left, and the other two in his rear, and they several times entered the first line and relieved the regiments in front of them when hard pressed. A section of Sumner's battery was brought up and placed in the open space in the woods, where it did good service during the rest of the day.

The enemy several times attempted to retake the crest, advancing with boldness, but were each time repulsed. They then withdrew their battery to a point more to the right, and formed columns on both our flanks. It was now about noon, and a lull occurred in the contest which lasted about two hours, during which the rest of the corps was coming up. General Wilcox's division was the first to arrive. When he reached the base of the mountain, General Cox advised him to consult General Pleasanton as to a position. The latter indicated that on the right, afterwards taken up by General Hooker. General Wilcox was in the act of moving to occupy this ground, when he received an order from General Reno to move up the old Sharpsburg road and take a position to its right, overlooking the turnpike. Two regiments were detached to support General Cox, at his request. One section of Cooke's battery was placed in position near the turn of the road, (on the crest,) and opened fire on the enemy's batteries across the gap. The division was proceeding to deploy to the right of the road, when the enemy suddenly opened (at one hundred and fifty yards) with a battery which enfiladed the road at this point, drove off Cook's cannoneers with their limbers, and caused a temporary panic in which the guns were nearly lost. But the 79th New York and 17th Michigan promptly rallied, changed front under a heavy fire, and moved out to protect the guns with which Captain Cook had remained. Order was soon restored, and the division formed in line on the right of Cox, and was kept concealed as much as possible under the hillside until the whole line advanced. It was exposed not only to the fire of the battery in front, but also to that of the batteries on the other side of the turnpike, and lost heavily.

Shortly before this time Generals Burnside and Reno arrived at the base of the mountain; and the former directed the latter to move up the divisions of Generals Sturgis and Rodman to the crest held by Cox and Wilcox, and to move upon the enemy's position with his whole force as soon as he was informed that General Hooker (who had just been directed to attack on the right) was well advanced up the mountain.

General Reno then went to the front and assumed the direction of affairs, the positions having been explained to him by General Pleasanton. Shortly before this time I arrived at the point occupied by General Burnside, and my headquarters were located there until the conclusion of the action. General Sturgis had left his camp at 1 p. m., and reached the scene of action about 3½ p. m. Clark's battery, of his division, was sent to assist Cox's left, by order of General Reno, and two regiments (2d Maryland and 6th New Hampshire) were detached by General Reno and sent forward a short distance on the left of the turnpike. His division was formed in rear of Wilcox's, and Rodman's division was divided; Colonel Fairchilds's brigade being placed on the extreme left, and Colonel Harland's, under General Rodman's personal supervision, on the right.

My order to move the whole line forward and take or silence the enemy's batteries in front was executed with enthusiasm. The enemy made a desperate resistance, charging our advancing lines with fierceness, but they were everywhere routed and fled.

Our chief loss was in Wilcox's division. The enemy's battery was found to be across a gorge and beyond the reach of our infantry; but its position was made untenable, and it was hastily removed and not again put in position near us. But the batteries across the gap still kept up a fire of shot and shell.

General Wilcox praises very highly the conduct of the 17th Michigan in this advance—a regiment which had been organized scarcely a month, but which charged the advancing enemy in flank in a manner worthy of veteran troops; and also that of the 45th Pennsylvania, which bravely met them in front.

Cook's battery now reopened fire. Sturgis's division was moved to the front of Wilcox's, occupying the new ground gained on the further side of the slope, and his artillery opened on the batteries across the gap. The enemy made an effort to turn our left about dark, but were repulsed by Fairchilds's brigade and Clark's battery.

At about 7 o'clock the enemy made another effort to regain the lost ground, attacking along Sturgis's front and part of Cox's. A lively fire was kept up until nearly 9 o'clock, several charges being made by the enemy and repulsed with slaughter, and we finally occupied the highest part of the mountain.

General Reno was killed just before sunset, while making a reconnoissance to the front, and the command of the corps devolved upon General Cox. In General Reno the nation lost one of its best general officers. He was a skilful soldier, a brave and honest man.

There was no firing after 10 o'clock, and the troops slept on their arms ready to renew the fight at daylight; but the enemy quietly retired from our front during the night, abandoning their wounded, and leaving their dead in large numbers scattered over the field While these operations were progressing on the left of the main column, the right under General Hooker was actively engaged. His corps left the Monocacy early in the morning, and its advance reached the Catoctin creek about 1 p. m. General Hooker then went forward to examine the ground.

At about 1 o'clock General Meade's division was ordered to make a diversion in favor of Reno. The following is the order sent:

"SEPTEMBER 14—1 *p. m.*

"GENERAL: General Reno requests that a division of yours may move up on the right (north) of the main road. General McClellan desires you to comply with this request, holding your whole corps in readiness to support the movement, and taking charge of it yourself.

"Sumner's and Banks's corps have commenced arriving. Let General McClellan be informed as soon as you commence your movement.

"GEORGE D. RUGGLES,

"*Colonel, Assistant Adjutant General, and Aide-de-Camp.*

"Major General HOOKER."

Meade's division left Catoctin creek about two o'clock, and turned off to the right from the main road on the old Hagerstown road to Mount Tabor church, where General Hooker was, and deployed a short distance in advance, its right resting about one and a half mile from the turnpike. The enemy fired a few shots from a battery on the mountain side, but did no considerable damage. Cooper's battery "B," 1st Pennsylvania artillery, was placed in position on high ground at about three and a half o'clock, and fired at the enemy on the slope, but soon ceased by order of General Hooker, and the position of our lines prevented any further use of artillery by us on this part of the field. The first Massachusetts cavalry was sent up the valley to the right to observe the movements, if any, of the enemy in that direction, and one regiment of Meade's division was posted to watch a road coming in the same direction. The other divisions were deployed as they came up, General Hatch's on the left, and General Ricketts's, which arrived at 5 p. m., in the rear. General Gibbon's brigade was detached from Hatch's division by General Burnside, for the purpose of making a demonstration on the enemy's centre, up the main road, as soon as the movements on the right and left had sufficiently progressed. The 1st Pennsylvania rifles of General Seymour's brigade were sent forward as skirmishers to feel the enemy, and it was found that he was in force. Meade was then directed to advance his division to the right of the road, so as to outflank them if possible, and then to move forward and attack, while Hatch was directed to take with his division the crest on the left of the old Hagerstown road, Ricketts's division being held in reserve. Seymour's brigade was sent up to the top of the slope, on the right of the ravine through which the road runs; and then moved along the summit parallel to the road, while Colonel Gallagher's and Colonel Magilton's brigades moved in the same direction along the slope and in the ravine.

The ground was of the most difficult character for the movement of troops, the hillside being very steep and rocky, and obstructed by stone walls and timber. The enemy was very soon encountered, and in a short time the action became general along the whole front of the division. The line advanced steadily up the mountain side, where the enemy was posted behind trees and rocks, from which he was gradually dislodged. During this advance Colonel Gallagher, commanding 3d brigade, was severely wounded; and the command devolved upon Lieutenant Colonel Robert Anderson.

General Meade having reason to believe that the enemy were attempting to outflank him on his right, applied to General Hooker for re-enforcements. General Duryea's brigade of Ricketts's division was ordered up, but it did not arrive until the close of the action. It was advanced on Seymour's left, but only one regiment could open fire before the enemy retired and darkness intervened.

General Meade speaks highly of General Seymour's skill in handling his brigade on the extreme right, securing by his manœuvres the great object of the movement, the outflanking of the enemy.

While General Meade was gallantly driving the enemy on the right, General Hatch's division was engaged in a severe contest for the possession of the crest on the left of the ravine; it moved up the mountain in the following order: two regiments of General Patrick's brigade deployed as skirmishers, with the other two regiments of the same brigade supporting them. Colonel Phelps's brigade in line of battalions in mass at deploying distance, General Doubleday's brigade in the same order bringing up the rear. The 21st New York having gone straight up the slope instead of around to the right, as directed, the 2d United States sharpshooters was sent out in its place. Phelps's and Doubleday's brigades were deployed in turn as they reached the woods, which began about half up the mountain. General Patrick with his skirmishers soon drew the fire of the enemy, and found him strongly posted behind a fence which bounded the cleared space on the top of the ridge, having on his front the woods through which our line was advancing, and in his rear a cornfield full of rocky ledges, which afforded good cover to fall back to if dislodged.

Phelps's brigade gallantly advanced, under a hot fire, to close quarters, and after ten or fifteen minutes of heavy firing on both sides (in which General Hatch was wounded while urging on his men) the fence was carried by a charge, and our line advanced a few yards beyond it, somewhat sheltered by the slope of the hill.

Doubleday's brigade, now under the command of Lieutenant Colonel Hoffman, (Colonel Wainwright having been wounded,) relieved Phelps, and continued firing for an hour and a half; the enemy behind ledges of rocks, some thirty or forty paces in our front, making a stubborn resistance, and attempting to charge on the least cessation of our fire. About dusk Colonel Christian's brigade of Ricketts's division came up and relieved Doubleday's brigade, which fell back into line behind Phelps's. Christian's brigade continued the action for thirty or forty minutes, when the enemy retired, after having made an attempt to flank us on the left, which was repulsed by the 75th New York and 7th Indiana.

The remaining brigade of Ricketts's division (General Hartsuff's) was moved up in the centre, and connected Meade's left with Doubleday's right. We now had possession of the summit of the first ridge which commanded the turnpike on both sides of the mountain, and the troops were ordered to hold their positions until further orders, and slept on their arms. Late in the afternoon General Gibbon, with his brigade and one section of Gibbon's battery, (B, 4th artillery,) was ordered to move up the main road on the enemy's centre. He advanced a regiment on each side of the road, preceded by skirmishers, and followed by the other two regiments in double column; the artillery moving on the road until within range of the enemy's guns, which were firing on the column from the gorge.

The brigade advanced steadily, driving the enemy from his positions in the woods and behind stone walls, until they reached a point well up towards the top of the pass, when the enemy, having been re-enforced by three regiments, opened a heavy fire on the front and on both flanks. The fight continued until 9 o'clock, the enemy being entirely repulsed; and the brigade, after having suffered severely, and having expended all its ammunition, including even the cartridges of the dead and wounded, continued to hold the ground it had so gallantly won until 12 o'clock, when it was relieved by General Gorman's brigade of Sedgwick's division, Sumner's corps, (except the 6th Wisconsin, which remained on the field all night.) General Gibbon, in this delicate movement, handled his brigade with as much precision and coolness as if upon parade, and the bravery of his troops could not be excelled.

The 2d corps (Sumner's) and the 12th corps (Williams's) reached their final positions shortly after dark. General Richardson's division was placed near Mount Tabor church, in a position to support our right, if necessary; the 12th corps and Sedgwick's division bivouacked around Bolivar, in a position to support our centre and left.

General Sykes's division of regulars and the artillery reserve halted for the night at Middletown. Thus, on the night of the 14th the whole army was massed in the vicinity of the field of battle, in readiness to renew the action the next day, or to move in pursuit of the enemy. At daylight our skirmishers were advanced, and it was found that he had retreated during the night, leaving his dead on the field, and his wounded uncared for.

About fifteen hundred prisoners were taken by us during the battle, and the loss to the enemy in killed was much greater than our own, and, probably, also in wounded. It is believed that the force opposed to us at Turner's gap consisted of D. H. Hill's corps, (15,000,) and a part, if not the whole, of Longstreet's, and perhaps a portion of Jackson's, probably some 30,000 in all.

We went into action with about 30,000 men, and our losses amounted to 1,568 aggregate, (312 killed, 1,234 wounded, and 22 missing.)

On the next day I had the honor to receive the following very kind despatch from his excellency the President:

"WAR DEPARTMENT,
"*Washington, September* 15, 1862—2.45 *p. m.*

"Your despatch of to-day received. God bless you, and all with you; destroy the rebel army if possible.

"A. LINCOLN.

"Major General McCLELLAN."

"ANTIETAM."

On the night of the battle of South Mountain, orders were given to the corps commanders to press forward the pickets at early dawn. This advance revealed the fact that the enemy had left his positions, and an immediate pursuit was ordered: the cavalry, under General Pleasonton, and the three corps under Generals Sumner, Hooker, and Mansfield, (the latter of whom had arrived that morning and assumed command of the 12th, Williams's corps,) by the national turnpike and Boonsboro'; the corps of Generals Burnside and Porter (the latter command at that time consisting of but one weak division, Sykes's) by the old Sharpsburg road, and General Franklin to move into Pleasant valley, occupy Rohrersville by a detachment, and endeavor to relieve Harper's Ferry.

Generals Burnside and Porter, upon reaching the road from Boonsboro' to Rohrersville to re-enforce Franklin, or to move on Sharpsburg, according to circumstances.

Franklin moved towards Brownsville and found there a force of the enemy, much superior in numbers to his own, drawn up in a strong position to receive him. At this time the cessation of firing at Harper's Ferry indicated the surrender of that place.

The cavalry overtook the enemy's cavalry in Boonsboro', made a daring charge, killing and wounding a number, and capturing 250 prisoners and two guns.

General Richardson's division of the 2d corps pressing the rear guard of the enemy with vigor, passed Boonsboro' and Keedysville, and came upon the main body of the enemy, occupying in large force a strong position a few miles beyond the latter place.

It had been hoped to engage the enemy during the 15th. Accordingly, instructions were given that if the enemy were overtaken on the march they should be attacked at once; if found in heavy force and in position, the corps in advance should be placed in position for attack, and await my arrival. On reaching the advanced position of our troops, I found but two divisions, Richardson's and Sykes's, in position; the other troops were halted in the road; the head of the column some distance in rear of Richardson.

The enemy occupied a strong position on the heights, on the west side of Antietam creek, displaying a large force of infantry and cavalry, with numerous batteries of artillery, which opened on our columns as they appeared in sight on the Keedysville road and Sharpsburg turnpike, which fire was returned by Captain Tidball's light battery, 2d United States artillery, and Pettit's battery, 1st New York artillery.

The division of General Richardson, following close on the heels of the retreating foe, halted and deployed near Antietam river, on the right of the Sharpsburg road. General Sykes, leading on the division of regulars on the old Sharpsburg road, came up and deployed to the left of General Richardson, on the left of the road.

Antietam creek, in this vicinity, is crossed by four stone bridges—the upper one on the Keedysville and Williamsport road; the second on the Keedysville and Sharpsburg turnpike, some two and a half miles below; the third about a mile below the second, on the Rohrersville and Sharpsburg road; and the fourth near the mouth of Antietam creek, on the road leading from Harper's Ferry to Sharpsburg, some three miles below the third. The stream is sluggish, with few and difficult fords. After a rapid examination of the position, I found that it was too late to attack that day, and at once directed the placing of the batteries in position in the centre, and indicated the bivouacs for the different corps, massing them near and on both sides of the Sharpsburg turnpike. The corps were not all in their positions until the next morning after sunrise.

On the morning of the 16th, it was discovered that the enemy had changed the position of his batteries. The masses of his troops, however, were still concealed behind the opposite heights. Their left and centre were upon and in front of the Sharpsburg and Hagerstown turnpike, hidden by woods and irregularities of the ground; their extreme left resting upon a wooded eminence near the cross-roads to the north of J. Miller's farm; their left resting upon the Potomac. Their line extended south, the right resting upon the hills to the south of Sharpsburg, near Shaveley's farm.

The bridge over the Antietam, described as No. 3, near this point, was strongly covered by riflemen protected by rifle-pits, stone fences, &c., and enfiladed by artillery. The ground in front of this line consisted of undulating hills, their crests in turn commanded by others in their rear. On all favorable points the enemy's artillery was posted and their reserves hidden from view by the hills, on which their line of battle was formed, could manœuvre unobserved by our army, and from the shortness of their line could rapidly re-enforce any point threatened by our attack. Their position, stretching across the angle formed by the Potomac and Antietam, their flanks and rear protected by these streams, was one of the strongest to be found in this region of country, which is well adapted to defensive warfare.

On the right, near Keedysville, on both sides of the Sharpsburg turnpike, were Sumner's and Hooker's corps. In advance, on the right of the turnpike and near the Antietam river, General Richardson's division of General Sumner's corps was posted. General Sykes's division of General Porter's corps was on the left of the turnpike and in line with General Richardson, protecting the bridge No. 2, over the Antietam. The left of the line, opposite to and some distance from bridge No. 3, was occupied by General Burnside's corps.

Before giving General Hooker his orders to make the movement which will presently be described, I rode to the left of the line to satisfy myself that the troops were properly posted there to secure our left flank from any attack made along the left bank of the Antietam, as well as to enable us to carry bridge No. 3.

I found it necessary to make considerable changes in the position of General Burnside's corps, and directed him to advance to a strong position in the immediate vicinity of the bridge, and to reconnoitre the approaches to the bridge carefully. In front of General Sumner's and Hooker's corps, near Keedysville, and on the ridge of the first line of hills overlooking the Antietam, and between the turnpike and Fry's house on the right of the road, were placed Captain Taft's, Languer's, Von Kleizer's and Lieutenant Weaver's batteries of twenty-pounder Parrott guns. On the crest of the hill in the rear and right of bridge No. 3, Captain Weed's three-inch and Lieutenant Benjamin's twenty-pounder batteries. General Franklin's corps and General Couch's division held a position in Pleasant valley in front of Brownsville, with a strong force of the enemy in their front. General Morell's division of Porter's corps was *en route* from Boonsboro', and General Humphrey's division of new troops *en route* from Frederick, Maryland. About daylight on the 16th the enemy opened a heavy fire of artillery on our guns in position, which was promptly returned; their fire was silenced for the time, but was frequently renewed during the day. In the heavy fire of the morning, Major Arndt, commanding first battalion first New York artillery, was mortally wounded while directing the operations of his batteries.

It was afternoon before I could move the troops to their positions for attack, being compelled to spend the morning in reconnoitring the new position taken up by the enemy, examining the ground, finding fords, clearing the approaches, and hurrying up the ammunition and supply trains, which had been delayed by the rapid march of the troops over the few practicable approaches from Frederick. These had been crowded by the masses of infantry, cavalry and artillery pressing on with the hope of overtaking the enemy before he could form to resist an attack. Many of the troops were out of rations on the previous day, and a good deal of their ammunition had been expended in the severe action of the 14th.

My plan for the impending general engagement was to attack the enemy's left with the corps of Hooker and Mansfield, supported by Sumner's, and if necessary by Franklin's; and, as soon as matters looked favorably there, to move the corps of Burnside against the enemy's extreme right, upon the ridge running to the south and rear of Sharpsburg, and having carried their position, to press along the crest towards our right; and whenever either of these flank movements should be successful, to advance our centre with all the forces then disposable.

About 2 p. m. General Hooker, with his corps, consisting of General Ricketts's, Meade's and Doubleday's divisions, was ordered to cross the Antietam at a ford, and at bridge No. 1, a short distance above, to attack and, if possible, turn the enemy's left. General Sumner was ordered to cross the corps of General Mansfield (the 12th) during the night, and hold his own (the 2d) corps ready to cross early the next morning. On reaching the vicinity of the enemy's left a sharp contest commenced with the Pennsylvania reserves, the advance of General Hooker's corps, near the house of D. Miller. The enemy were driven from the strip of woods where he was first met. The firing lasted until after dark, when General Hooker's corps rested on their arms on ground won from the enemy.

During the night General Mansfield's corps, consisting of Generals Williams's and Green's divisions, crossed the Antietam at the same ford and bridge that General Hooker's troops had passed, and bivouacked on the farm of J. Poffenberger, about a mile in rear of General Hooker's position. At daylight on the 17th the action was commenced by the skirmishers of the Pennsylvania reserves. The whole of General Hooker's corps was soon engaged, and drove the enemy from the open field in front of the first line of woods into a second line of woods beyond, which runs to the eastward of and nearly parallel to the Sharpsburg and Hagerstown turnpike.

This contest was obstinate, and as the troops advanced the opposition became more determined and the number of the enemy greater. General Hooker then ordered up the corps of General Mansfield, which moved promptly toward the scene of action.

The first division, General Williams's, was deployed to the right on approaching the enemy; General Crawford's brigade on the right, its right resting on the Hagerstown turnpike; on his left General Gordon's brigade. The second division, General Green's, joining the left of Gordon's, extended as far as the burnt buildings to the north and east of the white church on the turnpike. During the deployment, that gallant veteran General Mansfield fell mortally wounded, while examining the ground in front of his troops. General Hartsuff, of Hooker's corps, was severely wounded, while bravely pressing forward his troops, and was taken from the field.

The command of the twelfth corps fell upon General Williams. Five regiments of first division of this corps were new troops. One brigade of the second division was sent to support General Doubleday.

The one hundred and twenty-fourth Pennsylvania volunteers were pushed across the turnpike into the woods beyond J. Miller's house, with orders to hold the position as long as possible.

The line of battle of this corps was formed, and it became engaged about seven a. m., the attack being opened by Knapp's (Pennsylvania,) Cothran's (New York,) and Hampton's (Pittsburg) batteries. To meet this attack the enemy had pushed a strong column of troops into the open fields in front of the turnpike, while he occupied the woods on the west of the turnpike in strong force. The woods (as was found by subsequent observation) were traversed by outcropping ledges of rock. Several hundred yards to the right and rear was a hill which commanded the debouche of the woods, and in the fields between was a long line of stone fences, continued by breastworks of rails, which covered the enemy's infantry from our musketry. The same woods formed a screen behind which his movements were concealed, and his batteries on the hill and the rifle works covered from the fire of our artillery in front.

For about two hours the battle raged with varied success, the enemy endeavoring to drive our troops into the second line of wood, and ours in turn to get possession of the line in front.

Our troops ultimately succeeded in forcing the enemy back into the woods near the turnpike, General Green with his two brigades crossing into the woods to the left of the Dunbar church. During this conflict General Crawford, commanding first division after General Williams took command of the corps, was wounded and left the field.

General Green being much exposed and applying for re-enforcements, the thirteenth New Jersey, twenty-seventh Indiana, and the third Maryland were sent to his support with a section of Knapp's battery.

At about nine o'clock a. m. General Sedgwick's division of General Sumner's corps arrived. Crossing the ford previously mentioned, this division marched in three columns to the support of the attack on the enemy's left. On nearing the scene of action the columns were halted, faced to the front, and established by General Sumner in three parallel lines by brigade, facing toward the south and west; General Gorman's brigade in front, General Dana's second, and General Howard's third, with a distance between the lines of some seventy paces. The division was then put in motion and moved upon the field of battle, under fire from the enemy's concealed batteries on the hill beyond the roads. Passing diagonally to the front across the open space and to the front of the first division of General Williams's corps, this latter division withdrew.

Entering the woods on the west of the turnpike, and driving the enemy before them, the first line was met by a heavy fire of musketry and shell from the enemy's breastworks and the batteries on the hill commanding the exit from the woods; meantime a heavy column of the enemy had succeeded in crowding back the troops of General Green's division, and appeared in rear of the left of Sedgwick's division. By command of General Sumner, General Howard faced the third line to the rear preparatory to a change of front to meet the column advancing on the left; but this line now suffering from a destructive fire both in front and on its left, which it was unable to return, gave way towards the right and rear in considerable confusion, and was soon followed by the first and second lines.

General Gorman's brigade, and one regiment of General Dana's, soon rallied and checked the advance of the enemy on the right. The second and third lines now formed on the left of General Gorman's brigade, and poured a destructive fire upon the enemy.

During General Sumner's attack, he ordered General Williams to support him. Brigadier General Gordon, with a portion of his brigade, moved forward, but when he reached the woods, the left of General Sedgwick's division had given way; and finding himself, as the smoke cleared up, opposed to the enemy in force with his small command, he withdrew to the rear of the batteries at the second line of woods. As General Gordon's troops unmasked our batteries on the left, they opened with canister; the batteries of Captain Cothran, 1st New York, and I, 1st artillery, commanded by Lieutenant Woodruff, doing good service. Unable to withstand this deadly fire in front and the musketry fire from the right, the enemy again sought shelter in the woods and rocks beyond the turnpike.

During this assault Generals Sedgwick and Dana were seriously wounded and taken from the field. General Sedgwick, though twice wounded, and faint from loss of blood, retained command of his division for more than an hour after his first wound, animating his command by his presence.

About the time of General Sedgwick's advance, General Hooker, while urging on his command, was severely wounded in the foot and taken from the field, and General Meade was placed in command of his corps. General Howard assumed command after General Sedgwick retired.

The repulse of the enemy offered opportunity to rearrange the lines and reorganize the commands on the right, now more or less in confusion. The batteries of the Pennsylvania reserve, on high ground, near I. Poffenburger's house,

shot. This advance gave us possession of Piper's house, the strong point contended for by the enemy at this part of the line, it being a defensible building several hundred yards in advance of the sunken road. The musketry fire at this point of the line now ceased. Holding Piper's house, General Richardson withdrew the line a little way to the crest of a hill, a more advantageous position. Up to this time the division was without artillery, and in the new position suffered severely from artillery fire which could not be replied to. A section of Robertson's horse battery, commanded by Lieutenant Vincent, 2d artillery, now arrived on the ground and did excellent service. Subsequently a battery of brass guns, commanded by Captain Graham, 1st artillery, arrived, and was posted on the crest of the hill, and soon silenced the two guns in the orchard. A heavy fire soon ensued between the battery further to the right and our own. Captain Graham's battery was bravely and skilfully served, but unable to reach the enemy, who had rifled guns of greater range than our smooth-bores, retired by order of General Richardson, to save it from useless sacrifice of men and horses. The brave general was himself mortally wounded while personally directing its fire.

General Hancock was placed in command of the division after the fall of General Richardson. General Meagher's brigade, now commanded by Colonel Burke, of the 63d New York, having refilled their cartridge-boxes, was again ordered forward, and took position in the centre of the line. The division now occupied one line in close proximity to the enemy, who had taken up a position in the rear of Piper's house. Colonel Dwight Morris, with the 14th Connecticut and a detatchment of the 108th New York, of General French's division, was sent by General French to the support of General Richardson's division. This command was now placed in an interval in the line between General Caldwell's and the Irish brigades.

The requirements of the extended line of battle had so engaged the artillery that the application of General Hancock for artillery for the division could not be complied with immediately by the chief of artillery or the corps commanders in his vicinity. Knowing the tried courage of the troops, General Hancock felt confident that he could hold his position, although suffering from the enemy's artillery, but was too weak to attack, as the great length of the line he was obliged to hold prevented him from forming more than one line of battle, and, from his advanced position, this line was already partly enfiladed by the batteries of the enemy on the right, which were protected from our batteries opposite them by the woods at the Dunker church.

Seeing a body of the enemy advancing on some of our troops to the left of his position, General Hancock obtained Hexamer's battery from General Franklin's corps, which assisted materially in frustrating this attack. It also assisted the attack of the 7th Maine, of Franklin's corps, which, without other aid, made an attack against the enemy's line, and drove in skirmishers who were annoying our artillery and troops on the right. Lieutenant Woodruff, with battery I, 2d artillery, relieved Captain Hexamer, whose ammunition was expended. The enemy at one time seemed to be about making an attack in force upon this part of the line, and advanced a long column of infantry towards this division; but on nearing the position, General Pleasonton opening on them with sixteen guns, they halted, gave a desultory fire, and retreated, closing the operations on this portion of the field. I return to the incidents occurring still further to the right.

Between 12 and 1 p. m. General Franklin's corps arrived on the field of battle, having left their camp near Crampton's pass at 6 a. m., leaving General Couch with orders to move with his division to occupy Maryland heights. General Smith's division led the column, followed by General Slocum's.

It was first intended to keep this corps in reserve on the east side of the Antietam, to operate on either flank or on the centre, as circumstances might require; but on nearing Keedysville, the strong opposition on the right, developed by the attacks of Hooker and Sumner, rendered it necessary at once to send this corps to the assistance of the right wing.

On nearing the field, hearing that one of our batteries, (A,) 4th United States artillery, commanded by Lieutenant Thomas, who occupied the same position as Lieutenant Woodruff's battery in the morning, was hotly engaged without supports, General Smith sent two regiments to its relief from General Hancock's brigade. On inspecting the ground, General Smith ordered the other regiments of Hancock's brigade, with Frank's and Cowen's batteries, 1st New York artillery, to the threatened position. Lieutenant Thomas and Captain Cothran, commanding batteries, bravely held their positions against the advancing enemy, handling their batteries with skill.

Finding the enemy still advancing, the 3d brigade, of Smith's division, commanded by Colonel Irwin, 49th Pennsylvania volunteers, was ordered up, and passed through Lieutenant Thomas's battery, charged upon the enemy, and drove back the advance until abreast of the Dunker church. As the right of the brigade came opposite the woods it received a destructive fire, which checked the advance and threw the brigade somewhat into confusion. It formed again behind a rise of ground in the open space in advance of the batteries.

General French having reported to General Franklin that his ammunition was nearly expended, that officer ordered General Brooks, with his brigade, to re-enforce him. General Brooks formed his brigade on the right of General French, where they remained during the remainder of the day and night, frequently under the fire of the enemy's artillery.

It was soon after the brigade of Colonel Irwin had fallen back behind the rise of ground that the 7th Maine, by order of Colonel Irwin, made the gallant attack already referred to.

The advance of General Franklin's corps was opportune. The attack of the enemy on this position, but for the timely arrival of his corps, must have been disastrous, had it succeeded in piercing the line between Generals Sedgwick's and French's divisions.

General Franklin ordered two brigades of General Slocum's division, General Newton's and Colonel Torbert's, to form in column to assault the woods that had been so hotly contested before by Generals Sumner and Hooker. General Bartlett's brigade was ordered to form as a reserve. At this time General Sumner, having command on the right, directed further offensive operations to be postponed, as the repulse of this, the only remaining corps available for attack, would peril the safety of the whole army.

General Porter's corps, consisting of General Sykes's division of regulars and volunteers and General Morell's division of volunteers, occupied a position on the east side of Antietam creek, upon the main turnpike leading to Sharpsburg, and directly opposite the centre of the enemy's line. This corps filled the interval between the right wing and General Burnside's command, and guarded the main approach from the enemy's position to our trains of supply. It was necessary to watch this part of our line with the utmost vigilance, lest the enemy should take advantage of the first exhibition of weakness here to push upon us a vigorous assault, for the purpose of piercing our centre and turning our rear, as well as to capture or destroy our supply trains. Once having penetrated this line, the enemy's passage to our rear could have met with but feeble resistance, as there were no reserves to re-enforce or close up the gap.

Towards the middle of the afternoon, proceeding to the right, I found that Sumner's, Hooker's, and Mansfield's corps had met with serious losses. Several general officers had been carried from the field severely wounded, and the aspect of affairs was anything but promising. At the risk of greatly exposing our centre, I ordered two brigades from Porter's corps, the only available troops, to re-enforce the right. Six battalions of Sykes's regulars had been thrown forward across the Antietam bridge on the main road to attack and drive back the enemy's sharpshooters, who were annoying Pleasonton's horse batteries in advance of the bridge; Warren's brigade, of Porter's corps, was detached to hold a position on Burnside's right and rear; so that Porter was left at one time with only a portion of Sykes's division and one small brigade of Morell's division (but little over three thousand men) to hold his important position.

General Sumner expressed the most decided opinion against another attempt during that day to assault the enemy's position in front, as portions of our troops were so much scattered and demoralized. In view of these circumstances, after making changes in the position of some of the troops, I directed the different commanders to hold their positions, and being satisfied that this could be done without the assistance of the two brigades from the centre, I countermanded the order, which was in course of execution.

General Slocum's division replaced a portion of General Sumner's troops, and positions were selected for batteries in front of the woods. The enemy opened several heavy fires of artillery on the position of our troops after this, but our batteries soon silenced them.

On the morning of the 17th General Pleasonton, with his cavalry division and the horse batteries, under Captains Robertson, Tidball, and Lieutenant Haines, of the 2d artillery, and Captain Gibson, 3d artillery, was ordered to advance on the turnpike towards Sharpsburg, across bridge No. 2, and support the left of General Sumner's line. The bridge being covered by a fire of artillery and sharpshooters, cavalry skirmishers were thrown out, and Captain Tidball's battery advanced by piece and drove off the sharpshooters with canister sufficiently to establish the batteries above mentioned, which opened on the enemy with effect. The firing was kept up for about two hours, when, the enemy's fire slackening, the batteries were relieved by Randall's and Van Reed's batteries, United States artillery. About 3 o'clock Tidball, Robertson, and Haines returned to their positions on the west of Antietam, Captain Gibson having been placed in position on the east side to guard the approaches to the bridge. These batteries did good service, concentrating their fire on the column of the enemy about to attack General Hancock's position, and compelling it to find shelter behind the hills in rear.

General Sykes's division had been in position since the 15th, exposed to the enemy's artillery and sharpshooters. General Morell had come up on the 16th, and relieved General Richardson on the right of General Sykes. Continually, under the vigilant watch of the enemy, this corps guarded a vital point.

The position of the batteries under General Pleasonton being one of great exposure, the battalion of the 2d and 10th United States infantry, under Captain Pollard, 2d infantry, was sent to his support. Subsequently four battalions of regular infantry, under Captain Dryer, 4th infantry, were sent across to assist in driving off the sharpshooters of the enemy.

The battalion of the 2d and 10th infantry, advancing far beyond the batteries, compelled the cannoneers of a battery of the enemy to abandon their guns. Few in numbers, and unsupported, they were unable to bring them off. The heavy loss of this small body of men attests their gallantry.

The troops of General Burnside held the left of the line opposite bridge No. 3. The attack on the right was to have been supported by an attack on the left. Preparatory to this attack, on the evening of the 16th, General Burnside's corps was moved forward and to the left, and took up a position nearer the bridge.

I visited General Burnside's position on the 16th, and after pointing out to him the proper dispositions to be made of his troops during the day and night, informed him that he would probably be required to attack the enemy's right on the following morning, and directed him to make careful reconnoissances.

General Burnside's corps, consisting of the divisions of Generals Cox, Wilcox, Rodman, and Sturgis, was posted as follows: Colonel Brooks's brigade, Cox's division, on the right. General Sturgis's division immediately in rear. On the left was General Rodman's division, with General Scammon's brigade, Cox's division, in support.

General Wilcox's division was held in reserve.

The corps bivouacked in position on the night of the 16th.

Early on the morning of the 17th I ordered General Burnside to form his troops, and hold them in readiness to assault the bridge in his front, and to await further orders.

At 8 o'clock an order was sent to him by Lieutenant Wilson, topographical engineers, to carry the bridge, then to gain possession of the heights beyond, and to advance along their crest upon Sharpsburg and its rear.

After some time had elapsed, not hearing from him, I despatched an aid to ascertain what had been done. The aid returned with the information that but little progress had been made. I then sent him back with an order to General Burnside to assault the bridge at once, and carry it at all hazards. The aid returned to me a second time with the report that the bridge was still in the possession of the enemy. Whereupon I directed Colonel Sackett, inspector general, to deliver to General Burnside my positive order to push forward his troops without a moment's delay, and, if necessary, to carry the bridge at the point of the bayonet; and I ordered Colonel Sackett to remain with General Burnside and see that the order was executed promptly.

After these three hours' delay, the bridge was carried at one o'clock by a brilliant charge of the 51st New York and 51st Pennsylvania volunteers. Other troops were then thrown over, and the opposite bank occupied, the enemy retreating to the heights beyond.

A halt was then made by General Burnside's advance until 3 p. m., upon hearing which, I directed one of my aids, Colonel Key, to inform General Burnside that I desired him to push forward his troops with the utmost vigor, and carry the enemy's position on the heights; that the movement was vital to our success; that this was a time when we must not stop for loss of life, if a great object could thereby be accomplished. That if, in his judgment, his attack would fail, to inform me so at once, that his troops might be withdrawn and used elsewhere on the field. He replied that he would soon advance, and would go up the hill as far as a battery of the enemy on the left would permit. Upon this report, I again immediately sent Colonel Key to General Burnside with orders to advance at once, if possible to flank the battery, or storm it and carry the heights; repeating that if he considered the movement impracticable, to inform me so, that his troops might be recalled. The advance was then gallantly resumed, the enemy driven from the guns, the heights handsomely carried, and a portion of the troops even reached the outskirts of Sharpsburg. By this time it was nearly dark, and strong re-enforcements just then reaching the enemy from Harper's Ferry, attacked General Burnside's troops on their left flank, and forced them to retire to a lower line of hills nearer the bridge.

If this important movement had been consummated two hours earlier, a position would have been secured upon the heights, from which our batteries might have enfiladed the greater part of the enemy's line, and turned their right and rear, our victory might thus have been much more decisive.

The following is the substance of General Burnside's operations as given in his report:

Colonel Crook's brigade was ordered to storm the bridge. This bridge, No. 3, is a stone structure of three arches with stone parapets. The banks of the stream on the opposite side are precipitous, and command the eastern approaches to the bridge. On the hill-side, immediately by the bridge, was a stone fence running parallel to the stream; the turns of the roadway, as it wound up the hill, were covered by rifle-pits and breastworks of rails, &c. These works, and the woods that covered the slopes, were filled with the enemy's riflemen, and batteries were in position to enfilade the bridge and its approaches.

General Rodman was ordered to cross the ford below the bridge. From Colonel Crook's position it was found impossible to carry the bridge.

General Sturgis was ordered to make a detail from his division for that purpose. He sent forward the 2d Maryland and the 6th New Hampshire. These regiments made several successive attacks in the most gallant style, but were driven back.

The artillery on the left were ordered to concentrate their fire on the woods above the bridge. Colonel Crook brought a section of Captain Simmons's battery to a position to command the bridge. The 51st New York and 51st Pennsylvania were then ordered to assault the bridge. Taking advantage of a small spur of the hills which ran parallel to the river, they moved towards the bridge. From the crest of this spur they rushed with bayonets fixed and cleared the bridge.

The division followed the storming party, also the brigade of Colonel Crook's as a support. The enemy withdrew to still higher ground, some five or six hundred yards beyond, and opened a fire of artillery on the troops in the new position on the crest of the hill above the bridge.

General Rodman's division succeeded in crossing the ford after a sharp fire of musketry and artillery, and joined on the left of Sturgis, Scammon's brigade crossing as support. General Wilcox's division was ordered across to take position on General Sturgis's right.

These dispositions being completed about 3 o'clock, the command moved forward, except Sturgis's division, left in reserve. Clark's and Durell's batteries accompanied Rodman's division; Cook's battery with Wilcox's division, and a section of Simmons's battery with Colonel Crook's brigade. A section of Simmons's battery and Mullenburgh's and McMullan's batteries were in position. The order for the advance was obeyed by the troops with alacrity. General Wilcox's division, with Crook in support, moved up on both sides of the turnpike leading from the bridge to Sharpsburg, General Rodman's division, supported by Scammon's brigade, on the left of General Wilcox. The enemy retreated before the advance of the troops. The 9th New York, of General Rodman's division, captured one of the enemy's batteries and held it for some time. As the command was driving the enemy to the main heights on the left of the town, the light division of General A. P. Hill arrived upon the field of battle from Harper's Ferry, and with a heavy artillery fire made a strong attack on the extreme left. To meet this attack the left division diverged from the line of march intended, and opened a gap between it and the right. To fill up this it was necessary to order the troops from the second line. During these movements General Rodman was mortally wounded. Colonel Harland's brigade, of General Rodman's division, was driven back. Colonel Scammon's brigade, by a change of front to rear on his right flank, saved the left from being driven completely in. The fresh troops of the enemy pouring in, and the accumulation of artillery against this command, destroyed all hope of its being able to accomplish anything more.

It was now nearly dark. General Sturgis was ordered forward to support the left. Notwithstanding the hard work in the early part of the day, his division moved forward with spirit. With its assistance the enemy were checked and held at bay.

The command was ordered to fall back by General Cox, who commanded on the field the troops engaged in this affair beyond the Antietam. The artillery had been well served during the day. Night closed the long and desperately contested battle of the 17th. Nearly two hundred thousand men and five hundred pieces of artillery were for fourteen hours engaged in this memorable battle.

We had attacked the enemy in a position selected by the experienced engineer then in person directing their operations. We had driven them from their line on one flank, and secured a footing within it on the other. The army of the Potomac, notwithstanding the moral effect incident to previous reverses, had achieved a victory over an adversary invested with the prestige of recent success. Our soldiers slept that night conquerors on a field won by their valor and covered with the dead and wounded of the enemy.

The night, however, brought with it grave responsibilities. Whether to renew the attack on the 18th, or to defer it, even with the risk of the enemy's retirement, was the question before me.

After a night of anxious deliberation and a full and careful survey of the situation and condition of our army, the strength and position of the enemy, I concluded that the success of an attack on the 18th was not certain. I am aware of the fact that, under ordinary circumstances, a general is expected to risk a battle if he has a reasonable prospect of success; but at this critical juncture I should have had a narrow view of the condition of the country had I been willing to hazard another battle with less than an absolute assurance of success. At that moment—Virginia lost, Washington menaced, Maryland invaded—the national cause could afford no risks of defeat. One battle lost, and almost all would have been lost. Lee's army might then have marched as it pleased on Washington, Baltimore, Philadelphia, or New York. It could have levied its supplies from a fertile and undevastated country; extorted tribute from wealthy and populous cities; and nowhere east of the Alleghanies was there another organized force able to arrest its march.

The following are among the considerations which led me to doubt the certainty of success in attacking before the 19th:

The troops were greatly overcome by the fatigue and exhaustion attendant upon the long continued and severely contested battle of the 17th, together with the long day and night marches to which they had been subjected during the previous three days.

The supply trains were in the rear, and many of the troops had suffered from hunger. They required rest and refreshment.

One division of Sumner's and all of Hooker's corps, on the right, had, after fighting most valiantly for several hours, been overpowered by numbers, driven back in great disorder, and much scattered, so that they were for the time somewhat demoralized.

In Hooker's corps, according to the return made by General Meade, commanding, there were but 6,729 men present on the 18th; whereas, on the morning of the 22d, there were 13,093 men present for duty in the same corps, showing that previous to and during the battle 6,364 men were separated from their command.

General Meade, in an official communication upon this subject, dated September 18, 1862, says:

"I enclose a field return of the corps made this afternoon, which I desire you will lay before the commanding general. I am satisfied the great reduction in the corps since the recent engagements is not due solely to the casualties of battle, and that a considerable number of men are still in the rear, some having dropped out on the march, and many dispersing and leaving yesterday during the fight. I think the efficiency of the corps, so far as it goes, good. To resist an attack in our present strong position I think they may be depended on, and I hope they will perform duty in case we make an attack, though I do not think their morale is as good for an offensive as a defensive movement."

One division of Sumner's corps had also been overpowered, and was a good deal scattered and demoralized. It was not deemed by its corps commander in proper condition to attack the enemy vigorously the next day.

Some of the new troops on the left, although many of them fought well during the battle, and are entitled to great credit, were, at the close of the action, driven back, and their morale impaired.

On the morning of the 18th General Burnside requested me to send him another division to assist in holding his position on the other side of the Antietam, and to enable him to withdraw his corps if he should be attacked by a superior force. He gave me the impression that if he were attacked again that morning he would not be able to make a very vigorous resistance. I visited his position early, determined to send General Morell's division to his aid, and directed that it should be placed on this side of the Antietam, in order that it might cover the retreat of his own corps from the other side of the Antietam, should that become necessary, at the same time it was in position to re-enforce our centre or right, if that were needed.

Late in the afternoon I found that, although he had not been attacked, General Burnside had withdrawn his own corps to this side of the Antietam, and sent over Morell's division alone to hold the opposite side.

A large number of our heaviest and most efficient batteries had consumed all their ammunition on the 16th and 17th, and it was impossible to supply them until late on the following day.

Supplies of provisions and forage had to be brought up and issued, and infantry ammunition distributed.

Finally, re-enforcements to the number of 14,000 men—to say nothing of troops expected from Pennsylvania—had not arrived, but were expected during the day.

The 18th was, therefore, spent in collecting the dispersed, giving rest to the fatigued, removing the wounded, burying the dead, and the necessary preparations for a renewal of the battle.

Of the re-enforcements, Couch's division, marching with commendable rapidity, came up into position at a late hour in the morning. Humphrey's division of new troops, in their anxiety to participate in the battle which was raging, when they received the order to march from Frederick at about half past three p. m., on the 17th, pressed forward during the entire night, and the mass of the division reached the army during the following morning. Having marched more than twenty-three miles after half past four o'clock on the preceding afternoon, they were, of course, greatly exhausted, and needed rest and refreshment. Large re-enforcements expected from Pennsylvania never arrived. During the 18th orders were given for a renewal of the attack at daylight on the 19th.

On the night of the 18th the enemy, after passing troops in the latter part of the day from the Virginia shore to their position behind Sharpsburg, as seen by our officers, suddenly formed the design of abandoning their position, and retreating across the river. As their line was but a short distance from the river, the evacuation presented but little difficulty, and was effected before daylight.

About 2,700 of the enemy's dead were, under the direction of Major Davis, assistant inspector general, counted and buried upon the battle-field of Antietam. A portion of their dead had been previously buried by the enemy. This is conclusive evidence that the enemy sustained much greater loss than we.

Thirteen guns, thirty-nine colors, upwards of fifteen thousand stand of small arms, and more than six thousand prisoners, were the trophies which attest the success of our army in the battles of South Mountain, Crampton's Gap, and Antietam.

Not a single gun or color was lost by our army during these battles.

Corps and divisions.	General officers.		Other officers.		Enlisted men.			Aggregate.			Grand aggregate.
	Killed.	Wounded.	Killed.	Wounded.	Killed.	Wounded.	Missing.	Killed.	Wounded.	Missing.	
1st corps, Maj. Gen. Hooker:											
1st division	...	...	...	...	...	...	...	98	669	95	862
2d division	...	...	...	...	...	...	...	157	898	137	1,188
3d division	...	...	...	...	...	...	...	97	449	23	569
Total	...	...	...	...	...	...	...	348	2,016	255	2,619
2d corps, Maj. Gen. Sumner:											
1st division	...	1	20	39	192	860	24	212	900	24	1,136
2d division	...	2	...	...	355	1,577	321	355	1,579	321	2,255
3d division	...	1	21	50	272	1,271	203	293	1,322	203	1,818
Total	...	4	41	89	819	3,708	548	860	3,801	548	5,209
5th corps, Maj. Gen. F. J. Porter:											
1st division	...	...	...	...	...	...	...	...	...	...	...
2d division	...	...	...	2	13	92	1	13	94	1	108
Artillery reserve	...	...	1	...	7	13	1	8	13	1	22
Total	...	...	1	2	20	105	2	21	107	2	130
6th corps, Maj. Gen. Franklin:											
1st division	...	...	...	...	...	...	...	5	58	2	65
2d division	...	...	...	...	...	...	...	65	277	31	373
Total	...	...	...	...	...	...	...	70	335	33	438
th corps, Maj. Gen. Burnside:											
1st division	...	...	2	20	44	264	7	46	284	7	337
2d division	...	...	7	29	121	493	20	128	522	20	670
3d division	...	...	8	40	212	743	70	220	783	70	1,073
4th division	...	...	5	7	33	145	23	38	152	23	213
Total	...	...	22	96	410	1,645	120	432	1,741	120	2,293
12th corps, (Gen. Banks.) Brig. Gen. Williams commanding:											
1st division	...	...	9	35	151	827	54	160	862	54	1,076
2d division	...	...	6	26	107	481	30	113	507	30	650
Artillery	...	...	...	...	1	15	1	1	15	1	17
Total	...	...	15	61	259	1,323	85	274	1,384	85	1,743
Maj. Gen. Couch's division	...	...	...	1		8			9		9
Brig. General Pleasonton, cavalry division	...	...	...	...	...	...	...	5	23	...	28
Grand total	...	4	79	249	1,508	[illegible]	755	2,010	9,416	1,043	12,469

HEADQUARTERS ARMY OF THE POTOMAC,
Camp near Sharpsburg, September 29, 1862.

General Ransom's and Jenkins's brigade....................	3,000	"
Forty-six regiments not included in above....................	18,400	"
Artillery, estimated at 400 guns	6,000	"
Total	97,445	"

These estimates give the actual number of men present and fit for duty.

Our own forces at the battle of Antietam were as follows:

1st corps	14,856	men.
2d corps..	18,813	"
5th corps (one division not arrived)	12,930	"
6th corps	12,300	"
9th corps	13,819	"
12th corps	10,126	"
Cavalry division..	4,320	"
Total in action	87,164	"

When our cavalry advance reached the river on the morning of the 19th, it was discovered that nearly all the enemy's forces had crossed into Virginia during the night, their rear escaping under cover of eight batteries, placed in strong positions upon the elevated bluffs on the opposite bank. General Porter, commanding the 5th corps, ordered a detachment from Griffin's and Barnes's brigades, under General Griffin, to cross the river at dark, and carry the enemy's batteries. This was gallantly done under the fire of the enemy; several guns, caissons, &c., were taken, and their supports driven back half a mile.

The information obtained during the progress of this affair indicated that the mass of the enemy had retreated on the Charlestown and Martinsburg roads, towards Winchester. To verify this, and to ascertain how far the enemy had retired, General Porter was authorized to detach from his corps, on the morning of the 20th, a reconnoitring party in greater force. This detachment crossed the river, and advanced about a mile, when it was attacked by a large body of the enemy lying in ambush in the woods, and driven back across the river with considerable loss. This reconnoissance showed that the enemy was still in force on the Virginia bank of the Potomac, prepared to resist our further advance.

It was reported to me on the 19th that General Stuart had made his appearance at Williamsport with some four thousand cavalry and six pieces of artillery, and that ten thousand infantry were marching on the same point from the direction of Winchester. I ordered General Couch to march at once with his division, and a part of Pleasonton's cavalry, with Franklin's corps, within supporting distance, for the purpose of endeavoring to capture this force. General Couch made a prompt and rapid march to Williamsport, and attacked the enemy vigorously, but they made their escape across the river.

I despatched the following telegraphic report to the general-in-chief:

"HEADQUARTERS ARMY OF THE POTOMAC,
" *Sharpsburg, September* 19, 1862.

"I have the honor to report that Maryland is entirely freed from the presence of the enemy, who has been driven across the Potomac. No fears need now be entertained for the safety of Pennsylvania. I shall at once occupy Harper's Ferry.

"G. B. McCLELLAN,
" *Major General, Commanding.*

"Major General H. W. HALLECK,
" *Commanding United States Army.*"

On the following day I received this telegram:

"WASHINGTON, *September* 20, 1862—2 *p. m.*

"We are still left entirely in the dark in regard to your own movements and those of the enemy. This should not be so. You should keep me advised of both, so far as you know them.

"H. W. HALLECK
"*General-in-Chief.*

"Major General G. B. McCLELLAN."

To which I answered as follows:

"HEADQUARTERS ARMY OF THE POTOMAC,
"*Near Sharpsburg, September* 20, 1862—8 *p. m.*

"Your telegram of to-day is received. I telegraphed you yesterday all I knew, and had nothing more to inform you of until this evening. Williams's corps (Banks's) occupied Maryland heights at 1 p. m. to-day. The rest of the army is near here, except Couch's division, which is at this moment engaged with the enemy in front of Williamsport; the enemy is retiring, *via* Charlestown and Martinsburg, on Winchester. He last night reoccupied Williamsport by a small force, but will be out of it by morning. I think he has a force of infantry near Shepherdstown.

"I regret that you find it necessary to couch every despatch I have the honor to receive from you in a spirit of fault-finding, and that you have not yet found leisure to say one word in commendation of the recent achievements of this army, or even to allude to them.

"I have abstained from giving the number of guns, colors, small arms, prisoners, &c., captured, until I could do so with some accuracy. I hope by to-morrow evening to be able to give at least an approximate statement.

"G. B. McCLELLAN.
"*Major General, Commanding.*

"Major General HALLECK,
"*General-in-Chief, Washington.*"

On the same day I telegraphed as follows:

"HEADQUARTERS ARMY OF THE POTOMAC,
"*September* 20, 1862.

"As the rebel army, now on the Virginia side of the Potomac, must in a great measure be dependent for supplies of ammunition and provisions upon Richmond, I would respectfully suggest that General Banks be directed to send out a cavalry force to cut their supply communication opposite Washington. This would seriously embarrass their operations, and will aid this army materially.

"G. B. McCLELLAN,
"*Major General, Commanding.*

"Major General H. W. HALLECK,
"*Commanding United States Army.*"

Maryland heights were occupied by General Williams's corps on this day, and on the 22d General Sumner took possession of Harper's Ferry.

It will be remembered that at the time I was assigned to the command of the forces for the defence of the national capital, on the 2d day of September, 1862, the greater part of all the available troops were suffering under the disheartening influences of the serious defeat they had encountered during the brief and unfortunate campaign of General Pope. Their numbers were greatly reduced by casualties, their confidence was much shaken, and they had lost something of that "*esprit du corps*," which is indispensable to the efficiency of an army.

Moreover, they had left behind, lost, or worn out, the greatest part of their clothing and camp equipage, which required renewal before they could be in proper condition to take the field again.

The intelligence that the enemy was crossing the Potomac into Maryland was received in Washington on the 4th of September, and the army of the Potomac was again put in motion, under my direction, on the following day, so that but a very brief interval of time was allowed to reorganize or procure supplies.

The sanguinary battles of South Mountain and Antietam fought by this army a few days afterwards, with the reconnoissances immediately following, resulted in a loss to us of ten general officers, many regimental and company officers, and a large number of enlisted men, amounting in the aggregate to fifteen thousand two hundred and twenty, (15,220.) Two army corps had been sadly cut up, scattered, and somewhat demoralized in the action on the 17th.

In General Sumner's corps alone forty-one (41) commissioned officers and eight hundred and nineteen (819) enlisted men had been killed; four (4) general officers, eighty-nine (89) other commissioned officers, and three thousand seven hundred and eight (3,708) enlisted men had been wounded, besides five hundred and forty-eight (548) missing; making the aggregate loss in this splendid veteran corps, in this one battle, five thousand two hundred and nine, (5,209.)

In General Hooker's corps the casualties of the same engagement amounted to two thousand six hundred and nineteen. (2,619.)

The entire army had been greatly exhausted by unavoidable overwork, fatiguing marches, hunger, and want of sleep and rest, previous to the last battle.

When the enemy recrossed the Potomac into Virginia the means of transportation at my disposal were inadequate to furnish a single day's supply of subsistence in advance.

Many of the troops were new levies, some of whom had fought like veterans, but the morale of others had been a good deal impaired in those severely contested actions, and they required time to recover as well as to acquire the necessary drill and discipline.

Under these circumstances I did not feel authorized to cross the river with the main army over a very deep and difficult ford in pursuit of the retreating enemy, known to be in strong force on the south bank, and thereby place that stream, which was liable at any time to rise above a fording stage, between my army and its base of supply.

I telegraphed on the 22d to the general-in-chief as follows:

"As soon as the exigencies of the service will admit of it, this army should be reorganized. It is absolutely necessary, to secure its efficiency, that the old skeleton regiments should be filled up at once, and officers appointed to supply the numerous existing vacancies. There are instances where captains are commanding regiments, and companies are without a single commissioned officer."

On the 23d the following was telegraphed to the general-in-chief:

"Headquarters Army of the Potomac,
"*Near Shepherdstown, September 23*, 1862—9.30 *a. m.*

"From several different sources I learn that General R. E. Lee is still opposite to my position at Leestown, between Shepherdstown and Martinsburg, and that General Jackson is on the Opequan creek, about three miles above its mouth, both with large forces. There are also indications of heavy re-enforcements moving towards them from Winchester and Charlestown. I have therefore ordered General Franklin to take position with his corps at the cross-roads about one mile northeast of Bakersville, on the Bakersville and Williamsport road, and General Couch to establish his division near Downsville, leaving sufficient force at Williamsport to watch and guard the ford at that place. The fact of the enemy's remaining so long in our front, and the indications of an advance of re-enforcements, seem to indicate that he will give us another battle with all his available force.

"As I mentioned to you before, our army has been very much reduced by casualties in the recent battles, and in my judgment all the re-enforcements of old troops that can possibly be dispensed with around Washington and other places should be instantly pushed forward by rail to this army. A defeat at this juncture would be ruinous to our cause. I cannot think it possible that the enemy will bring any forces to bear upon Washington till after the question is decided here; but if he should, troops can soon be sent back from this army by rail to re-enforce the garrison there.

"The evidence I have that re-enforcements are coming to the rebel army consists in the fact that long columns of dust extending from Winchester to Charlestown and from Charlestown in this direction, and also troops moving this way, were seen last evening. This is corroborated by citizens. General Sumner with his corps and Williams's (Banks's) occupies Harper's Ferry and the surrounding heights. I think he will be able to hold his position till re-enforcements arrive.

"G. B. McCLELLAN,
"*Major General.*

"Major General HALLECK,
"*General-in-Chief, Washington.*"

On the 27th I made the following report:

"HEADQUARTERS ARMY OF THE POTOMAC,
"*September 27, 1862—10 a. m.*

"All the information in my possession goes to prove that the main body of the enemy is concentrated not far from Martinsburg, with some troops at Charlestown; not many in Winchester. Their movements of late have been an extension towards our right and beyond it. They are receiving re-enforcements in Winchester, mainly, I think, of conscripts—perhaps entirely so.

"This army is not now in condition to undertake another campaign, nor to bring on another battle, unless great advantages are offered by some mistake of the enemy, or pressing military exigencies render it necessary. We are greatly deficient in officers. Many of the old regiments are reduced to mere skeletons. The new regiments need instruction. Not a day should be lost in filling the old regiments—our main dependence—and in supplying vacancies among the officers by promotion.

"My present purpose is to hold the army about as it is now, rendering Harper's Ferry secure and watching the river closely, intending to attack the enemy should he attempt to cross to this side.

"Our possession of Harper's Ferry gives us the great advantage of a secure debouche, but we cannot avail ourselves of it until the railroad bridge is finished, because we cannot otherwise supply a greater number of troops than we now have on the Virginia side at that point. When the river rises so that the enemy cannot cross in force, I purpose concentrating the army somewhere near Harper's Ferry, and then acting according to circumstances, viz: moving on Winchester, if from the position and attitude of the enemy we are likely to gain a great advantage by doing so, or else devoting a reasonable time to the organization of the army and instruction of the new troops, preparatory to an advance on whatever line may be determined. In any event, I regard it as absolutely necessary to send new regiments at once to the old corps, for purposes of instruction, and that the old regiments be filled at once. I have no fears as to an attack on Washington by the line of Manassas. Holding Harper's Ferry as I do, they will not run the risk of an attack on their flank and rear while they have the garrison of Washington in their front.

"I rather apprehend a renewal of the attempt in Maryland should the river remain low for a great length of time, and should they receive considerable addition to their force. I would be glad to have Peck's division as soon as possible. I am surprised that Sigel's men should have been sent to Western Virginia withou my knowledge. The last I heard from you on the subject was that they were at my disposition. In the last battles the enemy was undoubtedly greatly superior to us in number, and it was only by very hard fighting that we gained the advantage we did As it was, the result was at one period very doubtful, and we had all we could do to win the day. If the enemy receives considerable re-enforcements and we none, it is possible that I may have too much on my hands in the next battle. My own view of the proper policy to be pursued is to retain in Washington merely the force necessary to garrison it, and to send everything else available to re-enforce this army The railways give us the means of promptly re-enforcing Washington should it become necessary. If I am re-enforced, as I ask, and am allowed to take my own course, I will hold myself responsible for the safety of Washington. Several persons recently from Richmond say that there are no troops there except conscripts, and they few in number. I hope to give you details as to late battles by this evening. I am about starting again for Harper's Ferry.

"G. B. McCLELLAN,
"*Major General Commanding.*

"Major General HALLECK,
"*General-in-Chief, Washington.*"

The work of reorganizing, drilling, and supplying the army, I beagn at the earliest moment. The different corps were stationed along the river in the best positions to cover and guard the fords. The great extent of the river front from near Washington to Cumberland, (some one hundred and fifty miles,) together with the line of the Baltimore and Ohio railroad, was to be carefully watched and guarded, to prevent, if possible, the enemy's raids. Reconnoissances upon the Virginia side of the river, for the purpose of learning the enemy's positions and movements, were made frequently, so that our cavalry, which from the time we left Washington had performed the most laborious service, and had from the commencement been deficient in numbers, was found totally inadequate to the requirements of the army.

This overwork had broken down the greater part of the horses; disease had appeared among them, and but a very small portion of our original cavalry force was fit for service.

To such an extent had this arm become reduced, that when General Stuart made his raid into Pennsylvania on the 11th of October with two thousand men, I could only mount eight hundred men to follow him.

Harper's Ferry was occupied on the 22d, and in order to prevent a catastrophe similar to the one which had happened to Colonel Miles, I immediately ordered Maryland, Bolivar, and Loudon heights to be strongly fortified. This was done as far as the time and means at our disposal permitted.

The main army of the enemy, during this time, remained in the vicinity of Martinsburg and Bunker hill, and occupied itself in drafting and coercing every able-bodied citizen into the ranks, forcibly taking their property, where it was not voluntarily offered, burning bridges, and destroying railroads.

On the first day of October, his excellency the President honored the army of the Potomac with a visit, and remained several days, during which he went through the different encampments, reviewed the troops, and went over the battle-fields of South Mountain and Antietam. I had the opportunity during this visit to describe to him the operations of the army since the time it left Washington, and gave him my reasons for not following the enemy after he crossed the Potomac.

On the 5th of October, the division of General Cox (about 5,000 men) was ordered from my command to Western Virginia.

On the 7th of October I received the following telegram:

"WASHINGTON, D. C., *October* 6, 1862.

"I am instructed to telegraph you as follows: The President directs that you cross the Potomac and give battle to the enemy, or drive him south. Your army must move now, while the roads are good. If you cross the river between the enemy and Washington, and cover the latter by your operation, you can be re-enforced with 30,000 men. If you move up the valley of the Shenandoah, not more than 12,000 or 15,000 can be sent to you. The President advises the interior line between Washington and the enemy, but does not order it. He is very desirous that your army move as soon as possible. You will immediately report what line you adopt, and when you intend to cross the river; also to what point the re-enforcements are to be sent. It is necessary that the plan of your operations be positively determined on, before orders are given for building bridges and repairing railroads. I am directed to add, that the Secretary of War and the general-in-chief fully concur with the President in these instructions.

"H. W. HALLECK, *General-in-Chief.*

"Major General MCCLELLAN."

At this time General Averill, with the greater part of our efficient cavalry, was in the vicinity of Cumberland, and General Kelly, the commanding officer, had that day reported that a large force of the enemy was advancing on Colonel Campbell, at Saint John's river. This obliged me to order General Averill to proceed with his force to the support of Colonel Campbell, which delayed his return to the army for several days.

On the 10th of October Stuart crossed the river at McCoy's Ferry, with 2,000 cavalry and a battery of horse artillery, on his raid into Maryland and Pennsylvania, making it necessary to use all our cavalry against him. This exhausting service completely broke down nearly all of our cavalry horses, and rendered a remount absolutely indispensable before we could advance on the enemy.

The following were the dispositions of troops made by me to defeat the purposes of this raid:

General Averill, then at Green Spring, on the upper Potomac, was ordered to move rapidly down upon the north side of the river, with all his disposable cavalry, using every exertion to get upon the trail of the enemy, and follow it up vigorously.

General Pleasonton, with the remaining cavalry force, was ordered to take the road by Cavetown, Harmon's gap, and Mechanicsville, and cut off the retreat of the enemy should he make for any of the fords below the position of the main army. His orders were to pursue them with the utmost rapidity, not to spare his men or horses, and to destroy or capture them if possible.

General Crook, at that time commanding Cox's division, at Hancock, en route for Western Virginia, was ordered to halt, place his men in cars, and remain in readiness to move to any point above should the enemy return in that direction, keeping his scouts well out on all the roads leading from the direction of Chambersburg to the upper Potomac.

The other commanders between Hancock and Harper's Ferry were instructed to keep a vigilant watch upon all the roads and fords, so as to prevent the escape of the rebels within these limits.

General Burnside was ordered to send two brigades to the Monocacy crossing, there to remain in cars, with steam up, ready to move to any point on the railroad to which Stuart might be aiming, while Colonel Rush, at Frederick, was directed to keep his lancers scouting on the approaches from Chambersburg, so as to give timely notice to the commander of the two brigades at the Monocacy crossing.

General Stoneman, whose headquarters were then at Poolsville, occupying with his division the different fords on the river below the mouth of the Monocacy, was directed to keep his cavalry well out on the approaches from the direction of Frederick, so as to give him time to mass his troops at any point where the enemy might attempt to cross the Potomac in his vicinity. He was informed of General Pleasonton's movements.

After the orders were given for covering all the fords upon the river, I did not think it possible for Stuart to recross, and I believed that the capture or destruction of his entire force was perfectly certain; but owing to the fact that my orders were not in all cases carried out as I expected, he effected his escape into Virginia without much loss.

The troops sent by General Burnside to the Monocacy, owing to some neglect in not giving the necessary orders to the commander, instead of remaining at the railroad crossing, as I directed, marched four miles into Frederick, and there remained until after Stuart had passed the railroad, only six miles below, near which point it was said he halted for breakfast.

General Pleasonton ascertained, after his arrival at Mechanicsville, that the enemy were only about an hour ahead of him, beating a hasty retreat towards the mouth of the Monocacy. He pushed on vigorously, and, near its mouth, overtook them with a part of his force, having marched seventy-eight miles in twenty-four hours, and having left many of his horses broken down upon the road. He at once attacked with his artillery, and the firing continued for several hours, during which time he states that he received the support of a small portion of General Stoneman's command, not sufficient to inflict any material damage upon the enemy.

General Stoneman reports that, in accordance with his instructions, he gave all necessary orders for intercepting the return of the rebels, and Colonel Staples, commanding one of his brigades, states that he sent two regiments of infantry to the mouth of the Monocacy, and one regiment to White's ford; that on the morning of the 12th, about ten o'clock, he, by General Stoneman's order, marched the remaining three regiments of his command from Poolsville towards the mouth of the Monocacy; that before getting into action he was relieved by General Ward, who states that he reported to General Pleasonton with his command, while the enemy was crossing the river, and was informed by him (General Pleasonton) that he was too late, and that nothing could be done then.

General Pleasanton, in his report of this affair, says: "It was at this time that Colonel Ward reported to me from General Stoneman's division, with a brigade of infantry, a regiment of cavalry, and a section of artillery. I told him that his command could be of no use, as the enemy had then crossed the river. These are the only troops that I knew of, that were in that vicinity, and this was the first intimation I received that any troops were endeavoring to assist me in capturing the rebels. I succeeded in preventing the enemy from crossing at the mouth of the Monocacy, and drove him to White's ford, three miles below. Had White's ford been occupied by any force of ours previous to the time of the occupation by the enemy, the capture of Stuart's whole force would have been certain and inevitable. With my small force, which did not exceed one-fourth of the enemy's, it was not practicable for me to occupy that ford while the enemy was in front."

It would seem from the report of General Stoneman, that the disposition he made of his troops, previous to the arrival of Stuart, was a good one. He stationed two regiments at the mouth of Monocacy, and two regiments at White's ford, the latter in the very place where the crossing was made, and the former only three miles off, with a reserve of three regiments at Poolsville, some six miles distant. General Pleasonton's report shows that from the time the firing commenced until the enemy were across the river was about four and a half hours. General Stoneman states that he started the reserve from Poolesville at about nine o'clock, but it appears, from the report of General Pleasonton, that it did not reach him until half past one.

At the time I received the order of October 6, to cross the river and attack the enemy, the army was wholly deficient in cavalry, and a large part of our troops were in want of shoes, blankets, and other indispensable articles of clothing, notwithstanding all the efforts that had been made since the battle of Antietam, and even prior to that date, to refit the army with clothing, as well as horses. I at once consulted with Colonel Ingalls, the chief quartermaster, who believed that the necessary articles could be supplied in about three days. Orders were immediately issued to the different commanders who had not already sent in their requisitions, to do so at once, and all the necessary steps were forthwith taken by me to insure a prompt delivery of the supplies. The requisitions were forwarded to the proper department at Washington, and I expected that the articles would reach our depots during the three days specified; but day after day elapsed, and only a small portion of the clothing arrived. Corps commanders, upon receiving notice from the quartermasters that they might expect to receive their supplies at certain dates, sent the trains for them, which, after waiting, were compelled to return empty. Several instances occurred where these trains went back and forth from the camps to the depots, as often as four or five different times, without receiving their supplies, and I was informed by one corps commander that his wagon train had travelled over 150 miles, to and from the depots, before he succeeded in obtaining his clothing.

The corps of General Franklin did not get its clothing until after it had crossed the Potomac, and was *moving* into Virginia. General Reynolds's corps was delayed a day at Berlin, to complete its supplies, and General Porter only completed his on reaching the vicinity of Harper's Ferry.

I made every exertion in my power, and my quartermasters did the same, to have these supplies hurried forward rapidly; and I was repeatedly told that they had filled the requisitions at Washington, and that the supplies had been forwarded. But they did not come to us, and *of* course were inaccessible to the army. I did not fail to make frequent representation of this condition of things to the general-in-chief, and it appears that he referred the matter to the Quartermaster General, who constantly replied that the supplies had been promptly ordered. Notwithstanding this, they did not reach our depots.

The following extracts are from telegrams upon this subject:

"HEADQUARTERS ARMY OF THE POTOMAC,
"*October* 11, 1862—9 *a. m.*

* * * * * * * *

"We have been making every effort to get supplies of clothing for this army, and Colonel Ingalls has received advices that it has been forwarded by railroad; but, owing to bad management on the roads, or from some other cause, it comes in very slowly, and it will take a much longer time than was anticipated to get articles that are absolutely indispensable to the army, unless the railroad managers forward supplies more rapidly.

"GEORGE B. McCLELLAN,
"*Major General.*

"Major General H. W. HALLECK,
"*General-in-Chief, Washington.*"

"HEADQUARTERS ARMY OF THE POTOMAC,
"*October* 11, 1862.

"I am compelled again to call your attention to the great deficiency of shoes, and other indispensable articles of clothing, that still exists in some of the corps in this army. Upon the assurances of the chief quartermaster, who based his calculation upon information received from Washington, that clothing would be forwarded at certain times, corps commanders sent their wagons to Hagerstown and Harper's Ferry for it. It did not arrive as promised, and has not yet arrived. Unless some measures are taken to insure the prompt forwarding of these supplies, there will necessarily be a corresponding delay in getting the army ready to move, as the men cannot march without shoes. Everything has been done that can be done at these headquarters to accomplish the desired result.

"GEORGE B. McCLELLAN,
"*Major General, Commanding.*

"Major General H. W. HALLECK,
"*Commander-in-Chief, Washington.*"

"HEADQUARTERS ARMY OF THE POTOMAC,
"*October* 15, 1862—7 *p. m.*

* * * * * * * *

"I am using every possible exertion to get this army ready to move. It was only yesterday that a part of our shoes and clothing arrived at Hagerstown. It is being issued to the troops as rapidly as possible.

"GEORGE B. McCLELLAN,
"*Major General.*

"Major General H. W. HALLECK,
"*General-in-Chief.*"

"HEADQUARTERS ARMY OF THE POTOMAC,
"*October* 15, 1862—7.30 *p. m.*

"General Franklin reports that there is by no means as much clothing as was called for at Hagerstown. I think, therefore, you had better have additional supplies, especially of shoes, forwarded to Harper's Ferry as soon as possible.

"R. B. MARCY, *Chief of Staff.*

"Colonel R. INGALLS,
"*Care of Colonel Rucker, Quartermaster, Washington.*"

"HEADQUARTERS ARMY OF THE POTOMAC,
"*October* 16, 1862.

"General J. F. Reynolds just telegraphs as follows: 'My quartermaster reports that there are no shoes, tents, blankets, or knapsacks at Hagerstown. He was able to procure only a complete supply of overcoats and pants, with a few socks, drawers, and coats. This leaves many of the men yet without a shoe. My requisitions call for 5,255 pairs of shoes.'

"Please push the shoes and stockings up to Harper's Ferry as fast as possible.

"R. B. MARCY, *Chief of Staff.*

"Colonel R. INGALLS,
"*Care of Colonel Rucker, Quartermaster, Washington.*"

"HEADQUARTERS ARMY OF THE POTOMAC,
"*Camp near Knoxville, Maryland, October* 9, 1862.

"You did right in sending clothing to Harper's Ferry. You will not be able to send too much or too quickly. We want blankets, shoes, canteens, &c., very much.

"RUFUS INGALLS,
"*Lieutenant Colonel and Aide-de-Camp, Chief Quartermaster.*

"Colonel C. G. SAWTELLE,
"*Depot Quartermaster, Washington.*"

"HEADQUARTERS ARMY OF THE POTOMAC,
"*Camp near Knoxville, Maryland, October* 10, 1862.

"Shipments to Hagerstown must be made direct through, to avoid the contemptible delays at Harrisburg. If Colonel Crosman was ordered to send clothing, I hope he has sent it, for the suffering and impatience are excessive.

"RUFUS INGALLS,
"*Lieutenant Colonel and Aide-de-Camp, Chief Quartermaster.*

"Captain AUGUSTUS BOYD,
"*Quartermaster, Philadelphia.*"

"HEADQUARTERS ARMY OF THE POTOMAC,
"*Camp near Knoxville, October* 13, 1862.

"Has the clothing arrived yet? If not, do you know where it is? What clothing was taken by the rebels at Chambersburg? Did they capture any property that was en route to you? Have we not got clothing at Harrisburg? Send an agent over the road to obtain information, and hurry up the supplies. Reply at once.

"RUFUS INGALLS,
"*Lieutenant Colonel and Aide-de-Camp, Chief Quartermaster.*

"Captain GEORGE H. WEEKS,
"*Depot Quartermaster, Hagerstown.*"

"SHARPSBURG, *October* 15, 1862.

"I have just returned from Hagerstown, where I have been for the clothing for the corps. There was nothing there but overcoats, trowsers, and a few uniform coats and socks. There were not any shoes, blankets, shirts, or shelter tents. Will you please tell me where and when the balance can be had. Shall I send to Harper's Ferry for them to-morrow? The corps surgeon has just made a requisition for 15 hospital tents. There are none at Hagerstown. Will you please to inform me if I can get them at Harper's Ferry?

"FIELDING LOWRY,
"*Captain and Quartermaster.*

"General INGALLS."

"HAGERSTOWN, *October* 15, 1862.

"I want at least ten thousand (10,000) suits of clothing in addition to what I have received. It should be here now.

"G. W. WEEKS,
"*Assistant Quartermaster.*

"Colonel INGALLS, *Quartermaster.*"

"HARPER'S FERRY, *October* 22, 1862.

"We have bootees, 12,000; greatcoats, 4,000; drawers and shirts are gone; blankets and stockings nearly so; 15,000 each of these four articles are wanted.

"ALEX. BLISS,
"*Captain and Assistant Quartermaster.*

"General INGALLS,
"*Chief Quartermaster, &c.*"

"McCLELLAN'S HEADQUARTERS,
"*October* 24, 1862—11 *a. m.*

"Please send to Captain Bliss, at Harper's Ferry, 10,000 blankets, 12,000 caps, 5,000 overcoats, 10,000 pairs bootees, 2,000 pairs artillery and cavalry boots, 15,000 pairs stockings, 15,000 drawers, and 15,000 pants. The clothing arrives slowly. Can it not be hurried along faster? May I ask you to obtain authority for this shipment?

"RUFUS INGALLS,
"*Lieutenant Colonel and Aide-de-Camp, Chief Quartermaster.*

"Captain D. G. THOMAS,
"*Military Storekeeper, Washington.*"

"HAGERSTOWN, *October* 30.

"Clothing has arrived this morning. None taken by rebels. Shall I supply Franklin, and retain portions for Porter and Reynolds until called for?

"G. W. WEEKS,
"*Captain and Assistant Quartermaster.*

"Colonel INGALLS."

The following statement, taken from a report of the chief quartermaster with the army, will show what progress was made in supplying the army with clothing from the 1st of September to the date of crossing the Potomac on the 31st of October, and that a greater part of the clothing did not reach our depots until after the 14th of October:

Statement of clothing and equipage received at the different depots of the army of the Potomac from September 1, 1862, to October 31, 1862.

Received at the depot—	Drawers.	Forage caps.	Stockings.	Sack coats.	Cavalry jackets.	Canteens.	Flannel shirts.	Haversacks.	Trowsers, (mounted.)	Boots.	Shelter tents.
From September 1 to October 6.	10,700	4,000	6,200	4,190	3,000	6,000	6,200	6,000	4,200	4,200	11,100
From October 6 to October 15 ..	17,000	11,000	22,025	......	500	10,221	18,325	12,989	1,000	6,000	3,000
From October 15 to October 25..	40,000	19,500	65,200	......	1,250	9,000	18,876	5,000	2,500	3,600	9,000
From October 25 to October 31..	30,000	......	30,000	......	1,500	3,008	2,200	9,900	5,000	20,040	......
Total	97,700	34,500	123,425	4,190	6,250	28,229	45,301	33,889	12,700	33,840	23,100

Statement of clothing and equipage received, &c.—Continued.

Received at the depot—	Camp kettles.	Mess pans.	Overcoats, (foot.)	Artillery jackets.	Blankets.	Overcoats (mounted.)	Felt hats.	Infantry coats.	Trowsers. (foot.)	Bootees.	Knit shirts.
From September 1 to October 6.	799	2,030	3,500	1,200	20	1,200	2,200	2,000	2,000	2,000	
From October 6 to October 15...	1,302	2,100	12,000	500	......	875	7,000	12,060	9,500	7,000	2,655
From October 15 to October 25..	1,891	4,500	14,770	1,750	6,500	3,500	......	22,500	39,620	52,900	2,424
From October 25 to October 31..	......	......	......	1,000	4,384	2,015	......	7,500	25,000	......	11,595
Total....................	3,995	8,630	30,270	4,450	10,904	7,590	9,200	44,060	76,120	61,900	16,674

Colonel Ingalls, chief quartermaster, in his report upon this subject, says:

"There was great delay in receiving our clothing. The orders were promptly given by me and approved by General Meigs, but the roads were slow to transport, particularly the Cumberland Valley road.

"For instance, clothing ordered to Hagerstown on the 7th October for the corps of Franklin, Porter, and Reynolds did not arrive there until about the 18th, and by that time, of course, there were increased wants and changes in position of troops. The clothing of Sumner arrived in great quantities near the last of October, almost too late for issue, as the army was crossing into Virginia. We finally left 50,000 suits at Harper's Ferry, *partly on the cars just arrived*, and partly in store."

The causes of the reduction of our cavalry force have already been recited. The difficulty in getting new supplies from the usual sources led me to apply for and obtain authority for the cavalry and artillery officers to purchase their own horses. The following are the telegrams and letters on this subject:

"HEADQUARTERS ARMY OF THE POTOMAC,
"*October* 12, 1862—12.45 *p. m.*

"It is absolutely necessary that some energetic means be taken to supply the cavalry of this army with remount horses. The present rate of supply is (1,050) ten hundred and fifty per week for the entire army here and in front of Washington. From this number the artillery draw for their batteries.

"GEORGE B. McCLELLAN,
"*Major General, Commanding.*

"Major General HALLECK,
"*General-in-Chief.*"

The general-in-chief, in a letter to me dated Washington, D. C., October 14, 1862, replies to this despatch in the following language:

"I have caused the matters complained of in your telegrams of the 11th and 12th to be investigated.

* * * * * * * * * *

"In regard to horses, you say that the present rate of supply is only 150 per week for the entire army here and in front of Washington. I find from the records that the issues for the last six weeks have been 8,754, making an average per week of 1,459."

One thousand and fifty (1,050) is the number stated in the original despatch, now in my possession; and as not only figures were used, but the number was written out in full, I can hardly see how it is possible for the telegraphic operator to have made a mistake in the transmission of the message.

"HEADQUARTERS ARMY OF THE POTOMAC,
"*October* 14, 1862—7 *p. m.*

* * * * * * * * * * * *

"With my small cavalry force it is impossible for me to watch the line of the Potomac properly, or even make the reconnoissances that are necessary for our movements. This makes it necessary for me to weaken my line very much, by extending the infantry to guard the innumerable fords. This will continue until the river rises, and it will be next to impossible to prevent the rebel cavalry raids. My cavalry force, as I urged this morning, should be largely and immediately increased, under any hypothesis, whether to guard the river, or advance on the enemy, or both.

"GEORGE B. McCLELLAN,
"*Major General.*

"Major General H. W. HALLECK,
"*Commander-in-Chief.*"

The following is an extract from the official report of Colonel Ingalls:

"Immediately after the battle of Antietam efforts were made to supply deficiencies in clothing and horses. Large requisitions were prepared and sent in. The artillery and cavalry required large numbers to cover losses sustained in battle, on the march, and by diseases. Both of these arms were deficient when they left Washington. A most violent and destructive disease made its appearance at this time, which put nearly 4,000 animals out of service. Horses reported perfectly well one day would be dead lame the next, and it was difficult to foresee where it would end, or what number would cover the loss. They were attacked in the hoof and tongue. No one seemed able to account for the appearance of this disease. Animals kept at *rest* would recover in time, but *could not be worked.* I made application to send west and purchase horses at once, but it was refused, on the ground that the outstanding contracts provided for enough, *but they were not delivered sufficiently fast,* nor in sufficient numbers until late in October and early in November I was authorized to buy 2,500 late in October, but the delivery was not completed until in November, after we had reached Warrenton."

In a letter from General Meigs, written on the 14th of October, and addressed to the general-in-chief, it is stated: "There have been issued, therefore, to the army of the Potomac, since the battles in front of Washington, to replace losses, (9.254) nine thousand two hundred and fifty-four horses."

What number of horses were sent to General Pope before his return to Washington I have no means of determining; but the following statement made upon my order, by the chief quartermaster with the army, and who had means for gaining accurate information, force upon my mind the conclusion that the Quartermaster General was in error:

"HEADQUARTERS ARMY OF THE POTOMAC,
"*Chief Quartermaster's Office, October* 31, 1862.

"Horses purchased since September 6, 1862, by Colonel Ingalls chief quartermaster, and issued to the forces under the immediate command of Major General George B. McClellan............	1,200
"Issued and turned over to the above force by Captain J. J. Dana, assistant quartermaster, (in Washington)....................	2,261
"Issued to forces at and near Washington which have since joined the command..	352
"Total purchased by Colonel Ingalls and issued and turned over by Captain Dana to the forces in this immediate command........	3,813

"Issued by Captain J. J. Dana, assistant quartermaster, to the forces in the vicinity of Washington	3,363
"Grand total purchased by Colonel R. Ingalls, chief quartermaster, and issued and turned over by Captain J. J. Dana, assistant quartermaster, to the entire army of the Potomac and the forces around Washington	7,176

About 3,000 horses have been turned over to the quartermaster's department by officers as unfit for service; nearly 1,500 should now be turned over also, being worn out and diseased.

Respectfully submitted.

"FRED. MYERS,
"*Lieutenant Colonel and Quartermaster.*"

This official statement, made up from the reports of the quartermasters who received and distributed the horses, exhibits the true state of the case, and gives the total number of horses received by the army of the Potomac, and the troops around Washington, during a period of eight weeks as (7,176) seven thousand one hundred and seventy-six, or (2,078) two thousand and seventy-eight less than the number stated by the Quartermaster General.

Supposing that (1,500) fifteen hundred were issued to the army under General Pope previous to its return to Washington, as General Meigs states, there would still remain (578) five hundred and seventy-eight horses which he does not account for.

The letter of the general-in-chief to the Secretary of War on the 28th of October, and the letter of General Meigs to the general-in-chief on the 14th of October, convey the impression that, upon my repeated applications for cavalry and artillery horses for the army of the Potomac, I had received a much greater number than was really the case.

It will be seen from Colonel Myers's report that, of all the horses alluded to by General Meigs, only (3,813) three thousand eight hundred and thirteen came to the army with which I was ordered to follow and attack the enemy. Of course the remainder did not in the slightest degree contribute to the efficiency of the cavalry or artillery of the army with which I was to cross the river. Neither did they in the least facilitate any preparations for carrying out the order to advance upon the enemy, as the general-in-chief's letter might seem to imply.

During the same period that we were receiving the horses alluded to about (3,000) three thousand of our old stock were turned into the quartermaster's department, and 1,500 more reported as in such condition that they ought to be turned in as unfit for service; thus leaving the active army some 700 short of the number required to make good existing deficiencies, to say nothing of providing remounts for men whose horses had died or been killed during the campaign and those previously dismounted. Notwithstanding all the efforts made to obtain a remount, there were, after deducting the force engaged in picketing the river, but about a thousand serviceable cavalry horses on the 21st day of October.

In a letter dated October 14, 1862, the general-in-chief says:

"It is also reported to me that the number of animals with your army in the field is about 31,000. It is believed that your present proportion of cavalry and of animals is much larger than that of any other of our armies."

What number of animals our other armies had I am not prepared to say, but military men in European armies have been of the opinion that an army to be efficient, while carrying on active operations in the field, should have a cavalry force equal in numbers to from one-sixth to one-fourth of the infantry force. My cavalry did not amount to one-twentieth part of the army, and hence the necessity of giving every one of my cavalry soldiers a serviceable horse.

Cavalry may be said to constitute the *antennæ* of an army. It scouts all the roads in front, on the flanks and in the rear of the advancing columns, and constantly feel the enemys. The amount of labor falling on this arm during the Maryland campaign was excessive.

To persons not familiar with the movements of troops, and the amount of transportation required for a large army marching away from water or railroad communications, the number of animals mentioned by the general-in-chief may have appeared unnecessarily large; but to a military man, who takes the trouble to enter into an accurate and detailed computation of the number of pounds of subsistence and forage required for such an army as that of the Potomac, it will be seen that the 31,000 animals were considerably less than was absolutely necessary to an advance.

As we were required to move through a country which could not be depended upon for any of our supplies, it became necessary to transport everything in wagons, and to be prepared for all emergencies. I did not consider it safe to leave the river without subsistence and forage for ten days.

The official returns of that date show the aggregate strength of the army for duty to have been about 110,000 men of all arms. This did not include teamsters, citizen employés, officers' servants, &c., amounting to some 12,000, which gave a total of 122,000 men.

The subsistence alone of this army for ten days required for its transportation 1,830 wagons at 2,000 pounds to the wagon, and 10,980 animals.

Our cavalry horses at that time amounted to 5,046, and our artillery horses to 6,836.

To transport full forage for these 22,862 animals for ten days required 17,832 additional animals; and this forage would only supply the entire number (40,694) of animals with a small fraction over half allowance for the time specified.

It will be observed that this estimate does not embrace the animals necessary to transport quartermasters' supplies, baggage, camp equipage, ambulances, reserve ammunition, forage for officers' horses, &c., which would greatly augment the necessary transportation.

It may very truly be said that we did make the march with the means at our disposal, but it will be remembered that we met with no serious opposition from the enemy; neither did we encounter delays from any other cause. The roads were in excellent condition, and the troops marched with the most commendable order and celerity.

If we had met with a determined resistance from the enemy, and our progress had been very much retarded thereby, we would have consumed our supplies before they could have been renewed. A proper estimate of my responsibilities as the commander of that army did not justify me in basing my preparations for the expedition upon the supposition that I was to have an uninterrupted march. On the contrary, it was my duty to be prepared for all emergencies; and not the least important of my responsibilities was the duty of making ample provision for supplying my men and animals with rations and forage.

Knowing the solicitude of the President for an early movement, and sharing with him fully his anxiety for prompt action, on the 21st of October I telegraphed to the general-in-chief as follows:

"HEADQUARTERS ARMY OF THE POTOMAC,
"*October* 21, 1862.

"Since the receipt of the President's order to move on the enemy, I have been making every exertion to get this army supplied with clothing absolutely necessary for marching.

"This, I am happy to say, is now nearly accomplished. I have also, during the same time, repeatedly urged upon you the importance of supplying cavalry and artillery horses to replace those broken down by hard service, and steps have been taken to insure a prompt delivery.

"Our cavalry, even when well supplied with horses, is much inferior in numbers to that of the enemy, but in efficiency has proved itself superior. So forcibly has this been impressed upon our old regiments by repeated successes, that the men are fully persuaded that they are equal to twice their number of rebel cavalry.

"Exclusive of the cavalry force now engaged in picketing the river, I have not at present over about one thousand (1,000) horses for service. Officers have been sent in various directions to purchase horses, and I expect them soon. Without more cavalry horses our communications, from the moment we march, would be at the mercy of the large cavalry force of the enemy, and it would not be possible for us to cover our flanks properly, or to obtain the necessary information of the position and movements of the enemy, in such a way as to insure success. My experience has shown the necessity of a large and efficient cavalry force.

"Under the foregoing circumstances, I beg leave to ask whether the President desires me to march on the enemy at once, or to await the reception of the new horses, every possible step having been taken to insure their prompt arrival.

"GEO. B. McCLELLAN,
"*Major General Commanding.*

"Major General H. W. HALLECK,
"*General-in-Chief, Washington.*"

On the same day General Halleck replied as follows:

"WASHINGTON, *October* 21, 1862—3 *p. m.*

"Your telegram of 12 m. has been submitted to the President. He directs me to say that he has no change to make in his order of the 6th instant.

"If you have not been, and are not now, in condition to obey it, you will be able to show such want of ability. The President does not expect impossibilities; but he is very anxious that all this good weather should not be wasted in inactivity. Telegraph when you will move, and on what lines you propose to march.

"H. W. HALLECK,
"*General-in-Chief.*

"Major General GEO. B. McCLELLAN."

From the tenor of this despatch I conceived that it was left for my judgment to decide whether or not it was possible to move with safety to the army at that time; and this responsibility I exercised with the more confidence in view of the strong assurances of his trust in me, as commander of that army, with which the President had seen fit to honor me during his last visit.

The cavalry requirements, without which an advance would have been in the highest degree injudicious and unsafe, were still wanting.

The country before us was an enemy's country, where the inhabitants furnished to the enemy every possible assistance; providing food for men and forage for animals, giving all information concerning our movements, and rendering every aid in their power to the enemy's cause.

It was manifest that we should find it, as we subsequently did, a hostile district, where we could derive no aid from the inhabitants that would justify dispensing with the active co-operation of an efficient cavalry force. Accordingly I fixed upon the first of November as the earliest date at which the forward movement could well be commenced.

The general-in-chief, in a letter to the Secretary of War, on the 28th of October, says: "In my opinion, there has been no such want of supplies in the army under General McClellan as to prevent his compliance with the orders to advance against the enemy."

Notwithstanding this opinion, expressed by such high authority, I am compelled to say again that the delay in the reception of necessary supplies up to that date had left the army in a condition totally unfit to advance against the enemy—that an advance, under the existing circumstances, would, in my judgment, have been attended with the highest degree of peril, with great suffering and sickness among the men, and with imminent danger of being cut off from our supplies by the superior cavalry force of the enemy, and with no reasonable prospect of gaining any advantage over him.

I dismiss this subject with the remark that I have found it impossible to resist the force of my own convictions, that the commander of an army who, from the time of its organization, has for eighteen months been in constant communication with its officers and men, the greater part of the time engaged in active service in the field, and who has exercised this command in many battles, must certainly be considered competent to determine whether his army is in proper condition to advance on the enemy or not; and he must necessarily possess greater facilities for forming a correct judgment in regard to the wants of his men, and the condition of his supplies, than the general-in-chief in his office at Washington city. The movement from Washington into Maryland, which culminated in the battles of South Mountain and Antietam, was not a part of an offensive campaign, with the object of the invasion of the enemy's territory and an attack upon his capital, but was defensive in its purposes, although offensive in its character, and would be technically called a "defensive-offensive campaign."

It was undertaken at a time when our army had experienced severe defeats, and its object was to preserve the national capital and Baltimore, to protect Pennsylvania from invasion, and to drive the enemy out of Maryland. These purposes were fully and finally accomplished by the battle of Antietam, which brought the army of the Potomac into what might be termed an accidental position on the upper Potomac.

Having gained the immediate object of the campaign, the first thing to be done was to insure Maryland from a return of the enemy; the second, to prepare our own army, exhausted by a series of severe battles, destitute to a great extent of supplies, and very deficient in artillery and cavalry horses, for a definite offensive movement, and to determine upon the line of operations for a further advance.

At the time of the battle of Antietam the Potomac was very low, and presented a comparatively weak line of defence unless watched by large masses of troops.

The reoccupation of Harper's Ferry, and the disposition of troops above that point, rendered the line of the Potomac secure against everything except cavalry raids. No time was lost in placing the army in proper condition for an advance, and the circumstances which caused the delay after the battle of Antietam have been fully enumerated elsewhere.

I never regarded Harper's Ferry or its vicinity as a proper base of operations for a movement upon Richmond. I still considered the line of the Peninsula as the true approach, but, for obvious reasons, did not make any proposal to return to it.

On the 6th of October, as stated above, I was ordered by the President, through his general-in-chief, to cross the Potomac and give battle to the enemy, or drive him south. Two lines were presented for my choice:

1st. Up the valley of the Shenandoah, in which case I was to have 12,000 to 15,000 additional troops.

2d. To cross between the enemy and Washington—that is, east of the Blue Ridge—in which event I was to be re-enforced with 30,000 men.

At first I determined to adopt the line of the Shenandoah, for these reasons: The Harper's Ferry and Winchester railroad and the various turnpikes converging upon Winchester afforded superior facilities for supplies. Our cavalry being weak, this line of communication could be more easily protected. There was no advantage in interposing at that time the Blue Ridge and the Shenandoah between the enemy and myself.

At the period in question the Potomac was still very low, and I apprehended that, if I crossed the river below Harper's Ferry, the enemy would promptly check the movement by re-crossing into Maryland, at the same time covering his rear by occupying in strong force the passes leading through the Blue Ridge from the southeast into the Shenandoah valley.

I anticipated, as the result of the first course, that Lee would fight me near Winchester, if he could do so under favorable circumstances; or else that he would abandon the lower Shenandoah, and leave the army of the Potomac free to act upon some other line of operations.

If he abandoned the Shenanhoah, he would naturally fall back upon his railway communications. I have since been confirmed in the belief that, if I had crossed the Potomac below Harper's Ferry in the early part of October, General Lee would have re-crossed into Maryland.

As above explained, the army was not in condition to move until late in October, and in the mean time circumstances had changed.

The period had arrived when a sudden and great rise of the Potomac might be looked for at any moment; the season of bad roads and difficult movements was approaching, which would naturally deter the enemy from exposing himself very far from his base, and his movements all appeared to indicate a falling back from the river towards his supplies. Under these circumstances, I felt at liberty to disregard the possibility of the enemy's re-crossing the Potomac, and determined to select the line east of the Blue Ridge, feeling convinced that it would secure me the largest accession of force, and the most cordial support of the President, whose views, from the beginning, were in favor of that line.

The subject of the defence of the line of the upper Potomac, after the advance of the main army, had long occupied my attention. I desired to place Harper's Ferry and its dependencies in a strong state of defence, and frequently addressed the general-in-chief upon the subject of the erection of field-works and permanent bridges there, asking for the funds necessary to accomplish the purpose. Although I did my best to explain, as clearly as I was able, that I did not wish to erect permanent works of masonry, and that neither the works nor the permanent bridges had any reference to the advance of the army, but solely to the permanent occupation of Harper's Ferry, I could never make the general-in-chief understand my wishes, but was refused the funds necessary to erect the field-works, on the ground that there was no appropriation for the erection of permanent fortifications; and was not allowed to build the permanent bridge, on the ground that the main army could not be delayed in its movements until its completion.

Of course I never thought of delaying the advance of the army for that purpose, and so stated repeatedly. On the 25th of October I sent to the general-in-chief the following telegram:

"HEADQUARTERS ARMY OF THE POTOMAC,
"*October 25, 1862—10.45 p. m.*

"As the moment is at hand for the advance of this army, a question arises for the decision of the general-in-chief, which, although perhaps impliedly decided by the President in his letter of the 13th, should be clearly presented by me, as I do not regard it as in my province to determine it.

"This question is the extent to which the line of the Potomac should be guarded, after the army leaves, in order to cover Maryland and Pennsylvania from invasion by large or small parties of the enemy.

"It will always be somewhat difficult to guard the immediate line of the river, owing to its great extent and the numerous passages which exist.

"It has long appeared to me that the best way of covering this line would be by occupying Front Royal, Strasburg, Wardensville and Moorefield, or the debouches of the several valleys in which they are situated.

"These points, or suitable places in their vicinity, should be strongly intrenched and permanently held. One great advantage of this arrangement would be the covering the Baltimore and Ohio railroad, and an essential part of the system would be the construction of the link of railway from Winchester to Strasburg, and the rebuilding of the Manassas Gap railway bridge over the Shenandoah.

"The intrenchment of Manassas Junction would complete the system for the defence of the approaches to Washington and the upper Potomac. Many months ago I recommended this arrangement; in fact, gave orders for it to be carried into effect. I still regard it as essential under all circumstances.

"The views of the chief engineer of this army, in regard to the defences and garrison of Harper's Ferry and its defences, are in your possession.

"The only troops under my command, outside of the organization of the army of the Potomac, are the Maryland brigade, under General Kenly; the 54th Pennsylvania, Colonel Voss; 12th Illinois cavalry, and Colonel Davis's 8th New York cavalry; total, 2,894 infantry, one battery, and about 900 cavalry men.

"There are also two of my regiments of cavalry (about 750 men) guarding the Baltimore and Ohio railroad between Hancock and Cumberland.

"As I have no department, and command simply an active army in the field, my responsibility for the safety of the line of the Potomac and the States north of it must terminate the moment I advance so far beyond that line as to adopt another for my base of operations. The question for the general in-chief to decide, and which I regard as beyond my province, is this:

"1st. Shall the safety of Harper's Ferry and the line of the Potomac be regarded as assured by the advance of the army south of the Blue Ridge, and the line left to take care of itself?

"2d. If it is deemed necessary to hold the line, or that hereinbefore indicated in advance of it, how many troops shall be placed there, at what points, and in what numbers and of what composition at each, and whence shall they be supplied—*i. e.*, from the army, or from other sources?

"Omitting the detached troops mentioned above, and the small garrisons of Boonsboro' and Frederick, the last returns show the strength of this army for duty to be about (116,000) one hundred and sixteen thousand officers and men. This includes the divisions of Stoneman and Whipple, but does not include Heintzelman, Sigel, and Bayard.

"If Harper's Ferry and the river above are rendered fully secure, it is possible that the active army, if it supplies the garrison, may be reduced so much as to be inadequate to the purposes contemplated. If it is preserved intact, Maryland, Pennsylvania, and the Baltimore and Ohio railroad may be unduly exposed.

"I leave the decision of these grave questions to the general-in-chief. I know nothing of the number of troops at Baltimore, &c.

"An important element in the solution of this problem is the fact that a great portion of Bragg's army is probably now at liberty to unite itself with Lee's command.

"I commence crossing the river at Berlin in the morning, and must ask a prompt decision of the questions proposed herein.

"GEORGE B. McCLELLAN,
"*Major General, Commanding.*

"Major General HALLECK,
"*General-in-Chief, Washington.*

To which I received the following reply:

"WASHINGTON, *October* 26, 1862—1.35 *p. m.*

"In addition to the command which you had when I came here, you also have the greater part of that of Major General Pope. Moreover, you have been authorized to use any troops within your reach in General Wool's department, and in Western Virginia. General Banks's command is also under your direction, with the single restriction that he is not to remove troops from Washington till he has notified me of his orders.

"Since you left Washington I have advised and suggested in relation to your movements, but I have given you no orders; I do not give you any now. The government has intrusted you with defeating and driving back the rebel army in your front. I shall not attempt to control you in the measures you may adopt for that purpose. You are informed of my views, but the President has left you at liberty to adopt them or not, as you may deem best.

"You will also exercise your own discretion in regard to what points on the Potomac and the Baltimore and Ohio railroad are to be occupied or fortified. I will only add that there is no appropriation for *permanent* intrenchments on that line. Moreover, I think it will be time enough to decide upon fortifying Front Royal, Strasburg, Wardensville, and Moorefield, when the enemy is driven south of them, and they come into our possession.

"I do not think that we need have any immediate fear of Bragg's army. You are within (20) twenty miles of Lee's, while Bragg is distant about (400) four hundred miles.

"H. W. HALLECK,
"*General-in-Chief.*

"Major General G. B. McCLELLAN."

On the 29th I sent the following:

"HEADQUARTERS ARMY OF THE POTOMAC,
"*October* 29, 1862—1.15 *p. m.*

"On the 25th instant I sent you a despatch requesting you to decide what steps should be taken to guard the line of the Potomac when this army leaves here. To this I received your reply that I had been intrusted by the President with defeating and driving away the rebel army; that you had given me no orders heretofore—did not give me any then, &c. Under these circumstances I have only to make such arrangements for guarding this extended line as the means at my disposal will permit, at the same time keeping in view the supreme necessity of maintaining the moving army in adequate force to meet the rebel army before us.

"The dispositions I have ordered are as follows, viz: Ten thousand men to be left at Harper's Ferry; one brigade of infantry in front of Sharpsburg; Kenley's brigade of infantry at Williamsport; Kelly's brigade, including Colonel Campbell's 54th Pennsylvania infantry, at Cumberland; and between that point and Hancock. I have also left four small cavalry regiments to patrol and watch the river and the Baltimore and Ohio railroad from Cumberland down to Harper's Ferry.

"I do not regard this force as sufficient to cover securely this great extent of line, but I do not feel justified in detaching any more troops from my moving columns; I would, therefore, recommend that some new regiments of infantry and cavalry be sent to strengthen the forces left by me.

"There should be a brigade of infantry and section of artillery in the vicinity of Cherry run, another brigade at Hancock, an additional brigade at Williamsport, one regiment at Hagerstown and one at Chambersburg, with a section of artillery at each place if possible. This is on the supposition that the enemy retain a considerable cavalry force west of the Blue Ridge; if they go east of it, the occupation of the points named in my despatch of the 25th instant will obviate the necessity of keeping many of these troops on the river.

"There are now several hundred of our wounded, including General Richardson, in the vicinity of Sharpsburg, that cannot possibly be moved at present.

"I repeat, that I do not look upon the forces I have been able to leave from this army as sufficient to prevent cavalry raids into Maryland and Pennsylvania, as cavalry is the only description of troops adequate to this service, and I am, as you are aware, deficient in this arm.

"G. B. McCLELLAN,
"*Major General, Commanding.*

"Major General HALLECK,
"*General-in-Chief, Washington.*"

To which I received on the 30th this reply:

"WASHINGTON, *October* 30, 1862—11.30 *a. m.*

"Your telegram of yesterday was received late last evening. The troops proposed for Thoroughfare gap will be sent to that place whenever you are in position for their cooperation, as previously stated, but no new regiments can be sent from here to the upper Potomac. The guarding of that line is left to your own discretion with the troops now under your command.

"H. W. HALLECK,
"*General-in-Chief.*

"Major General G. B. MCCLELLAN."

I accordingly left the 12th corps at Harper's Ferry, detaching one brigade to the vicinity of Sharpsburg. General Morell was placed in command of the line from the mouth of the Antietam to Cumberland; General Slocum in command of Harper's Ferry and the line east of the mouth of the Antietam.

The orders given to these officers were as follows:

"HEADQUARTERS ARMY OF THE POTOMAC,
"*October* 29, 1862—1 *p. m.*

"The general commanding directs that you send one brigade of your corps to march at once to the position now occupied by General F. J. Porter's corps, in front of Sharpsburg, to watch and guard the line of the river, the ford near the mouth of the Antietam creek to the mouth of the Opequan creek.

"The officer in command will also take steps to afford proper protection to the sick and wounded in the hospitals in the vicinity of Sharpsburg and Boonsboro'. The regiment now at Boonsboro' will be placed under his orders. General Kenley, at Williamsport, will guard the river from the mouth of the Opequan alone, including the ford at the mouth of the Opequan.

"The commanding general also directs that you take immediate steps to establish the remainder of your corps as follows, viz: one brigade on Maryland heights, one brigade on Loudon heights, with the remainder on Bolivar heights and at Harper's Ferry.

"These dispositions should be made at once, so that General Couch can move with his corps. Please acknowledge the receipt of this.

"R. B. MARCY,
"*Chief of Staff.*

"General H. W. SLOCUM,
"*Commanding Army Corps, Harper's Ferry.*"

"HEADQUARTERS ARMY OF THE POTOMAC,
"*October* 31, 1862.

"GENERAL: I am instructed by the commanding general to say to you, that he has selected you to perform the highly important and responsible duty of taking charge of and commanding the troops left for the defence of the line of the Potomac river, from the mouth of the Antietam to Cumberland, as well as any other troops that may hereafter be sent for the protection of the Maryland and Pennsylvania frontier within the limits of the lines herein specified. The force which has been left to guard the line is not deemed adequate to prevent cavalry raids, but it is all that the commanding general feels authorized to detach from the army of the Potomac at the present time, and it devolves upon you to make the best use of this force in your power. You will have four cavalry regiments under your command, which should be so distributed along the river as to watch all the available fords, and give timely notice to the infantry of the approach of any force of rebels.

"You will afford all the protection in your power to the Baltimore and Ohio railroad.

"You will endeavor to prevent any cavalry raids into Maryland and Pennsylvania.

"You will take steps to have all the sick and wounded of our army, as well as of the rebel army within your lines, properly taken care of until they can be sent to general hospitals, or discharged, or paroled.

"You will make your headquarters at Hagerstown, and occasionally visit the different parts of your line.

"You will please report promptly to these headquarters everything of importance that occurs within the limits of your command.

"The three brigades now at Cumberland, Williamsport, and Sharpsburg, including the fifty-fourth Pennsylvania volunteers, near Cumberland, will be under your command. They are commanded by Generals Kelly, Kenley, and Gordon.

"Very respectfully, your obedient servant,

"S. WILLIAMS,
"*Assistant Adjutant General.*

"General G. W. MORELL,
"*Commanding Upper Potomac.*"

On the 25th of October the pontoon bridge at Berlin was constructed, there being already one across the Potomac, and another across the Shenandoah, at Harper's Ferry.

On the 26th two divisions of the ninth corps, and Pleasonton's brigade of cavalry, crossed at Berlin and occupied Lovettsville.

The first, sixth, and ninth corps, the cavalry, and the reserve artillery, crossed at Berlin between the 26th of October and the 2d of November.

The second and fifth corps crossed at Harper's Ferry between the 29th of October and the 1st of November. Heavy rains delayed the movement considerably in the beginning, and the first, fifth and sixth corps were obliged to halt at least one day at the crossings to complete, as far as possible, necessary supplies that could not be procured at an earlier period.

The plan of campaign I adopted during this advance was to move the army, well in hand, parallel to the Blue Ridge, taking Warrenton as the point of direction for the main army; seizing each pass on the Blue Ridge by detachments, as we approached it, and guarding them after we had passed as long as they would enable the enemy to trouble our communications with the Potomac. It was expected that we would unite with the eleventh corps and Sickles's division near Thoroughfare gap. We depended upon Harper's Ferry and Berlin for supplies until the Manassas Gap railway was reached; when that occurred the passes in our rear were to be abandoned, and the army massed ready for action or movement in any direction.

It was my intention if, upon reaching Ashby's or any other pass, I found that the enemy were in force between it and the Potomac in the valley of the Shenandoah, to move into the valley and endeavor to gain their rear.

I hardly hoped to accomplish this, but did expect that by striking in between Culpeper Court House and Little Washington I could either separate their army and beat them in detail, or else force them to concentrate as far back as Gordonsville, and thus place the army of the Potomac in position either to adopt the Fredericksburg line of advance upon Richmond, or to be removed to the Peninsula, if, as I apprehended, it were found impossible to supply it by the Orange and Alexandria railroad beyond Culpeper.

On the 27th of October the remaining divisions of the ninth corps crossed at Berlin, and Pleasonton's cavalry advanced to Purcellville. The concentration of the sixth corps, delayed somewhat by intelligence as to the movements of the enemy near Hedgesville, &c., was commenced on this day, and the first corps was already in motion for Berlin.

On the 28th the first corps and the general headquarters reached Berlin

On the 29th the reserve artillery crossed and encamped near Lovettsville. Stoneman's division, temporarily attached to the ninth corps, occupied Leesburg; Averill's cavalry brigade moved towards Berlin from Hagerstown; two divisions of the ninth corps moved to Wheatland, and one to Waterford. The second corps commenced the passage of the Shenandoah at Harper's Ferry, and moved into the valley east of Loudon heights.

On the 30th the first corps crossed at Berlin and encamped near Lovettsville, and the second corps completed the passage of the Shenandoah. The fifth corps commenced its march from Sharpsburg to Harper's Ferry.

On the 31st the second corps moved to the vicinity of Hillsborough; the sixth corps reached Boonsboro'; the fifth corps reached Harper's Ferry, one division crossing the Shenandoah.

On the 1st of November the first corps moved to Purcellville and Hamilton; the second corps to Woodgrove; the fifth corps to Hillsborough; the sixth corps reached Berlin, one division crossing. Pleasonton's cavalry occupied Philomont, having a sharp skirmish there and at Bloomfield.

On November 2 the second corps occupied Snicker's gap; the fifth corps, Snickersville; the sixth corps crossed the Potomac and encamped near Wheatland; the ninth corps advanced to Bloomfield, Union, and Philomont. Pleasonton drove the enemy out of Union. Averill was ordered to join Pleasonton. The enemy offered no serious resistance to the occupation of Snicker's gap, but advanced to gain possession of it with a column of some 5,000 to 6,000 infantry, who were driven back by a few rounds from our rifled guns.

On the 3d the first corps moved to Philomont, Union, Bloomfield, &c.; the second corps to the vicinity of Upperville; the fifth corps remained at Snicker's gap; the sixth corps moved to Purcellville; the ninth corps moved towards Upperville. Pleasonton drove the enemy out of Upperville after a severe fight.

On the 4th the 2d corps took possession of Ashby's gap; the 6th corps reached Union; the 9th corps, Upperville; the cavalry occupied Piedmont. On the 5th the 1st corps moved to Rectortown and White Plains; one division of the 2d corps to the intersection of the Paris and Piedmont with the Upperville and Barber's road; the 6th corps to the Aldie pike, east of Upperville;

the 9th corps beyond the Manassas railroad, between Piedmont and Salem, with a brigade at Manassas gap. The cavalry under Averill had a skirmish at Manassas gap, and the brigade of Pleasonton gained a handsome victory over superior numbers at Barber's Cross Roads. Bayard's cavalry had some sharp skirmishing in front of Salem.

On the 6th the 1st corps advanced to Warrenton; the 2d corps to Rectortown; the 5th corps commenced its movement from Snicker's gap to White Plains; the 9th corps to Waterloo and vicinity on the Rappahannock; the 11th corps was at New Baltimore, Thoroughfare and Hopewell's gaps; Sickles's division guarding the Orange and Alexandria railroad from Manassas Junction towards Warrenton Junction; the cavalry near Flint hill; Bayard to cut off what there might be in Warrenton, and to proceed to the Rappahannock station.

November 7th: General Pleasonton was ordered to move towards Little Washington and Sperryville, and thence towards Culpeper Court House.

November 8th: the 2d corps moved half way to Warrenton; the 5th corps to New Baltimore.

November 9: the 2d and 5th corps reached Warrenton; the 6th corps, New Baltimore.

Late on the night of the 7th I received an order relieving me from the command of the army of the Potomac, and directing me to turn it over to General Burnside, which I at once did.

I had already given the orders for the movements of the 8th and 9th; these orders were carried into effect without change.

The position in which I left the army, as the result of the orders I had given, was as follows:

The 1st, 2d, and 5th corps, reserve artillery, and general headquarters, at Warrenton; the 9th corps on the line of the Rappahannock, in the vicinity of Waterloo; the 6th corps at New Baltimore; the 11th corps at New Baltimore, Gainesville, and Thoroughfare gap; Sickles's division of the 3d corps, on the Orange and Alexandria railroad, from Manassas Junction to Warrenton Junction; Pleasonton across the Rappahannock at Amissville, Jefferson, &c., with his pickets at Hazel river, facing Longstreet, six miles from Culpeper Court House; Bayard near Rappahannock station.

The army was thus massed near Warrenton, ready to act in any required direction, perfectly in hand, and in admirable condition and spirits. I doubt whether, during the whole period that I had the honor to command the army of the Potomac, it was in such excellent condition to fight a great battle. When I gave up the command to General Burnside, the best information in our possession indicated that Longstreet was immediately in our front near Culpeper; Jackson, with one, perhaps both, of the Hills, near Chester and Thornton's gaps, with the mass of their force west of the Blue Ridge.

The reports from General Pleasonton on the advance indicated the possibility of separating the two wings of the enemy's forces, and either beating Longstreet separately, or forcing him to fall back at least upon Gordonsville, to effect his junction with the rest of the army.

The following is from the report of General Pleasonton:

"At this time, and from the 7th instant, my advance pickets were at Hazel river, within six miles of Culpeper, besides having my flank pickets towards Chester and Thornton's gaps extended to Gaines's Cross Roads and Newby's Cross Roads, with numerous patrols in the direction of Woodville, Little Washington, and Sperryville.

"The information gained from these parties, and also from deserters, prisoners, contrabands, as well as citizens, established the fact of Longstreet, with his command, being at Culpeper, while Jackson, with D. H. Hill, with their respective commands, were in the Shenandoah valley, on the western side of the

Blue Ridge, covering Chester and Thornton's gaps, and expecting us to pass through and attack them.

"As late as the 17th of November, a contraband just from Strasburg came in my camp and reported that D. H. Hill's corps was two miles beyond that place, on the railroad to Mount Jackson. Hill was tearing up the road and destroying the bridges, under the impression that we intended to follow into that valley, and was en route for Staunton.

"Jackson's corps was between Strasburg and Winchester. Ewell and A. P. Hill were with Jackson. Provisions were scarce, and the rebels were obliged to keep moving to obtain them."

Had I remained in command, I should have made the attempt to divide the enemy as before suggested, and could he have been brought to a battle within reach of my supplies, I cannot doubt that the result would have been a brilliant victory for our army.

On the 10th of November General Pleasonton was attacked by Longstreet, with one division of infantry and Stuart's cavalry, but repulsed the attack.

This indicates the relative position of our army and that of the enemy at the time I was relieved from command.

It would be impossible to participate in operations, such as those described in the foregoing pages, without forming fixed opinions upon subjects connected with the organization of our armies, and the general conduct of military operations.

This report would be incomplete without a brief allusion to some general considerations which have been firmly impressed upon me by the events which have occurred.

To my mind the most glaring defect in our armies is the absence of system in the appointment and promotion of general and other officers, and the want of means for the theoretical instruction of the mass of officers. The expansion of the army was so great and so rapid at the commencement of the existing war that it was perhaps impossible, in the great scarcity of instructed officers, to have adopted any other course than that which was pursued; but the time has arrived when measures may be initiated to remedy existing defects, and provide against their recurrence.

I think that the army should be regarded as a permanent one; that is to say, its affairs should be administered precisely as if all who belonged to it had made it their profession for life; and those rules for promotion, &c., which have been found necessary in the best foreign armies to excite honorable emulation, produce an *esprit du corps* and procure efficiency, should be followed by us.

All officers and soldiers should be made to feel that merit—that is to say, courage, good conduct, the knowledge and performance of the duties of their grade, and fitness to exercise those of a superior grade—will insure to them advancement in their profession, and can alone secure it for them.

Measures should be adopted to secure the theoretical instruction of staff officers at least, who should, as far as possible, be selected from officers having a military education, or who have seen actual service in the field.

The number of cadets at the Military Academy should be at once increased to the greatest extent permitted by the capacity of the institution. The regular army should be increased and maintained complete in numbers and efficiency.

A well-organized system of recruiting and of depots for instruction should be adopted, in order to keep the ranks of the regiments full, and supply promptly the losses arising from battle or disease. This is especially necessary for the artillery and cavalry arms of the service, which, from the beginning of the war, have rendered great services, and which have never been fully appreciated by any but their comrades. We need also large bodies of well-instructed engineer troops.

In the arrangement and conduct of campaigns the direction should be left to professional soldiers. A statesman may, perhaps, be more competent than a soldier to determine the political objects and direction of a campaign; but those once decided upon, everything should be left to the responsible military head, without interference from civilians. In no other manner is success probable. The meddling of individual members of committees of Congress with subjects which, from lack of experience, they are of course incapable of comprehending, and which they are too apt to view through the distorted medium of partisan or personal prejudice, can do no good, and is certain to produce incalculable mischief.

I cannot omit the expression of my thanks to the President for the constant evidence given me of his sincere personal regard, and his desire to sustain the military plans which my judgment led me to urge for adoption and execution. I cannot attribute his failure to adopt some of those plans, and to give that support to others which was necessary to their success, to any want of confidence in me; and it only remains for me to regret that other counsels came between the constitutional commander-in-chief and the general whom he had placed at the head of his armies—counsels which resulted in the failure of great campaigns.

If the nation possesses no generals in service competent to direct its military affairs without the aid or supervision of politicians, the sooner it finds them and places them in position the better will it be for its fortunes.

I may be pardoned for calling attention to the memorandum submitted by me to the President on the 4th of August, 1861; my letter to him of July 7, 1862; and other similar communications to him and to the Secretary of War. I have seen no reason to change in any material regard the views there expressed.

After a calm, impartial, and patient consideration of the subject—a subject which demands the closest thought on the part of every true lover of his country—I am convinced that by the proper employment of our resources it is entirely possible to bring this war to a successful military issue. I believe that a necessary preliminary to the re-establishment of the Union is the entire defeat or virtual destruction of the organized military power of the confederates; and that such a result should be accompanied and followed by conciliatory measures; and that by pursuing the political course I have always advised, it is possible to bring about a permanent restoration of the Union—a re-union by which the rights of both sections shall be preserved, and by which both parties shall preserve their self-respect, while they respect each other.

In this report I have confined myself to a plain narrative of such facts as are necessary for the purposes of history.

Where it was possible, I have preferred to give these facts in the language of despatches, written at the time of their occurrence, rather than to attempt a new relation.

The reports of the subordinate commanders, hereto annexed, recite what time and space would fail me to mention here: those individual instances of conspicuous bravery and skill by which every battle was marked. To them I must especially refer, for without them this narrative would be incomplete, and justice fail to be done. But I cannot omit to tender to my corps commanders, and to other general officers under them, such ample recognition of their cordial co-operation and their devoted services as those reports abundantly avouch.

I have not sought to defend the army which I had the honor to command, nor myself, against the hostile criticisms once so rife.

It has seemed to me that nothing more was required than such a plain and truthful narrative to enable those whose right it is to form a correct judgment on the important matters involved.

This report is, in fact, the history of the army of the Potomac.

During the period occupied in the organization of that army, it served as a barrier against the advance of a lately victorious enemy, while the fortifications of the capital were in progress; and under the discipline which it then received it acquired strength, education, and some of that experience which is necessary to success in active operations, and which enabled it afterwards to sustain itself under circumstances trying to the most heroic men. Frequent skirmishes occurred along the lines, conducted with great gallantry, which inured our troops to the realities of war.

The army grew into shape but slowly; and the delays which attended on the obtaining of arms, continuing late into the winter of 1861–'62, were no less trying to the soldiers than to the people of the country. Even at the time of the organization of the Peninsula campaign, some of the finest regiments were without rifles; nor were the utmost exertions on the part of the military authorities adequate to overcome the obstacles to active service.

When, at length, the army was in condition to take the field, the Peninsula campaign was planned, and entered upon with enthusiasm by officers and men. Had this campaign been followed up as it was designed, I cannot doubt that it would have resulted in a glorious triumph to our arms, and the permanent restoration of the power of the government in Virginia and North Carolina, if not throughout the revolting States. It was, however, otherwise ordered, and instead of reporting a victorious campaign, it has been my duty to relate the heroism of a reduced army, sent upon an expedition into an enemy's country, there to abandon one and originate another and new plan of campaign, which might and would have been successful if supported with appreciation of its necessities, but which failed because of the repeated failure of promised support, at the most critical, and, as it proved, the most fatal moments. That heroism surpasses ordinary description. Its illustration must be left for the pen of the historian in times of calm reflection, when the nation shall be looking back to the past from the midst of peaceful days.

For me, now, it is sufficient to say that my comrades were victors on every field save one, and there the endurance of but little more than a single corps accomplished the object of the fighting, and, by securing to the army its transit to the James, left to the enemy a ruinous and barren victory.

The army of the Potomac was first reduced by the withdrawal from my command of the division of General Blenker, which was ordered to the Mountain department, under General Frémont. We had scarcely landed on the Peninsula when it was further reduced by a despatch revoking a previous order giving me command at Fortress Monroe, and under which I had expected to take ten thousand men from that point to aid in our operations. Then, when under fire before the defences of Yorktown, we received the news of the withdrawal of General McDowell's corps of about 35,000 men. This completed the overthrow of the original plan of the campaign. About one-third of my entire army (five divisions out of fourteen, one of the nine remaining being but little larger than a brigade) was thus taken from me. Instead of a rapid advance which I had planned, aided by a flank movement up the York river, it was only left to besiege Yorktown. That siege was successfully conducted by the army, and when these strong works at length yielded to our approaches, the troops rushed forward to the sanguinary but successful battle of Williamsburg, and thus opened an almost unresisted advance to the banks of the Chickahominy. Richmond lay before them, surrounded with fortifications, and guarded by an army larger than our own; but the prospect did not shake the courage of the brave men who composed my command. Relying still on the support which the vastness of our undertaking and the grand results depending on our success seemed to insure us, we pressed forward. The weather was stormy beyond precedent: the deep soil of the Peninsula was at times one vast morass; the Chickahominy rose to a higher stage than had been known for years before. Pursuing the advance, the crossings were seized, and the right wing extended to effect a junction with reenforcements now promised and earnestly desired, and upon the arrival of which the complete success of the campaign seemed clear. The brilliant battle of Hanover Court House was fought, which opened the way for the first corps, with the aid of which, had it come, we should then have gone into the enemy's capital. It never came. The bravest army could not do more, under such overwhelming disappointment, than the army of the Potomac then did. Fair Oaks attests their courage and endurance when they hurled back, again and again, the vastly superior masses of the enemy. But mortal men could not accomplish the miracles that seemed to have been expected of them. But one course was left—a flank march in the face of a powerful enemy to another and better base—one of the most hazardous movements in war. The army of the Potomac, holding its own safety, and almost the safety of our cause, in its hands, was equal to the occasion. The seven days are classical in American history; those days in which the noble soldiers of the Union and Constitution fought an outnumbering enemy by day, and retreated from successive victories by night, through a week of battle, closing the terrible series of conflicts with the ever-memorable victory of Malvern, where they drove back, beaten and shattered, the entire eastern army of the confederacy, and thus secured for themselves a place of rest and a point for a new advance upon the capital from the banks of the James. Richmond was still within our grasp, had the army of the Potomac been re-enforced and permitted to advance. But counsels, which I cannot but think subsequent events proved unwise, prevailed in Washingson, and we were ordered to abandon the campaign. Never did soldiers better deserve the thanks of a nation than the army of the Potomac for the deeds of the Peninsula campaign, and although that meed was withheld from them by the authorities, I am persuaded they have received the applause of the American people.

The army of the Potomac was recalled from within sight of Richmond, and incorporated with the army of Virginia. The disappointments of the campaign on the Peninsula had not damped their ardor nor diminished their patriotism. They fought well, faithfully, gallantly, under General Pope; yet were compelled to fall back on Washington, defeated and almost demoralized.

The enemy, no longer occupied in guarding his own capital, poured his troops northward, entered Maryland, threatened Pennsylvania, and even Washington itself. Elated by his recent victories, and assured that our troops were disorganized and dispirited, he was confident that the seat of war was now permanently transferred to the loyal States, and that his own exhausted soil was to be relieved from the burden of supporting two hostile armies. But he did not understand the spirit which animated the soldiers of the Union. I shall not, nor can I living, forget that when I was ordered to the command of the troops for the defence of the capital, the soldiers, with whom I had shared so much of the anxiety, and pain, and suffering of the war, had not lost their confidence in me as their commander. They sprang to my call with all their ancient vigor, discipline, and courage. I led them into Maryland. Fifteen days after they had fallen back defeated before Washington, they vanquished the enemy on the rugged height of South Mountain, pursued him to the hard-fought field of Antietam, and drove him, broken and disappointed, across the Potomac into Virginia.

The army had need of rest. After the terrible experiences of battles and marches, with scarcely an interval of repose, which they had gone through from the time of leaving for the Peninsula; the return to Washington; the defeat in Virginia; the victory at South Mountain, and again at Antietam, it was not surprising that they were in a large degree destitute of the absolute necessaries to effective duty. Shoes were worn out; blankets were lost; clothing was in rags: in short, the army was unfit for active service, and an interval for rest and equipment was necessary. When the slowly forwarded supplies came to us I led the army across the river, renovated, refreshed, in good order and discipline and followed the retreating foe to a position where I was confident of decisive victory, when, in the midst of the movement, while my advance guard was actually in contact with the enemy, I was removed from the command.

I am devoutly grateful to God that my last campaign with this brave army was crowned with a victory which saved the nation from the greatest peril it had then undergone. I have not accomplished my purpose if, by this report, the army of the Potomac is not placed high on the roll of the historic armies of the world. Its deeds ennoble the nation to which it belongs. Always ready for battle, always firm, steadfast, and trustworthy, I never called on it in vain; nor will the nation ever have cause to attribute its want of success, under myself, or under other commanders, to any failure of patriotism or bravery in that noble body of American soldiers.

No man can justly charge upon any portion of that army, from the commanding general to the private, any lack of devotion to the service of the United States government, and to the cause of the Constitution and the Union. They have proved their fealty in much sorrow, suffering, danger, and through the very shadow of death. Their comrades dead on all the fields where we fought have scarcely more claim to the honor of a nation's reverence than their survivors to the justice of a nation's gratitude.

I am, sir, very respectfully, your obedient servant,

GEORGE B. McCLELLAN,
Major General, United States Army.

Brigadier General L. THOMAS,
Adjutant General, United States Army.

WAR DEPARTMENT,
Adjutant General's Office, Washington, December 22, 1863.

I certify that the above is a true copy of the original report on file in this office.

E. D. TOWNSEND,
Assistant Adjutant General.

www.ingramcontent.com/pod-product-compliance
Lightning Source LLC
Chambersburg PA
CBHW031738230426
43669CB00007B/386

* 9 7 8 3 3 3 7 8 1 0 4 8 1 *